A SHORT HISTORY OF THE
ROMAN EMPIRE

BY J. WELLS

A SHORT HISTORY OF ROME TO THE DEATH OF AUGUSTUS
OXFORD AND ITS COLLEGES

BY R. H. BARROW

SLAVERY IN THE ROMAN EMPIRE

A SHORT HISTORY OF THE ROMAN EMPIRE
TO THE DEATH OF
MARCUS AURELIUS

BY

J. WELLS, M.A., D.C.L.
LATE WARDEN OF WADHAM COLLEGE, OXFORD

AND

R. H. BARROW, M.A., B.Litt.
FORMERLY SENIOR SCHOLAR OF EXETER COLLEGE, OXFORD

WITH EIGHT MAPS

SECOND EDITION

METHUEN & CO. LTD.
36 ESSEX STREET W.C.
LONDON

First Published . . . . *June 25th 1931*
Second Edition 1935

PREFACE

THE late Dr. Wells intended to write a ' Short History of the Roman Empire to the Death of Marcus Aurelius ' which would continue his well-known *Short History of Rome to the Death of Augustus*. He lived to complete about a third of the work.

The publishers asked me to finish the book and I agreed to do so. To attempt a short history of the early Empire is rash enough ; it was more rash to attempt to finish the work of so lucid and skilful a writer as Dr. Wells.

Dr. Wells intended to reprint in this book the chapters on Augustus contained in his earlier book. But they seemed too slender a basis on which to rest a history of the early Empire, and I have ventured to write two new chapters. Chapters III–X are the work of Dr. Wells, though some passages have been slightly altered and paragraphs have been inserted. But the original point of view, e.g. as to the character of Tiberius, has been preserved. The chapters on Roman Britain were written by Dr. Wells. At the time of his death they were in the hands of Miss M. V. Taylor, F.S.A., who had undertaken to revise them. She has very kindly done so for me, and as a result of her comments and suggestions many alterations have been made and many paragraphs have been completely rewritten. But responsibility for errors in the rewritten parts rests with me.

For Chapters I, II, XI–XVI, XIX- XXII, the appendices and maps I must take responsibility. The footnotes indicate my chief debts ; to make mention of all would be impossible, and I hope that this will be regarded as sufficient acknowledgement. But I must record my gratitude to Mr. H. C. Oakley, M.A., of the City of London School, who read many of the chapters in manuscript ; I owe much to his criticism and encouragement. The chapters on Social Life and Economic Conditions are not meant to do more than raise topics for further elaboration. The maps do not claim to make unnecessary the use of an ancient atlas and the Ordnance Survey Map of Roman Britain.

April, 1931   R. H. B.

PREFACE TO THE SECOND EDITION

VARIOUS mis-statements or obscurities which occurred in the first edition have been corrected, and several misprints removed. For drawing my attention to these I am grateful to Mr. G. H. Stevenson, Mr. J. P. V. D. Balsdon, Mr. Norman Whatley, Rev. E. Evans, and Mr. H. C. Oakley.

April, 1935.   R. H. B.

CONTENTS

APPENDICES

TABLES

LIST OF MAPS

12

A SHORT HISTORY OF THE ROMAN EMPIRE

CHAPTER I

THE ESTABLISHMENT OF THE PRINCIPATE
THE PRINCIPATE OF AUGUSTUS, 27 B.C.–A.D. 14

IN August 29 B.C. Caesar Octavianus arrived in Rome from Egypt ; his rivals had one by one been defeated, and by virtue of his triumviral power he was constitutionally [1] commander of the Roman legions and hence master of the Roman world. On him all eyes were turned, for on him the future depended ; what use would he make of his power ? From that date the Empire may be said to begin, and by the labours of this man, who at this time was thirty-four years old, a form of government was constructed which was destined to last in fact for five hundred years and in name and influence for centuries more ; it gave such peace as the world has seldom or never known since. Such was the use which Augustus made of his power.

The Causes of the Empire. Whence came this power ? The Empire was the direct and logical outcome of the failure of the Republic, and in that failure the origins of Octavian's power must be sought. The fall of the Republic was brought about by the weakness of the central government, the Senate ; and this weakness, caused in part by conservatism and in part by selfishness, displayed itself in a refusal to shoulder the responsibility of governing a growing empire. It is true that this empire was often forced upon the government by circumstances, but this is no excuse. Historically the weak-

[1] For another view, cf. Greenidge, *Roman Public Life*, p. 338.

I   I

ness of the central government was the cause of two processes of development, one constitutional, the other military, and these processes converged to lead to the same result, namely, the great military command.

The Great Military Commands. (i) Nobility and office were in the early days of the Republic closely connected, and the holders of office were concerned with the administration of the internal affairs of the city. At first, when Rome acquired new lands, she increased the number of her magistrates and sent them to the new provinces as governors. But increase of magistrates meant also the enlargement of the nobility, and aristocratic exclusiveness resented the admission of men who did not come from families already ennobled by office. But, for one reason or another, expansion was forced upon Rome, and from time to time the Senate devised means to govern the new dependencies with as little alteration of the existing machinery of administration as was possible. At times, however, the Senate deliberately refused to adopt a policy of expansion, even when military or political considerations recommended it : but circumstances in the end proved too powerful. Further, the men sent to govern the dependencies were often unfitted for the work ; appointed in the first place as magistrates they were later placed in charge of armies ; they were unpaid, and therefore rewarded themselves by plundering the provincials. Thus the refusal of the Senate to adapt the machinery of the State to meet new responsibilities led to inefficiency, till the people lost patience, and, taking control into their own hands, voted to capable generals extraordinary powers to deal with pressing emergencies ; by the Gabinian and Manilian laws Pompey held power which foreshadowed that of the Emperor. This precedent once set was difficult to recall, and the great command became a common feature of the last years of the Republic.[1]

(ii) In the early days of the Republic the citizen-farmer was also the soldier ; he fought a brief campaign in defence of the State and returned to his land. Wars, however,

[1] See further, F. B. Marsh, *The Founding of the Roman Empire,* 2nd ed., 1927.

became more frequent ; they were fought at a distance from home, and they lasted for more than one season ; if the State was to have soldiers without at the same time ruining agriculture, some other system of recruiting must be devised. The defeat of Hannibal had two important effects on Roman history ; it committed Rome to further expansion in the Mediterranean and it poured cheap slave labour into Italy. For the moment slave labour tended to replace free labour on the farms, and for this and other reasons a landless rabble gathered in the towns. In 107 B.C. the State needed soldiers and Marius undertook to find an army with which to carry on campaigns hitherto mishandled. He threw over the principle that the possession of land should be the requisite qualification for service in the army and called for volunteers, whom he readily obtained from the landless population. But the armies thus raised directed their allegiance not to the State but to their own commander, whose prime object it now became after a victorious campaign to obtain rewards for his men. To obtain them and to protect himself against loss of power or possible prosecution he must take some part in politics ; if he could not exert his influence here constitutionally, then he must use threats of force. The Senate in desperation to save the constitution could only appeal to some other commander of an army. From the long conflict which ensued Julius Caesar emerged supreme ; he was Emperor in all but name. Yet the old machinery of the constitution continued to function—but under his control. The conspirators dreamed that if he were removed they could galvanize this machinery to life once more. But it was obsolete ; the power now lay with the leader of the army, and when Antony, through alienating Roman sentiment by his schemes of Oriental power, was defeated, Octavian, heir to the power of Julius Caesar his ' father ', was left master of the Roman legions. The Senate had accomplished its own downfall ; the Senate as much as the people had created the great command.

The Character of Octavian. Octavian presents many contrasts with Julius Caesar in origin, character and aims. Julius was an aristocrat, indifferent to tradition and almost cosmopolitan in outlook; he saw his object clearly defined, and he moved along the straightest path to it, pursuing a course to its logical end. Octavian, born in 63 B.C., belonged to a typically bourgeois Italian family, into which his father was the first to bring the honours of curule office. And Octavian, though he did more for the provinces than Caesar had the time to do, was Italian in his point of view. His character, too, did not present the same clear-cut lines as that of Julius Caesar. His strong point was his adaptiveness; hence it was difficult to forecast what course he would take as circumstances changed. Abstract principles or logical consistency did not weigh against the expediency of the moment. There is no reason, for example, to believe that he was by nature cruel, yet he did not shrink from the proscriptions when they served his purpose. By sheer opportunism he realized his aims.

In stature he was not tall; he stood about five feet nine inches, but was well proportioned. He was handsome and his eyes were keen and penetrating and difficult to meet.[1] His health was not robust, yet good enough to stand campaigns and a life of ceaseless care. He had received the usual education, though he never spoke Greek fluently. On occasion hot-tempered, he was aware of this; he could endure rebukes from his friends and was modest enough to seek or accept their advice. His statues suggest nothing if not dignity—the dignity which comes from self-control and confidence in success.

The Problem confronting Octavian. Octavian's power was absolute; the world wanted peace, which was the restoration of law. Would Octavian use his power to restore the peaceful working of the laws? Now Octavian, though Caesar's heir, was his severest critic. Caesar had left the constitution apparently intact, and relying on his soldiers had ignored it; he was murdered because he outraged Roman veneration for the State. Octavian learnt the lesson; the old constitution must not only remain but must really function. Yet Pompey, too, came to grief when by laying aside his great command he left the constitution to work freely once more. Here was

[1] Suet. *Octav.* 79.

another lesson for Octavian ; he could not surrender his command, otherwise chaos would follow. Further, his own position was closely bound up with the working of the State ; he needed its help to reward his soldiers and to administer the world.

His own power, therefore, must in the last resort rest on the army ; yet the State machinery must work as freely as was consistent with the security of his own position. And so in 27 B.C. Augustus (for in this year Octavian took this title) drew up the first form of his government—his first attempt to solve the problem set before him.

The First Form of the Principate. In January 27 B.C. Augustus laid down the powers which he held by virtue of his triumviral office. In the words of the *Monumentum Ancyranum* (p. 54) 'rempublicam ex mea potestate in senatus populique Romani arbitrium transtuli'. But in the same month certain powers were restored to him ; he was given—

I. Proconsular imperium for ten years (he had already received it in 43 B.C.) and on this power the Principate finally rested. It was essentially the same power as that which had been conferred on Pompey. It carried with it command of all the armies of the provinces, but no control of Rome and Italy. Now the armies were stationed in the frontier provinces where there was of course most need for them. Thus Augustus by assuming command of these provinces really acquired control of foreign policy and decided the question of peace or war.

II. The consulship. In 27 B.C. he held the consulship for the seventh time and continued to hold it annually till 23 B.C. By virtue of this office he acquired imperium in Rome and Italy together with control of the machinery of government.

The 'Princeps', i.e. Princeps civitatis—for so Augustus wished to be known—was thus a magistrate and a citizen among citizens. He says of himself, ' In authority I excelled all ; but, as far as power is concerned, I had no more of it than those who were my colleagues in each magistracy.' [1] He held powers which had existed under the Republic, though

[1] *Mon. Anc.* 34. 'Auctoritate' (not 'dignitate') is the newly-discovered reading. For the *Monumentum Ancyranum*, see p. 54.

they had not all been concentrated in the hands of one man. In one further respect, however, there was a difference ; for the fact that he held consular imperium made him superior to other provincial governors.

The Revised Form of the Principate, 23 B.C.   But after four years' trial Augustus discovered a serious flaw in the working of his plan   His tenure of the consulship tended to alienate republican sentiment ; it gave him duties which no doubt took up too much time ; but, more important, it reduced the number of those who having held the consulship would be available as proconsular governors of provinces.   This was a serious matter ; for the civil wars had depleted the families ennobled by office, and, if he halved the supply of consuls, he would have difficulty in providing governors for the provinces, at any rate from the nobility.   Only twice again, therefore, did he hold the consulship, and that for special reasons, as we shall see.   But by refusing the consulship[1] he laid aside important powers.   These he recovered by two means—

I. In 36 B.C. the sacrosanctity attaching to the office of tribune had been conferred on Octavian ; in 30 B.C. this had been augmented by the *ius auxilii* and the right to judge cases of appeal.   In 23 B.C. Augustus assumed the full *tribunicia potestas*[2] which gave him authority in Rome and Italy ; and to call attention to it he dated the years of his reign by his annual holding of the power.   This power associated the Princeps with the people whose champion the tribune had been ; further, by virtue of it he was able to summon the Senate and lay before it any proposal he wished or to veto another's measure.   He could not legally hold the tribunate itself, for by Caesar's adoption he had become a patrician, nor would it be convenient to him to become a member of a body of ten.   The *tribunicia potestas*, however, did not make up for the loss of the consulship, and so—

II. In 23 B.C. and the following years Augustus caused special privileges to be conferred on himself.   These included (*a*) the *imperium maius* which gave power superior to that of any other holder of imperium and so gave the right to interfere

---

[1] *Mon. Anc.* 5, 'consulatum tum datum annuum et perpetuum non accepi ', 22 B.C.   [2] *J.R.S.* xvii. (1927) 2, p. 227.

in the administration of the senatorial provinces,[1] (b) the right
of proposing the first motion at meetings of the Senate (*ius
primae relationis*) ; (c) the right to issue magisterial edicts
(*ius edicendi*) ; (d) the privilege of the twelve fasces, i.e. he
was given the insignia of the consulship and therefore shared
the dignity of the office ; (e) the right to propose candidates for
election to the magistracies. These and other miscellaneous
privileges were later gathered together in a single law and
were conferred by it on succeeding Emperors.[2]

The Titles of the Emperor. The name ' Augustus ' conferred
in B.C. 27 gave no powers ; it was, however, a mark of distinction ; it separated him from other magistrates, and, since
it was an epithet used particularly of the gods, it perhaps
drew attention to his kinship with the deified Caesar. That
the supreme ruler should somehow be in close association
with the gods was almost necessary according to Eastern
notions ; of the worship of the Emperor something will be said
later. The title ' Princeps ' showed how Augustus wished his
position to be regarded ; he was chief citizen, and he refused
to be called *dominus*. As Pontifex Maximus (12 B.C.) Augustus
identified himself with the old State religion, and, as will be
seen hereafter, attached great importance to the office.
' Pater Patriae ', conferred in 2 B.C., was held by most succeeding Emperors. ' Imperator ' had been assumed by Julius
Caesar immediately after his cognomen. Augustus treated
it as a praenomen ; it signified the possession of *imperium
proconsulare*. The letters ' Imp.' combined with a numeral
after the name meant that he had been so often hailed as
' imperator ' by the soldiers after victories in the field. Thus
in A.D. 14 Augustus' full title was Imp. Caesar [3] Divi Filius
Augustus, Pontifex Maximus, Consul xiii, Imp. xx, Tribunicia
Potestate xxxvii, Pater Patriae.

---

[1] Cf. Dio, liii. 32 ; *J.R.S.* xvii. (1927) 1, p. 43.
[2] The so-called *lex de imperio Vespasiani*, of which considerable
fragments remain, conferred these powers on Vespasian, cf. Tac.
Hist. iv. 3. 'Romae senatus cuncta principibus solita Vespasiano
decernit.'
[3] From Tiberius to Vitellius ' Caesar ' comes after the individual
name ; from Vespasian onwards it precedes it, e.g. Imp. Caesar Vespasianus Aug.

Certain Characteristics of the Emperor's Position. By using the forms and institutions of the Republic Augustus sought to make his supreme position less obvious and so less unacceptable to the Romans. Though his supremacy was clear to all, he had the tact, which Caesar lacked, not to obtrude it. But, just because the Emperor's powers were expressed in republican forms, his position suffered from certain defects. The very preservation of those forms tempted deluded aristocrats to believe that the Republic itself could be restored, and the early Emperors had to meet opposition from this quarter. Further, if Augustus was a citizen among citizens with no sanction of hereditary succession or divine right to support his supremacy, it was tempting for others, perhaps more nobly born than he was, to secure the same position for themselves. Again, the Emperor was a magistrate ; according to republican use, when a magistrate laid down his power, a successor would be elected. The supremacy of Augustus would end with his life ; what would happen then, for no magistrate nominated his successor ? The Principate lacked any theory of succession. These defects were early apparent to Augustus and exercised his attention throughout his reign, as we shall see.

The Diarchy. In spite of the Emperor's predominance the Senate was not left powerless, though, partly through its own inefficiency, its power gradually decreased. The aim of Augustus was to secure its co-operation in the running of the Empire ; without its help it would be difficult for him to succeed, for from its ranks he must draw the governors and administrators whom he needed ; his own position, too, would be greatly strengthened if he were associated in the work of government with the Senate, whose prestige was still great. The sharing of the government by the Emperor and Senate has earned for the constitution the name of 'diarchy ', though it was function rather than sovereign power that was divided.

I. By an arrangement made in 27 B.C. the Senate took responsibility for the government of certain of the provinces, the remainder being administered by nominees of the Emperor. To its own provinces the Senate appointed governors ; and from the field of senators the Emperor made his own appointments. The governor of a senatorial province might be an ex-consul or an ex-praetor ; he was called by the title of proconsul and he was assisted by quaestors and legati. The more important imperial provinces were governed by senators, whether ex-consuls or ex-praetors ; no matter what their status they were known as ' legati Augusti pro praetore '. The less important, e.g. Raetia, Noricum, Thrace (after 46 A.D.), were entrusted to procurators of equestrian rank. It must be remembered that there were no legions in senatorial provinces (except Africa), and that the Emperor by virtue of the *maius imperium* specially conferred on him exercised a general supervision over all provinces, senatorial included.[1]

II. The Senate controlled Italy and Rome, though in a few years Augustus made other arrangements for Rome, when senatorial management proved inefficient.

III. *Senatusconsulta* now acquired the force of law without the necessity of ratification by the people. Thus the Senate had greater legislative power now than under the Republic. The Emperor could of course issue edicts, rescripts, etc.

IV. Judicial powers were now granted to the Senate, which became a high court of law under the presidency of the consul.[2] The Emperor also reserved the right to pass judgment on any case, calling in as assessors a body of experts (*consilium*) whom he chose periodically, though till the reign of Hadrian this *consilium* was quite unofficial. The *quaestiones perpetuae* still continued to function.

V. The Senate retained the *aerarium Saturni*, now under praetors (23 B.C.) instead of quaestors.[3] Into it the taxes from the senatorial provinces and from Italy were paid ; for a short time the taxes were farmed, as under the Republic,

[1] How far-reaching this interference was has recently been proved by the discovery of the Augustan Edicts from Cyrene, dated 7–6 B.C. Cyrenaica was a senatorial province, and the edicts deal with such a matter as the trial of civil suits between Greeks in the province. See *J.R.S.* xvii. (1927) 1, p. 33 ; and xix. (1929) 2, p. 219.

[2] When this happened is uncertain. It is probable that the jurisdiction of the Senate developed slowly, but was recognized by the end of the reign of Augustus.

[3] See Appendix iv.

but soon the provinces themselves were made responsible for their collection. The *aerarium* defrayed the cost of public religious ceremonies, the maintenance of public buildings and the construction of roads. But alongside this treasury the Emperor instituted his own, which was called the *fiscus* [1] (though perhaps it was not centralized at Rome till the reign of Claudius). It received the land taxes from the imperial provinces and other dues to be mentioned presently (p. 34), and it paid for the upkeep of the army and navy, the imperial provinces, the corn supply and other expenses. From 27 B.C. both treasuries issued gold and silver coinage, copper ceasing for a time ; but from 15 B.C. the Emperor coined gold and silver, the Senate copper ; and, since the value of copper coinage was in excess of the value of the metal, the *aerarium* gained considerably. Later, imperial control became greater, and local mints more important.

Augustus treated the Senate with studied deference. He consulted it on many points and in the closing years of his reign he set up a *consilium* [2] of senators—a committee with which he discussed matters which would later be brought up in the Senate.

The Emperor's Interference with the Senate. Control of Elections. Thus in some respects the Senate now had greater powers than under the Republic. And Augustus was perfectly sincere in his wish that within the limits defined it should function freely, if also efficiently. At the same time he had to take long views with regard to the efficient administration of the Empire, and to this end he found it necessary to in-

[1] The personal property of the Emperor was called *patrimonium* and was distinct from the *fiscus*. Later it passed, like Crown property, to his successor, being regarded as imperial rather than private or fiscal.

[2] This *consilium* should be kept distinct from the informal judicial *consilium* mentioned above. The political *consilium* was a recognized Standing Committee in the reigns of Augustus and Tiberius, though its membership changed periodically under Augustus ; after Tiberius the term means an informal committee summoned from time to time to advise the Emperor on particular points. Cf. e.g. Juv. iv. 73 ; Tac. *Ann*. xv. 25 ; Hist. Aug. *Vita Pii*, vi. 11 ; *Vita Marci*, xxii. 3. The judicial *consilium* began as an informal advisory committee, and was given official position by Hadrian (p. 245).

fluence the constitution of the Senate. I. He reduced its numbers from 900 to 600 (28 B.C.) and fixed the property qualification of a senator at a million sesterces ; on other occasions also (8 B.C. and A.D. 14) he revised the roll. II. The senatorial career normally implied the following steps : vigintivirate, i.e. boards of officials performing minor magisterial duties, military tribunate, quaestorship, aedileship or tribunate, praetorship, consulate. The quaestorship was the lowest office which gave admission to the Senate, in which a man's rank depended on the last office held. Augustus reserved the right to place a man who had not passed through the lower grades into a grade which would give membership of the Senate, generally the praetorian (*adlectio*). III. The people continued to elect the magistrates ; by controlling the elections, therefore, Augustus would be able to influence the constitution of the Senate. He did this (*a*) by *commendatio*, i.e. by expressing his approval of certain candidates who were therefore duly elected [1] ; (*b*) by *nominatio*, i.e. by nominating as many candidates as there were vacancies ; (*c*) by the bestowal of the *latus clavus*, the broad band which members of senatorial families wore on the tunic. A candidate for the vigintivirate had to be of senatorial rank ; by bestowing the *latus clavus* on men outside this rank, he made them eligible for the vigintivirate, and so set them on the lowest rung of a senatorial career.

The People. Under the new regime the people still retained in theory some of its powers, though in practice they meant little. Judicial powers were now taken from the people. The assembly, however, still met to elect magistrates and to pass laws, but, as has been seen, the elections could be controlled by the Emperor and legislation by the assembly became very infrequent. The *comitia* for a long time conferred the tribunican power, but this was a mere formality, for the preliminary vote of the Senate was necessary. The powers which the people originally exercised thus passed into the Emperor's hands ; the mob at Rome was quite incapable of serious government, and in default of representative institu-

[1] He did not 'commend' candidates for the Consulship.

tions it was natural and right that the people should become extinct as a political force.

THE IMPERIAL CIVIL SERVICE. (i) *Proconsulars*. The reason for the Emperor's control of the elections may be briefly explained. The Senate possessed a civil service in the magistrates; Augustus had no such help, though the major work of administration fell on him. By degrees, therefore, he must build one up through the constitutional means at his disposal. For the government of his provinces and for the command of legions he needed men who would be loyal to him. During the first few years of his reign he tried to appoint to these posts personal friends or members of his family whom he could trust; as these died and his share of the proconsular provinces became greater, he found that he had to exercise increasing control of the elections to secure the right men. And so in A.D. 2 he had recourse to the plan of appointing *consules suffecti* to succeed the consuls of the year after six months of office. This doubled the supply of consulars and increased the supply of men who, since they owed advancement to the Emperor's intervention, were likely to be loyal to him. *Adlectio, nominatio*, the appointment of *consules suffecti* all tended to render the Senate subservient to him.

(ii) *The Equites*. To fill the subordinate posts of the civil service Augustus organized the Equites as an official class, giving them increasing prominence in the latter years of his reign. The qualifications for admission to this class were the equestrian census of four hundred thousand sesterces, free birth (a qualification often waived) and good character; the son of a senator automatically became a knight till he reached the age of twenty-five. Augustus revived the old ceremony of *transvectio equitum*, the parade of the knights, for which they were organized in six squadrons (*turmae*). The Emperor read out the names of the *ordo*, and omission of any knight's name meant that for some reason or other his membership was cancelled. Knights now received the right to wear the *trabea* and a gold ring, and special seats were reserved for them in the theatre. The old feud between the equestrian and senatorial classes on the matter of the control of the law-courts was now closed ; for Augustus gave to the equites exclusively the right to sit as jurors.[1] They were enrolled in three panels (*decuriae*), while a fourth, composed of men possessing half the equestrian census, heard less important civil suits. Thus the *ordo* was recognized as a distinct official class. To it Augustus threw open varied and interesting careers in the government service. The equites now furnished the subordinate officers in the army, holding the posts of *praefectus* or *tribunus* of an auxiliary cohort, *tribunus* of a legion, *praefectus* of a squadron of auxiliary cavalry (*ala*).[2] These army posts were regarded as qualifying service for a vast number of financial and administrative appointments as procurators in the provinces, both imperial and senatorial. Promotion took place from grade to grade, though the equestrian career was not so clearly defined as the senatorial. When new provinces were added to the Empire, e.g. Egypt, Noricum, Raetia, Augustus appointed knights as governors ; and newly created posts, such as the command of the fleet or the control of the corn supply, were filled from this class. The Prefecture of the Praetorian Guard was the crown of the equestrian career and normally won for its holder *ornamenta consularia* when the post was resigned. But it cannot be emphasized too strongly that the knights were entirely dependent on the Emperor ; they owed their position and appointment to him ; they held their posts during his pleasure and they could not hand on their equestrian status to their sons.

Freedmen in the Emperor's Service. The fiction that the Emperor was only a citizen, albeit a magistrate, deprived him of such ministers and public servants as a monarch could command. Apart from the machinery of government inherited from the Republic, the Emperor must depend on his own household for administrative help. Every Roman of means maintained slave or freedmen stewards and bailiffs to

[1] Greenidge, *op. cit.*, p. 404, expresses some doubt on this.

[2] Men of senatorial rank not yet old enough to enter the Senate (age 25 years) became knights and as such served as officers, but no career in the army was open to them. If a knight served as a centurion —and service in this rank became very attractive—he automatically surrendered his equestrian status.

keep accounts and administer his property, and on such freedmen Augustus relied for help as secretaries and accountants (*procuratores fisci*), particularly, perhaps, after the deaths of Maecenas and Agrippa, his ministers for many years. Such freedmen were often well educated and entirely fitted for their duties. Thus a very important branch of the civil service arose, which in time included secretariates of great influence and dignity (p. 88). These officials were often extremely able, and certain Emperors who could not attract to themselves the allegiance of the official classes tended to rely too much on them ; but on the whole it may be said that the State was well served by these freedmen administrators.

Maecenas and Agrippa. In his rise to power Augustus received the advice and loyal assistance of two men who continued their service without jealousy or discontent for many years of his reign. M. Vipsanius Agrippa (63–12 B.C.) was the constant adviser of Octavian in the difficult years immediately following the murder of Caesar. In the war with Sextus Pompeius, at Perusia, later in Gaul and Spain and Illyria he devoted his untiring energy to the cause of his master ; he never asked for reward and agreed to whatever plans his master made for him. If Cassius Dio's account records truth, Agrippa urged Octavian not to establish the Principate, but to restore the Republic as it was. Yet he did his best to make the Principate a success. C. Cilnius Maecenas, *circ.* 65–8 B.C., was utterly unlike the blunt and rugged Agrippa. He was luxurious, even effeminate ; he could nevertheless show resolution and enterprise. The peace of Brundisium was due to his diplomacy. During the war with Sextus Pompeius he was for part of the time in charge of Rome, invested with full authority to act without reference to Octavian. His influence in favour of his master was in later years very powerful ; he gathered round him men of ability and literary talent and turned them into apostles of the new regime ; Vergil, Horace, Propertius were useful allies in the work of reconciling men to the Principate. Without the help of these two men it is doubtful whether Augustus could have succeeded in his vast labour of reorganization.

Conspiracies against Augustus. Something will be said

later about the ' opposition under the Empire '. Here we may
note that the first Emperor was not immune from threats.
Conspiracies were formed against him, though we know little
about them. Fannius Caepio, together with Terentius Varro
Murena, the Emperor's colleague in the consulate, formed a
plot against the life of the Emperor in 23 B.C. It was detected
in good time ; Augustus regarded the matter in serious light
and executed Caepio and Murena. In A.D. 4 Cn. Cornelius
Cinna made a similar attempt, but on this occasion Augustus
granted pardon, on the advice of Livia, his wife. Other
conspiracies need not detain us ; it must be remembered,
however, that Augustus had to face much opposition, even
though it did not always take the form of attempts on his
life.

The Reorganization of the Roman World. A brief account
has now been given of Augustus' reconstruction of the government. While he was solving this problem—and the solution
was not found in a moment—other pressing work had to be
done. The civil wars had thrown the world out of joint ;
at home and abroad reorganization was imperative in every
department of life. We may now describe Augustus' social
and moral legislation [1] and the measures which he took to
provide for the well-being of Rome and Italy.

Religious Reforms. It was the purpose of Augustus to
direct men's eyes to the future rather than to permit them
to dwell on the past. Yet he knew Roman conservatism of
thought. In his reconstruction of the constitution he had
clothed his new power beneath republican forms ; in the
same way he sought to revive old religious usages to give
sanction to the new imperial order. He aimed at encouraging
a weary world, which had long suffered disaster and therefore
was ready to receive whatever comfort religion could give,
to believe that a new era had dawned and that he was
peculiarly the agent chosen by the gods to inaugurate it. No
small part of his success as Emperor was due to the readiness
with which Rome responded. Yet his motive was not wholly

---

[1] *Mon. Anc.* 8. ' Legibus novis latis et multa exempla maiorum
exolescentia iam ex nostro usu reduxi et multarum rerum exempla
imitanda posteris tradidi.'

political ; he himself was superstitious and he revered the past. In his struggle with Antony he stood forth as the champion of Roman character and religion against the influences of the East, and as Emperor he tried to spread the confidence in Roman destiny which he sincerely felt. He rebuilt temples and revived ceremonies. ' Eighty and two temples of the gods I repaired in the city in obedience to a decree of the Senate '[1] (28 B.C.). For the temples had fallen into ruin in the troublous times of the last century, which were sent, said the poets, as a punishment for neglected piety and virtue. ' 'Tis no wonder that cobwebs have covered the shrines, and rank grass possesses the deserted courts.' [2] In restoring public worship Augustus gave prominence to three cults, all of which bore reference in some way to himself or his descent. To Mars Ultor he built a temple ; it was vowed at Philippi to the god who avenged Caesar's murder, but the title of the god perhaps gained a wider significance after the triumph over the Parthians in 19 B.C. The cult of Venus Genetrix, the mother of the Roman race and, in particular, of the Julian family, was fostered by the Emperor and the poets. Apollo, under whose care Augustus regarded himself, received much honour, including a new temple on the Palatine [3] ; ' tuus iam regnat Apollo ' says Vergil, speaking of the new Augustan age. Further, the influence of the sacred colleges was revived ; the Emperor became a member of the various orders, fratres Arvales, augurs, fetiales and others,[4] and took an active part in their rites ; the Vestal virgins, too, were restored to their ancient dignity.

In 17 B.C., at the height of his success, Augustus revived the *ludi saeculares*, originally introduced in time of plague and sacred to Dis Pater and Proserpina, deities of the underworld. He changed their character, dedicating them to Apollo and Diana ; they were to be celebrated every 110 years as a thanksgiving to the gods and a memorial of the new era. For the preceding year had seen extensive social and moral legis-

---

[1] *Mon. Anc.* 20.
[2] Prop. ii. 6, 35, and cf. Horace's well-known lines, ' Delicta maiorum immeritus lues, Romane, donec templa refeceris ', etc., *Odes*, iii. 6.
[3] Described in Propertius, ii. 31.   [4] *Mon. Anc.* 7.

lation to which a religious significance was now to be given, and at the festival itself the Emperor's grandsons were formally adopted by him. The *carmen saeculare*, which Horace composed to be sung by a chorus of boys and girls, is still extant. In 12 B.C. Augustus took the office of Pontifex Maximus, entreated to do so by the multitude, and thus the supreme political ruler became also the highest religious authority. Combined with the tribunician power the office completed the sacred character of the Principate.

To help him in the restoration of old Roman cults and Roman virtues the Emperor enlisted the poets and literary men of the day ; these Maecenas gathered round him and inspired with the ideals of the Principate ; Horace, Vergil, Propertius were his friends. In these writers there is no hostility to the Republic ; they see the culmination of its glories in the Principate. But while they admire past heroes, they admire also the manner of life which fashioned them— the simplicity of country life; and the Georgics of Vergil— 'tua, Maecenas, haud mollia iussa'[1]—were a powerful plea for the simplicity of character which in this corrupt age Augustus strove to restore.

Moral Reforms. For it was evident that the salvation of society depended on the encouragement of a healthier morality. But unfortunately the performance of religious ceremonies had little to do with morality, as the Emperor discovered, and he was compelled to resort to legislation, urged to do so, it was said, by the Senate. The immorality of the day was sapping the life of Roman society and, through the resulting disinclination to marry, was endangering the perpetuation of the Roman stock. And so Augustus attempted to restore family life, with its virtues and responsibilities, to its former position of dignity. By a series of Julian laws passed in 18 B.C.[2] he regulated the conditions of divorce and imposed penalties on the unmarried and on the married who had no children ; a bachelor could not receive a legacy, and the

---

[1] iii. 41.

[2] He did not assume *Censoria potestas* or hold the office of Censor, *Mon. Anc.* 6. He held three censuses, in 28 and 8 B.C. and A.D. 14, by virtue of his consular imperium. Cf. *Mon. Anc.* 8.

childless married man paid to the State half of any legacy left to him. Immorality, which hitherto could be punished only as a matter of private injury, now became an offence against the State. Many years later, in A.D. 9, these penalties were reinforced by a system of rewards, embodied in the *Lex Papia Poppaea*. The father of three children at Rome obtained privileges (*ius trium liberorum*), chief of which were exemption from certain taxes and preference in standing for offices, even the highest, e.g. the governorships of provinces.

Augustus strove to check extravagance by sumptuary laws, which extended to such details as the amount which might be spent on a *cena* suitable to various occasions. He encouraged the wearing of the heavy and formal *toga*, which in the prevailing slackness had fallen into disuse even at State functions. He forbade women to attend athletic games and in the theatre he assigned to them seats apart from the men ; places were also set apart for senators, knights and freedmen.

Angry protests naturally followed the passing of these laws ; Augustus, however, stood firm, and there is little doubt that he received much support from quarters which viewed with dismay the prevailing laxity. Whether his legislation produced any effect it is difficult to say [1] ; his own sincerity perhaps had some influence,[2] but it is clear that the penalties were often evaded and no example was set by the Emperor's own family and friends. The consuls who proposed the *Lex Papia Poppaea* were bachelors ; Maecenas' luxury was proverbial, and the immorality of Julia, the Emperor's daughter, was notorious. Perhaps that part of his legislation which affected slaves and freedmen had the most lasting results ; these will be discussed in a later chapter.

New Buildings in Rome. No attempt can be made here to describe in detail the change in the appearance of Rome during this reign. It was the boast of Augustus that he found it a city of brick and left it a city of marble. His aim was to make the capital worthy of the Empire, and the

---

[1] The *Mon. Anc.* says that in 28 B.C. the number of citizens was 4,063,000 and in A.D. 14 4,937,000.

[2] Cf. Horace, *Odes*, iii. 1–6.

example which he set in replanning parts of the city and
erecting buildings of dignified architecture was followed by
private owners who, thanks to the Augustan peace, could
now afford to turn their houses into palaces set in spacious
gardens. The example set by Augustus and his friends was
ambitious. The forum of Augustus, built on land purchased
for the purpose, was roughly a rectangle of about 400 feet
by 300 feet : it was built to give room for law courts
and other needs of the growing city ; its chief feature was
the temple of Mars Ultor, and along its sides statues of
all those who from earliest days had won the honour of
a triumph were set up. Round it ran a wall nearly 140
feet high. The Campus Esquilinus, hitherto used as a burial
ground, was reclaimed and turned into a park, and the Campus
Agrippae, part of the Campus Martius, was laid out as public
gardens by Agrippa. As early as 28 B.C. Augustus erected
a Mausoleum in the Campus Martius, where it had become
the custom to bury men of distinction ; it was 'a dynastic
rather than a personal' monument (p. 54). Agrippa, who
contributed much to the rebuilding of Rome, was responsible
for a group of buildings in the Campus Martius. The Pantheon—a huge rotunda preceded by a portico—was dedicated
to Venus and Mars and glorified the Julian *gens* : it was
rebuilt by Hadrian (p. 248). Close at hand Agrippa built
also the Thermae called by his name, and the Stagnum, an
artificial lake fed by the waters of the Aqua Virgo, an aqueduct also erected by Agrippa. The Porticus Octaviae was
built by Augustus in the name of Octavia, his sister ; within
its enclosure there were temples, and later a library was
added by Octavia in memory of her son, Marcellus (p. 27) ;
in his memory also the Theatre of Marcellus was built. The
new temple of Apollo and the repairing of many others has
already been mentioned (p. 16), and the building of aqueducts by Agrippa and Augustus will be noticed later.

*Restoration of Order, and the Administration of Rome and
Italy.* It was part of Augustus' original design to leave Rome
and Italy in the hands of the Senate while he devoted himself
to the provinces. But, as the inefficiency of the Senate
became evident, he was compelled to take over one depart-

ment after another. Indeed it was his policy to give the
Senate complete independence within a limited sphere and to
justify his encroachment on their powers by their inefficiency ;
at the same time it is only fair to the Senate to remember that
the Emperor's superior power and the unity of control which
he was able to exert gave him great advantages. In 22 B.C.
there was a severe shortage of corn ; Augustus refused the
people's demand that he should become dictator and consul
for life, but he took over the *cura annonae* and by means of
his control of Egypt relieved the famine.[1]   Between 18 B.C.
and A.D. 6 he appointed *curatores* to organize the corn supply.
In A.D. 6 another shortage occurred, and he appointed a
praefectus annonae, of equestrian rank, to organize the supply
of corn and regulate its market price and to arrange for
distribution to some 200,000 persons in Rome.   The expenses
were defrayed by the fiscus.   The water supply also passed
into imperial control, though not so soon.   In 33 B.C. Agrippa,
as aedile, took over the system of aqueducts ; he organized
a gang of 240 of his own slaves and trained them as watermen ;
on his death he bequeathed the staff to Augustus, who handed
it over to the Senate and created a *cura aquarum*.   In the
reign of Augustus four new aqueducts were built.   The final
step was taken by the Emperor Claudius who brought the
system directly under the control of an imperial *procurator
aquarum*.

To guard the city against fire Augustus took over the fire-
brigade from the aediles in A.D. 6 ; he organized it in seven
cohortes vigilum, composed chiefly of freedmen under a *praefectus* of equestrian rank.   He also appointed *curatores operum
publicorum* to maintain the fabric of public buildings ; they
were senators of praetorian rank responsible to him.   And
in 20 B.C. *curatores viarum*, of praetorian and equestrian rank,
were charged with the upkeep of the roads of Italy ; the
system of State couriers—*cursus publicus*—with relays of
horses ready at intervals on the main roads was tentatively
begun in this reign and greatly developed later.   But the
two most important officials yet remain to be mentioned,
though their influence did not reach its height till later times.

[1] *Mon. Anc.* 5.

By ancient right the consul had the power to appoint a *prae-fectus urbi* to represent him in Rome during his absences. Augustus revived the office, appointing a man of senatorial rank to maintain order with the help of three urban cohorts and to exercise certain judicial powers. Agrippa discharged this office in 21 B.C. during the absence of Augustus in the East, and, when Augustus and Agrippa were both absent in 16–13 B.C., Statilius Taurus was *praefectus urbi*. Under Augustus the office was temporary ; in the next reign it became permanent and very important. Further, the new office of *praefectus praetorio*, of equestrian rank, commanded great power and dignity ; the *praefectus* was in charge of the praetorian cohorts, the Emperor's guard, which were organized in 28 B.C. and were stationed in Italy during the reign of Augustus, in Rome during the reign of Tiberius and after. His power extended beyond Italy ; he could issue army orders, and, in later reigns, was at the head of the civil service. He occupied the nearest position to the throne, and this fact reveals the military character of the Principate. Augustus realized the danger which might come from so powerful an office, and he appointed two *praefecti*, hoping thus to reduce its power. Later Emperors adopted this and other expedients, as will be seen ; but none the less the power of the praetorian prefect was often the decisive factor in the making of Emperors.

The Army. The chief military changes which Augustus introduced were : (i) the maintenance of a standing army ; (ii) the organization of the *auxilia* ; (iii) the distribution of the legions in permanent camps in the frontier provinces.

I. After his great victories Augustus settled many of his veterans on lands chiefly in the north of Italy and in the neighbourhood of the great roads (41, 36, 30 B.C.). But at the close of the civil wars there still remained about sixty legions. These he reduced gradually to (probably) twenty-eight, and at the end of his reign the army list contained twenty-five legions.[1] Great changes were introduced in the method of recruiting and the conditions of service. The

---

[1] By the time of Marcus Aurelius thirteen new legions had been created, and eight had ceased to exist.

legions were recruited chiefly from Italy and the western provinces, that is, from the most Romanized parts of the Empire, though the East provided a certain number of recruits. On enlistment the legionary took an oath of allegiance to his Emperor and became a Roman citizen ; many of the rights of citizenship, however, he could not exercise till after his discharge. After a service of twenty years (after A.D. 5) he might receive his discharge,[1] though there existed no absolute right to it. To provide pensions for time-expired soldiers Augustus instituted the *aerarium militare*, which he endowed with an enormous sum, and maintained by the taxes on inheritances and on sales (p. 34). Legionary service became a career which offered many attractions : the pay was good—225 denarii a year—and was augmented by gifts—*donativa*—given occasionally by Augustus and periodically by later Emperors ; there were chances of distinction and promotion, and for its veterans the State undertook to provide land or a gratuity. A legion numbered about 5,500 men with 120 horsemen and attached to it were *auxilia*, infantry or cavalry or both. Over each legion a *legatus legionis* was set. This was a new post created by Augustus and must be kept distinct from the *legatus Augusti pro praetore* who governed an imperial province and controlled all the military forces within it. The legions bore numbers and names ; certain numbers appear twice or thrice in the army list, for their number depended on the circumstances of their origin, but the title differentiated them ; for example, at Augustus' death the V Alaudae was stationed in Lower Germany, the V Macedonica in Moesia.[2]

II. The *auxilia*, which perhaps equalled the legionaries in number, were recruited from the less Romanized provinces and served for twenty-five years for a pay of seventy denarii a year, Roman citizenship being given on discharge. They were organized in *cohortes* or *alae* which bore distinctive titles

---

[1] On his discharge he received a *diploma militare* specifying his service and the rights to which he was entitled.

[2] Names were given for various reasons. Some legions took their title from their insignia, e.g. Alaudae ; others from their enemy, e.g. Scythica ; to others general names were given, e.g. Victrix, Rapax, etc.

taken generally from the country of recruitment; the units had no separate status of their own, being brigaded with a legion. They were stationed generally in a country remote from their homes, though this was not always the case, for service in the home-country popularized the service. But the danger of allowing clan-regiments to serve in their native country became apparent in later years (p. 156).

III. There was now a permanent army of about 280,000 men besides the specialist corps to be mentioned presently. The army, which was none too large for its duties, was stationed in permanent camps in the frontier provinces. This was a system which had very important results. On the one hand, it was attractive for the men, and in some respects made for efficiency, since the soldiers became familiar with local conditions. Further, round the camp grew up settlements of traders—*canabae*; from them small towns developed, in which the ex-soldier frequently settled, and thus Roman influence and town life was spread in remote districts. On the other hand, there was a tendency for officers and men to make themselves too comfortable and to resent a change of station, while if the troops were left too long in the same district they identified themselves with local interests. The advantages and disadvantages of the system became apparent in the course of the first century.

Besides the legions and the *auxilia*, the praetorians, urban cohorts and *vigiles* formed part of the regular army. The praetorians, recruited from the most urbanized parts of Italy, numbered 9,000, organized in nine cohorts; service was for sixteen years, and the pay was originally 500 denarii, though this was raised considerably. The status of the three urban cohorts was much the same as that of the legionaries. Augustus also employed a bodyguard of Batavians and Germans, but these must be counted as part of his personal staff rather than of the army.

The Fleet. In Republican times Rome possessed no permanent fleet. But Augustus owed his position to a naval battle, and he was alive to the need of a permanent fleet for defence and for police work. The Roman Empire was built up round the Mediterranean Sea, and its frontiers were for

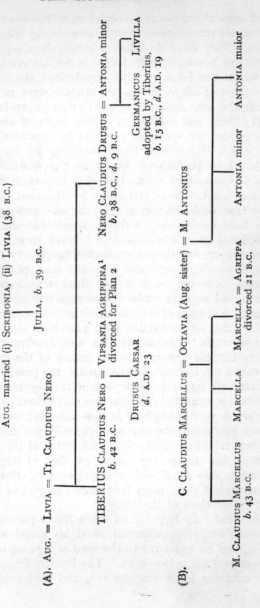

THE FAMILY OF AUGUSTUS

(A). AUG. = LIVIA = TI. CLAUDIUS NERO

AUG. married (i) SCRIBONIA, (ii) LIVIA (38 B.C.)

JULIA, b. 39 B.C.

TIBERIUS CLAUDIUS NERO = VIPSANIA AGRIPPINA¹
b. 42 B.C.   divorced for Plan 2

NERO CLAUDIUS DRUSUS = ANTONIA minor
b. 38 B.C., d. 9 B.C.

GERMANICUS   LIVILLA
adopted by Tiberius,
b. 15 B.C., d. A.D. 19

DRUSUS CAESAR
d. A.D. 23

(B). C. CLAUDIUS MARCELLUS = OCTAVIA (Aug. sister) = M. ANTONIUS

M. CLAUDIUS MARCELLUS   MARCELLA   MARCELLA = AGRIPPA   ANTONIA minor   ANTONIA maior
b. 43 B.C.   divorced 21 B.C.

¹ Daughter of Agrippa and Pomponia, who was daughter of Atticus.

AUGUSTUS' DYNASTIC PLANS

First Plan. M. CLAUDIUS MARCELLUS = JULIA
                  d. 23 B.C.   *m.* 25 B.C.

Second Plan.
      AGRIPPA = JULIA
     d. 12 B.C. *m.* 21 B.C.

GAIUS   LUCIUS   AGRIPPINA = GERMANICUS   AGRIPPA POSTUMUS   JULIA
adopted into Aug. family 17 B.C.   C. CAESAR (CALIGULA)   (unsuitable)
d. A.D. 4   *d.* A.D. 2

Third Plan. TIBERIUS = JULIA, to provide protector for Gaius and Lucius. Julia banished 2 B.C.
                  m. 11 B.C.
and TIBERIUS, adopted A.D. 4, invested with special powers A.D. 13.

the most part waterways—the North Sea, the Channel, the Atlantic, the Black Sea, the Red Sea, the Rhine, the Danube, the Euphrates.[1] Permanent naval bases were established by Augustus at Misenum, to police the West, and at Ravenna to operate in Eastern waters ; there was also a base of less importance at Forum Julii. Later Emperors developed the fleet, and Classes Britannica, Africana, Pontica and others are known, besides the flotillas on the Rhine and Danube. But the fleet never enjoyed the same prestige as the army. It was manned in the time of Augustus by slaves, officered by freedmen and commanded by a knight ; but during the first two centuries of the Empire its importance increased with corresponding improvement in the status of its personnel.

The Family of Augustus ; the First Plan to Found a Dynasty. Augustus married three times. His first wife is of no political importance. His second wife, Scribonia, whom he married to please Sextus Pompeius, her relative, need not concern us, except in that she bore Augustus a daughter, Julia, who was destined to play a prominent part in his plan for the succession. In 38 B.C. he divorced Scribonia to marry Livia, who was a woman noted for her ability and beauty, and who retained the affection of her husband to the end. Now Livia had been divorced from her former husband, Tiberius Claudius Nero, and by this marriage she had two sons, Tiberius Claudius Nero (born 42 B.C.) and Nero Claudius Drusus (born 38 B.C.). Thus in 38 B.C. Augustus had one daughter and two stepsons. Livia bore him no children.

Octavia, the sister of Augustus, a woman of great gentleness, had married C. Claudius Marcellus ; their children were M. Claudius Marcellus (born 43 B.C.) and two daughters, both named Marcella. Octavia had for political reasons later married M. Antonius, and her two daughters were both named Antonia. Thus Augustus had a daughter, two stepsons, one nephew and four nieces. To secure the succession for his family he arranged marriages and divorces among his kindred and friends without scruple as failure attended one plan after another.

His first plan was the marriage of his nephew Marcellus with

[1] Cf. Tac. *Ann.* i. 9.

his daughter Julia.   Amid great jubilation the marriage took place in 25 B.C.   Now Agrippa, who had already married Marcella, had perhaps entertained hopes of succeeding to the Principate, and this sign of favour conferred on Marcellus was a blow to him.   In 23 B.C. Augustus fell ill.   He handed to his colleague in the consulship a list of the military forces and a statement of the finances of the Empire as though restoring the power to the Senate ;   to Agrippa he handed his signet ring, by this act commending him as his successor ;   Marcellus was obviously too young.   But Augustus recovered, and on learning that there had been friction between Agrippa and Marcellus he assigned to Agrippa a mission in the East.   But Augustus' dynastic plan failed ;   the young Marcellus—' heu, miserande puer '—died in 23 B.C. at Baiae.   His death called forth the famous lines of Vergil which so touched his mother, Octavia, that she fainted as the poet recited them.

The Second Plan.   Still Augustus hoped for a successor in the direct line.   To this end he made Agrippa divorce Marcella [1] and marry Julia (21 B.C.).   In 18 B.C. he conferred the tribunician power (renewed in 13 B.C.) on Agrippa, who already (before 22 B.C.) had received proconsular imperium ;   thus he made him consort in the imperial power.   To Agrippa and Julia there were born three sons and two daughters, the eldest being Gaius and Lucius.   These two boys were adopted into the Emperor's family in 17 B.C., and were thus marked out as successors to the Principate.   In 12 B.C. Agrippa died and, though the succession was not thus imperilled, it was felt that the young sons of Julia needed a protector, for Augustus was in feeble health.   Augustus then caused his stepson, Tiberius, to divorce his wife, Agrippina, the daughter of Agrippa and Pomponia, in order to marry Julia, daughter of Augustus and widow of Agrippa.

Tiberius and Drusus ; Julia ; Gaius and Lucius.   Tiberius and his brother Drusus had already achieved much distinction in warfare on the northern frontier, as we shall see later.   In 13 B.C. Tiberius held the consulship and about

---

[1] Agrippa married I. Pomponia, the daughter of Atticus, the friend of Cicero—their daughter was Vipsania Agrippina, who married Tiberius the Emperor ;   II. Marcella ;   III. Julia.

9 B.C. was invested with the proconsular imperium, and three years later with the *tribunicia potestas* for five years. He was thus elevated to the position which Agrippa had held. In 9 B.C. Drusus died, and his death was a severe loss to Augustus. Tiberius and Julia's sons Gaius and Lucius now remained nearest in the succession. But Tiberius realized that he was intended to be merely the protector of Gaius and Lucius and not to be Emperor ; for, though he was now consort, he was not adopted into the imperial family. Sent on a mission to Armenia he refused to carry it out and went into voluntary retirement at Rhodes. This desertion by Tiberius was a disappointment to Augustus, who felt that he had been betrayed by the man upon whom he had come to depend, though perhaps he never really liked his reserved nature.

Yet another grief awaited Augustus. The open profligacy of Julia had long been notorious in Rome, and at last rumours of it reached her father's ears. For years he had been endeavouring to reform the morals of Roman society by every method in his power. His anger was unrestrained ; he banished his daughter to the island of Pandateria (2 B.C.), her lovers were driven into exile and one was put to death.

Meantime Gaius and Lucius grew up. Gaius received proconsular *imperium* and the consulship, and was sent on the mission to Armenia. Lucius had assumed the *toga virilis* in 2 B.C., and both men were proclaimed *principes juventutis* by the equites,[1] a title which in future marked out a successor to the Principate who was as yet too young to be a Senator. But disaster followed quickly. Lucius died at Massilia in A.D. 2, and Gaius received a wound at the siege of Artagira and died in Lycia in A.D. 4 (p. 38).[2]

The Third Plan. No alternative remained to Augustus but to recognize Tiberius as his successor, for Agrippa Postumus, the brother of Gaius and Lucius, was scarcely suitable. Yet even so, Augustus seems to have clung to other hopes. Drusus, Tiberius' brother, for whom Augustus had entertained a real affection, had married the younger Antonia, Octavia's daughter, and their son was Germanicus ; Augustus married

---

[1] Cf. *Mon. Anc.* 14.

[2] *Ibid.* 'Filios meos, quos iuvenes mihi eripuit fortuna, ...'

him to Agrippina, daughter of Agrippa and Julia. But he had
to restore Tiberius to public life ; in A.D. 4 he adopted him
and the young Agrippa Postumus [1] as his sons, but he insisted
that Tiberius should in turn adopt Germanicus. Tiberius
was invested with the tribunician power for ten years, and
later, in A.D. 13, a special law was brought in by which he
received proconsular power equal to that of the Emperor, while
his tribunician power was extended indefinitely ; his position
was therefore secured. Thus Augustus, after many vain
designs, was forced to adopt Tiberius as his heir. He never
liked him personally, but he saw that there was no one else
capable enough to succeed to the Principate. ' Hoc reipublicae causa facio,' he said of the adoption ; in one sense
the words were no compliment to Tiberius ; in another sense
they reflect credit both upon him and upon their speaker.

The Worship of the Emperor. Before Augustus' reorganization of the provinces is described, a brief account must be
given of the honours which were paid to him as a god, for, as
will be seen, the influence of Emperor-worship was very great.
The reasons for the growth of this cult, which to the ancient
world was so natural and to us is so strange, cannot here be
discussed in detail ; the following points must suffice. In
the East the distinction between man and god had never
been so clear-cut as in the West ; eponymous heroes are
common in Greek cult ; Oriental nations willingly deified
their rulers during their lifetimes, and, after Alexander had
conquered the East, they were willing to transfer this honour
to him and to his successors. The worship of kings in the
Hellenistic Age was common enough and was highly organized
with a definite political purpose. When Rome succeeded
to the rule of the East, her provincial governors sometimes
received divine honours, and temples were in some cases built
to them.

Meantime in Roman religion there were kindred elements,
though Roman restraint prevented extravagance. The
Manes were honoured with offerings placed on the tomb,
which was an altar, and there is much evidence that, particularly among the populace, the title *deus* and *dea* was regularly

[1] He soon proved unsatisfactory and was banished.

applied to the dead. Even Cicero in all seriousness wished to raise a temple to his daughter Tullia and to pay her divine honours ; he had the support, he maintained, of the Stoic philosophers, for whom virtue conferred divinity. The amazing popularity of Julius Caesar and the extravagant adulation paid to him caused the next step to be taken ; in his lifetime he was hailed as a god, and at his death the devotion of the people, fostered by Antony and later by Octavian, resulted in the foundation of the cult of Divus Julius, which spread into Italy.

When Octavian became master of the world, similar honours were offered to him by the provinces and the populace at home. After Actium he travelled through the East, which was willing to deify him at once. He moulded his policy with characteristic discretion. He allowed temples to be built to him in Bithynia and Asia on condition that his name was associated with that of the goddess Rome and that no Roman took part in the cult. In the course of time the Western provinces followed suit, till by his death most provinces had at least one temple in his honour. Meantime the populace at Rome begged that a temple should be built to him in the capital itself, and the praises of the Court poets had not scrupled to use the terms ' deus ' and ' divus '.[1] Augustus refused the temple, but he yielded to popular wish in reviving the worship of the *lares compitales* which Julius Caesar had abolished. This cult of the *lares*, who were two in number and were protectors of the locality, was organized in every ' region ' in Rome and was devotedly carried on by the lower classes. By the side of the *lares* the *genius* of Augustus was now placed, and thus the Emperor's cult was established in Rome and linked to one of the oldest and most characteristic elements in Roman religion. Guilds sprang up for the celebration of the chief days of his life and priests of the cult (*flamines*) offered prayer for his safety. For the maintenance of the cult in the townships of Italy and the provinces a special order—the *seviri Augustales*—composed chiefly of freedmen, was instituted. More will be said of

[1] Verg. *Ecl.* i. 7 ; *Georg.* i. 42 ; *Aen.* i. 290. Hor., *Odes*, i. 2, 45 ; iii. 5, 1 ; iv. 5, 32 ; *Ep.* ii. 1, 15. Ovid, *Pont.* ii. 8, 9 ; iv. 9, 111.

this order when life in the municipalities is described (p. 345) ; but here it may be said that great success attended the institution, which evoked the loyalty and the public spirit of the class for which it was intended.

In this way, briefly, Emperor-worship was established. But Augustus was careful to link it to old beliefs and ritual and so gave less offence to Roman sentiment. Nor did he evolve the plan at once, or realize to the full, perhaps, its political utility. It fulfilled several purposes. Among the Romans it gave a religious sanction to the new order of things and invested the Emperor's person with divine sacredness. In the provinces, where the worship of Rome was organized round a central *ara* established in the main town (p. 33), it gave unity to tribes or small political units by superimposing a common loyalty. It afforded a common bond to the different nationalities and cults of East and West. Through it the provincials expressed their gratitude for the *pax Romana*, and the very expression of gratitude strengthened their allegiance. Further, religion is conservative ; once the cult was firmly established it was a valuable method of ensuring the continuance of the political idea, the Principate, of which the worship of Rome and Augustus was the religious expression.

CHAPTER II

THE REORGANIZATION OF THE PROVINCES—THE DEATH OF AUGUSTUS

IN the following chapter, which attempts to describe the work of Augustus in the provinces, the following divisions will be observed, corresponding roughly to chronological order :—

I. The main principles on which the government of the provinces was now based. Some of these were clearly envisaged early in the reign, others took shape gradually according as circumstances demanded.

II. The settlement of the lands already acquired by the Republic ; the definition of frontiers and the problems of their defence. With this task Augustus was perpetually occupied till 16 B.C. Though, of course, similar problems arose later for his decision, after that year hís attention was given chiefly to—

III. The security of the Empire on its northern side. The problem was to discover the most suitable frontier and to organize its military defences. The solution devised by Augustus, speaking generally, was final, but it was only reached at the cost of infinite patience, severe fighting and tragic disappointment.

I. GENERAL PRINCIPLES. The amazing prosperity of the provinces, with few exceptions, during the early Empire was due to a new spirit of government which was answered in the provinces by a new attitude towards the governing power. The government now made the welfare of its subjects its first consideration and reaped its reward in the loyalty of every part of the Empire.

In making himself responsible for Syria, Gaul and Hither Spain, Augustus was able to set a new example in provincial government, while in exercising a general control of the senatorial provinces he influenced the character of their administration. The tendency was for more capable and experienced men to be appointed to governorships ; and their tenure of office, certainly in the imperial provinces, was longer. Salaries were now fixed and liberal enough to attract good men and to minimize the temptation to exploit the provincials. Further, it became more dangerous for the governors to attempt high-handed methods, for the number of Roman citizens in the provinces increased and Roman citizens could appeal to Caesar. Citizenship became more common, chiefly for three reasons : i, the new army system of Augustus created citizens ; ii, communities were not seldom granted the *civitas*, although Augustus himself was sparing in such grants [1] ; iii, the magistrates of *municipia* with Latin rights gained citizenship for themselves and their families at the expiration of their office. Again, the policy of the Roman Government was to encourage local self-government, and the growth of this tended to limit the governor's authority

[1] Suet. *Octav.* 40.

(p. 35). Lastly, the so-called provincial *concilia*, recognized in almost every province in the reign of Augustus, might act as a check upon an overbearing governor.

Provincial Concilia. Local assemblies of tribes or cities connected by common bonds of race or cult had from the earliest days existed in Eastern lands, and are, of course, familiar in Greek history ; but the tendency of the Roman government had been to suppress their activities. When Augustus was asked to allow temples to be built to him in Asia and Bithynia, he saw an opportunity to turn his worship to political account. The cities of Asia and Bithynia in particular were subject to local jealousies. In 27 B.C. Augustus revived the κοινά, or assemblies, made them representative of several localities and gave them the charge of the maintenance of his worship. Thus he hoped to fuse local rivalries in a common interest, and the plan to some extent worked. In 25 B.C. Galatia was made a province and Ancyra became the meeting-place of its *concilium* and the seat of Emperor-worship for the province. The system was followed, as we shall see, in most provinces East and West,[1] and on the annexation of new territory in later reigns the erection of an altar to Rome and Augustus (i.e. the reigning Emperor) became almost equivalent to the planting of the flag. The purpose of the meeting was primarily religious, but local affairs were also discussed and in time the *concilium* gained such importance that it sent deputations to the Emperor and in some cases actually prosecuted with success oppressive governors. But two points must be emphasized. The political nature of the *concilium* was a matter of slow growth and of secondary importance and could not have been deliberately contemplated. Further, the *concilium* was not in theory recognized as part of the machinery of provincial government. But its moral influence on the province was considerable ; membership and still more the office of priest reflected great glory on individuals and districts, and called forth public and private generosity. Games and festivals were held periodically with great pomp and magnificence. There can

[1] E.g. Tarraco (26 B.C. ?), Lugdunum (12 B.C.), Ara Ubiorum, Camulodunum, Flaviae Arae were meeting-places of the Assembly.

be little doubt that the existence of a central meeting-place, with its activities and its Emperor-worship, did much to foster loyalty and to spread Roman civilization.

The System of Taxation. One of the first tasks of Augustus was the reorganization of the finance of the Empire, and the scheme evolved by him remained the basis of the taxation till the time of Diocletian. We may deal first with Italy.

(A) Italy. The Italians had long ceased to pay tribute ; the revenues from the provinces relieved them from the burden, and it would have been an unbearable insult if Augustus had reimposed it on them. He had not the courage to do so. But, if he could not tax capital where it lay, he could tax it when it changed hands. In spite of angry protests he imposed (i) the *vicesima hereditatum*, a tax of 5 per cent. on inheritances, paid by Roman citizens in Italy and the provinces, (ii) the *centesima rerum venalium*, a tax of I per cent. on goods sold at auctions and on contracts of sale, (iii) a tax of 4 per cent. on the sale of slaves, *quinta et vicesima mancipiorum venalium.* Besides these taxes Italy contributed to the revenue by (*a*) harbour dues, *portoria*, restored by Julius Caesar ; (*b*) the *vicesima libertatis*, a tax of 5 per cent. on manumission, dating from 357 B.C. ; (*c*) *vectigal* or *scriptura* paid by State lands.

(B) The provinces. If Augustus was to reorganize the finances, the first thing necessary was a general survey of the resources of the Empire. The scanty information which we have suggests that this was done with characteristic Roman thoroughness ; under the supervision of Agrippa geographers, surveyors and valuers started on this gigantic work. In 27 B.C. Augustus himself held a census in Gaul, but that the census was general is stated by St. Luke, our sole authority.[1] The provinces were subject both to direct and indirect taxation : (i) the *tributum soli*, a tax on the value of land and fixed property, was paid by every property-holder according to a fixed assessment ; it extended to provincials, individual Roman citizens and bodies of Roman citizens, i.e. townships with Roman rights, except those having *Ius Italicum* which placed them in the same category

[1] ii. I.

as Italy ; (ii) the *tributum capitis*, a tax on income derived from movable property, was paid by provincials, though in poor provinces, e.g. Britain, this was simply a poll-tax. Indirect taxes were also paid in the form of customs and harbour dues, while imperial domains brought in revenue from the lessees of land, mines, pasturage, forests and the like.

II. THE SETTLEMENT OF THE PROVINCES. The overseas empire of Rome had grown up by degrees, and as a result the dependent communities stood in various relationships towards their mistress. In the midst of a conquered territory there might exist (i) *civitates liberae et foederatae*, i.e. cities or whole regions which were guaranteed independence for ever according to a *foedus* ; (ii) *civitates liberae sine foedere*, which enjoyed independence during Rome's pleasure. Such cities were free from the provincial governor's control. Again, *coloniae* and *municipia* were scattered over the Empire. Originally *colonia* meant a new foundation by Roman citizens, while a *municipium* denoted an existing community now for the first time organized as a township according to a charter which conferred either full Roman rights or *ius Latinum* (p. 341). Many *municipia* with *ius Latinum*, however, had later received full Roman citizenship, and thus the distinction between *colonia* and *municipium* tended to disappear, as far as political rights were concerned, though new foundations continued to be called *coloniae* and were proud of the title. Further, Rome had availed herself of the services of client princes, particularly on the frontiers. It was economical to leave a native prince on his throne and to entrust the security of the frontier to him ; it was understood, however, that Rome's engagement was with the individual prince only, and that on his death she could, if she wished, turn his kingdom into a province.

In our review of the provinces all these types of community will be met, and it will be noticed that the *civitas* becomes more widely spread, that the client princes disappear, that uniformity of status becomes more general, since the free communities and the dependent communities are put more on a level, and that the provinces draw closer in status to

Italy as privilege is more widely conferred. At the same
time it must be noted with what care Rome respected local
traditions and observances whenever they did not conflict
with the progress of Roman civilization.

Interest, too, may be derived from a study of the frontier
system. · Under the Republic there were no permanent army
and no permanent camps. By creating a standing army and
stationing it in camps and by defining the ' bounds of empire ',
Augustus laid the foundations of a frontier system. In it
there were frequently two elements : (i) the boundary,
represented either by an imaginary line or by geographical
features which might be of defensive value ; (ii) a buffer
State in the hands of a friendly king ; beyond lay the enemy.
The allied State tended to be annexed by Rome, especially
under the successors of Augustus, and the frontier and the
enemy were brought together. This made necessary a
change of frontier policy and a new system of defence, which
was elaborated by the Flavian and Antonine Emperors.

The East. Augustus spent two periods in the East engaged
in the work of reorganization. After Actium he pursued
Antony to Egypt and remained in the East till 29 B.C., undoing
the agreements which Antony had made with client or independent kings in furtherance of his or Cleopatra's Oriental
empire. Again in 22–19 B.C. he visited Greece and Asia
Minor, and on this occasion scored a great diplomatic victory
over the Parthians.

In ASIA MINOR there were in 27 B.C. only three provinces,
Asia, Bithynia and Cilicia, the rest of the country being
occupied by native kings. Over Galatia, Pisidia, Lycaonia
and Pamphylia ruled Amyntas, who had won the favour of
Antony. On the death of Amyntas in 25 B.C. *Galatia* became
an imperial province, embracing Pisidia and Lycaonia, and
Pamphylia also became a province. In these districts, which
had been little civilized by the Hellenistic kings who ruled
them, Roman influence spread rapidly ; roads, cities, theatres
and aqueducts bear witness to the growth of prosperity.
The rest of Asia Minor was not organized in provinces till
after the death of Augustus. Pontus, parts of Cilicia and
many city-states on the Euxine continued under the rule of

client kings, and Lycia still remained a loose confederacy of cities. Armenia, which also remained as a kingdom, became a perpetual problem to Rome. It was a land difficult to hold, and by ties of race and civilization was more akin to Persia than to Rome ; its fate depended for many years on whatever relations existed between Parthia and Rome.

Relations between Rome and Parthia. After the victories of Pompey in the East and the annexation of Syria by the Romans, the two great powers came into open opposition. In assisting the client king of Armenia, the Romans provoked the hostility of Parthia, and were defeated at Carrhae under Crassus, 53 B.C. Some years later Antony attempted an expedition against King Phraates and with difficulty extricated his army from an awkward situation. His impending struggle with Octavian prevented further attempt, though he had already succeeded in placing one of his sons on the Armenian throne, having put Artavasdes, its king, to death and driven his son Artaxes into exile. Augustus delayed the settlement of the Parthian problem, though Roman sentiment, reflected in the *Odes* of Horace,[1] strongly demanded retribution for the disaster at Carrhae. But no doubt he saw clearly the difficulties of a Parthian expedition, and in a few years the internal feuds of the Parthians, which so often aided the Roman cause, gave him the opportunity to retrieve the disgrace of the loss of the standards. In 23 B.C. Phraates, King of Parthia, demanded the return of his infant son, carried off by Tiridates, who for a brief time had replaced Phraates on the throne. The child was bartered against the spoils of Carrhae ; Agrippa was sent to negotiate the exchange, which on the appearance of Augustus in the East in 20 B.C. was finally concluded. Poets celebrated this victory [2] and coins were struck with the legend 'signis Parthicis receptis'. In this year also Armenia was for a short time recovered. King Artaxes had been restored, but had made himself unpopular, and a demand was made to the Emperor that Tigranes, his brother, who had been educated

[1] iii. 5, 4.
[2] E.g. Verg. *Aen.* vii. 606; viii. 726. Hor. *Odes*, iv. 15, 7. Cf. *Mon. Anc.* 29.

at Rome, should take his place.   This was naturally acceptable at Rome, and Tiberius was sent to depose the one prince
and set up the other ;   which he did.   Tigranes, however,
soon died, and again there was a struggle between the parties
favourable to Rome and to Parthia.   Again, Tiberius was
sent, but he refused to go further than Rhodes (p. 28).   Four
years later the grandson of the Emperor, Gaius Caesar, was
commissioned to arrange the affairs of the East.   On an
island in the Euphrates he met the Parthian king Phraataces,
son of Phraates, who renounced all claim to Armenia ; he then
proceeded to Armenia to assert Roman rule there, but was
wounded at Artagira and died some months later.   For the
remaining years of this reign Armenia was left to the feuds
of contending parties, and in later reigns became the bone of
contention between the two powers (p. 123).   The character-
istically Roman plan of interposing buffer states would seem
in this case to have failed.[1]

SYRIA.   Syria was by far the most important of the Eastern
provinces, and it was with good reason, therefore, that
Augustus classed it as imperial.   On it depended the safety
of the Euphrates frontier ;   hence four legions were stationed
in the province, and the governor, who was always a man of
experience, was responsible for the safety of the ' unarmed '
provinces which lay round it.   The troops were stationed
not on the frontier but in the cities, which it was necessary
to protect against the hill-tribes ;   and as a result discipline
suffered (pp. 128, 264).   The towns of Syria—for example,
Tyre, Berytus, Apamea—were prosperous ;   manufactures and
commerce brought them great wealth, while Antioch became
proverbial for her luxury.   Bordering on Syria lay the
kingdom of Judaea.

JUDAEA.   To begin with, Rome definitely favoured the
Jews, and, when favour could no longer be given, indulgence
took its place.   When the Jews rebelled against Antiochus
Epiphanes in 167 B.C. Rome supported them, for it was
always her plan to support a small nation against her enemies.
But, as she became mistress in the East, she found it neces-

---

[1] Cf. Tac. *Ann.* ii. 56.   ' Ambigua gens ea antiquitus hominum
ingeniis et situ terrarum.'

sary to decide the destiny of the Jews herself. After Pompey took Jerusalem in 63 B.C., Rome followed her usual policy of setting up a native ruler in her own interests, and the power was given to Antipater, father of Herod the Great, who afterwards succeeded to the throne. Herod tried to conciliate the Jews ; he restored the Temple (' forty and six years was this temple in building ') ; his rule was good, and as a reward the Romans gave him the districts of Ituraea, Trachonitis, Auranitis and Batanea. But, because of his friendliness to Rome and his violation of Jewish traditions, he was never accepted by the strict Jews. On his death in 4 B.C. his kingdom was divided among three of his sons.[1] One of these, Archelaus, obtained Judaea, Samaria and Idumaea, but after some years of misgovernment he was deposed. Judaea then became a Roman province in A.D. 6, and was governed by a procurator of equestrian rank [2] ; no legions were stationed in it, but a body of about 3,000 local troops, chiefly Syrian Greeks, was raised.

The Treatment of the Jews by the Romans. The Romanizing process so successful elsewhere in the Empire made no headway against the stubborn national spirit, based on religious fanaticism, which the Jews fostered. They had been treated with unusual indulgence. Tribute was imposed on them as a matter of course ; but religious control was in the hands of the Synhedrion of which the High Priest was president. This body had powers of civil jurisdiction, but no power of death in criminal cases. Money was coined by the Jews themselves in the name of the Roman ruler, but it bore no image.[3] All possible tolerance was shown to their religion, and the Emperors—Augustus in particular—sent presents to the High Priest for the adornment of the Temple. Every Jew was exempt from military service, and the handful of Roman soldiers in Jerusalem were ordered to leave their standards at Caesarea. Romans who were guilty of pro-

---

[1] Though Augustus added Gaza and the Greek towns beyond Jordan to Syria. [2] Pontius Pilate, A.D. 26–37.
[3] The imperial currency circulated in Judaea : the Jewish coinage was for the Temple tribute and the use of the strict Jews who would not touch a coin bearing the Emperor's superscription.

vocative acts towards the Jews were punished with the greatest severity. Rome carried her indulgent policy to extremes ; and Mommsen remarks that it was sheer stupidity and ill-applied parsimony not to put a governor of high rank with legionary troops in Judaea to keep this turbulent people in check. At any rate Roman tolerance called forth no similar answer. The Herodians, it is true, were favourable to Rome, but they were not numerous and they were hated by the extremists, the Zealots. Hence there was constant trouble and even war between different parts of the country, till finally open rebellion broke out in A.D. 66 (p. 143).

EGYPT. After the death of Cleopatra, Augustus appropriated Egypt and turned it into an imperial preserve. It was neither regarded as a province nor governed nor organized as such. Protected on all sides by sea or desert it would have proved an almost unconquerable stronghold for a rebellious general in command of even a small army ; and since Rome was dependent on Egyptian harvests for a good proportion of her corn supply, it would have been dangerous for the Emperor to permit even the possibility of the supply being cut off. Hence Augustus took every precaution. He placed over Egypt a knight, responsible to himself only, in command of three legions ; no senator was allowed to set foot in the country even as a visitor. Cornelius Gallus, the first prefect of Egypt, was bold enough to allow his name and deeds to be inscribed on the pyramids. He was tried by the Senate for treason, suspended from his office and was driven by disgrace to commit suicide. While elsewhere it was Roman policy to encourage city life and local self-government, in Egypt every effort was taken to prevent the development of political or national self-consciousness; there was naturally no *concilium*. The peasants were virtually serfs ; they continued to pay the heavy corn tax imposed by the Ptolemies, though perhaps irrigation schemes carried out by Augustus made it more easily borne. But a poll-tax was also imposed and ruthlessly exacted. Land in private ownership was absorbed by the Emperor ; even the temple lands were appropriated, compensation being given to the priests by an annual subsidy. The old manufacturing monopolies of the

Ptolemies were done away with in the interest of Roman traders, but the new currency system introduced by Augustus destroyed any chance of Egypt ever taking her place in the commercial system of the Empire. The country went from bad to worse under Roman rule. The cities already in existence were prosperous, chiefly as centres of trade routes. Alexandria, situated on the main lines of commerce, attracted to herself the wares, and the learning, of East and West. All races, philosophies and religions were to be found here; scholars gathered in her library and merchants in her markets; here was the Empire in epitome. But Egypt herself, her lands and natural wealth, was the domain of the Emperor, preserved for the production of revenue.

The development of Roman trade with the East will receive notice later, but here mention may be made of an expedition sent by Augustus in 25 B.C. into ARABIA FELIX to secure control of the routes of the Red Sea, and to open up trade, especially with India. The expedition, led by Aelius Gallus in command of half the army of Egypt, does not appear to have been entirely successful. It reached, it is true, the capital of the Sabaean kings, Mariba, but its retreat was somewhat ignominious. But there is little doubt that it helped Roman merchants to secure a foothold in some of the Red Sea ports.

CRETE and CYRENE together made up a senatorial province and enjoyed tranquillity under Roman rule. CYPRUS, at first imperial, was allotted to the Senate in 22 B.C.; it will hereafter be the scene of troublesome Jewish outbreaks which frequently were accompanied by ruthless massacres (p. 229).

GREECE received such favour from imperial Rome as no other land. Whether that favour took the wisest form is doubtful; at any rate Greece lapsed more and more into stagnation, perhaps helped by the very freedom granted to her. Augustus divided Macedonia and Greece, which hitherto had made up one province, into two senatorial provinces. *Macedonia*, of which Thessalonica was the capital, now included Thessaly, Aetolia, Acarnania and probably Epirus. Colonies of veterans were settled at many places, e.g.

Dyrrhachium, Epidamnus, Pella, Philippi, and *concilia* met
at Thessalonica and at Larissa. The Thessalian cities formed
a loose confederacy to which Julius Caesar had granted
independence; Augustus withdrew this privilege, leaving
them, however, the right to hold gatherings at Larissa. The
remainder of Greece formed the province of *Achaia*, Corinth
being the head-quarters of the proconsul. But within the
province certain cities remained *liberae et foederatae*, for the
Romans were always sentimentalists where Greece was
concerned, and perhaps against their better judgment they
allowed such famous cities as Athens, Thespiae, Tanagra,
Plataea, Delphi and Sparta to remain free and even to retain
dependencies of their own. Thus Athens possessed among
other places Delos, Lemnos, Scyros, Imbros and Salamis,
and Sparta controlled North Laconia. On the site where
his army encamped at the battle of Actium Augustus founded
a new town, Nicopolis, formed not by a settlement of veterans
but by gathering together the neighbouring villages into a
free and sovereign city; dominion over Acarnania, Leucas
and part of Aetolia was given to her, and on the promontory
opposite to the town a temple to Apollo was built, and quin-
quennial Actian games were held.

While Augustus was in Spain in 25 B.C., he issued orders
to reorganize AFRICA, to which he never went himself. To
the Roman province of Africa, which was quite small, Julius
Caesar had added Numidia, the kingdom of Juba, after the
battle of Thapsus, 46 B.C.; and Augustus, after restoring
the country to Juba's son for a short time, confirmed this.
Africa now embraced the strip of coast from Cyrenaica to
the river Ampsaga. A proconsul of consular rank was placed
in charge; his position was in one way unique, for he was the
only governor of a senatorial province to command an army.
The famous Third Augustan Legion was stationed successively at Ammaedara, Tebessa and (after Trajan) at Lambaesis; its main task was to repel the desert tribes of the
inland, and in this it was very successful, though it was but
a fraction of the forces maintained by France in Africa to-day.
Its other task was the Romanizing of the province; the
efforts of its architects and engineers and the labours of its

men may be seen in many places of Africa, and particularly at Lambaesis. Indeed it is only lately that we have realized the prosperity to which the towns of Africa rose, especially in the second and third centuries of our era. When Augustus made his changes, there remained strong elements of the Berber civilization and language besides those of the Phoenicians. True to her custom Rome did not interfere; she adapted Punic institutions to suit her requirements, and partly by peaceful penetration but also by the planting of colonies Roman civilization spread. Carthage, destroyed by the Republican Senate, was restored as a *colonia* and became the chief town of the province. Ut ca received *civitas* from Augustus and became the rival of Carthage, and among other well-known towns which later became colonies may be mentioned Hadrumetum, Leptis Magna, Thugga; in Africa as elsewhere military stations developed into small towns. Yet even in the fifth century A.D. the Semitic language of the Carthaginians was common; St. Augustine found it necessary to appoint as bishop of a place fifty miles from Hippo a man who could speak Punic. This mixture of Roman and Phoenician elements gave rise to a vigorous intellectual life, and Roman Africa contributed noted names both to Latin literature and to Church History.[1]

To the west of Numidia lay two kingdoms, Iol and Tingis, which towards the end of the struggle between Octavian and Antony had been united under King Bocchus. In 33 B.C. this king died and for a few years the Roman government appointed no successor. However in 25 B.C. Augustus set up as king of both countries the son of Juba (of Numidia), also called Juba, and married him to a daughter of Antony and Cleopatra. Their son, Ptolemy, succeeded to the throne in A.D. 23 and ruled till A.D. 40; two provinces were then formed under the names of MAURETANIA TINGITANIS and MAURETANIA CAESARIENSIS,[2] each governed by a procurator of equestrian rank with auxiliary forces at his disposal. These countries were never developed to the same extent as Africa Proconsularis.

[1] E.g. Apuleius, Tertullian, Arnobius, Cyprian, Augustine.
[2] See pp. 81, 91.

The wild tribes of North-west SPAIN had never really been conquered and for the first years of the reign of Augustus gave much trouble. Rebellions in Cantabria and Asturia were suppressed by Statilius Taurus (29–25 B.C.), only to break out again more seriously in 22 B.C. and again in 20–19 B.C. On this last occasion Agrippa with difficulty suppressed the hill-tribes, whose stubbornness had become proverbial.[1] Hence, though Spain was not exposed to any external enemy (except occasionally the Mauri), it was found necessary to keep three legions in the peninsula. Perhaps about 25 B.C., three provinces were formed. *Baetica,* which was the most civilized, was assigned to the Senate and governed by a proconsul of praetorian rank ; it contained a number of towns of which the chief were Gades (Cadiz), Corduba (Cordova), Astigis and Hispalis (Seville). *Tarraconensis,* covering more than half the total area of Spain, was placed under a *legatus pro praetore* who had Tarraco as his head-quarters ; here also was the seat of the worship of Rome and Augustus, and here, too, the provincial council met. Augustus encouraged the wild tribes to settle in the lowlands by the foundation of towns, of which Caesar Augusta (Saragossa), Lucus Augusti, Augusta Asturica (Astorga) may be mentioned. The third province was *Lusitania* with Emerita Augusta (Merida), a colony of veterans, as its capital. It also was placed under a *legatus pro praetore.* The Romanization of Spain was slowly brought about by the foundation of colonies and the gradual penetration of trade. It was a country of great value to the Romans, for it provided minerals, corn, oil and, above all, recruits (pp. 163, 322).

SARDINIA and CORSICA originally were assigned to the Senate. In A.D. 6, however, the Emperor was forced to take them into his own hands, for they became the head-quarters of pirates and therefore had to receive a military guard. Except for a brief interval in Nero's reign the province remained imperial.

III. THE PROVINCES OF THE NORTHERN FRONTIER. We now pass to a group of provinces which must be reviewed together, for they are all closely connected with the problem

---

[1] See e.g. Hor. *Odes,* ii. 6, 2 ; iii. 8, 21, etc.

of the Northern Frontier. There is a temptation to believe that even at the beginning of our period GAUL was already an integral and Romanized part of the Empire ; but it should be remembered that in the reign of Augustus the legions were stationed there as much to control the Gallic tribes as to keep out the Germans. The republican province of Transalpine Gaul, which had been acquired chiefly as a means of communicating between Italy and Spain, was bounded by the stretch of the river Rhone from Geneva to Vienne, and by the Cevennes extending towards the Pyrenees. Caesar's conquest of the rest of the country was quite recent and the work of organization remained to be done. Augustus divided the whole of the country into four provinces. The old province of Gaul now became *Narbonensis* ; it was naturally the most Romanized and was given to the Senate. The unit of the tribe, which in the other Gallic provinces was preserved, was here broken up and its place taken by cities ; Nemausus (Nîmes), Arelate (Arles), Narbo, the capital, and Massilia, an ancient foundation, are the well-known cities of this province. The other three provinces, which were imperial, were *Aquitania*, in the south-west, *Lugdunensis* in the centre and *Belgica* on the north-east. Care was taken that this division of territory should not follow racial distribution ; thus, Aquitania, though chiefly Iberian, and Belgica, in the main Teutonic, each received some Celtic lands. Originally these three provinces were commanded by a single governor with a *legatus* in each district (e.g. Drusus 13–9 B.C., Tiberius 9–7 B.C., Germanicus A.D. 13–17) and for this reason were known as the *Tres Galliae* ; after A.D. 17 each province received an independent *legatus*.

In the three new provinces it was the policy of the government to preserve the system of cantons ; sixty-four of these *civitates* were recognized and a chief village appointed for purposes of administration.[1] These villages developed into small towns, many of importance ; but so strong was the tribal feeling that the names of the towns tended to disappear, while the tribe names have survived. Thus, Lutetia was the centre of the Parisii, and the town is now Paris ; Avaricum,

[1] Tac. *Ann.* iii. 44.

the centre of the Bituriges, is called Bourges.[1] To the town
of Lugdunum, within easy reach of all the provinces and at
the meeting of the Rhone and the Saône, a position of great
importance was given. She possessed Roman citizenship
and the right to coin gold, and as head-quarters of the governor
and the centre of the great road system elaborated by Agrippa
for the country she became the political and commercial
capital of the *Tres Galliae*. Further, in 12 B.C. there was
erected the famous *ara Romae et Augusti*, dedicated on
1 August by Drusus ; on it were inscribed the names of the
sixty-four *civitates* entitled to send representatives to the
concilium and to choose a priest for the cult of the Emperor [2] ;
some fragments of the altar have survived and its representation may be seen on coins of the time.

We may now deal with the provinces on the NORTHERN
FRONTIER itself. The problem before Augustus was the
discovery of a natural frontier, which should mark clearly
the limits of Roman *imperium* and at the same time be suitable for defence ; for the menace of the Northern tribes had
made itself increasingly apparent during the closing years of
the Republic. This frontier was found, eventually, in the
Rhine and the Danube, though, as we shall see later, the line
of these two rivers was overstepped in places for varying
periods during the first two centuries.

The first task lay close at hand. Incursions were still made
by Alpine tribes into the North of Italy ; for its peace it was
necessary to crush these tribes once for all and to pursue
their kinsmen into RAETIA.[3] Drusus, the stepson of the
Emperor, defeated the Raetians in the Alps in 16 B.C.[4] and
pushed on by the Brenner pass to the river Inn. He was
joined by Tiberius[5] with an army marching from Gaul,
which defeated the Vindelici close to Lake Constance and
reached the Danube. The territory thus subdued was

[1] Cf. also Samarobriva, Ambiani, Amiens : Condevincum, Namnetes,
Nantes : Durocortorum, Remi, Rheims.
[2] Dio, liv. 32.
[3] Roughly, Eastern Switzerland and the Tyrol.
[4] Cf. Hor. *Odes*, iv. 4, 17 ; iv. 14, 9, 14.
[5] For an account of Tiberius as a soldier, see Velleius Paterculus, ii.
94–98, 104–115, 120–122, who served under him.

formed into an imperial province under a procurator. Few towns were founded, the most noteworthy being Augusta Vindelicorum (Augsburg), and little was done to Romanize the province. No legions were stationed there till the reign of Marcus Aurelius ; the commander of the Rhine armies was responsible for keeping peace. Meantime the remaining Alpine tribes were subdued ; the remains of a monument— the *Tropaeum Alpium,*—set up to commemorate the subjugation of forty-six Alpine and Raetian tribes, still survive at La Turbie, above Monaco. One district in the Western Alps was for some time ruled by its own Prince, Cottius, who was friendly to Rome and was given the title of *praefectus civitatium.*

To the east of Raetia lay the kingdom of NORICUM,[1] rich in minerals. Its conquest took place in 16 B.C. when the Noricans and Pannonians invaded Istria, the tongue of land at the North of the Adriatic, and were defeated by P. Silius, the proconsul of Illyricum. The country was then included in the Empire, but probably was not organized as a province till some years later, perhaps in the reign of Claudius. Towns sprang up rapidly, for Roman influence had already made some headway. No troops were stationed in Noricum ; the governor of Pannonia, to the east, was responsible for its safety. The importance of Raetia and Noricum in the scheme of frontier protection is to be found chiefly in the direct communication which they gave between the garrisons of the Rhine and the Middle Danube.

In republican times ILLYRICUM[2] had been very imperfectly conquered ; as recently as 48 and 44 B.C. Roman eagles had been captured by the wild tribes of the country, and Octavian felt it incumbent to overrun the whole of this district. In 35 B.C. he subdued the piratical tribes of the Adriatic coast and marched against the Iapydes who had raided the North of Italy ; such insecurity had the civil wars brought about. Octavian penetrated as far north as Siscia, in Pannonia,[3] which he took by siege, returning to Rome at the end of the

---

[1] Roughly, Austria.
[2] Western Yugo-Slavia (Bosnia and Montenegro).
[3] Carinthia and Western Hungary.

year. But in 34 B.C. he had to hasten back to rescue his general, Fufius Geminus, from defeat by the Pannonians, and, marching south, repulsed a combined army of Dalmatian tribes at Promona. He then returned to Rome to enter on his second consulship, 33 B.C., commissioning Statilius Taurus to complete the subjugation of Dalmatia. Illyricum now stretched as far north as the river Save, and was assigned in 27 B.C. to the Senate ; many colonies were soon settled, e.g. Pola, Salonae, Emona. But the Pannonians soon gave trouble again ; in 13 B.C. Agrippa, invested with extraordinary powers, was sent to keep them in check, and on his death in 12 B.C. he was succeeded by Tiberius. It was clear that Illyricum was too turbulent to be left to senatorial administration, and at this time it was restored to the Emperor. By constant warfare Tiberius advanced the frontier northwards to Poetovio, and this enlargement of Illyricum led to its division into two provinces, PANNONIA and DALMATIA, both imperial. But still the subjugation of these territories was incomplete. In A.D. 6, while Tiberius was engaged in warfare in Germany and was on the eve, it seemed, of a decisive victory there (p. 52), news reached him of serious rebellions in Pannonia and Dalmatia, caused by excessive taxation. In each province the insurgent leader bore the name of Bato. In Dalmatia the rebels were momentarily checked by the *legatus*, M. Valerius Messalinus, and in Pannonia by the military commander of Moesia, but they succeeded in uniting their armies near Sirmium. Tiberius hastened to Siscia ; legionaries, auxiliaries, newly raised levies under Germanicus and contingents from Thracian princes poured into the country ; at Rome the alarm was great. However, the Pannonian Bato was induced to turn traitor, and later he fell into the hands of his Dalmatian namesake, who after exacting full retribution was eventually defeated by Germanicus, A.D. 8. Throughout the campaign Germanicus showed himself an able general, and a brilliant career seemed marked out for him. Tiberius meantime completed the subjugation of Dalmatia, whence he was summoned back to Germany by news of the defeat of Varus (p. 52).

South of the Lower Danube there lay two tracts of land,

THRACE and MOESIA,[1] inhabited by tribes often at war with one another, though derived from the same stock and speaking in some cases the same language. So long as their feuds served merely to weaken them, Rome watched in patience ; when, however, the northern districts of Macedonia were menaced, Rome had to intervene. Beyond Thrace, as far as the Danube, lived the Moesians, and north of the river, the Dacians ; as the movements of one of these peoples affected the peace of another and eventually the security of Macedonia, Augustus made it his policy to push forward Roman dominion up to the Danube. In 29 B.C. the Bastarnae, who occupied the districts north of the Lower Danube, broke into Thrace, and the governor of Macedonia, Marcus Licinius Crassus, fearing for the safety of his province, crossed into Moesia and pursued the invaders. After defeating them he carried on a difficult campaign against the tribes of Moesia, conquering the powerful Serdi and taking their capital Serdica (Sofia). He probably left a tribal king to rule Moesia before he turned back to Thrace to interfere in a feud between the Bessi and Odrysae. The Odrysian king was entrusted with the task of preserving peace in Thrace, and it was not till A.D. 46 that the country was made into a Roman province. Moesia was not organized as a province till the reign of Claudius ; under Domitian it was divided into two provinces, Moesia superior and Moesia inferior, the line of division following the course of the river Cibrus. On the coast of Moesia and Thrace there were already towns founded centuries before by Greek colonists ; they contained a very mixed population, and Ovid, who was banished by Augustus to Tomi, makes it clear in his descriptions of life in that town that conditions were somewhat barbaric. On the other hand, the towns which sprang up as a result of Roman civilization, chiefly in the west of the provinces, were Latin in speech and manners.

We have now seen something of the effort which Rome expended to organize her dominions and to secure adequate

[1] Thrace covers southern Bulgaria, Turkey, and the Greek Coast at the head of the Aegean Sea. Moesia is, roughly, Serbia, Northern Bulgaria and the Dobruja.

4

frontier protection for the ring of provinces which encircled
the Mediterrancan Sca. It remains to tell of Augustus'
attempt to define the frontier in the north-west corner of the
Empire and to carry the frontier from the Danube to the
North Sea.

The German Frontier. Julius Caesar had already crossed
the Rhine and had also ' pointed the way to Britain'.
Augustus did for a moment contemplate the invasion of
Britain, but he abandoned the idea when the Pannonian
rebellion showed that his recent conquests needed consolidation. But the definition of the German frontier was imperative, though difficult, and we shall see how Augustus felt
his way to one solution of it, though another was finally
forced upon him by circumstances. If the pacification of
Gaul was to be successful, it was clear that raids by the
German tribes must be checked. Such raids occurred in
29 B.C. when the Suevians crossed the Rhine, perhaps to
support a rising of the Morīni, and again in 16 B.C., when the
Sugambri, Tencteri and Usipĕtes succeeded in defeating a
Roman army commanded by M. Lollius. Augustus hurried
into Gaul and appointed Tiberius as its military commander.
His first activities were directed against Raetia and Noricum
(p. 47). He was succeeded in 12 B.C. by his brother Drusus,
then about 25 years old and very popular with the soldiers.
To him belongs the credit of a series of brilliant campaigns
into the heart of Germany.

The Campaigns of Drusus, 12 B.C. *to* 9 B.C. North of the
Rhine there are three rivers running, roughly, parallel with
it, the Amisia (Ems), the Visurgis (Weser), and the Albis
(Elbe). Drusus' plan was to advance from river to river till
he reached the Albis which he proposed to make the frontier ;
such a frontier would have the merit of being shorter than the
Rhine and would link up more directly with the Danube.
His aim was to subdue first the more westerly tribes situated
between the Rhine and the Albis and to deal with the inland
tribes later. Accordingly in 12 B.C. he marched to the Lower
Rhine and defeated the Usipĕtes, who were established in
the western angle of the Rhine and the river Luppia (Lippe).
In this year, probably, he joined the Rhine to the Lakes,

where the Zuider Zee now is, by a canal which gave the Rhine fleet easy access to the North Sea, and perhaps prevented the junction of the Batavians with the Frisians and Chauci. His ships sailed by the sea to the Amisia, in which river they defeated those of the Bructeri and subsequently invaded the lands of the Chauci, north of the Amisia. In the following year he turned his attention to the inland tribes. Starting from Castra Vetera he marched with little opposition through the territory of the Cherusci to the Visurgis, and narrowly extricating himself from an ambush reached the Luppia again in safety; on its banks the fort of Aliso was built. The next year was occupied by a campaign against the Chatti. In the meantime forts were being built on the Rhine. Fifty are said to have been established between the sea and Vindonissa (Windisch); of these Castra Vetera (near Xanten), Moguntiacum (Mainz), Argentoratum (Strasbourg), Bonna (Bonne) may be mentioned, but it must be remembered that the exact dating of many of the Rhine forts is impossible.

In 9 B.C., in spite of bad omens at Rome, Drusus again penetrated into German territory. Passing through the Chatti and the Suevi, he reached the Albis and erected a trophy on its banks. But his ambitious schemes were doomed; at the river a woman of giant stature is said to have barred his way and to have prophesied his speedy death. And this soon befell; for he died within a short time as a result of injuries received in a fall from his horse. Tiberius arrived in time to see his brother's end. Thus a promising career was cut short, and the conquest of Germany, which he planned, though it is doubtful whether he could have accomplished it, was postponed for ever. Great honours were given to Drusus, among them the title of ' Germanicus '. His body was carried to Rome where Augustus and Tiberius delivered funeral speeches in his praise.[1]

Tiberius in Germany. On the death of Drusus, Tiberius, invested with proconsular power and placed in charge of the Tres Galliae and the Rhine armies, continued the work of pacification for a year or so. In 7 B.C. he was recalled to

[1] There is extant a poem addressed to his Mother, the *Consolatio ad Liviam*, of which the authorship is unknown.

Rome to receive his second consulship, and from Rome he
went into retirement at Rhodes (p. 28). In Germany a
series of commanders of the Rhine armies experienced varying
fortunes, till in A.D. 4 Tiberius, restored to favour with the
Emperor after the deaths of Gaius and Lucius, was again
sent to Germany. In the next two years he crushed rebellions
among the Cherusci and Chauci and advanced against the
Langobardi. He, too, used a fleet and reached the territory
north of the Albis, so that even the Semnones and Charydes
and Cimbri sought his friendship.[1] In A.D. 6, however, his
attention was diverted in another direction. The Marcomanni, who had appropriated the lands of the Boii (Bohemia),
had been welded into a compact and powerful State by the
far-sighted policy of their king Maroboduus. He had trained
a strong army, but was ready to make peace with Rome. If,
however, the Roman frontier was to stretch from the Elbe to
the Danube, a powerful State between Germany and Noricum
would have been a perpetual menace. His defeat, therefore,
was decided upon, and Cn. Sentius Saturninus advanced from
Germany to meet the army which Tiberius led from Carnuntum
with a view to a simultaneous attack. Sudden news, however,
prevented the operations ; revolts in Pannonia and Dalmatia
required every soldier available. The suppression of these
revolts lasted three years (p. 48), and in the meantime Publius
Quinctilius Varus was placed in command of the Rhine armies.

The Defeat of Varus, A.D. 9. Varus had come from the
province of Syria, which he entered a poor man and quitted
wealthy. He imagined that in Germany he would have the
same easy task of government as in Syria, and he attempted
to impose taxes and deal summarily with offending Germans.
His sense of security blinded him to the real state of affairs.
For Arminius, the chieftain of the Cherusci, who had seen
service in the Roman army and had received the rank of
knight, was plotting rebellion with the leaders of the Chatti,
Marsi and Bructeri ; yet he retained the confidence of
the Romans. In A.D. 9 Varus with three legions was in camp
on the Visurgis, where Arminius and his fellow-conspirators

[1] See *Mon. Anc.* 26. Augustus' claim to have ' pacified ' Germany
' ad ostium Albis ' is somewhat exaggerated.

were frequently his guests. Winter was approaching and Varus left his summer quarters intending to make, probably, for Aliso, but he turned aside from his route to deal with some local disturbance ; his way led through dense forests. This was the chance for which the rebels had waited. In the depths of the Teutoberg forest, near Osnabruck, the Romans were defeated, and defeat was turned into a massacre. Three legions were wiped out and Varus committed suicide.[1]

This was a greater disaster than that of Carrhae. Its implications for Germany were incalculable. The peoples beyond the Rhine asserted their independence, and there was great fear that they might invade Germany south of the Rhine and perhaps unsettle the Gauls. Maroboduus, too, might join the rebels. Luckily the energy of the remaining Rhine legions secured the river and Maroboduus preferred to remain at peace. The Varian disaster was a terrible blow to Augustus ; he could ill afford three legions ; the work of Drusus was undone and the disgrace would have a lasting effect on the half-conquered peoples of Gaul. ' Quinctili Vare, legiones redde ' was his constant moan, and on the anniversary of the defeat he observed deep mourning. Meantime troops of every kind, including freedmen, were rushed to Germany, and in A.D. 10 Tiberius, with Germanicus on his staff, was once more in command of a Rhine army of eight legions. His immediate task was the defence of the river, and though he crossed it he attempted no offensive operations. In A.D. 13 Germanicus succeeded him, and adopted a more vigorous policy. But the story of his success or failure will be told in a later chapter.

The Death of Augustus. In A.D. 9 Augustus reached the age of seventy-one years ; in that year the terrible defeat of Varus took place, and the Emperor, already feeble in health, never recovered from the shock. He knew that his end was near and that his work was done. By A.D. 13 he had assured Tiberius' position as his successor ; there remained one task. In A.D. 14 Augustus began the third census of his reign, and,

---

[1] The legions were the XVIIth, XVIIIth, XIXth. These numbers were never again included in the Roman Army list. The *Mon. Anc.* is silent about the defeat of Varus.

contrary to his expectations, he lived to complete it with
Tiberius' help. Thus in his last year he was able to review
the Empire of his creation. The census completed, he
accompanied Tiberius on the first stage of his journey to
Illyricum ; on his way back from Beneventum he fell ill and
died at Nola, 19 August. Suetonius gives many details of
the cheerfulness of the enfeebled Emperor as he lay knowing
that death was near. He asked his friends whether he had
played the farce of life well, and his last words were to Livia,
his wife : ' Livia, nostri coniugii memor vive ac vale.'
Whether Tiberius, who hurried back, arrived in time to find
his father-in-law alive is uncertain.[1] The body of the
Emperor was taken to Rome, and after stately funeral honours
was placed in the Mausoleum which he had built and where
lay the bodies of Marcellus, Octavia, his grandsons, and his
friend Agrippa.

The Res Gestae and the Breviarium. The papers which
Augustus left included, besides his will, two important
documents. The *breviarium totius imperii* furnished careful
statistics of the Empire—the moneys in the fiscus and the
debts due to it, and details of the troops ; an appendix
contained maxims and counsels for the guidance of his successor, among them the warnings that the frontiers should
not be extended nor citizenship given too freely. The *Res
Gestae* briefly described his own achievements from his nine-
teenth year onwards. It was intended to be inscribed on
brass pillars placed outside his Mausoleum ; but copies were
also set up in the centres of the Emperor's cult in the
provinces, and one of these, in Latin and Greek, has been
preserved at Ancyra.[2] The inscription gives in the most
direct and simple manner the Emperor's account of his
imperial trust ; though couched in the first person, there

---

[1] Suet. *Oct.* 98 implies that he did ; Tac. *Ann.* i. 5 and Dio, lvi. 31
imply the reverse.
[2] Hence its more common name, the *Monumentum Ancyranum.*
Both versions are slightly incomplete, though one often fills gaps in
the other. Fragments have been found also at Apollonia and Antioch
in Pisidia. It is uncertain when the record was compiled ; it makes
little reference to events which happened in and after A.D. 6.

is none of the pride of egotism. It is in itself the best commentary on his work.

After a century of disorder Augustus restored peace. Without terrorism he carried through a revolution. The Principate lasted for three hundred years, yet no one saw it come. He was no soldier, yet he reorganized the army and doubled the Empire. No doubt he left some things half done; the East was soon to give trouble, and the Empire suffered through the want of any theory of succession to the throne. But Augustus achieved what Caesar did not; he gave peace and security.[1]

The ' Ara Pacis Augustae '. The Augustan peace is worthily commemorated in a monument of which some important and beautiful fragments remain. In July 13 B.C. the Senate decreed that an altar should be dedicated to Pax Augusta to celebrate the return of Augustus from the Western provinces; it was dedicated in 9 B.C.[2] Placed in the Campus Martius—the very site chosen is significant—the altar was surrounded by a small court about 35 feet by 38 feet; the marble walls of the court, two of which had entrances about 11 feet wide, were covered inside and outside with beautiful reliefs. Inside, festoons of fruit and foliage and flowers covered the surface; outside, the upper portion was given up to historical scenes, and the ideas embodied fitly symbolize the main themes of the Augustan peace. One of the most perfectly preserved reliefs shows a figure of Terra Mater with her children on her knees. Once more the earth may yield her increase. She sits upon a rock; round her are flowers and ears of corn; at her feet are a bull and a sheep, symbols of agriculture and pasturage. At each side two figures ride, one upon a swan, the other upon a sea-dragon; they have been interpreted as the ' Aurae ' blowing from the sea and from the river.[3] Fragments of another relief show the figures of Rome, Mars and Faunus; along the walls unbroken by an entrance processions move in stately dignity; priests and lictors are followed by Roman citizens with women and

---

[1] Cf. Tac. *Ann.* i. 9.   [2] *Mon. Anc.* 12.
[3] Cf. Hor. *Carm. Saec.* 29.

children : here are members of the priestly colleges, now restored to their ancient honour. Another scene shows an ideal figure [1] taking part in sacrificial rite ; in the background is a landscape with the temple of the Penates on the Velian Hill. Peace, a prosperous countryside, the ancient faith of Rome, which alone is the secret of the serene confident dignity of the sculptures themselves—these are the themes of a ' work inspired by the purest and most honourable patriotism, that of a nation which felt its mission to be one not of self-glorification or dominion, but of putting an end to war and violence and initiating the reign of peace. In that mood Virgil sang of the new Empire in verses which medieval readers could only interpret as a prophecy of the reign of Christ ; and the calm sweet music of the Virgilian hexameter is pitched in the same key and develops the same motive as the tender yet dignified sculpture of the Altar of Peace.' [2]

CHAPTER III

THE PRINCIPATE OF TIBERIUS, A.D. 14–37

*T*HE *Accession of Tiberius*, A.D. 14. Tacitus, who was born not quite half a century later, and who certainly must have talked with men who remembered the change of rulers in A.D. 14, gives a vivid picture of the state of Rome at the time ; a few ' talked idly of the blessings of Liberty ', but the majority only feared the disturbance of peace. Officials and non-officials, Senate and people alike, hurried to take the oath to the new Emperor. His professed unwillingness to allow the Senate to vote him this position may well have been genuine ; he was always, except in the field, averse to decisive and clear speech. But in the end he ceased to refuse, and the Lex de Imperio was passed, recognizing *de jure* the powers he already had *de facto* ; Cassius Dio definitely tells us that it was passed for ten years, and then renewed quite formally.

---

[1] Representing the Senate.
[2] R. G. Collingwood, *Roman Britain*, p. 78.

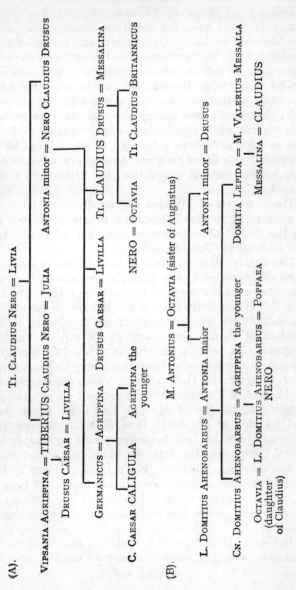

THE JULIO-CLAUDIAN EMPERORS

(A).

TI. CLAUDIUS NERO = LIVIA

VIPSANIA AGRIPPINA = TIBERIUS CLAUDIUS NERO = JULIA   ANTONIA minor = NERO CLAUDIUS DRUSUS

DRUSUS CAESAR = LIVILLA

GERMANICUS = AGRIPPINA   DRUSUS CAESAR = LIVILLA   TI. CLAUDIUS DRUSUS = MESSALINA

C. CAESAR CALIGULA   AGRIPPINA the younger   NERO = OCTAVIA   TI. CLAUDIUS BRITANNICUS

(B).

M. ANTONIUS = OCTAVIA (sister of Augustus)

L. DOMITIUS AHENOBARBUS = ANTONIA maior   ANTONIA minor = DRUSUS

Cn. DOMITIUS AHENOBARBUS = AGRIPPINA the younger   DOMITIA LEPIDA = M. VALERIUS MESSALLA

OCTAVIA = L. DOMITIUS AHENOBARBUS = POPPAEA   MESSALINA = CLAUDIUS
(daughter   NERO
of Claudius)

Divisions of Reign of Tiberius. Tacitus has described,[1]
with even more than his usual conciseness, the periods of
the life of Tiberius. ' His conduct and his reputation were
excellent while he was in private life or in command under
Augustus ; he hid his true character and hypocritically pretended virtue while Germanicus and Drusus were alive ; so,
too, while his mother survived, he was a mixture of good and
evil ; his cruelty was abominable, but he kept his vices in
concealment while Sejanus was alive, whether he looked on
him as a favourite or as a danger ; finally he gave himself up
completely to a life of guilt and debauchery, when he followed
only his own natural disposition, free alike from shame and
from fear.'

The character of Tiberius will be discussed later ; but it
is convenient to divide his reign into four periods marked
by the deaths of Germanicus (A.D. 19), of Livia (A.D. 29),
and of Sejanus (October, A.D. 31).

The Rivalry of the Julian and the Claudian Families. It
is no exaggeration to say that the rivalries in the family of
Augustus were the curse of the first century of the Empire,
and this is especially true of the life and reign of Tiberius.
He came to the throne an embittered man owing to the misconduct of his wife Julia, and to the way in which, under
Augustus, his position and his very life had been made to
depend on the fortunes of the two young Caesars, the grandsons of Augustus. The first period of his reign was dominated
by his fear of the ' blood of Augustus '. The most pressing
danger was the life of Agrippa Postumus, whom Augustus
had adopted at the same time that he adopted Tiberius,
although later he had been compelled to banish him for
brutal incapacity, the form in which he showed the strain
of madness hereditary in Julia's family. Even in the lifetime of Augustus conspiracies in his name had been talked
of, and the plot to carry him off to the German legions
on Augustus' death was only frustrated by his immediate
murder.

Two years later (A.D. 16), Clemens, the slave of Agrippa
Postumus, who had planned this bold stroke, came forward

[1] *Ann.* vi. 51.

himself to personate his master, and was suppressed with difficulty. How dangerous such pretenders can be, when the rights of succession are uncertain, is well seen in the trouble caused to our own king, Henry VII, by the impostor Perkin Warbeck, who also personated a young prince, removed by murder.

Germanicus and Agrippina. The danger to Tiberius from his nephew and adopted son, Germanicus, seemed to be, and to some extent was, much more serious. That prince united in himself the double popularity of being the son of the much-loved Drusus and of having married Agrippina, the grand-daughter of Augustus. He was in command, too, of Rome's most powerful army, that of the Rhine, with extended authority over Rome's greatest province, all three divisions of imperial Gaul; Tacitus records that the mutinous legions at once, though informally, offered to make him Emperor. He himself refused the suggestion with horror, and there is no doubt that he was completely loyal to his uncle, although, as will be seen later, he sometimes injudiciously ventured on acts inconsistent with the position of a subject; an heir-apparent is always in a difficult relation to a reigning prince, as has been seen again and again in English history.

Whether his wife Agrippina was equally loyal to Tiberius is more doubtful, but it is significant in her favour that, even when she was finally accused openly (in A.D. 29), no definite charge of conspiracy was put forward against her or her sons. On the other hand, there is no doubt that she was a 'bad subject', and that there was some truth in Tiberius' rebuke to her, 'Si non dominaris, filiola, iniuriam te accipere existimas.' It was not without reason that her husband on his death-bed begged her ' not to provoke the stronger by jealousy of their power '. It may be added finally that the relations between Tiberius and his nephew were embittered by the mutual jealousy of Livia and of Agrippina ; under an absolute ruler women's influence becomes a great political force.

The Mutinies on the Frontiers. The rivalries in the Imperial house mattered the more because in theory the Principate was not hereditary, and the forces which had founded the rule of Caesar and Augustus were always liable to break loose, and to destroy what they had created. It was the legions which had brought the Empire into being, and already in A.D. 14 military discipline showed signs of breaking down ; both in Pannonia and on the Rhine there were serious mutinies. The immediate causes of these were partly temporary. In the face of the danger of the Pannonian Revolt (A.D. 6–9), and of the alarm caused by the defeat of Varus (A.D. 9), Augustus had relaxed the rules as to enlistment, and had filled up his legions with a lower class of recruits ; we are definitely told that the chief mutineer in Pannonia had been a leader of a theatrical claque, and that in Germany freedmen had been enrolled in the army. And the same crises had rendered necessary the suspension of the ordinary rules as to retirement on pension, and undue detention with the eagles was a prominent grievance in both armies.

But there were other grievances of a more permanent character ; the demand for higher pay and still more the jealousy of the greater privileges of the Praetorians are significant hints of the dangerous part which the legions were to play later.

. For the moment the dangers were easily met. An appeal to the superstition of the Pannonian legions, an appeal in Germany to their loyalty to the family of Augustus and to their jealousy of the provincials, helped to bring about a ready acceptance of the concessions made, viz. that ordinary service should cease at the end of sixteen years, and that any later service for four years as *vexillarii* should be lightened of fatigue duties and confined to actual fighting. Even these concessions, however, were cancelled by Tiberius next year, on the ground that the finances of the State required that the legionaries should serve twenty full years with the eagles.

Early Constitutional Changes. The soldiers were thus easily pacified, and occupation was found for their ' idle hands ' in renewed hostilities in Germany, to be described later. Meanwhile in Rome changes were carried out without difficulty, which removed still more of the old Republican constitution. These were :

(*a*) Divine honours were at once (A.D. 14) voted to Augustus,

and a brotherhood of the leading men of the State
(the *Sodales Augustales*) was set up to attend to his
worship.

(b) The people lost their right of electing magistrates, which
was transferred to the Senate. This had become so
much a form that the change only provoked 'empty
talk'.

(c) In A.D. 15 the provinces of Achaia and Macedonia were
transferred from the Senate's control to an imperial
governor, and the Senate by voting this as a measure
of relief to the provincials, recognized the superiority
of imperial rule.

The Beginnings of Delation. Much more formidable was
the beginning of the system of political prosecutions which
was to become so terrible an evil throughout the first period
of the Roman Empire. The crime of treason (*maiestas laesa*)
had been defined first by Saturninus [1] (100 B.C.), whose law
was passed to protect tribunes in the exercise of their power.
It had been renewed from time to time under the Republic,
and under Augustus had been definitely extended to include
'words' (*famosi libelli*) as well as acts. Under Augustus
it had been little employed, but Tiberius in A.D. 15 definitely
directed that the laws were to be enforced.

Its extension from written to spoken words was easy, and
the charge of treason in words soon became a common feature
in all political trials; hence before the end of the reign of
Tiberius, and again in the last period of Nero, Rome was under
the shadow of a universal spy system, when no man's life
was safe. There is no reason to suppose that Tiberius contemplated this extension from the first; on the contrary,
to begin with he quashed frivolous charges, as will be seen.
But he was smarting under personal attacks on his character—
in which Roman society always indulged freely [2]—and as a
soldier he had a genuine love of discipline. Unfortunately

[1] It is significant that the great instrument of imperial tyranny
begins with the tribune who first formed political alliance with the
popular army leader.

[2] 'Despotism tempered by epigrams' is a feature common to
Ancient and to Modern History.

the arrangements of the Roman State were only too favourable to the abuse of judicial forms for political purposes ; a
prosecutor who obtained a conviction was entitled to gain
personal advantage at the expense of the man whom he
convicted, e.g. the Roman franchise could be obtained by
a prosecutor who succeeded in depriving another man of it
by judicial sentence. The law under the Empire allowed
a successful *delator* part [1] of the confiscated property of the
condemned. Hence, as Tacitus says, *delatio* became a profession ' in which poor men became rich, insignificant men
became dangerous, and brought destruction first on other
men and then on themselves'.

The beginnings of the evil were frivolous. One man was
accused of treason for employing a low-class actor in the
worship of Augustus, another for perjuring himself by the
name of Augustus, and a third for showing a cheap loyalty
by putting the head of Tiberius on a statue of his predecessor.
All these charges were quashed by the Emperor, who observed
with grim humour, that the deified Augustus could take care
of himself, ' deorum iniurias dis curae'.

The Trial of Libo Drusus. There may have been more
real danger to the Emperor from Libo Drusus, who was
accused of treason in A.D. 16. There is no doubt that among
the noble houses there was still jealousy of the position which
the Julio-Claudian family had gained, and the prosecutions
of the nobles, both in this and in the three following reigns,
may have had some justification in actual plots. Libo
Drusus represented some of the oldest families in Rome, e.g.
that of Pompey the Great, and he was even connected with
the Imperial house. The new features in his trial were the
treacherous friend, who acted as ' agent provocateur', the
foolish young noble, and the use of the supernatural. In
the motives of the accused and in his methods of proceeding,
' Black Magic ' played a part ; e.g. he was charged with
attempting to raise the dead. All these evils recur repeatedly
in later trials. One result of the condemnation of Drusus
was legislation against the professors of the black arts (*mathe-*

---

[1] Usually one-fou th ; hence their nickname ' quadruplatores ';
but sometimes they received more.

matici magique [1]) in Italy, two of whom were executed, while as a class they were banished.

Foreign Policy, A.D. 14–19. But, as usual under the Empire, the events of real importance were those that were happening outside Italy ; it is the Roman world rather than the city and the court of Rome which are of most interest to students of history. Augustus had left an autograph memorandum on the state of the Empire (p. 54), in which he definitely urged a policy of non-aggression. This policy Tiberius adopted as his own ; he called it his ' rule ' (*praeceptum*).[2] Soldier though he was, he knew that the resources of Rome in men and in money were dangerously near exhaustion, and he always avoided war if possible. But at the beginning of his reign, he was compelled to engage in very important military operations on the Rhine frontier ; these perhaps seemed necessary in order fully to restore Roman prestige, shattered by the defeat of Varus, and also to restore the morale of the legions ; the most important motive, however, was probably the ambition of Germanicus ; it was too much to expect that a young and capable soldier would at once acquiesce in inactivity.

The course of these campaigns and their results will be described later in a separate chapter ; it must suffice to say here that, at a terrible expense of men and money, the Germans were taught that Rome was still formidable and the Rhine frontier was secured.

The recall of Germanicus from Germany (A.D. 17) was rendered easier by the grant of a splendid triumph and by his appointment with a *maius imperium* over all the Eastern provinces. This was rendered necessary by the breaking out afresh of the ever-recurring struggle with Parthia over Armenia, as well as by minor troubles. The settlement of the Armenian question must be reserved for a special chapter on Rome's policy towards Parthia. The other acts of Germanicus may be taken separately.

Germanicus in the East, A.D. 17–19. His policy was one

---

[1] Tac. *Ann.* ii. 32.

[2] Tac. *Agric.* 13. 'Consilium id divus Augustus vocabat, Tiberius praeceptum.'

of conciliation throughout. In Greece he respected the traditional rights of Athens as an ' allied town ' by appearing with only one lictor ; he travelled through the Aegean, redressing grievances and winning favour by his interest in the antiquities of every kind ; he set up a popular king in Armenia, and sweetened the reduction of Cappadocia and Commagene to the status of Roman provinces [1] by some remission of tribute. He met the Parthian king on the Euphrates and peace was established on terms of mutual concession. In the next year (A.D. 19) he travelled up the Nile as far as the First Cataract ' to study the antiquities '. Even to visit Egypt without the Emperor's leave was illegal, for by the rules of Augustus no senator was allowed to enter it. But Germanicus was even more careless of the mis-construction of his acts ; he opened the State granaries and gained popularity by lowering prices. There is no reason to think that he was more than injudicious, even when he definitely exceeded his powers and trenched on the Emperor's prerogative by striking silver coins with his own head on them, to commemorate the settlement of the Armenian throne ; but he forgot how differently all his popular acts might be construed by a suspicious ruler, only recently come to power. It is not surprising that Tiberius had thought it desirable to prevent Germanicus going too far by removing a governor of Syria, who was friendly to him, and by appointing to the vacancy Cn. Piso, a man notorious for his self-confidence and his obstinacy.

Death of Germanicus, 10 *October A.D.* 19. Even before Germanicus went to Egypt, there had been serious trouble between Germanicus and Piso as governor of Syria ; the subordinate behaved with gross rudeness and went so far as to criticize the behaviour of his superior ; and the bitter-ness was inflamed by the quarrels of Agrippina and Plancina, the wife of Piso, who unfortunately was a special friend of the Empress-mother, Livia.

---

[1] This was part of the regular Roman policy ; the native dependent ruler paved the way for direct Roman rule. But the annexation of Commagene was not maintained ; it did not become a province finally till A.D. 72.

Piso clearly lost his head and exceeded the instructions of Tiberius ; his tampering with the army was as suspicious as it was futile, for the army remained devoted to Germanicus. There were dark stories, too, of magic practices against the life of Germanicus, who unfortunately had fallen ill on his return from Egypt.

Finally Piso left Syria and Germanicus died, appealing to his friends to avenge him, for he believed himself to have been poisoned by Piso. Of this crime no proof was ever produced, and it is, to say the least, unlikely that it was ever committed. But Piso proceeded to put himself still more in the wrong by attempting to recover by force the province from which Germanicus had driven him. In this attempt he failed, and he committed the further mistake of allowing Agrippina and the friends of Germanicus to return to Rome before him. Hence on his return he was prosecuted both for misconduct in his province and also for his attack on it after his expulsion ; it was clear that his case was hopeless, though the additional charge of poisoning quite broke down. He anticipated condemnation by committing suicide.

The rumour, repeated by Tacitus, that Tiberius had promised to save him, and that he was murdered in prison because he was intending to produce compromising documents to show the Emperor's complicity, is probably a mere piece of contemporary scandal. Would the cautious and experienced Tiberius have allowed a guilty agent to possess written proof ? But there was no doubt that the Emperor and his mother showed no sympathy with the popular mourning for Germanicus.

His death delivered Tiberius from a not unnatural anxiety, but it also cast a shadow over his whole reign ; the impression of his merciless cruelty, which Augustus was said to have shared,[1] was confirmed. With Germanicus disappears from history the last lovable member of the Julio-Claudian house ; he was not the great general painted by Tacitus, who even compares him to his advantage with Alexander the Great, but he was a kindly as well as a capable man.

[1] Cf. Suetonius, *Tib.* 21, ' miserum populum Romanum qui sub tam lentis maxillis erit '.

5

Troubles in Thrace and in Africa. Two more sets of events fall into this first period of the reign of Tiberius, both of which had important sequels in the period that followed.

In Africa the Romans had a problem to face different from that either of the Rhine or of the Euphrates. Their neighbours across this frontier were not a danger to the whole Empire like the Germans, nor a semi-civilized but organized power like the Parthians ; tribes like the Musulamii were to the Romanized provinces of Africa and Numidia what the tribes on the North-West Frontier are to the British in India ; they did not as a rule invade, but they were always ready to make raids. And at this time (A.D. 17) they were rendered more troublesome than usual by the presence of a leader who knew Roman weaknesses. The Roman system of employing men of the conquered tribes as ' auxiliaries ' produced excellent troops, but also from time to time most formidable adversaries ; men like Jugurtha in the days of the Republic, like Arminius now, like Civilis fifty years later, had learned in the Roman service how to beat their teachers. Such a deserter was Tacfarinas, who for seven years gave the Romans in North Africa the same kind of trouble that the Mad Mullah, in the days before the Great War, gave the English in Somaliland. Formidable as a ravager, he was now (A.D. 19), as always, easily beaten in a pitched battle ; but till he was caught, as we shall see later, Roman Africa had no peace.

The trouble in Thrace (A.D. 19) was of a different kind. Augustus had there divided the country between two native princes, Rhescuporis and his nephew Cotys ; it was the same policy of ' Divide et Impera ' which had been pursued two centuries before in Numidia, and it had the same results. Rhescuporis murdered his rival, but he was no Jugurtha, and he was easily reduced and taken to Rome. The kingdom was once more divided, and a further step in Romanization was made by the introduction of a Roman resident.

The African War, renewed A.D. 20–24. The difficulty in Africa very quickly revived, and the campaign opened, as so often happens on the frontiers of big empires, with ' a regrettable incident ' ; a whole Roman cohort allowed itself to be disgracefully beaten (A.D. 20), and discipline had to be restored by ' decimating ' the offending troops. The campaign then followed its usual course ; Tacfarinas was again worsted in a pitched battle, but continued his ravages, and the trouble called for serious measures. Hence the Senate (A.D. 21) agreed that the command in Africa should not go in the usual way to one of the two senior consulars who had not had a consular province, but should be filled by special appointment ; the choice was left to the Emperor, whose influence secured the appointment of Blaesus, the uncle of the rising favourite, Sejanus. He conducted the campaign of A.D. 22 with scientific vigour. The methods employed by Lord Kitchener in the Boer War were anticipated by him ; a triple advance engaged Tacfarinas on all fronts ; he was cut off from his refuge in the deserts on the south-east, while Cirta in the west of Romanized Africa was secured from attack ; flying columns pursued his broken forces, and ' block-houses ' in the enemies' country secured in the winter what the summer operations had gained. The success was so great that Tiberius allowed Blaesus to receive the title of ' Imperator ' from his victorious troops—the last time this title was given outside the imperial house. But the war was not ended till two years later, when the Romans by a ucky surprise succeeded in killing Tacfarinas.

The Roman province of Africa then settled down, and already under Tiberius became one of the granaries of the Roman Empire.

The Romanization of Thrace. The settlement of A.D. 19 in Thrace produced its natural result. The attractions of Roman civilization soon gained a party among the natives, and the fighting instincts of many more were satisfied by admission to the Roman *auxilia* ; but there was a strong party for independence and the old ways of life, and in A.D. 21, and still more in A.D. 26, there were serious risings. The danger was always present that the mountain tribes of the Balkans beyond Mons Haemus, the northern boundary of Thrace, would be brought in. But the legions of Moesia were at hand to assist, and the risings were put down without much difficulty. Twenty years later Thrace became a province (*A.D.* 46) and a fruitful recruiting ground for the legions.

Rebellion in Gaul, A.D. 21.   Much more serious than the troubles either in Africa or in Thrace was the Gallic rebellion, which broke out in the same year as the first of the Thracian risings.   This was serious enough to be thought at Rome to require the presence of the Emperor himself, although, judging the danger more rightly, he refused to leave Rome. Indeed national feeling had already become so weak in Gaul that the risings were only partial, breaking out first in the West, in the region of the Loire, and then among the Aedui and the Treveri.   The lack of national character in them is indicated by the fact that both the chief rebel leaders—Julius Florus and Julius Sacrovir—were Roman citizens ; but one of them, to judge by his name, ' Sacrovir ', was a Druid, and the Romans, both in Gaul and in Britain, found in Druidism the most serious obstacle to the spread of their civilization. The first rising was put down by the local forces, the urban cohort (No. XIII) which was always on duty at Lyons ; it was the proud boast of the Romans that they kept the whole of the vast region of Gaul in subjection with 1,200 men.   But the second part of the rising was more dangerous ; its main motive was social discontent.   Gaul, apart from the heaviness of the tribute, was deeply in debt to Roman financiers, who from the days of Cicero [1] onwards, exploited the wealth of the great Western province ; hence the rebellion began, as so often, with a massacre of the Roman traders.   A considerable success was gained by the capture of Augustodunum (the modern Autun), where the school of Roman culture, founded by Augustus, had drawn pupils from the noblest families in Gaul ; these were seized, and furnished valuable hostages for winning support in every part of Gaul.   But the rebels had underrated Rome's resources ; she used the forces of the north-west to crush the rest of Gaul ; it was

----

[1] Cicero (*Pro Fonteio*, v. 11) speaking in 69 B.C. says ' referta Gallia negotiatorum est . . . nummus in Gallia nullus sine civium Romanorum tabulis commovetur '.   This, of course, refers to Gallia Narbonensis, but Caesar's conquests had opened the way for Roman trade and finance all over Gaul.

the old policy of Caesar, who won Gaul by securing the expulsion of the Germans, and then in 52 B.C. brought back the Germans into Gaul to aid him in putting down the national rebellion of Vercingetorix. Now the Roman legions on the Rhine, not Germans of course, but the guard against Germany, swept down to crush the unwarlike Gauls whom they despised ; Silius, the old lieutenant of Germanicus, with the legions of Upper Germany, easily defeated the forces of Sacrovir. Unfortunately the Roman victory was abused by Silius, who three years later was exiled for extortion in his province.

The Provinces in general under Tiberius. But the provincial troubles which have been sketched were exceptional ; the blessings of the Pax Romana were being enjoyed all over the Roman world, and the facts recorded by Tacitus about the provinces indicate wise government gratefully accepted. ' Happy is the country that has no history ' may or may not be true ; but it certainly is true that silence in the history of conquered provinces is fair evidence that the rule of the conquerors was acquiesced in as fair and just. The suffering caused by the terrible earthquake in Asia in A.D. 17, which destroyed large parts of at least twelve cities, was met by a remission of all Roman taxes for five years, while Sardis, which had suffered most, received a liberal relief-grant from the Emperor. The dependent communities also found in Rome a tribunal where their internal troubles could be impartially considered ; so a long-standing dispute between the Lacedaemonians and the Messenians, which had broken out at intervals over at least seven centuries, was decided in favour of the Messenians (A.D. 25) ; and the cities of Asia found in the Senate an equally impartial tribunal, to regulate the rights of asylum in the temples, then as always so fruitful a source of trouble in the East (A.D. 22). The province of Asia showed its gratitude by voting a new temple to Tiberius, who joined with him in this honour his mother Livia and the Senate ; the temple after some dispute was placed at Smyrna. But, though the Emperor allowed this honour to be voted, he refused to permit it to be taken as a precedent ; when Baetica asked to be allowed to follow the example of Asia,

Tiberius flatly refused ; he called the Senate to witness that he was satisfied to be only a man, and to do his duty as a man and an Emperor. While, however, Tiberius refused any great extension of Emperor-worship, he was careful to maintain the old respect for Rome ; Cyzicus was deprived of its position as a ' free state ' for neglecting the worship of Augustus ; but perhaps the additional charge of outrages on Roman citizens may have moved the Emperor to action against the offending city.

Prosecutions of Provincial Governors. This care for the provinces showed itself in another way, which· is especially blamed by Tacitus, and which certainly had its evil side. From the very beginning of the reign of Tiberius prosecutions of governors for misconduct in the provinces became frequent. The Emperor's maxim was ' Boni pastoris esse tondere pecus, non deglubere ' : to diminish the temptation to extortion the Emperor was in the habit of keeping his governors for long periods in the provinces, so that they were not tempted to enrich themselves quickly at all costs, as had been the rule under the Republic. Josephus especially praises this custom of Tiberius.[1] In any case it was now the interest of the central government that the provinces should not be plundered.[2] In view of the record of noble Roman governors in the time of the Republic, we can well believe that many, if not most, of those condemned under Tiberius for *de repetundis* were guilty ; but the list is a long and dreary one, beginning with Granius Marcellus in A.D. 15 ; the most famous cases later are those of Silanus, condemned for extortion in Asia in A.D. 22 and of Silius mentioned above.

[1] Pontius Pilate is an instance ; he was procurator of Judaea for ten years ; but in this case the long tenure of office failed to prevent extortion. No doubt the indecision which marked the character of Tiberius as he grew older was another cause of this policy, but on the whole prolongation of tenure was in the interest of the provinces.

[2] Tacitus says nothing that bears out the statement of Suetonius that the Emperor himself plundered the provinces, robbing both communities and individuals ; the definite charge is that leading men in the provinces had their property confiscated on the mere charge of hoarding money ; this may well be an exaggeration of the troubles of the land crisis at the end of the reign of Tiberius (p. 75).

Growth of Delation. Misconduct in the provinces was only one, and by no means the most frequent, of the charges which became increasingly numerous as the reign of Tiberius proceeded, especially after the death of Drusus, the Emperor's son, in A.D. 23. Tacitus with reason complains of the dreariness of his subject—'cruel orders, continuous prosecutions, treacherous friendships, the ruin of the innocent'[1]; he draws a gloomy picture of the last days of Tiberius, when there was a reign of terror in Rome, when all classes alike, even leading senators, turned informers, whether 'to save themselves, or more often infected by the contagion of the malady'; private life, he says, became full of danger when chance words 'in foro, in convivio' were made matters of accusation. The number of those who perished is variously estimated, but there is no doubt that under Tiberius begins the systematic destruction of the old Roman nobility, which continued with intervals to the end of Nero's reign and, along with the Civil War of A.D. 68–69, cleared the ground for a new nobility under Vespasian.

To attempt to give an account of the various cases is impossible, and it would be painful to dwell on so gloomy a record ; as typical may be mentioned the execution of Clutorius Priscus, put to death (A.D. 21) for writing an elegy on the Emperor's son Drusus, who had recovered when the poet expected him to die, and the forced suicide of Cremutius Cordus, who had in his history called Cassius, the assassin of Caesar, 'the last of the Romans'. How eager were the informers can be seen from the story of Latiaris, who led on Sabinus, a friend of Agrippina, to express freely, as to a sympathizer, his pity for her and his indignation against the Emperor and his favourite Sejanus, while he had concealed his fellow-informers, all ex-praetors, in the roof, so that they might overhear and report the fatal words. There is a grim pleasure in noting that, four years later, the informer Latiaris himself met the same fate as his victim.

It seems difficult to acquit Tiberius, as some of his apologists do, of the largest share in the responsibility for these judicial murders. It is true that from time to time he interfered to

---

[1] iv. 33, *sub anno* A.D. 25.

save the accused, or to lighten the sentence ; but this hardly palliates his conduct ; he alone had this prerogative of mercy, and, if he failed to exercise it, condemnation was certain. And he saw to it that the *delatores* had their blood-money as their reward, even though from time to time the informers, as has just been said, were themselves condemned.

Political Uncertainty the Cause of the Reign of Terror. The explanation of the attitude of Tiberius to the *delatores* is probably simple ; nothing is so cruel as fear, and fear seems to dominate the greater part of the reign of Tiberius. This may be in part the explanation of his long retirement from Rome, which began as partial in A.D. 21 and was complete for the last eleven years of his reign. To what extent this fear was in any way justified, it is impossible for us to say ; but it is significant that of Suetonius' first six ' Caesars ' four at least [1] perished by violent deaths, and Augustus only escaped numerous conspiracies by the extraordinary fortune which marked the whole of his long life.

The uncertainty of the Roman succession was its bane. To quote Gibbon's stately prose—' The acknowledged right (i.e. of hereditary succession) extinguishes the hopes of faction, and the conscious security disarms the cruelty of the monarch '.[2] But this ' acknowledged right ' and ' conscious security ' were just what the second Roman Princeps lacked ; there were other members of the Imperial house who had almost as good claims as Tiberius, and other Roman nobles as well as Sejanus were quite ready to try for the prize of absolute power ; it was not an accident that the one period of peaceful government in Imperial Rome is the century which followed the accession of Vespasian, who had created a new nobility, free from the traditions and the ambitions of the old.

Various Pretenders to the Principate. Tiberius had at times shown himself arbitrary and cruel before the death of his son Drusus ; but it is after that event that Tacitus dates the evil development of his character. With a grown-up

[1] Whether Tiberius was a fifth it is impossible to say, but it seems probable.

[2] *Decline and Fall*, Cap. vii, *ad init.*

son, who had married Livilla the sister of Germanicus, and who had already three children, the Emperor might well have felt fairly secure. Drusus was given a share in the government, and in the year before his death (A.D. 23), after he had been twice consul, he was marked out as the Emperor's successor by the conferment on him of the *tribunicia potestas*. Whether if this prince had lived the Roman State would have fared better may be doubted ; his life was notoriously lax, and his partiality for the gladiatorial shows, though it endeared him to the bloodthirsty mob of Rome, may well have been a sign of a disposition which would have made him on the throne as terrible as his father, or as his nephew by marriage, Gaius.

This apparent settlement of the succession was ruined by the death of Drusus, A.D. 23, and from this time onward one fear after another possessed the Emperor. First of all, his alarm was aroused by the enthusiasm shown by Senate and people for the sons of Germanicus, who had been brought nearer to the throne by the death of Drusus. The intrigues of Sejanus inflamed this fear, and in A.D. 29, after the death of the Empress-mother, Livia, both the elder son Nero and his mother Agrippina were banished. Their deaths followed some years later ; when Nero died is uncertain ; Agrippina's death was postponed till A.D. 33.

The Rise and Fall of Sejanus. But meantime a new and real danger had arisen. Sejanus, the Prefect of the Praetorian Guard since A.D. 17, had wormed himself into the Emperor's confidence. He had increased his own power by concentrating the Guard, hitherto scattered over Italy, in a great camp on the north of Rome, just outside the Servian Agger, and he was looked upon as a formidable rival by Drusus. The death of that prince was generally attributed to the poison of Sejanus, who had seduced Livilla, the wife of Drusus, and had divorced his own, hoping that the Emperor would then allow him to marry Livilla. The Emperor put aside this request, but heaped honours and powers on Sejanus, who had shown his devotion by saving the Emperor's life at the risk of his own (A.D. 26). The favourite played upon the Emperor's jealousy of Agrippina and her sons, and is even stated to have succeeded in winning the younger of these, Drusus, to join in the intrigue against the elder, Nero. But the suspicions of Tiberius were at last awakened against Sejanus, and in A.D. 31 he suddenly struck down his favourite. A ' verbosa et grandis epistola ' came from Capreae to the Senate, denouncing Sejanus, who, all unsuspecting, thought his plans were going well. The favourite had no friends, and the man to whom all had been cringing was hurried to prison and executed. His body was torn to pieces by the mob, and his fall was followed by wholesale executions of his family and partisans. The terror of the Emperor thus led once more to a bloody slaughter.[1]

Life at Rome during the Reign of Tiberius. The three books of Tacitus which record events after the death of Drusus are mainly the dreary record of the judicial bloodshed which has just been described. So far as other events are mentioned at all, they are generally to the Emperor's credit. He showed that he realized how little can be done through mere legislation by discouraging futile prosecutions for luxury ; he pointed out how much more serious were the decay of agriculture in Italy and the dependence of Rome on corn supplies from abroad. ' Vita populi Romani per incerta maris cotidie volvitur.'

When great disasters occurred, as e.g. the fall of the temporary amphitheatre at Fidenae (A.D. 27), which killed or crippled 50,000 spectators, the Emperor contributed liberally to the relief of the sufferers, while legislation was passed against jerry-building contractors, whose aim was to make money from the people's love of shows. A similar liberality was shown nine years later, when the Emperor gave 100,000,000

---

[1] The story of Sejanus' rise and fall is one of the most dramatic of history ; it has a curious resemblance to that of Haman in the Book of Esther. Juvenal makes it a striking example of the ' Vanity of Human Wishes ', in his famous Tenth Satire (lines 56 f.). It is the subject also of one of the greatest of English tragedies, the ' Sejanus ' of Ben Jonson, which is full of spirited writing, either because of, or in spite of, its being largely made up of translations of the very words of Tacitus. Even those who question the accuracy of Tacitus' condemnation of Tiberius generally accept his account of the favourite as substantially correct.

sesterces to assist those whose houses had been burned in a
great fire on the Aventine. But nothing seems to have been
done on this occasion to secure better building in Rome, and
the only public works carried out by Tiberius were the temple
to Augustus and the restoration of the theatre of Pompeius.

The Emperor again acted with vigour and discretion when,
four years before his death, a financial crisis arose in Rome.
An attempt had been made suddenly to enforce laws of Julius
Caesar, which had been allowed to become obsolete ; they
seem to have forbidden the hoarding of money (not more
than 60,000 sesterces was to be kept by any one), and to have
required that a certain proportion of a man's capital—probably not less than half—should be invested in land in Italy.
This unexpected enforcement of the old laws caused creditors
to call in their debts, and a shortage of money at once resulted ;
this was the more marked, since, owing to recent judicial
confiscations of the goods of the condemned, a large part of
the money of Rome was in the hands of the Government.
Hence there were many wishing to sell while few could buy,
and panic ensued. The Emperor with wise generosity
remedied this by a grant of 100,000,000 sesterces, from which
debtors could borrow without interest, if they gave proper
security in land.

The End of Tiberius. But this and other minor acts of
good policy were quite insufficient to save the Emperor's
popularity. The upper classes were each and all afraid for
their lives, the lower classes had no affection for an Emperor
whom no one had seen for eleven years, and who stinted their
amusements.

The most important of the surviving members of the
Imperial house was the one son of Germanicus who was still
left, Gaius. The old Emperor could not make up his mind
whether to choose him as successor or to prefer his own
grandson Tiberius Gemellus, the son of Drusus. The character of Gaius was well known to him ; he said that Gaius
would be the Phaethon to ruin the whole world and he foretold that Gaius would kill young Tiberius. But Gaius was
a man, while Tiberius was a mere boy, and so the Emperor
spared him, Perhaps, as Josephus says, he even let it be

known that Gaius was to succeed. Gaius, though rightly called 'the best of slaves', resolved to put an end to this uncertainty ; he won over Macro, the Prefect of the Praetorian Guard, and waited only his opportunity to kill the Emperor.

The end came almost suddenly at the last, for the Emperor insisted on his ordinary course of life, when already seriously ill ; the result was a sudden collapse on 16 March, A.D. 37. Some said, however, that death was caused by violence, and that Gaius, to make sure of his succession, either poisoned the old Emperor, or smothered him when he had unexpectedly recovered from the fainting fit which had been thought to be fatal.

Character of Tiberius. The reign of Tiberius is in some ways the most melancholy period in the first two centuries of the Empire. Yet its horrors were not worse, as will be seen, than those of the latter parts of the reigns of Gaius and of Nero.

In contrast to these the story of Tiberius is the story of a man who, till well on in middle life, had played a creditable part, whose morals seem on the whole to have been better than those of most members of the Imperial house, and who, both in peace and still more in war, had done great things with at any rate considerable success. As Emperor, as has been seen, he often showed practical wisdom, and both in Rome and in the provinces, government was carried on effectively and often skilfully.

But the policy of Augustus, who for years had treated Tiberius merely as a pawn in his game, using him openly to secure the succession of his own family, and, regardless of his feelings, condemning him to a marriage with a woman whom he feared and loathed, had completely soured him by the time he came to the throne. Then the abuse of unlimited power brought its own punishment. The removal of his enemies one by one did not diminish his fears, but left him more miserable than ever ; there are few records more terrible than the opening words of his letter to the Senate in A.D. 32 : 'If I know what I am to write to you, or how I am to write, or what I should not write at the present time, may the gods and goddesses destroy me with a worse destruc-

tion than I experience every day.' Tacitus well says that
'the souls of tyrants are torn with the scars of their own
cruelty and lust'. Tiberius has passed down into history
as the typical tyrant, and yet, had he died before he came
to the throne or after the first few years of rule, he would
have left the reputation of a ruler of good character and of
more than ordinary ability.[1]

Tacitus' Character of Tiberius. It has been argued often,
especially of recent times, that Tacitus is systematically
unfair to Tiberius, that he blackened the character of a man
who, though unhappy and unfortunate, tried to do his duty
to the end, and that he revenged himself for the anxieties
and terrors which he had suffered in the reign of Domitian
by painting the darkest picture possible of the second Princeps.

The only positive evidence for this is the Roman coinage.
Both Titus and Domitian, and again Trajan, introduced
new series of types, in each of which Tiberius figures among
the other Emperors. Later he disappears from the series,
and the contrast is explained by the fact that 'Tacitus had
not yet damned his memory' (Mattingly). This inference
receives some confirmation from the fact that among the
imperial precedents quoted in the famous inscription giving
the *Lex de Imperio Vespasiani*, Tiberius' name occurs over
and over again, while that of Nero is omitted because his
'memory was condemned'.

It may be admitted that Tacitus, with consummate skill,
makes the worst of his indictment of Tiberius; when he
has to praise, he usually insinuates a bad motive, or he spoils
the effect of the good act by some damaging addition; so, too,
he certainly exaggerates. But the fact remains that almost
all the other evidence we have confirms the view of Tacitus.
Suetonius, of course, is a mere scandalmonger, but Seneca

[1] Nothing has been said about the abominable vices which Tiberius
was said to have practised in his retirement, and which have made the
name of Capreae a byword. Certainty, of course, is impossible, and
the scandalmongers of Rome were prepared to go any lengths in the
way of invention. It might be argued that his previous life before
he was Emperor rendered such evil improbable; on the other hand,
it is possible that a disillusioned man, who had lost all hope, might
in despair have given himself up to vices he had hitherto scorned.

speaks almost as strongly in condemnation as Tacitus, and both he and Pliny significantly contrast the early years of this reign with the later. The one exception is Velleius Paterculus who served in the army in Germany under Tiberius ; he speaks with enthusiasm about Tiberius, and gives a striking description of the devotion of the German armies to him ; but this statement seems hardly to agree with their readiness to make Germanicus Emperor in A.D. 14. And in any case the evidence of Velleius is more than suspect when it is remembered that he published his book in A.D. 30, that he was a warm admirer of Sejanus, whom he makes the 'Laelius' to the Emperor as Scipio, and that he probably perished among the friends of Sejanus in A.D. 31.

CHAPTER IV

THE PRINCIPATE OF GAIUS, A.D. 37-41

*T*HE *Accession of Gaius.* The accession of Gaius was a matter of course ; he had the support of the all-powerful Praetorian Prefect, and as the son of Germanicus he was universally popular. As he travelled to Rome, accompanying the body of Tiberius, he was greeted everywhere by enthusiastic crowds, and the Senate at once voted him the Principate, disregarding the wishes of Tiberius who in his will had made his grandson, Tiberius, now 18 years of age but not yet allowed to assume the *toga virilis*, co-heir with Gaius. And the first months of the new reign corresponded with this happy beginning. Gaius recalled the exiles and quashed all trials impending ; he affirmed that he would not listen to the *delatores* and burned all papers about the trials of his mother and his brothers (but, as was found later, he kept copies) ; he gave the magistrates full judicial powers and remitted taxation ; he even attempted to restore the popular elections which Tiberius had abolished (p. 61), but no one came to vote.

Family bitterness for a moment seemed to have ceased ; Gaius adopted his rival and cousin Tiberius, and gave him the style of *Princeps iuventutis*, and he rescued his uncle

Claudius, the future Emperor, from the obscurity in which he had hitherto been kept, and made him his colleague in the consulship.

It is a marked feature in the reigns of all the four early Emperors, that they begin brightly and end in gloom and terror. And this is what might have been expected. So long as an Emperor kept the allegiance of the soldiers, he was safe against conspiracy, and he had not much to fear from the individual assassin; he could therefore tyrannize as he pleased over the rest of the Roman world; such absolute power was too much for any ruler, especially when as in Rome he came from a stock thoroughly degenerate.

Gaius shows his True Character. With Gaius the disillusionment soon came. When he had been a few months on the throne, he had a severe illness; on his recovery he showed himself at once in his true character, which those who had known him from childhood had always understood; he was, as Suetonius says, no longer a Prince, he was a ' portent ' (*monstrum*).

It is admitted by Tacitus that he had the power of words; he was a fluent speaker, especially in invective, and some of his phrases were most happy; such was his nickname for his aged great-grandmother Livia, a ' Ulysses Stolatus ', and his description of the popular oratory of Seneca as ' sand without cement ' (*arena sine calce*). His assumptions of divinity were one of the chief manifestations of his madness; they were not, as with most Emperors, part of a settled policy, but a mere freak. So the heads of famous divine statues were removed, to make room for his own,[1] and the Emperor professed to hold familar talk with Jupiter in his temple. We are told that this claim of divinity was suggested to him that it might take the place of and avert a more dangerous intention to assume a crown and to make the ' Principate ' a ' kingship '.

On the other hand, the Emperor shocked Roman prejudices by childish display as well as by inordinate ambition. He

---

[1] Suetonius says that the famous Zeus of Phidias at Olympia was to be brought to Rome and suffer this indignity; but apparently it was saved by a portent.

showed himself in public dressed like a woman, and anticipated Nero by performing as a singer, a gladiator, a charioteer ;
it was only his death which prevented his public appearance
on the stage. His schemes for construction were on a scale
of the wildest extravagance ; it is true that one or two of
these were of practical use, e.g. a new aqueduct for Rome
was begun, and measurements were made for cutting the
Isthmus of Corinth ; but most of them were mere freaks,
e.g. to join the Capitoline and the Palatine, or to build a
town on the Alps. One of them was actually completed—a
mole, fully two miles long, from Baiae to the harbour of
Puteoli ; this was not intended, like Agrippa's harbour at the
Lucrine Lake, as a protection for shipping ; it was only a
bridge of boats, collected from all parts of Italy, and built
to satisfy the mad vanity of the Emperor.

The Emperor's Cruelty. To pay for these extravagances,
and for a more than Roman expenditure on the pleasures of
the table, he squandered in less than a year the vast treasure
(2,700,000,000 sesterces) which had been left by Tiberius,
and then proceeded to fill his exchequer by reckless taxation.
It is not worth while to go into details about follies so transi-
tory, but his tax of 2 per cent. on all sums disputed in
court may serve as an instance. Soldiers were used to
collect these taxes, and by a grim stroke of humour laws
inflicting heavy penalties were put forth, but in such small
letters and in such inconvenient places that the unhappy
offenders first heard of them when they had broken them.

Above all, the terrible weapon of Delation was again brought
into force, and men were executed freely to obtain their
wealth. The papers that the Emperor had burned were
produced in duplicate and used with deadly effect. And his
executions had a new and terrible feature, for torture was
freely used, and in his presence. Among the first victims
of Gaius were Tiberius Gemellus, his old rival and his son
by adoption, and Macro the Praetorian Prefect and his wife,
to whom he owed his throne. But it was especially against
the Senate that his prosecutions were directed ; he continued the work of destroying Rome's old nobility which
marked all the early Principate. The Emperor's attitude is

seen in the fact that, when he was in Gaul, he first ordered the Senate to make no proposals in his honour, and then threatened them because they had cheated him of a ' well-deserved triumph '.

It is not surprising that a conspiracy was formed against him (39 B.C.). His brother-in-law, Aemilius Lepidus, and his two sisters, Agrippina, the mother of the Emperor Nero, and Livilla (Julia) intrigued with Lentulus Gaetulicus, the commander of the legions on the Upper Rhine, who had ventured to defy even Tiberius at the end of his reign. The conspiracy, however, came to nothing, perhaps because the German armies had a hereditary reverence for the blood of Germanicus, and remembered Gaius as ' Caligula ',[1] the darling of the legions. At any rate, Lentulus and Lepidus were executed, and the princesses banished.

Gaius' Rule in the Provinces. Early in his reign the Emperor had made a change of far-reaching importance by taking away from the senatorial proconsul in Africa the command of the forces there. He also executed the King of Mauretania, Ptolemy (A.D. 40), and so prepared the way for the annexation of that country by Claudius in the first year of the next reign. On the other hand, he restored the Kingdom of Commagene, and presented Herod Agrippa I (the executioner of St. James) with the tetrarchies of his uncles, Philip and Herod Antipas.[2] There was no method in the measures of Gaius ; to set up or to pull down was a mere whim. But his most important acts away from Rome were in Gaul, and here they were even more a burlesque of policy.

Action on the Rhine frontier was suggested to him by the lack of recruits for his Batavian bodyguard, and he collected an enormous force in Gaul, and marched to the Rhine. His campaign consisted of a hurried crossing against an imaginary enemy, but he provided himself out of the slave market with captives for his ' triumph ', compelling them to grow their hair

[1] One of the methods by which Agrippina the elder endeared herself to the legions was by dressing the young Gaius in the uniform of a legionary ; hence his nickname ' Bootkin ', the diminutive of the soldier's boot (*caliga*).

[2] For these, cf. St. Luke iii. 1 ; Herod Antipas was the executioner of John the Baptist.

6

long and to dye it red, and even to learn some German. Almost more of a farce was the march to the shore of the English Channel in the following year (A.D. 40), on the pretext that the whole island had been handed over to him by a British runaway prince, the son of Cunobelinus (' Cymbeline '). Here the troops were suddenly ordered to collect shells as the ' spoils of the Ocean ',[1] promised a donation of 100 denarii per man, and then ' dismissed '. Besides these costly freaks the Emperor raised money in Gaul, by selling the furniture of his exiled sisters and of the imperial palace at Rome for exorbitant prices ; he also amused himself by setting up at Lugdunum (Lyons) a contest in Greek and Latin eloquence, where the luckless losers were compelled to furnish the prizes of the winners, while some of them even had to destroy their own productions by licking them out.

Gaius and the Jews. More serious in its possible results than the Emperor's freaks in Gaul was his treatment of the Jews. In the second year of his reign there were troubles in Egypt ; the Jews demanded the citizenship of Alexandria, the Alexandrians constantly persecuted them, and the arrival of the favourite of Gaius, Herod Agrippa, had led to further outbursts in Alexandria against the Jews. In the same year —A.D. 38—the enemies of the Jews demanded that the Emperor's statues should be placed in the Jewish synagogues at Alexandria, and even in the Holy of Holies in Jerusalem ; such a measure, it was said, was in accordance with Gaius' wishes. This outrage on Jewish religious feeling was unbearable ; the Jews in Palestine prepared to resist, and the Alexandrian Jews sent an embassy to plead their cause with

[1] The stories of these two sham campaigns rest on the authority of Suetonius and Dio, and they are also confirmed by allusions in Tacitus. ' The ancients represented the action of Gaius as pure lunacy, but their whole account of his reign is deliberate caricature.' Amminus, son of Cunobelinus, fled in exile to Boulogne and surrendered to Gaius, who regarded this act as the surrender of the whole island. ' The discovery of the conspiracy of Gaetulicus, Lepidus, Agrippina and Julia, in Oct. 39, greatly alarmed him, and perhaps the real reason for the abandonment of the invasion was the fear that further revolutionary movements might develop during what would necessarily be a prolonged absence from Rome.'—J. G. C. Anderson's edition of Furneaux's Tacitus, *Agricola*, p. xlv.

the Emperor, headed by the philosopher-theologian, Philo. His account of their interview with the Emperor is a curious blending of the comic and the tragic. They found Gaius superintending the reconstruction of one of his villas in the gardens of Maecenas ; Philo describes how his embassy, with the counter-embassy of the Alexandrians, pursued the Emperor from room to room, now attempting to plead their case, now answering his shrewd questions. Finally the Emperor broke off the interview, saying, ' Men who think me no god are more unfortunate than criminal '. Tacitus seems to imply that the outrage was to be persisted in and that the Jews were preparing to resist by force when the Emperor's death removed the cause of the trouble ; Philo and Josephus, better authorities, say that Gaius countermanded the order.

The Death of Gaius, A.D. 41. It was the soldiers, as has been said, on whom the Emperor's power rested, and the end of Gaius, like those of Tiberius and Nero, came at once when some of the soldiers began to fear for themselves. The lead was taken by Cassius Chaerea, a tribune of a praetorian cohort, whom the Emperor had repeatedly and grossly insulted. Taking their opportunity of finding the Emperor unguarded, the conspirators despatched him with thirty wounds ; the German bodyguard arrived too late to save him, but not too late to kill some of the assassins.

CHAPTER V

THE PRINCIPATE OF CLAUDIUS, A.D. 41-54

*T*HE *Accession of Claudius*. The assassination of Gaius resembled that of Julius Caesar in being the work of a few individuals, acting from personal motives, who had made no plans for following up their act ; hence Rome suddenly found itself without a head, and the only constitutional power in existence was that of the Senate and the two consuls. They, as nominal heads of the State, convened the Senate, and the tyranny of Gaius was denounced ; but there was no agreement as to what was to be done next ; some senators wished to declare the Republic restored, others were for the continuance of the Principate in a different family, and were prepared themselves to undertake the office. The four Urban Cohorts were ready to support the Senate, and received the watchword ' Liberty ' ; but action was necessary, and no action was taken. ' While the Senate deliberated, the Praetorian Guards had resolved ' (Gibbon). During the confusion some of them were plundering the Palace, and one of the plunderers found a man hiding behind a curtain ; dragging him out, he found that it was Claudius, the uncle of the late Emperor and the son of Drusus and brother of Germanicus. He presented him at once to his comrades, who carried their prize off to their camp ; they were delighted to have found a member of the popular branch of the Imperial house, for they were most unwilling to submit to the Senate ; their privileges and their pay depended on the maintenance of the Empire.

Claudius was at first uncertain whether he was being carried off for honour or for execution, but by the next day he had plucked up his courage, and, emboldened by his friend Herod Agrippa, he received the soldiers' oath of allegiance, and promised them a donation of 15,000 sesterces each ; as Suetonius says, ' Primus Caesarum fidem militis praemiis pigneratus '—a precedent which was only too consistently followed. The Senate had to yield, for the people were shouting for Claudius, and the Urban Cohorts were no match for the Praetorians and were, moreover, beginning to waver. Hence Claudius was accepted as Emperor.

His Previous Life. Tacitus lays stress on the accession of Claudius as an example of the ' mockery ' [1] in all human affairs ; ' by common talk, by popular expectation, by respect, all men were marked out for Empire more than the man whom Fortune held in the background as the Emperor to be '. Weak in health from his birth, with legs unable properly to support his weight, and with a stammering tongue and a slobbering mouth, he was disliked by his own mother Antonia, and under Augustus was kept in the background entirely, though the old Emperor rightly saw there was something in his ungainly step-grandson. Under Tiberius,

[1] *Ann.* iii. 18.

beyond the nominal honour of being an *Augustalis*, he received
no office ; he was not even admitted to the Senate. Gaius
took him as his colleague in his first consulship, and he now
married Valeria Messalina, who, as connected with Augustus
on both sides of her family, was a great match ; but such promotion brought its dangers, and Claudius probably only owed
his life to the fact that the Emperor made him a butt publicly
and privately. Hence, during the greater part of his life
Claudius had been left to slaves and freedmen, and both his
manners and his morals suffered ; he indulged in gluttony,
drunkenness, gaming, but he retained one redeeming feature,
his devotion to study.

There is no reason to doubt the unfavourable parts of this
picture, but it may well be the case that Claudius deliberately sought obscurity for the sake of safety ; this is the more
likely, for he certainly lacked physical courage ; when he
was Emperor, he disliked weapons as much as our own king,
James I, whom he strangely resembled both in his unattractive
qualities, moral as well as physical, and in his real though
somewhat pedantic learning.

Importance of Claudius. But the importance of the work
done in his reign is so great, and the wisdom of much of the
policy is so marked, that it may well be suspected that Claudius
was a much greater man than our authorities allow. They
were all prejudiced ; Suetonius as usual is a scandalmonger,
Seneca's satire is clearly inspired by personal dislike, and
Tacitus could not forgive an Emperor who did so much to
sweep away the remnants of the republican tradition which,
like all Roman literary men, the great historian held in such
reverence.[1]

It must never be forgotten that both in home affairs and
in foreign affairs Claudius ranks only second to Augustus as
an empire-builder ; to almost every great development his

---

[1] Against Seneca's bitter satire, the *Apocolocyntosis*, may be set
the gross flattery in the *Consolatio ad Polybium*, written to induce
Claudius to permit him to return from exile. And we should probably
have evidence for a much more favourable judgment from Tacitus,
had not *Annals* ix. and x. perished, the books which contained the
account of the earlier and better part of the Emperor's reign.

reign contributed something. Hence it is hardly likely that he was a mere pedantic dotard.

The Imperial Title. Claudius had not been adopted by the preceding Emperor, but he assumed the cognomen of Caesar, which henceforth in theory as in fact becomes a mere title, with a great and honourable history.[1] He strengthened his own family claim by deifying his grandmother Livia, and by special honours to his mother Antonia.

Beginnings of the Reign of Claudius. Like all the first Emperors, Claudius began his reign well, with at any rate a show of respect for the Senate and old Roman tradition. The 'acts' of Gaius were annulled, a general amnesty was proclaimed, the exiles were restored, including even those who had talked of restoring the Republic or who had been ready to take the Principate themselves. Only the actual assassins of Gaius were executed.

Claudius consulted the Senate in everything, and showed special courtesy to the magistrates. The law of *Maiestas* was dropped, and was not revived again till late in the time of Nero (p. 107). Special measures, too, were taken at once to remove the danger of the famine which threatened Italy ; the reckless interference of Gaius with the means of communication (cf. p. 80) had seriously interrupted the foreign supplies on which Rome depended.

Antiquarian Measures of Claudius. The Emperor was moved to a constitutional policy partly by prudence, but also, in part at any rate, by his antiquarian leanings. He gratified these by holding the Secular Games in A.D. 47, the 800th anniversary of the Founding of Rome. These were held every hundred and ten years (p. 16), and only sixty-four years had passed since Augustus had held them, but Claudius made a fresh start with a new method of calculation.[2]

---

[1] It is curious, however, that it was in ' regions Caesar never knew ', the Centre and the East of Europe, that ' Kaiser ' and ' Czar ' were established as titles.

[2] Claudius added three new letters to the alphabet (Tac. *Ann.* xiv. 14). An inverted digamma represented V, an antisigma (Ɔ) stood for BS or PS, and Ⱶ for U or I in words like ' maximus '. The first and third are met with in inscriptions of his time. These symbols soon disappeared from use.

Claudius as Censor, A.D. 47. So, too, he was not satisfied with performing the duties of censor, as Augustus did, holding the more ordinary office of consul ; he revived the censorship itself (A.D. 47), in which he is said to have made himself ridiculous by his fussiness. As censor, too, he extended the *pomerium*, the boundary of the city of Rome, a thing which had not been done since Sulla [1] ; it was the privilege of those who had added to the Empire, and Claudius claimed the honour as the conqueror of Britain. Antiquarian interests also are seen in his legislation (A.D. 47) to restore the old college of the *haruspices*, and in his creation, when he was censor, of new patrician families ; the old ones were dying out, and it was becoming difficult to fill certain offices which Roman conservatism in religious matters reserved for patricians alone. It was antiquarianism, too, which was the pretext for restoring (A.D. 44) the Senate's Treasury, the aerarium, to the care of quaestors, as under the Republic. [2] But this change really increased the Emperor's power, for the two quaestors appointed to the Treasury for a three-year term were chosen by the Emperor. And it was accompanied by a real diminution of the powers of the Republican officials, for the Emperor, at the time that he transferred the Treasury back to them, abolished the powers of the four *quaestores classici*, one of whom, [3] at any rate, the *quaestor Ostiensis*, still had retained important duties in connection with Rome's corn supply.

The Imperial Civil Service. The development of the powers of the Emperor's own officials was even more important. Since in theory the Emperor was only an ordinary citizen, entrusted with special powers, it was impossible for him to employ at Rome free-born Romans in the various financial departments under his control. Apart from his private property, the *patrimonium Caesaris*, he had the revenues of

[1] Tacitus says it was also done by Augustus, but the silence of the *Monumentum Ancyranum* refutes this.

[2] Augustus had given it to praetors, or at any rate men with praetorian rank.

[3] Another, the quaestor Gallicus, whose head-quarters were at Ariminum, seems to have had important powers in the Po valley.

the imperial provinces to receive and to spend. At first
there was a special *fiscus* for each province. But as time
went on, it became evident that central control was necessary, and this work had to be done at Rome and therefore
by freedmen. We are told that under Tiberius the imperial
Civil Service had been small,[1] but under Claudius for the
first time the *libertus a rationibus*, in charge of an Imperial
fiscus,[2] appears in the freedman, Pallas. He was one of
the most important men in the State, and, as Tacitus says,
his resignation of the Treasury under Nero (A.D. 55) was
satirically compared to the resignation of a magistrate.[3]

A corresponding organization of the Imperial services
went on in other departments. Side by side with Pallas,
and hardly less important, was Narcissus, the *libertus ab
epistolis*, who was in charge of all official correspondence ;
the *libertus a libellis*, who dealt with petitions of individuals,
was not quite so important.

These officials and others, e.g. Polybius, who was *libertus
a studiis*, i.e. the Emperor's librarian and literary secretary,
were his special advisers, and they gained enormous power
and consequently wealth.[4] This new organization tended
to efficiency, but it also increased the personal power of the
Emperor, and correspondingly diminished the powers of the
old magistrates.

Further Encroachments of the Emperor. The development
of the judicial power of the Emperor probably affected still
more seriously the lives and fortunes of individuals, though
in itself it was less important than the administrative
encroachments. In theory the Emperor had the right to
try criminal cases,[5] especially those that concerned his procurators, or cases of great importance, but in practice he

[1] ' Intra paucos libertos domus ', Tac. *Ann*. iv. 6.

[2] Tacitus (*Ann*. ii. 47 ; vi. 2) speaks of an imperial fiscus under
Tiberius, but he is thought to be using anachronistically the title of
his own day.

[3] Tac. *Ann*. xiii. 14, ' ire Pallantem ut eiuraret '.

[4] Pallas was proverbial for wealth, cf. Juvenal, i. 108. He is said
to have possessed 300,000,000 sesterces.

[5] E.g. Tiberius was asked to undertake the trial of Piso (p. 65),
but refused.

had usually 'remitted' them to the Senate. Claudius, however, devoted himself to this kind of activity, and allowed himself to be unduly influenced in it by his wives and his freedmen, e.g. in condemning Valerius Asiaticus (A.D. 47) to please Messalina. These trials *intra cubiculum* were most unpopular, and were formally given up by Nero at the beginning of his reign (cf. p. 98), though resumed by him later.

What the Emperor claimed for himself he extended to his officials. In A.D. 53 a *senatusconsultum* was passed, giving his procurators judicial power in financial cases ; by this they became at once prosecutor and judge.

This increased power of the Emperor was at once supported by and expressed in the increase in the number of the Guard. There had been nine cohorts only of these under Augustus, and inscriptions prove they had become twelve under Nero ; it is not unnatural to conjecture that the change was made by Claudius on his accession, which he owed to the Praetorians.

Public Works of Claudius. This increase of centralization and of the Emperor's power led, at first at any rate, to increased efficiency, though it had its bad side also, as will be seen later.

It has been already noticed that the Emperor had immediately on his accession to take measures for securing the food supplies of the Roman populace, and that he had further interfered with this department of government by transferring the powers of the quaestor Ostiensis (p. 87) to a procurator of his own. No doubt connected with these measures was the improvement of the harbour of Ostia, the most important of his public works. The old port of Rome at the river mouth had been silted up, and the corn-ships, on which Rome depended for its life, had to land their freights at Puteoli ; hence delay and increased expense. Julius Caesar had planned the improvement of the harbour at Ostia[1] ; Claudius now had a new harbour made, with a channel to the right bank of the Tiber, and protected it with three moles, one on each side and a third in deep water at the

---

[1] Suetonius, *Claud.* 20, says 'propter difficultatem omissum '; but more probably it was his death which prevented the work being carried out.

entrance ; on this there was a lighthouse, which was compared with the famous Alexandrian 'Pharos'. In the end this harbour, too, was allowed to silt up, but the recent excavations at Ostia have shown how important the town was ; its remains have been called 'a second Pompeii'.

Another work for the improvement of the corn supply of Italy was the cutting of a channel, three miles long, to carry off the water of the Lacus Fucinus (Lago Celano), and so prevent its shores being ruined for agriculture by periodic floods. This *emissarium* resembled that of the Alban Lake, but was far larger, and cost the labour of 30,000 men for eleven years.[1] Probably more effective than this second work was the legislation for improving the sea carriage of corn to Rome, by encouraging the construction of larger vessels.

Claudius also provided for the other great need of Rome by completing the aqueduct begun by Gaius ; this was far the finest of the Roman aqueducts, and brought the water at such a level that it could be carried to all the hills of Rome. Two of its arches still form the Porta Maggiore on the north side of Rome. The water-supply was under a *procurator aquarum*.

Constructive work of another kind for Italy was the care of the State roads ; it was under Claudius that the great Via Claudia was opened, Italy's line of communication, over the Brenner Pass, with the Danube Valley, and later the way by which the barbarian hosts poured south to conquer Italy.

Legislation of Claudius. The building up of a State is done in other ways than by material construction. Claudius on the judgment seat was often ingenious, and still more often injudicious ; but some of his laws were definite contributions to Roman jurisprudence. Such was the law forbidding usurers to lend money to a son in anticipation of the father's death, and the law for the protection of sick slaves, which made the killing of them murder, and

[1] Owing to Nero's neglect, the channel soon became blocked, but was reopened by Hadrian. By the third century, however, it was again blocked, and remained so till about sixty years ago ; since 1874 it has been working again, and some 40,000 acres have been recovered for cultivation.

gave them freedom if they recovered after they had been exposed in the temple of Aesculapius.

Claudius' Foreign Policy. Annexation of New Provinces. As usual under the early Empire, the work abroad was better than that done at home. Of the restoration of the German frontier (p. 152 ff.) and of the weakness shown in the East (p. 126), some account will be given elsewhere. It is interesting to notice that under this Emperor more provinces were permanently added to the Empire than by any other of the successors of Augustus. There were five annexations: Mauretania (A.D. 42), Britain (begun in A.D. 43), Judaea (A.D. 44), Thrace (A.D. 46), and Lycia (A.D. 43). The Emperor could afford to restore, as he did, Achaia and Macedonia to the Senate.

The annexations of Mauretania and Thrace have been already spoken of (pp. 43–49). There was hard fighting to reduce the former (A.D. 42), in which Suetonius Paulinus distinguished himself and gained the reputation which led to his appointment in Britain, the conquest of which will be spoken of in a separate chapter.

It will be remembered that in A.D. 6 Judaea had been placed under an imperial procurator (p. 39). At the beginning of the reign of Claudius the Kingdom of Judaea was restored to the line of Herod the Great, Herod Agrippa I being put on the throne. He was a favourite at the imperial court and was equally acceptable to the Jews and to the Greeks of the Hellenized cities of Judaea. However, his behaviour was not entirely satisfactory; he persisted in strengthening the fortifications of Jerusalem, till the Romans were compelled to interfere. The kingdom did not last long; in A.D. 44 Agrippa died, and the country was again placed under an imperial procurator. But, to placate the Jews, it was arranged that the nomination of the High Priest and the control of the Temple should be in the hands of Herod of Chalcis, brother of Agrippa (p. 143). Felix, brother of the freedman Pallas, was procurator from A.D. 52 to 60.

Extension of the Franchise and Colonization. But on the whole the management of the provinces under the Empire was good. Claudius went back to the bold traditions of

Julius Caesar, and, unlike the cautious Augustus, extended the franchise freely. No doubt there was venality in this too; the centurion at Jerusalem before whom St. Paul was brought was by no means the only one who ' by a great sum obtained this freedom '; but the enfranchising policy was a carrying out of a great principle. In Claudius' great speech to the Senate on the admission of the ' *Primores Galliae* ' to the ' *ius honorum* ' (*vid. inf.*), the antiquarian precedents are clumsy and pedantic, but they show that the Emperor really understood why it was that Rome had throughout the centuries gone on from strength to strength, why she had become the mistress of the Western World, and how it was that it could be said of her :

' Urbem fecisti quod prius orbis erat.'

An interesting instance of the enfranchising policy of Claudius is given us in an inscription (of the year A.D. 46), in which the Emperor decided that an Alpine tribe, the Anauni, who legally were only dependents (*attributi*) of the *municipium*, Tridentum, should be recognized as full Roman citizens ; they were by usage acquiring that right, and some of them even had been recruited in the Praetorian Guard. This unconscious assimilation, confirmed after an interval as a legal fact, is typical of the way in which Rome absorbed her subjects.

Augustus had counted 4,233,000 citizens in 8 B.C. ; Claudius in A.D. 48 counted nearly six millions.[1] Seneca, himself of a newly-enfranchised stock, could gibe at the Emperor for enfranchising nearly the whole barbarian world [2]; but Claudius was a statesman and Seneca a turner of elegant phrases and a philosopher, who by no means always practised what he preached.

It was not merely the extension of the franchise which was the work of Claudius. He—or his officers—did their best to forward Roman ideas and methods of government. Rome's colonies had been her stepping-stones to Empire,

---

[1] But the figures are uncertain in Tacitus, and Jerome gives nearly a million more.

[2] Clotho says ironically that Claudius might as well be spared ' dum hos pauculos, qui supersunt, civitate donaret '.

and Claudius continued outside Italy the policy which in earlier days had secured Italy. Famous towns like Trèves in Gaul and Cologne on the Rhine, Colchester in England, Ptolemais (Acre) in Palestine, and no less than six colonies in Mauretania, owed their origin to him. Cologne is especially noticeable ; as its name implies, it was ' the colony ', a new departure in that part of the world ; it marked the final development of Rome's long friendship with the Ubii.[1]

In some ways the best-known of the acts of Claudius for extending Romanization is his speech to the Senate which has been mentioned above (p. 92). The dislike of the Romans for Gallic senators had been shown when Julius Caesar admitted some of his newly-conquered subjects to that body ; Tacitus shows that it was still present in Claudius' time, and the memory even of the sack of Rome was recalled. The speech of the Emperor defending his act in admitting Gallic chiefs to the Senate is preserved to a large extent in an inscription now in the museum of Lyons, where no doubt the commemorative tablet had been set up.[2] It was only the chiefs of the Aedui, a tribe always philo-Roman, who were thus admitted to the Senate by Claudius, but the precedent was soon followed in a wider form.

Perhaps the concession may have been connected with another measure of Claudius in Gaul, the prohibition of Druidism ; this religion had always been national and anti-Roman in character, and Claudius seems to have made more

[1] But Tacitus, *Ann.* xii. 27, contemptuously puts down this important new departure to the influence of the Empress Agrippina, who had been born there. Cf. pp. 153-4.

[2] Tacitus, *Ann.* xi. 24, summarizes the speech, and greatly improve the Emperor's Latin. There is considerable discussion as to the exact nature of the Emperor's act. It was once thought that it was a revival of an old usage, creating an imperfect citizenship without the *ius honorum* (cf. the similar *civitas sine suffragio*) ; but there is no evidence for such a status under the Empire, and the old *civitas sine suffragio* had ceased to exist in the second century B.C. The view now usually held is that Claudius as Censor was using his right of *adlectio* in an unusual way, (1) by admitting wholesale, and (2) by admitting citizens of a new race and standing. The *primores Galliae* were chiefs with a large personal following and thus held an unusual position.

thorough the repressive policy against it which we find both under Augustus and under Tiberius.

Claudius and the Jews of Alexandria. It will be remembered that in the reign of Gaius riots broke out between the Jews and the Alexandrians, culminating in the embassy to the Emperor (p. 82). Immediately on Claudius' accession the slumbering hostility again burst out ; the Jews, who had been making secret preparations and had sent to their friends in Egypt and Syria for reinforcements, took the aggressive in attacking the Alexandrians, as they themselves had often been attacked. Again an embassy and a counter-embassy were sent to Rome, and Claudius' letter in reply to the Alexandrians has recently been discovered on a papyrus. ' I must reserve for myself ', he writes, ' an unyielding indignation against whoever caused this renewed outbreak ; but I tell you plainly that, if you do not desist from this baneful and obstinate mutual hostility, I shall perforce be compelled to show you what a beneficent prince can be when turned by just indignation. Wherefore I conjure you yet once again that on the one side the Alexandrians show themselves forbearing and kindly towards the Jews who for many years have dwelt in the same city and offer no outrage to them in the exercise of their traditional worship, but permit them to observe their customs as in the time of Divus Augustus, which customs I also after hearing both sides have confirmed ; and on the other side I bid the Jews not to busy themselves about anything beyond what they have held hitherto . . . but to profit by what they possess and to enjoy in a city not their own an abundance of all good things ; and not to introduce or invite Jews who sail down to Alexandria from Syria or Egypt, thus compelling me to conceive the greater suspicion ; otherwise I will by all means take vengeance on them as fomenting a general plague for all the world.' [1] Thus Claudius showed himself firm and impartial ; he would neither give the Jews the citizenship of Alexandria nor tolerate the Alexandrians' attacks on them.

Evil Side of Imperial Autocracy. So far the good side of the

[1] The translation is taken from *Jews and Christians in Egypt* by H. I. Bell, p. 29.

reign of Claudius has been sketched. But centralization and the growth of Imperial power had their evil side ; Tacitus [1] was speaking from bitter experience when he wrote, ' Impares libertini libertatis argumentum sunt ' ; he knew that the greater the power of the Emperor's own servants, the more the liberty of the State suffered. This was equally true of the women of the Emperor's household ; the wives of Claudius were an influence for evil even more powerful than his freedmen.

As with Tiberius, so with Claudius fear was a powerful motive for moving the Emperor. Already in the second year of his reign there had been a conspiracy against him, in which Camillus Scribonianus, the legate of Dalmatia, took a leading part ; but the legions, the Seventh and the Eleventh, remained faithful to the Emperor, earning thereby the honourable title of *Claudia Pia Fidelis*, and killed the legate. Among those who suffered death as the result was Paetus, taught ' how to die ' by his heroic wife, Arria. The natural cowardice of the Emperor was increased by this conspiracy, and the most trifling evidence, even based only on dreams,[2] was sufficient to secure a condemnation. It would be useless to attempt to describe the various trials. What is certain is that the evil influence of Messalina, the Emperor's wife, combined with that of the freedmen to pervert justice.

Influence of Messalina. She was especially bitter against any possible woman rival and secured the death of Julia, one of the surviving daughters of Germanicus, and of Poppaea, reputed the most beautiful woman in Rome. In the Emperor a curious tendency to cruelty developed ; he is said by Suetonius to have put to death thirty-five senators and more than 300 knights.

Messalina was prominent in stimulating this cruelty. Her name, too, has passed into a proverb for shameless debauchery ; as she was married at about 15, and executed eight years later (A.D. 48), it is difficult to credit all the stories about her, but it may safely be affirmed that she was a physical degenerate.

[1] *Germania*, 25.
[2] E.g. the condemnation of Appius Silanus, the stepfather of Messalina, was secured in this way.

Her fall is mysterious and a matter of much dispute. She certainly had incurred the jealousy of the great freedmen, and they seized the opportunity of a final outrageous act on her part to awaken the Emperor to a sense of her misconduct and of his own danger. Tacitus tells us that, not satisfied with the licence allowed by the complacent Emperor, she agreed to the request of her lover, the consul-designate, C. Silius, one of the handsomest men in Rome, that they should be formally married. The Emperor, who was at Ostia, was with difficulty brought to realize what had happened ; but finally becoming alarmed he took refuge with the Praetorians and proceeded to act. The guilty pair, surprised at his determined action, were abandoned by all. Silius met his death bravely with many of his friends ; Messalina, after vainly trying to see the Emperor in the hope that her charms would obtain pardon, met her death finally by assisted suicide.

The whole repulsive story bristles with improbabilities, but Tacitus devotes a whole chapter [1] to affirming its truth ; he affirms that the very outrageousness of the act tempted Messalina, and it is difficult to reject his account without accusing him of deliberate falsehood. One point may be added in confirmation of his account ; Messalina's act was perhaps part of a serious conspiracy, and not a mere result of unbridled passion ; she was related to the imperial family, and she may well have preferred to be Empress regnant with a young and handsome consort to remaining only Empress consort. It is significant that among the bridal guests, who were later punished as accomplices, were the Prefect of the *Vigiles* and the head of the imperial gladiatorial ' school '.

The Last Years of Claudius. The Emperor still had some six years to live, and during these he was a mere tool in the hands of his freedmen. The first concern of these minions was to find him a new wife. Three claimants were put

[1] xi. 27. He affirms that his account was based at once on the spoken and on the written evidence of contemporaries, and that ' nihil compositum miraculi causa '. This seems to answer the argument of those who attributed his story to the many enemies of Messalina, and especially to Agrippina, her successor as the wife of Claudius.

forward, each supported by a freedman ; Agrippina, the last surviving daughter of Germanicus, who was the choice of Pallas, won. The objection that she was the Emperor's own niece was overruled on the suggestion of L. Vitellius, the colleague of Claudius as censor and the father of the future Emperor, who proposed to the Senate that they should bring pressure on the Emperor to do—what he wished to do ; the personal charms of Agrippina and the fact of her being the representative of the Julian house had already won him over (A.D. 49).

Her influence at once became predominant, and the Emperor betrothed his daughter Octavia to Nero, the son of Agrippina, the future Emperor. The Empress was as unscrupulous as Messalina in securing condemnations, and drove her unsuccessful rival, Lollia Paulina, to suicide on the charge of using magic. But her main endeavour was to secure the succession for her son as against the Emperor's own son, Britannicus : it was the old rivalry between the Julian and the Claudian houses breaking out. once more, with the Claudian Emperor as wax in the hands of his wife.

In the next year (A.D. 50) Claudius was persuaded to adopt Nero ; then in A.D. 51, when he was only 13, the boy was allowed to take the *toga virilis*, was made consul-designate (for the year A.D. 58) and received immediately proconsular power outside Rome and the title of ' Princeps Iuventutis '. In A.D. 52, when Claudius left Rome for the *Latinae Feriae*, Nero was put in authority as Prefect of the City. Early in the following year he was married to the daughter of Claudius, Octavia. It was clear that his fortune was in the ascendant, and Agrippina succeeded in obtaining the all-important post of Prefect of the Praetorian Guards (A.D. 51) for her partisan Afranius Burrus. She herself adopted the Imperial style, and at the opening of the Fucine Lake in dress and in position rivalled the Emperor himself. She is the first princess in Rome whose head appears on the coins.[1]

---

[1] While she is Empress-consort, it is placed on the reverse, but during the first few months of her son's reign, in A.D. 54, it appears on the obverse : then with the breakdown of her influence it is on the reverse again.

Death of Claudius. But the old Emperor was thought to be anxious for his own family, and to be likely to favour Britannicus, who was supported by the freedman Narcissus ; this once all-powerful favourite knew that he had incurred Agrippina's deadly hatred by supporting her rival Lollia. Unfortunately for Claudius and the Claudian family, Narcissus was taken ill, and in his absence at the baths of Sinuessa Agrippina resolved to 'make sure' at once ; the convicted poisoner Locusta was employed to give a speedy poison, and the Emperor died on 13 September, A.D. 54 ; he was in his sixty-fourth year.

CHAPTER VI

THE PRINCIPATE OF NERO, A.D. 54–68

*T*HE *Beginnings of Nero's Reign.* Nero, like his predecessor, owed his position as Emperor to the Praetorian Guards, who had been secured to him through Burrus ; on the death of Claudius he had been at once carried to their camp and accepted on the promise of a donative ; the evil precedent set by Claudius was thus established. The decree of the Senate, formally conferring the Imperial powers on him, followed as a matter of course. As usual, all sorts of promises of good government and of the removal of abuses were made. The Emperor's speech was written for him by Seneca, and it was noticed that he was the first Emperor who was incapable of making a speech for himself. The main promises were :

(1) That the Emperor would not encroach on the jurisdiction of other courts, or try cases privately *intra cubiculum*.

(2) That the sale of favours and offices should be abolished.

(3) That his freedmen should not interfere in State affairs.

(4) That the powers of the Senate should be maintained and that, as by republican usage, the consuls should preside over that body.

(5) Cases concerning Italy and the senatorial provinces were to be tried in the consul's courts.

This speech was a condemnation of the evils which had

made the rule of Claudius, especially in his later years, so unpopular, and Seneca accompanied it by a bitter pasquinade, the *Apocolocyntosis*, in which he represented the reception of the new deity [1] in heaven, his denunciation there by Augustus, and his removal to the lower world. The twelve pages of brilliant Latin can still be read with real amusement; they effectually blasted for the time at any rate what reputation the dead Emperor still had.

The Quinquennium Neronis. On the whole the promises of good government were kept for a time, and the first ' five years ' of Nero's reign, except for the atrocious crimes which marked their beginning and their end, were, like the opening months of Gaius' reign, a contrast to the following decade. They are also praised highly in themselves, and the well-known *obiter dictum* of Trajan has been interpreted to mean that, in the opinion of that great Emperor, they were ' superior to the government of every other Emperor '.[2] Even if this exaggerated praise can be fairly deduced from Trajan's words, it is doubtful how far Nero himself deserves the credit for the good government. It seems pretty clear from our authorities that the Emperor spent his time mainly in self-indulgence, and that he left the management of affairs to his old tutor Seneca and to the Praetorian Prefect Burrus; these wise ministers had been chosen, not by him, but for him, by his mother Agrippina, but it is clear that from the very first they set themselves to free him from her influence and to check her reckless ambitions.

Nero and Seneca. To estimate the character of Seneca is hard. The contrast between his practice and his precept seems too glaring; there was perhaps some foundation for the charge on which he had been banished by Claudius— that he had had improper relations with Julia, the sister of Agrippina [3] and at any rate his enormous wealth (Tacitus

---

[1] Claudius had had divine honours voted to him at once after his death.

[2] The words [Aurelius Victor, *Caesar. Epit.* 5] are ' Quinquennium tantus fuit [Nero], augenda urbe maxime, ut merito Traianus saepius testaretur procul differre cunctos principes Neronis quinquennio '. It seems hard to get extreme commendation out of this, even as it stands, and in the context it may well have been limited.

[3] Cassius Dio says with Agrippina herself.

says he had accumulated 300,000,000 sesterces) suited ill with his philosophic teaching of renunciation. His reputation has been subject to the most astounding changes; he was the popular teacher of his own day, and yet Tacitus, half a century later, shows a barely concealed dislike for him and his style; he was greatly admired by the scholars of the Renaissance, both as a philosopher and as a dramatist; others have thought his well-turned epigrammatic sentences to be platitudes, and his dramas artificial rhetoric. Perhaps the fairest judgment is that he was certainly not a great man, but that he was above the standard of his time; and at least he understood how to die bravely.

He knew that he had a most unpromising pupil, born of a bad stock, and he seems to have tried by indulgence, and by giving Nero a taste for the minor arts, to keep him from developing his naturally cruel temper. We know, of course, that he failed, and there is a bitter irony in the fact that a treatise on 'Clemency' was dedicated, in the second year of his reign, to an Emperor who was to gain a reputation for cruelty. In its opening chapter Seneca gives the reason for his own failure; he puts into the mouth of Nero a speech describing his almighty power. 'These thousands of swords which my Peace keeps in the sheath will be drawn at my pleasure; it is for me alone to decide what nations shall be utterly cut off, what set free, what robbed of freedom, to decide what kings must be made slaves, what have their heads encircled with the royal diadem.' All this, and much more of the same kind, was only too true, and the temptation of absolute power soon proved too great for human nature.

The Quarrel with Agrippina. To begin with, Nero, who was young and timid, followed Seneca's advice; he needed his support against Agrippina, who at once showed that it was ambition to rule, not motherly affection, which had made her commit her crimes. The murder of her husband had been accompanied by the execution of her rival in Nero's affections, his aunt Domitia Lepida, who was accused of aiming at power by tampering with the slaves in South Italy. Narcissus too, who had tried to win Claudius to support Britannicus as his successor to the throne, was driven to

commit suicide. Poison removed Junius Silanus, the proconsul of Asia, who in spite of his sluggish temperament [1]
was feared by Agrippina, at once as a great-grandson of
Augustus and as a possible avenger of his brother, L. Silanus,
whose death she had secured in A.D. 49, in order that his
betrothed, Octavia, the daughter of Claudius, might be given
to her own son. Tacitus says that she would have proceeded
to other murders, had not Burrus and Seneca stopped her.
The clash with her son soon became open ; she tried to place
herself at his side at the reception of the Armenian ambassadors, but was prevented by the tact of Seneca, who told
Nero to rise to meet her, and then to postpone the audience.
This trifle was significant, but far more important was the
removal of Pallas, the partisan and perhaps the lover of
Agrippina, from the Treasury ; his place over it was taken
by a freedman, Claudius, the father [2] of Claudius Etruscus,
who was wise enough to keep out of politics, and so remained
in office till the time of Domitian.

Murder of Britannicus. Agrippina was not a woman to
submit to such a supersession. She openly taunted the
Emperor with ingratitude, and threatened to appeal to the
Praetorians on behalf of young Britannicus, who, she rightly
claimed, had been supplanted by Nero, only through her
influence over his father Claudius.

Nero's alarm was excited, and it was increased by the
sympathy shown for the boy, when Nero tried to hold him
up to ridicule at the Saturnalia ; called suddenly to sing,
Britannicus did not break down as Nero expected, but moved
his audience by a song only too appropriate to himself, the
lament [3] of a child deprived of his inheritance. Nero's fear
drove him to crime ; the skill of Locusta was once more
called into play, and Britannicus was poisoned when dining
with the Emperor and buried hurriedly to conceal the traces
of the crime.

[1] He was nicknamed by Gaius ' The Golden Sheep '.
[2] His other name is unknown, cf. p. 180.
[3] This has been supposed with some probability to be the fragment
of Ennius quoted in Cicero, *Tusc. Disp.* iii. 19, 44. The murder of
Britannicus is the subject of a play of Racine ; but in this a fictitious
love interest largely supersedes historical fact.

Agrippina now took up the cause of Nero's neglected wife, Octavia, but found that all her partisans deserted her, and that she herself was accused of treason. She met this charge with characteristic boldness, forced herself into the presence of the Emperor, and succeeded in obtaining the punishment of some of her accusers. Her power, however, was broken ; Nero still feared her, and did not venture to indulge his taste for public performances as a singer while she lived ; but otherwise her four remaining years of life were unimportant.

Nero and the Senate. Nero, freed from the influence of his mother, let his wise advisers rule, though his private life showed what might be expected later. A typical amusement was his passion for walking the streets at night, and playing 'the Mohawk'. Meanwhile the foreign policy of Rome, which had lost vigour in the latter days of Claudius, was strengthened ; both on the Eastern and on the Rhine frontiers Roman authority was vindicated (cc. viii, ix), and oppressive governors of provinces were punished. A series of trials, in which justice seems on the whole to have been done, was held before the Senate, where Tacitus [1] says 'adhuc manebat quaedam imago reipublicae'. Perhaps that of Cossutianus Capito, accused by the Cilicians (A.D. 58), may be especially mentioned, because he was afterwards conspicuous as a *delator* and because Tacitus says of him 'he thought he might be as reckless in his province as he had been in Rome ', a sentence which well illustrates the contrast between Imperial rule in Rome and in the provinces.[2] Some useful but comparatively unimportant legislation was passed. But the Imperial power automatically increased. The administration of the senatorial treasury (the *aerarium*) had broken down once more, and its control was transferred from the quaestors to *praefecti* appointed by the Emperor from among the ex-praetors (A.D. 56) ; Nero had also to assist it with a gift of 40,000,000 sesterces.

Nero's Finance Measures. More interesting, though they came to little, were Nero's finance proposals, made in the

[1] Tac. *Ann.* xiii. 28.
[2] He was soon restored by the influence of his father-in-law Tigellinus.

year A.D. 58. Moved by the ever-recurring complaints about the oppression of the *publicani*, he suddenly proposed, apparently on his own authority, a fundamental change in the system of taxation. ' All indirect taxes (*vectigalia*) were to be abolished.' [1] This change would have transferred all the burdens of the State to the provinces, for they alone paid direct taxes (*tributum*), but they would have had the compensatory advantage of ' Free Trade throughout the Empire '. Some have credited Nero with conceiving this great reform ; others (e.g. Merivale) think that the remission was limited to Italy. It is difficult to believe that Nero had at all thought out what his proposal involved ; it was simply a ' fine gesture ' on the part of a somewhat clever young prince, whose best quality was love of applause. At any rate it was dropped on the advice of his ' council ' (*seniores*) who urged that, if carried out, it would ' break up all authority '.

Some measures of financial reform, however, were passed ; the terms of the grants to the *publicani* were henceforth to be published,[2] claims more than a year old were not to be pressed by them, and suits against them were to be given priority in the provincial courts.

Reform of Coinage. It may be convenient to mention here the changes, slightly later in date, in the Roman coinage under Nero. A new system was introduced by which a set of coins in bronze was struck alongside those in gold, silver and copper on the Augustan standard. It is said to have been ' the most complete monetary system of ancient times ' (Mattingly), but it was too elaborate and was partially dropped even before the death of Nero. At the same time the technique of the coiners was improved ; the Neronian coins are the most artistic specimens of Roman mints. Much more important, however, were the changes in the weight and the purity of the coins ; the *aureus* and the *denarius* (silver) were both slightly reduced in weight, and about 10

[1] Tac. *Ann.* xiii. 50.
[2] The object of this was to give publicity to what had previously been secret : it may be compared with the recent attempts in the United States to check the powers of the great corporations by making them publish their terms of association.

per cent. alloy was added to the silver. Not improbably both these changes were made for reasons of policy ; the value of the precious metals was rising, and the diminution of weight in the coins made them correspond to their actual purchasing power ; the alloy also seems to have been introduced to re-establish the old relation between the values of gold and of silver.[1]

The changes did no harm at first, but the methods adopted were in the next century applied mistakenly with disastrous effects, when Emperors endeavoured to meet their obligations by debasing the coinage ; this process, however, was very gradual, and did not become marked till the time of Marcus Aurelius. After him the deterioration was rapid, and the Roman world suffered from the evils which the debasement of coinage always produces—uncertainty of values and destruction of all confidence. Nero himself is not likely to have had any voice in changes which, however important, were largely technical, and still less is it fair to blame him for the disastrous results later of the system of coin debasement. One more point as to the coinage may be noted, viz. that Nero for most of his reign took away from the Senate the coining of bronze and copper ; that body had enjoyed the privilege and the profits of issuing coins in these metals before his time, and only regained it after A.D. 63.

The Murder of Agrippina. Whatever the merits of the first ' five years ' of Nero's reign, and however much or little of the credit of them redounds to the Emperor himself, there is no doubt that from the year A.D. 59 onwards, his reign, as it appears in our ' literary ' sources, becomes mainly an orgy of frivolity, vice and cruelty. Nero needed no one to prompt him to evil, but he was urged on to it from A.D. 58 onwards by his new mistress, Poppaea, while his leading minister after A.D. 62 was the infamous Sophonius Tigellinus, who succeeded Burrus as Prefect of the Praetorians in that year ; he had previously been Praefectus Vigilum.

[1] The suggestion that the changes were made to make easier the exchange between Roman coins and the Greek ones current in the eastern provinces breaks down in view of the fact that there was a corresponding reduction at the same time in the value of the Greek coins.

Poppaea, the wife of M. Salvius Otho, afterwards Emperor, began by securing the removal of her husband to the province of Lusitania, where he was kept for ten years ; but she knew that she could not have her way with Nero, and especially that she could not secure the position of his lawful wife, while his terrible mother was alive ; hence she persistently urged him to the most shocking of his crimes, matricide. Working at once on his passion for her, his fears for his safety, and his fear of ridicule, she taunted him with being a mere ' baby prince ' (' pusillus princeps '). But Agrippina was not an easy victim ; she knew all that was to be known about poisons, and the Praetorians would not lay a finger on the great-granddaughter of Augustus. Hence a freedman, Anicetus, the commander of the fleet at Misenum, had to be called in.

The first attempt was to drown Agrippina by treachery ; after a pretended reconciliation with Nero at Baiae, she was induced to return to her villa at Bauli in a boat specially constructed for her honour ; it was really so contrived as to come to pieces on the way, and either crush her in the wreck or drown her. But the ' accident ' failed, and she escaped by swimming. Hoping to save herself still, she sent word to Nero to tell him of her ' providential escape '; Nero, however, was now desperate, and after an elaborate scene, contrived to make it appear that his mother's messenger had attempted to assassinate him, his assassins despatched Agrippina, who died with a courage worthy of a better woman. The whole story, told at the beginning of the Fourteenth Book of the *Annals*, is a masterpiece of Tacitean style, ranking high among the narratives of crime.

Of all the acts of Nero none so shocked the world. He himself did not venture to come to Rome for six months, although he received the congratulations first of the towns of Campania, and then of the Roman Senate on his ' escape '. If Suetonius may be believed, he himself confessed that his mother's ghost haunted him, and that, like Orestes, he was pursued by the Furies with their blazing torches.

Nero as Musician and Actor. Nero, now that his mother was dead, proceeded to indulge his childish passion for display.

On his return to Rome he performed in public as a charioteer and a musician, though not at first in a public theatre. Special games called the 'Iuvenalia' were instituted (A.D. 59), and he had no difficulty in inducing Romans of the highest birth and distinction, both men and women, to follow his example. This departure from old Roman ideas shocked his subjects generally almost as much as his matricide ; both Tacitus and Juvenal attack it fiercely. It was, however, some years before Nero actually appeared in a public theatre, at Naples (in A.D. 64). After that he performed in Rome, and then in the year A.D. 66 he started on a triumphal progress in Greece, where all the great games were held, whether it was the right year for them or not, in order that the Emperor might win his assured victories and receive his crowns. Nero was so delighted at the good taste of the Greeks that, at the end of A.D. 67, he solemnly conferred on the whole province immunity from taxation. It was only the growing danger of rebellion that forced him to return to Rome shortly after.

The story of Nero's childish vanity, which has been partially anticipated here, has its comic side. Tacitus tells us that soldiers, placed in the gangways of the theatres, flogged those who failed to applaud, or who applauded in the wrong place, and that some spectators were compelled to retain their seats till they became seriously ill. It was especially recorded that Vespasian was nearly put to death because he was so bad a courtier as to go to sleep when the Emperor was singing ; but, as Tacitus[1] says, he was reserved for ' a greater destiny ' ; knowing his value as a soldier, the more respectable courtiers interceded for him, and Nero agreed to pardon him, observing, with some humour, that his lack of taste was its own punishment.

Death of Octavia. The murder of Agrippina was only one step towards the attainment of Poppaea's ambition to be Empress-consort of Rome ; before this could be realized the Emperor must be freed from his wife, Octavia. She was accused of adultery, but the charge broke down, though her slaves were tortured in the endeavour to procure evidence ;

[1] *Ann.* xvi. 5.

she was therefore divorced because she had borne Nero no children, and banished to Campania. Popular feeling ran high in her favour, and Nero's fears, aroused by these demonstrations, were worked on by Poppaea; he therefore had Octavia removed to Pandateria, the island where Julia and her granddaughter Agrippina had met their well-deserved punishment; her innocence did not save her from the same fate, and her head was brought to Poppaea, who had at last attained her object.

Tacitus ends the sad story with a passage of bitter irony [1]: 'How long shall I go on telling how gifts were voted to the temples for crimes like these? Whoever learns the disasters of these times from us or from others may take it for granted that just as often as the Emperor ordered banishments or murders, just so often the gods were thanked; what were once the marks of victories were then the marks of public disaster.' He even exaggerates the pathos, perhaps intentionally, by understating the age of Octavia—making her 'barely twenty'. Her sad story is the subject of a Roman tragedy, of uncertain date, but probably not much after her time, which is printed among the plays of Seneca.

Nero's crimes against his own family created such horror and were so outrageous that it seems necessary to speak of them at some length. But it is impossible to give even the names of the long series of nobles murdered during the latter part of his reign; as typical may be mentioned Rubellius Plautus and Cornelius Sulla, who were banished, the one to Asia, the other to Gaul, and who later on were murdered (A.D. 62), and, three years later, Torquatus Silanus, a descendant of Augustus, against whom the charge was that he had among his freedmen men who bore the titles of *a rationibus* and *a libellis*, which were now becoming an imperial property. Plautus, too, had the misfortune to claim descent in part from Augustus; his death may be mentioned for the further reason that there was some talk of resistance; Nero's vice and cruelty were at last driving men in desperation to conspire. He had by this time freed himself from the little control that remained after his mother's death. As has

[1] *Ann.* xiv. 64.

been mentioned, Burrus died, perhaps by poison (A.D. 62) ; he was succeeded as the Prefect of the Guards by Tigellinus, jointly with Faenius Rufus, who as *Praefectus annonae* had won popularity by his admirable management of the corn supply. At the same time Seneca asked permission to retire from the Emperor's councils, surrendering his vast wealth to the Emperor ; but this retirement was not formally allowed, though the request was repeated later.

Nero's Waning Popularity. The success abroad which had marked the early days of Nero's reign was now clouded by repeated disasters ; Britain was nearly lost in Boudicca's bloody rebellion in A.D. 61 (cf. p. 280) ; in the next year the Roman army at Rhandeia (cf. p. 129) capitulated ignominiously to the Parthians ; in A.D. 66 the terrible revolt broke out in Judaea (cf. p. 142) which ended, four years later, in the destruction of Jerusalem. Such blows to the Empire were poorly compensated by the annexations of Pontus Polemoniacus (A.D. 63) and of the Cottian Alps.

Nero was, however, still popular with the common people, who sympathized with his love of shows and of pleasure, and for whose amusement he so liberally provided. Even to the last, as we shall see, many of them were devoted to him, in spite of the great disaster which now overtook Rome itself, and which for a time shook his popularity.

The Burning of Rome. On 19 July, A.D. 64, a fire broke out in the Circus, between the Palatine and the Caelian Hills, and raged for six days ; it was checked by pulling down the houses in its path, but broke out again and raged for three days more ; in the end, three of the fourteen *regiones* of Rome were totally destroyed, seven were almost destroyed, and only four escaped.

Popular opinion charged Nero with having caused the fire ; he was thought by some to have coveted the glory of rebuilding Rome, by others to have been tempted by the magnificent spectacle of a burning city. The latter reason, given by Cassius Dio,[1] is probably based simply on Nero's folly ; there seems no doubt that he did enjoy the disaster, and the story that he chanted the ' Capture of Troy ', dressed

[1] lxii. 16.

in a singer's robe, as he watched the flames, may be accepted ;
but Tacitus, who generally gives an account unfavourable
to Nero, leaves the question of the origin of the fire doubtful,
saying that authorities differed. It is in accordance with all
probability that popular fancy would play freely around such
a catastrophe.[1]

Results of the Fire. We may fairly suppose that the terrible
pestilence which happened next year was the result of the
fire ; exposure and lack of food and shelter would weaken
the population, and make them a ready prey to any infection.
But Nero or his ministers did their best to lighten the calamity ;
the Emperor opened his gardens to the homeless, provided
temporary shelters in the Campus Martius and elsewhere,
and lowered the price of corn.

More important were the wise regulations made for the
rebuilding of Rome. The old crooked streets were not
restored, but a new city was laid out with broad roads and
open spaces ; the height of the blocks of buildings (*insulae*)
was limited, and stone in part took the place of wood in
the new structures. Bounties, too, for speedy restoration
stimulated the activity of the builders. In fact Rome used
the opportunity given by the fire to make itself a fine city ;
in England a similar opportunity was foolishly thrown away
in 1666, when Wren's plan for a new and magnificent London
was rejected. To carry out this rebuilding heavy contributions were levied, not only in the provinces, but in Italy.

The rebuilding of Rome on a grander scale appealed to
Nero's artistic sense and to his love of display ; it seems
difficult, however, to give him much of the credit for the
new Rome ; he was busy building his ' Golden House ',
which stretched from the Palatine to the Esquiline and contained the famous colossal statue of himself, 120 feet high ;
enclosed within its walls were woods and fields and a lake
' like a sea '. His megalomania may be summed up in his
saying that ' at last he had begun to have a house fit for a
man '.

[1] We may compare the story, once officially recorded on ' The
Monument ', but now universally rejected, that the Great Fire of
London in 1666 was the work of the Roman Catholics.

The Persecution of the Christians. The regulations as to rebuilding are not likely to have been popular, and Nero was conscious that the feeling of Rome was for the time against him ; he therefore set himself to find a scapegoat in the new sect of Christians. The spread of this religion will be described elsewhere (Chap. xix) ; here it must suffice to say that the Christians were universally unpopular, and their denunciations of coming woe [1] probably gave colour to the belief that they were guilty of incendiarism.

The ghastly story is well known how Nero threw open his gardens, and displayed to the people his skill as a charioteer by the light of burning Christians ; the *tunica molesta*, in which they were clad as incendiaries, was carefully steeped in oil to make it blaze, just as petroleum is sprinkled over the clothes of the unhappy victims of a modern lynching.

The Conspiracy of Piso. The danger to Nero, however, was not from his temporary unpopularity with the sufferers from the fire. A conspiracy was formed in A.D. 65 to make Gaius Piso Emperor, a noble of great wealth and popular for his liberality ; it was joined by many of the leading men of Rome, and, what was especially formidable, by one of the Prefects of the Guards, Faenius Rufus, and by a considerable number of their officers. But the conspirators were too weak in character to be really dangerous ; the story as told in Tacitus is a pitiful tale of hesitation in action, of foolish ostentation at first, and then of despicable cowardice and treachery when the plot had been betrayed. Piso refused to attempt to save himself by a vigorous offensive when the soldiers were coming to arrest him, and committed suicide ; Faenius Rufus tried to escape by attacking his associates, but was in his turn convicted, and died the death of a coward. The only features which relieve the dismal story are the brave deaths of some of the conspirators. Tacitus especially mentions the dying words of one of the officers, Subrius Flavus, who told Nero : ' I used to be devoted to you, while you deserved it ; I began to hate you when you murdered your mother and your wife, and displayed yourself as a charioteer and an actor, and set Rome on fire.' He pointedly

[1] Cf. e.g. Revelation xviii. v. 8–9, 18.

omits, however, the elaborate speech which Seneca dictated
to his secretaries, when he was slowly dying. There is no
reason to suppose that the philosopher had really been one
of the conspirators, though some of them, it was said, had
intended to make him Emperor. His nephew too, the poet
Lucan, in spite of weakness at first, showed himself a brave
man ; he died repeating some of his own lines, which described a soldier dying a death like his own.[1] Tacitus empha-
sizes the weakness of the last generation of Roman nobility
by contrasting their treacherous efforts at self-preservation
with the heroism of the freed-woman Epicharis, who, having
been prominent in the plot, when tortured to make her reveal
her associates, baffled the utmost cruelties by enduring
repeated tortures, and in the end by strangling herself.

The detection of the conspiracy was followed by many
executions ; even Nero's friend and companion in pleasure,
his *arbiter elegantiae*, Petronius, was at the instigation of
Tigellinus compelled to commit suicide. Senators and other
leading men were executed without even the pretence of a trial.
Such of the Roman nobility as survived went from flattery to
flattery in the hope of saving themselves, even deifying the
wretched Poppaea, who died from a kick of Nero's (A.D. 65),
and the daughter she had borne him, who also died almost
at once. Nero, however, declined the divinity offered to
himself, as he considered it unlucky ; as Tacitus says, ' an
Emperor does not receive divine honours till he ceases to be
a man '.[2]

Thrasea and the Stoic Opposition. The gloom of the end
of Nero's reign is slightly relieved by the career of Paetus
Thrasea, in whom first the Stoic opposition to the Empire—
or at any rate, to its excesses—comes to the front. P. Clodius
Paetus Thrasea, to give him his full name, had been consul in
A.D. 56, and took for years a prominent part in the Senate ;
he prevented the judicial murder of the wretched Antistius
for libelling Nero (A.D. 62), and showed that he inherited
the prejudices as well as the virtues of the old nobility by
attempting to limit the customary rights of the provincial
concilia (p. 33) against their governors. He had the

[1] *Pharsalia*, iii. 635-641.   [2] *Ann.* xv. 74.

courage to dissent silently from the shameful congratulations given by the Senate to Nero on the murder of his mother, and he assisted in bringing to justice the notorious *delator*, Cossutianus Capito, accused of extortion in Cilicia (A.D. 58). When he found that he was powerless to check injustice and flattery, he absented himself from the Senate from A.D. 63 onwards ; what specially gave offence was that he had been absent when the deification of Poppaea was voted, and that he did not applaud Nero's ' divine voice '. Hence in A.D. 66 he was accused before the Senate of setting an example of ostentatious virtue, which was a reproach to Nero ; he was compared with Cato of Utica, who had by this time become the symbol of republican tradition. That Thrasea was a conspirator was not alleged even by his accusers ; the charge against him was merely negative : ' the gazettes of Rome are read only too carefully throughout the provinces and among the troops, to find what Thrasea has refused to do '.[1]

Thrasea refused to defend himself, or to allow the tribune, Arulenus Rusticus, to veto the proceedings in the Senate against him. He died by suicide, urging his wife Arria not to follow the example of her mother, the elder Arria (cf. p. 95). Another leading Stoic, Barea Soranus, and his daughter Servilia were executed at the same time, and Helvidius Priscus, the son-in-law of Thrasea, was banished.[2]

The End of Nero's Reign. One sign of apparent prosperity marked the closing years of Nero. The Parthian claimant for the throne of Armenia came to Rome to be invested with the crown by Nero (cf. p. 130), and he was received with extraordinary pomp. Shortly after this, Nero set out for Greece to win his artistic triumphs there (cf. p. 106) ; he only returned after an absence of more than a year, when his freedman Helius, who had been left in charge of Italy, compelled him to come back to face the dangers that were threatening. He entered Rome in triumph, and hung his 1,808 crowns on an obelisk in the Circus.

[1] 'Diurna populi Romani.' Tac. *Ann.* xvi. 22.

[2] For the Stoic opposition to Nero, in which these men and Thrasea were leaders, cf. Chapter vii. Helvidius was recalled by Galba in A.D. 68 and put to death by Vespasian (p. 170).

But his enemies were no longer the degenerate Roman nobility. The governors in the provinces were moving, and Vindex, who was legate in Gallia Lugdunensis, raised the standard of revolt ; ' where the Julian star had risen, there it set ' (Mommsen). Nero, who at first treated the news with contempt, awoke to the new seriousness of the crisis, when he heard that Galba in Spain was proclaimed Emperor. A courageous man might still have rallied the forces at his disposal, which were considerable, for troops were being gathered for a projected campaign against the Caucasus ; the Praetorians, too, would have supported the Emperor. But Nero's weakness was known ; the two commanders of the Guards, Tigellinus (who, however, was too ill to take much part), and Nymphidius Sabinus, proved traitors, and told their troops that Nero had already fled. Hence the cohort on guard deserted an Emperor who, they thought, had deserted them, and Nero in terror fled to the villa of his freedman Phaon outside Rome. Here, divided between fear of death and fear of being taken, he hesitated long ; true to his character to the last, he kept exclaiming : ' Qualis artifex pereo ' ; even when his pursuers were upon him, he had to be assisted to kill himself, and died quoting Homer (9 June, A.D. 68).

The last Emperor of the Julian family was buried by his old nurses and his concubine Acte, who seems to have loved him to the last.

Nero's Place in History. Nero was above all things a poser. The ability which he undoubtedly had was of a shallow kind, but it was such as struck men's attention. And his crimes were of the same character. After the first five years of his reign he was ever in the limelight. His memory was abhorred alike by corrupt Roman society, the members of which suffered from his cruelty, and by the respectable elements in Italy and the Roman world generally, whose prejudices he had shocked. Yet it is none the less true that in his reign the provinces in general prospered.

8

CHAPTER VII

REPUBLICAN FEELING UNDER THE EMPIRE

END of Republican Feeling. Tacitus [1] tells us that after Actium the war-weary Roman world accepted Augustus as ruler ' from love of peace and quiet ', and it may well be doubted whether there was ever a serious movement to restore the Republic. Conspiracies there certainly were, both against Augustus and against later Emperors, [2] but these seem to have been much more the attempts of ambitious nobles to take the Emperor's place for themselves than efforts to change the form of government. On two occasions only [3] was the restoration of the Republic proposed, once after the death of Gaius, and again at the time of the rebellion against Nero (pp. 83 and 131) ; the former movement was over in a few days ; the second which was much more formidable, as having armed force behind it, was probably only a cloak, in one province for a national revolt, in the other for personal ambition ; in both provinces it failed completely. The Republic in fact died at Philippi.

Survival of Republican Feeling in Society. But, though as a form of government the Republic was dead, it survived in several ways, interesting in themselves, and, indirectly at any rate, important. The uncertainty of the succession to the Principate at first prevented the growth of anything like a feeling of loyalty, for the members of the old Roman noble houses looked on themselves with reason as being as well-born and as entitled to rule as any member of the Julian or the Claudian house. Hence the tone of Roman Society was anti-Imperial, just as, under the second French Empire, the old Noblesse in the Faubourg St. Germain looked down on the Bonapartist government. Tacitus tells us of one noble lady, Junia, a sister of Brutus the ' Liberator ' and the wife of his colleague Cassius, who (A.D. 22) insulted the Emperor by omitting him altogether from her will, though she was very wealthy. This kind of hostility was not formidable ; but it manifested itself in the scandals spread

---

[1] *Ann.* i. 2.   [2] See pp. 14, 81, 95 e.g.   [3] But see also Dio lx. 15, 3.

in the 'banquets and clubs' of Rome about the Imperial house and its members. Seneca tells us that the Roman nobles preferred to 'risk their lives than lose their jests', inferior as these were ; as the best specimen of those retailed by Suetonius may be given the couplet on Nero's 'Golden House' :—

> Roma domus fiat ; Veios migrate, Quirites,
> Si non et Veios occupat ista domus.

The Principate was, as has been said, 'a despotism tempered by epigrams'.

The result of all this was unfortunate, for the hostility of the nobles deprived the Emperor of the strength which a loyal aristocracy can give to a monarch, and also made him more absolute, for, as Bacon says, 'a nobility attempers sovereignty'. This estrangement lasted till, after the time of Nero, the old Roman nobility had almost perished, partly through their own moral excesses, still more from the cruelty of Emperor after Emperor. A new period for the Roman aristocracy began with the Flavians. Vespasian, himself an Italian of middle-class birth, created a new nobility, which had learned the lesson of submission to authority and of moderation in life. But the evil influence of the old anti-Imperial nobility left a permanent mark on Roman history.

Aristocratic Bias in Roman Literature. Even in the times of the Republic, Roman men of letters had generally been on the side of the Senate against Caesar. Augustus, who knew the value of the written word, by his studied moderation and by his judicious patronage had won the men of letters to his side. But Tiberius was either too honest or too haughty for this, and the tendency of Roman literature again became anti-Imperial. A typical instance was the condemnation of Cremutius Cordus (p. 71), though the personal enmity of Sejanus was a partial cause of the severity against him. His books were burned by order of the Senate, and Tacitus [1] mocks the folly of those who think ' praesenti potentia extingui posse etiam sequentis aevi memoriam '. As he says, the views condemned by authority gained strength ; his own anti-Imperial bias is the reaction from the oppressive regulations

[1] *Ann.* iv. 35.

of the early Principate, and from the executions of men of letters by Domitian at the beginning of the historian's own career.

The anti-Imperialism of Tacitus. For there is no doubt that, in spite of his claims to impartiality,[1] Tacitus set himself to give the most unfavourable account possible of the Julio-Claudian Emperors ; by insinuating motives, by disparaging remarks on actions which he himself commends, by the careful repetition of charges which, according to his own account, were never substantiated, he blackens the character of Tiberius and his successors. The four Emperors who succeeded Augustus were probably no exceptions to the general low standard of morals in Rome ; but their vices are thrown into the strongest relief by the narrative of Tacitus. This partiality on the part of the historian is the more remarkable because he himself was a loyal servant of the Emperors, good and bad alike, and he more than once condemns those who, by useless protests against Imperial misdeeds, threw their lives away without benefiting anybody; so he indirectly censures Thrasea's silent protest against the murder of Agrippina.[2] This aristocratic bias affects almost all the records of the time : Suetonius, our other main Latin authority, was a scandalmonger, delighting in an evil story, and Cassius Dio, writing in Greek, at the beginning of the third century A.D., was dependent on the contemporary evidence. Much of this, e.g. the memoirs of the younger Agrippina,[3] would have been of the most lurid character, reflecting the hatreds and the ambitions of its composers and certainly most untrustworthy.

The Stoic Opposition under the Empire. But there was one section of the literary opposition to the Principate which must be treated with more respect, on the ground of the character of the members, if not of their impartiality. The antagonism between the Emperors from Nero to Domitian and the Stoic philosophers was recognized as a political factor by contemporaries and is reflected in the best literature

---

[1] *Ann.* i. 1. ' Sine ira et studio.'   [2] *Ann.* xiv. 12.

[3] Tacitus (*Ann.* iv. 53) mentions his use of these memoirs as material for the life of the Elder Agrippina ; it is to be noticed, however, that he carefully distinguishes these ' commentarii ' from the works of the regular historians.

of the time. Stoicism has been well called rather a religion than a system of philosophy, and it is as the former that it is especially important in Roman history. Little stress is laid by the great Roman Stoics on its physical and philosophic background, the idea of the Universe having for its first principle a creative fire, ultimately identical with the Deity who controls the whole course of mankind, and the idea of the divine Word, emanating from the Deity, and manifesting Him to men. The ideas on which the Romans laid stress were rather those of the Universal Reason, which is the voice of the Deity, and of the duty of Man, whose will is independent, to conform his life to this Universal Reason, and so to be prepared at any time to meet death, which comes in the course of nature, which delivers him from all pains, and which resolves him into the elements from which he came.

Looked at with suspicion as an importation from Greece under the Republic,[1] Stoicism had become the real religion of the better Romans under the Empire. So the Stoic Philosopher is a sort of father-confessor in times of trouble, as, e.g., Areus acts as 'consolator' to Livia on the death of Drusus ; and the great Roman lawyers found in the Universal Reason of the Stoics a justification of their conception of the Ius Naturale, and for their use of it in the expansion of Roman Law (p. 263).

But as the first century advanced, the Stoics began to come into collision with the Government. This was not necessary according to their principles, for the Stoic Philosopher, accepting the order of things as determined by the Divine Will, would naturally be prepared to live and work in any state, whatever its political form. But some of the Stoic ideals clashed with the practice, if not with the theory, of the Principate. Men with a high sense of duty could not be expected to approve acts that violated all accepted moral laws,[2] and the exaltation of the ideal 'Wise Man' of the

[1] Cato, the Censor, proposed the expulsion of the Stoic ambassador with his two philosopher colleagues (153 B.C.), and Cicero turned his wit in the *Pro Murena* on Cato of Utica for his unintelligent adoption of Stoic doctrines.

[2] Cf. the conduct of Thrasea in the Senate after the murder of Agrippina.

Stoics clashed with the vanity of the Emperors ; Cornutus,
who bluntly told Nero that the Emperor was proposing to
write far too many books, and that his proposed fertility
could not be justified by the example of the philosopher
Chrysippus, was fortunate to be only banished for his
frankness.[1]

The Stoics had now become almost a sect ; the genuine
philosophers had their imitators who wore the coarse cloak,[2]
and grew the long beard of their masters, but who were
really men of the world. The fact that the Stoics were
different from other men made them unpopular with the
Romans generally ; Cossutianus Capito,[3] in his attack on
Paetus Thrasea, invoked the old Roman dislike of the Stoics,
and openly said that their studied moderation was intended
to cast a reflexion on the wantonness of the Emperor.

And the opposition of the Stoics to the Principate was
intensified almost accidentally by the fact that the heroes of
the anti-Caesarian party, Cato of Utica and Brutus, were
both Stoics. Their birthdays, which were observed as feasts [4]
by their philosophic followers, were looked upon, not without
some reason, as occasions for Republican talk. There is,
however, no sufficient evidence that the Stoics as a whole
were actively disloyal ; this charge was never brought against
their most eminent leaders, Seneca and Paetus Thrasea ;
but it was part of the accusation against Rubellius Plautus [5]
(p. 107).

As was natural, a persecuted sect became more pronounced
in its opinions ; Plautus was advised by some of his friends
to resist the Emperor's order for his death, and there were
certainly Stoics among the Pisonian conspirators ; Arulenus
Rusticus, too, wished to defy the Emperor by vetoing as
tribune the proceedings against Thrasea. But it was only
under the Flavians that leading Stoics openly challenged the
Emperors ; Helvidius Priscus, the son-in-law of Thrasea,
was exiled and then executed by Vespasian for his Republican

[1] Cassius Dio, lxii. 29.
[2] Cf. Juvenal, iii. 115, for the ' maior abolla '.
[3] Tac. *Ann.* xvi. 22, ' rigidi et tristes quo tibi lasciviam exprobrent '.
[4] Juvenal, v. 36.   [5] Cf. *Ann.* xiv. 57.

rudeness, while under Domitian all the philosophers were banished from Italy (cf. pp. 170, 186).

But the new Roman nobility, under the Flavians, were content to practise Stoic virtues without emphasizing their philosophic theories or copying their political prejudices. Philosophy, it was said, came to the throne in the person of Marcus Aurelius ; but the majority of the Roman nobles did not identify themselves with the Stoic creed. Tacitus and Pliny,[1] who represent the best elements in Roman life and letters at the turn of the century, were ready to admire the bravery of the Stoics, but Tacitus [2] more than once condemns the excess to which they carried their protests against the Principate, and neither he nor Pliny were themselves Stoics.

Seneca and Lucan. The Stoic religion prepared men at least equally for death and for life, and suicide became almost frequent among the philosophers in the times of Nero. It was, at any rate, usual to anticipate the stroke of the executioner by a self-inflicted death. The two most famous examples of this are the philosopher Seneca and the poet Lucan ; their deaths have been already mentioned (p. 111), but a word must be said about their position in Roman literature.

Seneca was the fashionable preacher of his day. His letters and his treatises are full of good morals and common sense, expressed with an admirable neatness and conciseness. Probably no Latin writer can furnish so many excellent copy-book headings. Deep thought is not wanted in a sermon. Hence his wonderful popularity in his own day, though Tacitus [3] is contemptuous of his style. Lucan is probably now more admired than Seneca ; he died before he was twenty-six, and certainly deserves his place in Shelley's ' Adonaïs ', among ' the inheritors of unfulfilled renown '. His Republicanism was only the secondary cause of his taking part in the Pisonian conspiracy ; the young genius who

---

[1] Pliny especially admires the women of one family, the elder Arria, her daughter, Arria, the wife of Thrasea, and her daughter Fannia.

[2] Cf. *Agricola*, 42, ' plerique per abrupta, sed in nullum reipublicae usum, ambitiosa morte inclaruerunt '.

[3] He calls it ' amoenus et temporis eius auribus accommodatus '.

could not bear to be muzzled to gratify Nero's envy was more important than the sentimental admirer of Cato and Pompey : but Lucan certainly did his best to write down Caesar and to write up his opponents. The poet, however, was too much for the politician ; the comparison between Caesar and Pompey in the first book is an unsurpassable piece of rhetorical verse, and on the whole does justice to both rivals. Lucan, too, will always be remembered for his summings-up of events and careers in unforgettable phrases ; Quintilian well called him ' sententiis clarissimus '.[1] The Republican opposition to the Caesars has this to its credit, that it inspired Lucan and made him from a courtier into a poet.

NOTE ON SENECA

Apart from Seneca's political importance, it may be noticed :—

(1) That he holds enlightened views on slavery. A slave is a human being, and can do good and earn gratitude. He commends his correspondent Lucilius for making his slaves ' humble friends '.
(2) Hence he condemns gladiatorial shows.
(3) His attitude to God is at times almost Christian. ' Deo parere libertas est.' ' Ex animo illum (i.e. Deum), non quia necesse est, sequor.' [2]

But the story that Seneca learned from St. Paul is pure legend.

Seneca has been called a ' provincial Cicero ', and there is a curious resemblance in some points between the two. Both were literary men, who, by their command of language, gained a degree of political power which in Rome generally was only gained by men of action. Both forced their way into exclusive circles to which they did not belong by birth, and both identified themselves with the prejudices of the new class which they had entered. Both were kindly men in personal character, and showed in death a courage which they had not always showed in life.

---

[1] ' Sententia ' no doubt means in the first place a maxim ' quae satis apte et alio transfertur ', i.e., which can be used in other contexts, but Quintilian must also have had in mind lines such as ' Victrix causa deis placuit sed victa Catoni ' (i. 128) and ' momentumque fuit mutatus Curio rerum ' and ' Emere omnes, hic vendidit urbem ' (iv. 819, 824).

[2] *Dialogues*, vii. 15 ; *Epistles*, 96, 2.

CHAPTER VIII

THE EASTERN FRONTIER FROM THE DEATH OF AUGUSTUS

*T*HE *Augustan Policy in the East.* Augustus had beyond all other Romans the gift which Cavour said was the greatest quality in a statesman, ' Le tact des choses possibles '. His work on the Euphrates frontier lasted, for it was built on the old lines of Rome's Eastern policy as it had been developed by Pompey the Great ; the Syrian Desert and the Euphrates were the main boundaries of the Empire, and between the Roman provinces and the Parthian Empire lay a number of dependent kingdoms, governed by Roman nominees, who were generally Greeks, more or less orientalized.

This principle, the building on Greek foundations, was fundamental to the Roman Empire in the East. The Romans never obtained a real hold on any part of Asia except where the Greeks had been before them ; it should be added that nowhere has their work, however real it seemed for a time, been permanent outside Europe ; the ruins of the great buildings of Rome still remain in Asia Minor, in Africa, in Syria, even in Mesopotamia, but the civilization which saw them built has passed away.

The Parthian Empire. The Oriental reaction against Europe, which in the end undid the work in Asia of Greece and Rome, had begun with Mithradates of Pontus, but it only became really formidable in the Parthian Empire. The Parthians, whose native home was in Khorasan, on the south-east of the Caspian Sea, had made themselves free from the Seleucid Kings in the middle of the third [1] century B.C., and had about a century later expelled the Greek rulers from Mesopotamia. The successive kings, who all bore the name of ' Arsaces ', called themselves formally ' Philhellen ', and there were many Greek cities in their dominions ; but the

[1] Arsaces, the liberator, rebelled in 248 B.C., though the Parthian era of independence was dated ten years later. Mithradates I, who finally broke the power of the Seleucids and annexed Media and Mesopotamia, ruled Parthia from 170 to 138 B.C.

Parthians themselves, the ruling class, remained barbarian ; they were a feudal aristocracy, serving their king as cavalry and holding their lands by a kind of military tenure. Rome and Parthia represented two entirely different stages of civilization.

The Syrian desert even more than the Euphrates marked the frontier, and though Rome in the second century established a more or less permanent hold on certain provinces beyond it, yet, broadly speaking, the division between the two Empires remained almost as Augustus had left it. Each was strong for defence, Rome because her fortified towns could defy attacks of Parthian cavalry, unsupported almost by engines, Parthia because in the sultry plains of Mesopotamia a Roman legionary could not force a battle with the Parthian light horsemen, and was always in danger of being cut off by them in an unfavourable position.

Each power was conscious of its own weakness, and hence during the first century A.D. armed collisions were largely avoided ; it was the ambitious policy of Trajan in A.D. 113 that led to the campaigns of the second century. Hence the relations between the two powers were mainly diplomatic —at least till A.D. 100. But before an attempt is made to summarize these, it seems necessary to sketch briefly the line of dependent states which Rome set up between herself and Parthia.

Dependent States on the Eastern Frontier. First must be mentioned the great province of Galatia, which Pompey had given to his partisan Deiotarus, who forfeited it to Caesar. This was then given, first by Antony in 36 B.C. and then by Augustus in 31, to Amyntas, on whose death six years later it became a full Roman province. But it was rather an integral part of Asia Minor than a frontier province, and moreover it had a very strongly Romanized element in it ; it was the most important recruiting ground of the legions of the East. Of the dependent states proper, the most northerly was Pontus Polemoniacus, on the south of the Black Sea. To the south-east of this lay the much more important district of Lesser Armenia, stretching along the right (i.e. the west) bank of the Euphrates as far as the great crossing at Melitene.

Next to it, but only just touching the Euphrates, came Cappadocia, while on the other side of the Euphrates on the south-west frontier of Armenia proper, was the district of Sophene. Finally the rest of the frontier, as far as the northern border of the province of Syria, was occupied by the Kingdom of Commagene, important as commanding the other great Euphrates crossing at Samosata.

All these districts had become Roman by the time of Vespasian, who united Lesser Armenia and Sophene with Cappadocia, and Commagene with Syria. Cappadocia, as part of Asia Minor, had been made a regular province by Tiberius in A.D. 17, but the rulers of the other states were continually changed, according to the needs or the caprices of the Roman government. Their origin was various, but they were all Hellenized at least in part ; Polemo in Pontus had married a granddaughter of Antony, from whom also descended Cotys, who was made ruler of Lesser Armenia : a scion of the Herod family also is one of these royal tools of Roman rule. Judaea, it may be added, was only one of another set of similar princedoms, dependent on the province of Syria. The forces of these princelings were always at the disposal of the Roman Government.

It may be noted as an instance of Roman wisdom that the little dependent Kingdom of Bosporus in the Crimea was not incorporated in the Roman Empire, though Tacitus tells us that in A.D. 49 the Roman arms actually penetrated to within three days' march of the river Tanais (i.e. the Don). The native princes there, with some help in troops and subsidies from Rome, continued to rule till the fourth century, protecting the important trade route over the steppes to Asia.

Armenia. One of the dependent kingdoms, however, which lay between Rome and Parthia, had an entirely different history. Armenia remained a bone of contention between the two great Empires till they were both overwhelmed by the power of Islam in the seventh century. This long struggle was due to the position of Armenia ; lying as it did to the east of Asia Minor and to the north of Mesopotamia, it commanded both the great ford of the Euphrates at Melitene, from which the Roman provinces could be threatened, and the passes of Mt. Masius, through which an invader could pour down into the plains of Mesopotamia. Two policies towards Armenia were possible for Rome, for she could not leave it subject to Parthia, as this was inconsistent at once with safety and with Roman honour. Hence she had either to annex it or to control the kings who were set over it.

Difficulties in Annexing Armenia. The policy of annexation was given up by Augustus with his usual wisdom; Armenia was not hard to conquer, but it was very difficult to hold. The country was mountainous, and its people were averse to Roman ideas, having intermarried, as Tacitus says,[1] with the Parthians and being ' more inclined to slavery, since they knew nothing of liberty '. Hence, to make Armenia a province would have required a considerable Roman force, and would have been very expensive. And there was the further difficulty that the conquest of Armenia could not stand alone; to hold it safely it would have been necessary to annex also the whole valley of the Euphrates, and make the Roman boundary the Tigris. Unless this were done, a great wedge of hostile territory would have been left between the provinces of Syria and Armenia, and defence of them against a vigorous invader would have been very difficult. Hence Trajan, the one Emperor who really aimed at extension in the East, formed new provinces not only of Armenia, but of Assyria, Babylonia and Arabia (cf. pp. 216, 226). Such an extension was never possible as a permanence.

Policy of a Dependent Armenia. The Roman policy, therefore, as settled by Augustus and maintained with little alteration till the time of Trajan, was to control Armenia by controlling its king. But this policy of rule by a Roman nominee, which was easy on the west bank of the Euphrates, could never long be maintained on the East bank, for Roman nominees always became unpopular with true Orientals. How weak they were and how uncertain their rule can be judged from the fact that in the eighty-five years from the battle of Actium to the accession of Nero (A.D. 54), Rome had to interfere decisively no less than five times to secure control in Armenia. Tiberius in B.C. 20, Gaius Caesar from

[1] *Ann.* xiii. 34.

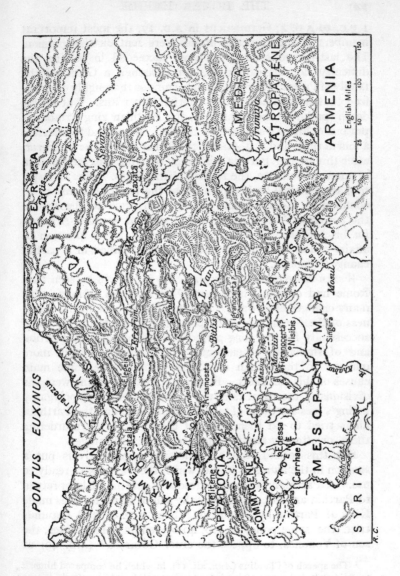

ARMENIA

English Miles

0 25 50   100   150

PONTUS EUXINUS

I B E R I A

MEDIA ATROPATENE

A S S Y R I A

MESOPOTAMIA

SYRIA

CAPPADOCIA

PONTUS

COMMAGENE

OSROENE

L. Sevan

L. Van

L. Urumija

Trapezus

Satala

Melitene

Zeugma

Edessa

Carrhae

Samosata

Rhandeia

Elegeia

Tigranocerta?

Bitlis

Artaxata

Artaxia

Nisibis

Singara

Nineveh

Mosul

Arbela

R.C.

1 B.C. to A.D. 4, Germanicus in A.D. 17, the most important
members of the Imperial house, were sent on this mission.
The last-named seemed to have succeeded in solving the
difficulty, for his candidate, Zeno, though a Greek of the
family of Polemo of Pontus, had become so thoroughly orientalized that he was acceptable to the Armenians.   But on his
death (probably about A.D. 34), the Parthian king Artabanus
put one of his own sons on the throne.   Rome had to interfere
a fourth time, and L. Vitellius, the father of the later Emperor,
after threatening Parthia with war, set up a king in Armenia
of a new nationality, the Iberian Mithradates.   This attempt,
too, after a time broke down, from the family dissensions so
common in the East, and when Nero came to the throne
the powerful Parthian king Vologeses had secured Armenia
for his brother, Tiridates, about A.D. 53.   This position of
affairs called for a fifth interference, and ended in a partial
change of policy.

Weakness of Parthian Empire.   So far it will be seen that
Rome had on the whole controlled Armenia, though with
many changes of fortune.   This was largely due to the weakness of the Parthians, which prevented them from ever using
successfully for any long period the advantages of position
and of similarity of customs, which made Armenia more
inclined to them than to Rome.   There were three main
causes of this weakness.   First and most important were the
divisions of the royal family.   Under a system of polygamy
a king's foes are those of his own household, and the Parthian
kings tried to rid themselves of these, either by murdering
them, or often by sending them to Rome as hostages.

But this second way of removing possible rivals put a
weapon in the hands of Rome, which she was always ready to
use.   A Parthian prince educated at Rome might later return
to Parthia as king.   Vonones, the son of Phraates, was made
King of Parthia by Augustus (about A.D. 8) and Claudius
tried the same policy in A.D. 49 by sending Meherdates, the
son of Vonones, to oppose the cruel Gotarzes [1] (A.D. 49) at

---

[1] The speech of Claudius (*Ann.* xii. 11), in which he compared himself
to Augustus and urged Meherdates ' not to think of himself as a tyrant
but as a ruler ', and of his subjects as ' fellow-citizens ', and so to

the request of the Parthian nobles. It must be added, however, that these pretenders never had long success; their connection with Rome was a weakness unforgivable by their countrymen.

The turbulence of these nobles was the second cause of Parthian weakness; they were always ready, like the feudal barons of Anglo-Norman England, to rebel and to set up another member of the royal house against the king. But whereas the English kings had in the growing strength of their towns a resource against the feudal lords, the Arsacidae found their towns, which were Greek, only another disruptive element; e.g. Seleucia, the successor to the position and prosperity of the ancient Babylon, held out for six years against three Parthian kings (A.D. 36–43).

And finally the Parthian rule was weak because the dependent provinces were always ready to rebel. Media and Hyrcania were held by a very uncertain tenure, and Rome's success for a time under Nero was rendered easier by an Hyrcanian revolt; Tacitus even tells us that envoys from this tribe on the shores of the Caspian came to Rome at this time to seek alliance and help. And the nations outside the Parthian empire, the Iberians in the Caucasus and the Scyths in Central Asia, were always a danger; Rome from time to time sought Iberian aid against Parthia.

The Struggle with Vologeses. Vologeses who came to the throne in A.D. 51, had made an arrangement with his brothers that, if they yielded the Parthian throne to him, he would provide them with princedoms; Pacorus was made satrap of Media, and Tiridates was provided for by seizing Armenia, which was in confusion and without a ruler once more at the end of the reign of Claudius. The struggle that followed is interesting and must be described in some detail,[1] partly

introduce into Parthia the maxims of good government he had learned at Rome, must be genuine in its delightful mixture of pedantry and self-deception.

[1] Tacitus, *Annals*, xiii.–xv., especially xiii. 35–41, xiv. 23–26 and xv. 1–31. The narrative of Tacitus is full of difficulties, both chronological and geographical; I have accepted in the main the views of Dr. B. W. Henderson (*Life and Principate of the Emperor Nero*, pp. 153–195). I cannot imagine a better introduction to the study of

because Tacitus describes it fully, but still more because it contains at least one striking character and several dramatic incidents, and because it led to a (comparatively) permanent settlement.

Nero's ministers, Seneca and Burrus, at once proceeded to act with decision on hearing of the Parthian aggression ; they sent Corbulo, the best general of the time, to the East, giving him a command in Cappadocia, and transferring to him two of the four Syrian legions. Corbulo found these absolutely disorganized, both physically and morally useless from long service on garrison duty in the Syrian towns.[1] It was nearly three years before he was able to assume the aggressive, and fortunately the Parthian king at this time was detained by the revolt of his son Vardanes. Corbulo, however, was finally able to advance in A.D. 57, in order to give his army the experience of an Armenian winter on the plateau of Erzerum, 6,000 feet above the sea.

Corbulo's Victories, *A.D.* 58–60. When his troops were ready, Corbulo assumed the offensive. In the first campaign (58) he pressed Tiridates hard, and then offered him the compromise that he should have the throne of Armenia, but have it as a gift from the Roman Emperor. As the Parthians refused this, Corbulo prepared for decisive action, and in the early summer of 59[2] he boldly advanced into Armenia, and captured its capital, Artaxata, in the north-

an ancient historian than to read his brilliant narrative side by side with the chapters, brilliant in another way, of Tacitus. But I have ventured to differ from him on the site of Tigranocerta, which I place with Kiepert at Sert, south-west of Lake Van, and north of Mt. Masius, not at Tel Ermen on the south of that range.

[1] It is worth noticing that the Roman distribution of troops was absolutely different in the East and in the West. On the Rhine and the Danube they were concentrated in great camps, for the barbarians opposite them were dangerous enemies ; in Syria there was little or no danger of invasion, but the populations of the towns were disorderly, and outbreaks of religious fanaticism might at any time call for repression by the strong hand of Rome (cf. Acts xx. St. Paul's rescue at Jerusalem). But this scattering of troops, though necessary, was very bad for discipline.

[2] Furneaux puts the capture of Artaxata in 58, and that of Tigranocerta in 59 ; this involves Corbulo's army wintering at Artaxata, which seems unlikely.

east corner of the country, and burned it ; then with a more daring stroke he cut himself off from his base, Trapezus, and marched southwards across Armenia to Tigranocerta, the other capital. It was a march as daring as that of Roberts from Kabul to the relief of Kandahar (in 1880), and it was crowned with success. The city surrendered, Tiridates was driven out of Armenia, and Corbulo was able to set up (A.D. 60) a Roman partisan as King of Armenia, Tigranes, the great-grandson of the last king of Cappadocia, Archelaus, and also of Herod the Great. He received a Roman garrison for his support.

Rome's Change of Policy. Annexation Proposed. So far all had gone well for Rome, but now fortune changed. This was partly due to the folly of Tigranes, who actually invaded Media, and provoked to action the Parthian king, who had seemed willing to keep quiet ; it was due still more to the change in the Roman command which gave Corbulo an incompetent successor. Vologeses drove Tigranes out of Armenia in 61, and we hear no more of him. Meantime Nero in Rome had decided on a bolder policy, and Caesennius Paetus was sent out as Governor to Cappadocia (Corbulo still commanded in Syria) with orders to conquer Armenia and make it a Roman province. He arrived in 62 and invaded Armenia with little success, and then fell back at the end of the year to Rhandeia on the river Arsamas (probably the Murad) near the frontier of Cappadocia. Here he thought he was safe, and allowed his force to be dangerously weakened by dispersing. When he was attacked and surrounded by Vologeses, he sent too late to ask the help of Corbulo in Syria, and, losing his head completely, though he had a camp abundantly provisioned, he surrendered to the Parthian, promising to evacuate Armenia. On this basis Vologeses was to send ambassadors to Rome to treat with Nero. Tacitus even compares the insults suffered by the beaten Romans to the disgrace of ' passing under the yoke '. Rhandeia was not as fatal as Carrhae, but it was even more disgraceful, for the Roman defeat was caused by cowardice as well as by incompetence ; Tacitus hints, too, that Corbulo deliberately delayed assisting Paetus till it was too late, from motives of jealousy. However this may be, the disaster also illustrated the weakness

9

of the new Roman frontier : Vologeses, 'moving on the inner lines ', was able to concentrate his forces against Paetus in Armenia much more quickly than Corbulo could reach him from Syria, marching as he did of necessity round two sides of the ' salient angle ' of Parthian territory.

The Roman Government set to work at once to wipe out the disgrace. Corbulo was given a *maius imperium* on the Eastern frontier ; a legion (the XVth) was summoned from Pannonia to strengthen his forces, and the ravaging of Armenia convinced the Parthian king and his brother that Rome was still formidable. They therefore now consented to the compromise rejected five years before (p. 128) : Tiridates came into the Roman camp, and laid down his crown before the statue of the Emperor, promising to go to Rome [1] to receive investiture of Armenia from Nero.

Peace between Rome and Parthia. This promise he carried out, though not at once. Starting in A.D. 65 and travelling as far as possible by land, he reached Italy after nine months. He was received with the greatest courtesy by Nero, and on the ' Golden Day ' in the Forum, Nero invested him with the crown of Armenia amid scenes of the greatest splendour. The peace thus made lasted, and for the next half-century there was no fighting between Rome and Parthia. The great expedition which Nero planned in A.D. 67 was to be not against Rome's old rival, but against the enemies of Parthia, the tribes of the Caucasus. This expedition of course was never made, but Vologeses did not forget his imperial ally, and the pretender who, after the Emperor's death, assumed in the East the name of Nero, found for a time shelter and support in the Parthian kingdom. It surely was not accidental that Nero, at once in his crimes and in his love of display the most Oriental of the Roman Emperors of the first two centuries, was the most successful in making a settlement with Rome's Oriental rival. It was indeed fortunate for Rome that Parthia was friendly during the troubled Year of the Four Emperors.

---

[1] This he had previously refused to do, because, as a Magian by religion, it was forbidden to him to pollute the sacred element, water, by crossing it.

CHAPTER IX

THE YEAR OF THE FOUR EMPERORS, A.D. 68–69, AND THE JEWISH REBELLION, A.D. 66–70

IMPORTANCE of the Death of Nero. The death of Nero marked the end of a period and the beginning of a new system in the Roman Empire. Hitherto all the Emperors had belonged to one family, though the succession had been most irregular ; but there was always a chance that, out of the devotion to the ' blood of Augustus ', which was a real feeling at any rate in the army, something might develop resembling the ' loyalty ' which has played so great a part in modern history. Henceforth, however, such a development was impossible ; it was clear that the Principate was a prize open to all, and Tacitus' famous epigram sums up one aspect of this : ' The secret was out that an Emperor could be made elsewhere than in Rome.' [1]

The Revolt of Vindex. The movement which led to the overthrow of Nero began in Gaul, where Vindex, the Governor of Aquitania, rose (in March A.D. 68) as the champion of the ' Senate and Liberty ', denouncing the crimes and follies of Nero. Whether this republican feeling was genuine,[2] or whether it was merely a cloak for a Gallic national movement, is much disputed ; probably both motives were present. At any rate Vindex put himself in communication with Sulpicius Galba, the Governor of Hispania Tarraconensis, who early in April was saluted by his soldiers as Emperor ; but he only declared himself the ' legate of the Senate and people of Rome ' ; Clodius Macer, the proconsul of Africa, rose at the same time, nominally, as his coins show, for the Republic,

[1] *Hist.* i. 4. ' Evolgato imperii arcano posse principem alibi quam Romae fieri.'

[2] This is Mommsen's view ; Vindex certainly is called by Pliny ' adsertor libertatis ', and his coins somewhat confirm this estimate of him. On the other hand, Tacitus repeatedly speaks of him as cloaking Gallic nationalism under a pretence of joining a Roman cause (cf. the conduct of Civilis, p. 157) ; his Gallic forces (i.e. provincial levies) are said to have been over 100,000 strong, and the fury with which they were attacked by the Roman legions seems to have been inspired by Roman hatred against rebellious provincials.

but no doubt really in his own interests. Feeling in Gaul
was very much divided ; Lugdunum, the old Roman colony,
remained loyal to Nero, but its rival, the newer colony of
Vienna, was for Vindex ; in the same way, while most of the
Gallic tribes joined him, the Treveri in the North held aloof.
No doubt their abstention was largely due to the attitude of
the German legions ; Verginius Rufus, commander on the
Upper Rhine, marched against Vindex ; he himself seems to
have had republican sympathies [1] and began to negotiate, but
his soldiers took the matter into their own hands, and attacked
and scattered the Gallic army with great slaughter ; Vindex
killed himself. Verginius was then offered the Empire by
his troops, but he declined, and finally declared for Galba,
who, on hearing of the death of Nero, ceased to hesitate, and
taking the name of ' Caesar ', set out with his troops for Rome
(early in July).

Galba as Emperor. It was not altogether meaningless that
Galba had at first declared himself ' the general of the Senate ' ;
he represented, as none of his successors did, the old nobility
of Rome, their virtues and their defects. He was descended
directly from one of the conspirators against Caesar, and
had some of the noblest blood of Rome in his veins ; he had
served with distinction throughout a long career, ending with
eight years of government in Spain, where he justified his
inactivity on the very sufficient ground that, under Nero, a
prominent noble was safer when he did nothing ; even so
there is a well-authenticated story that he was finally driven
to conspire by knowing that Nero had sent private instructions
for his murder. Though his moral character was stained by
some of the vices so common among the Roman nobles,
he had the old Roman virtues of honesty and justice, and
Tacitus has immortalized his memory by his untranslatable
summary : ' omnium consensu capax imperii nisi imperasset '.

From the very first, however, he began to make enemies ;
his favours to those in Gaul who had supported Vindex
alienated those more loyal to Rome, e.g. the colony of Lug-

---

[1] Cf. his own epitaph (Pliny, *Ep.* ix. 9) :
' Hic situs est Rufus, pulso qui Vindice quondam
Imperium adseruit non sibi sed patriae.'

dunum, and the German armies only sullenly acquiesced in the adhesion of their commander to Galba. He entered Rome in October, and, alike by his merits and by his faults, he began to weaken what little popularity he had. The State was bankrupt, and Galba set up a commission, of which the famous Agricola, the father-in-law of Tacitus, was a member, to recover the temple treasures embezzled under Nero. Such recovery was very unpopular, while it produced very little money, and men noted that Galba's own favourites, his lieutenant Titus Vinius, with whom he shared the consulship, the Praetorian Prefect Laco, and the Emperor's freedman Icelus, were as rapacious as Nero's creatures had been. And, however desirable good finance was, Galba lost popularity by refusing to pay the Praetorians the donative which Nymphidius Sabinus had promised in his name ; he said that he ' chose his soldiers and did not buy them ', a sentiment more honourable to his principles than to his tact. He gave offence alike by his mercy and by his severity.

Nymphidius met a well-deserved death, as did some other of Nero's favourites, but Tigellinus, the worst of them all, was spared for a time from the popular fury, though he was compelled to commit suicide later after the fall of Galba. The Emperor showed, too, the cruelty which was so often a marked feature in Roman character ; his entry into Rome was stained by serious bloodshed, for he ordered his cavalry to charge the men of Nero's new legion, enrolled from the fleet, when they pressed their demands on him with unseemly persistency.

The Adoption of Piso. Against this increasing unpopularity the support of the Senate was of little use, and when with the new year (A.D. 69) the news came that the German legions had hailed Aulus Vitellius, legate of Lower Germany, as Emperor, Galba resolved to strengthen himself by adopting a colleague. This step was often repeated in the coming century and with conspicuous success. But again Galba acted with more principle than prudence ; his choice fell on Calpurnius Piso, the brother of one of Nero's victims (p. 110), a man of the highest character ; but he had had no experience of political life, and the Emperor destroyed what chances of success his plan might have by again refusing a donative to the Praetorians. And there was a leader at hand, able and eager to take advantage of Galba's unpopularity and mistakes. Marcus Salvius Otho, the husband of Poppaea, who had been banished by Nero to Spain when he robbed him of his wife, is in character the strangest mixture of all the Roman Emperors ; stained as he was by every vice, he seems to have genuinely loved Poppaea, and he is said to have conspired against Nero to avenge the wrong done to him in her abduction ; prominent as he had been in every form of extravagance and luxury in the Roman Court, he had afterwards governed Lusitania for ten years with conspicuous honesty, and in the last year of his life he was to show himself a brave and capable soldier.

As he had not unnaturally hoped that his services to Galba, in aiding him to secure the throne would be rewarded by his being made the heir, he was rendered desperate by the choice of Piso, and he used his own popularity with the Praetorians to overthrow Galba. But now it was the common soldiers who made the plot, not, as in former reigns, the Prefects of the Guard ; as Tacitus says, ' two common soldiers (*manipulares*) undertook to transfer the Empire, and they did transfer it '.[1] On 15 January Otho left the old Emperor ' importuning the gods of an empire that he had already lost ' at a solemn sacrifice, and hurried to the Praetorian Camp. Galba had no forces with which to resist, and he and Piso were murdered, along with the three unpopular favourites, Vinius, Laco and Icelus.

Otho as Emperor. Otho was in Rome for two months only as Emperor. He was personally popular there, and, whatever may have been his own private feelings towards Nero, he was welcomed by the Praetorians and the mob of Rome as one of Nero's companions ; moreover, he allowed himself to be hailed as ' Nero ' in the theatre, and the statues of Nero to be restored. But he governed justly and treated the Senate with respect ; with the inconsistency which marks his career throughout, his conduct on the throne was as honourable as his method of getting it had been evil.

[1] Tac. *Hist.* i. 25.

He was, however, not left long to enjoy it or show what his real character might have been. It was true that the legions of the provinces east of Italy were prepared to support him, but the armies of Germany were against him ; they had most of the West with them and were much nearer to Italy, and so were able to strike at once. They had already declared for Vitellius when Galba was killed, and Vitellius for the moment had such superiority of numbers (he may well have had 100,000 men of all arms), that it seemed safe for him to divide his forces. Caecina and Valens, the two men to whom especially he owed [1] the Empire, were ordered to start at once (about the end of January), and to enter Italy from the north and from the north-west respectively ; Vitellius was to follow with the rest of his army. Caecina with part of the legions of the Upper German army advanced straight from Vindonissa, through what is now West Switzerland, and in March reached Italy over the Great St. Bernard Pass ; Valens, with a part of the Lower German army, had further to go, and took the route through Gaul and over the Mt. Genèvre. He did not reach Italy till a month after Caecina.

The Campaign of Bedriacum.[2] Caecina's rapid advance made Otho move from Rome at once, and, like Flaminius in the Second Punic War, he neglected the omens which recommended delay. But he was quite right to hasten ; even as it was, Caecina had already mastered the north bank of the Po, and seized the important town of Cremona. Otho therefore had to make the Po his line of defence, while he sent his fleet to threaten the coast of Gallia Narbonensis, and so compel Valens to divert part of his forces against this

[1] They each commanded a legion in the Upper and in the Lower German army respectively. Their previous record was bad ; Caecina had been punished by Galba for embezzling money, and Valens had been the leader in the assassination of the imperial legate, Fonteius Capito, in October, A.D. 68.

[2] The account of this campaign is given by Tacitus in the first half of *Histories*, Bk. II. I have followed as a rule the explanations of B. W. Henderson (in his *Civil War and Rebellion in the Roman Empire*) as before for the campaign of Corbulo (cf. p. 127). His chapters, read side by side with the account of Tacitus, furnish an admirable training in the sifting of evidence and a most interesting introduction to the principles of strategy and tactics.

attack. This strategy had some measure of success, for it cost Valens both a little delay and the detachment of some troops ; but Otho's brilliant use of the ' command of the sea ' was less successful than it deserved, owing to the incapacity of his generals and the unruliness of his troops,[1] who plundered friend and foe alike.

Otho with his main force crossed the Po east of Cremona, and took up his position at Bedriacum, a village near the Oglio, where two great roads met, one through Mantua to Aquileia, which some of the Pannonian army had already reached, and one through Hostilia on the Po to Ariminum and the great North Road of Rome. Caecina resolved to attempt a surprise, and placed an ambush at Locus Castorum, ten miles west from Otho's camp ; but the ambush was betrayed to Otho, and his generals, so far from being caught unprepared, themselves almost surrounded the attacking Vitellians, who escaped with severe loss. It was only the slowness of Suetonius Paulinus that saved them from destruction ; in this campaign he showed none of the desperate skill which had restored Rome's dominions in Britain eight years before (p. 280).

Otho had won the first success, but meantime Valens had arrived (early in April), and the Vitellians were once more much superior in force. Otho would probably have been well advised to wait ; the East, with unimpaired strength, was moving to support him, though ' too slowly owing to over-confidence ', and he had in his favour the command of the sea and the possession and name of the capital ; time thus was on his side. But his troops were impatient to attack, and he himself, though personally brave, hated fighting, and seems to have longed to ' get it over '.

Defeat and Death of Otho. He therefore planned to attack the enemy at once ; perhaps he ordered a direct march on Cremona, but more probably he intended by a flank march to

---

[1] This feature marks all the military operations of this year ; before he left Rome, Otho had with difficulty prevented his troops from massacring the Senate, owing to a false alarm of treachery, and in the fighting later the troops on both sides, from a not ill-founded distrust of their officers, were always more disposed to criticize than to obey.

seize a strong position [1] on the west of Cremona, and so to cut off the Vitellians at that town from their base in Gaul and from the advancing army of Vitellius. This was a brilliant plan, which Dr. Henderson well compares with the flank march of the Germans in 1870, by which they surrounded the French main army in Metz and finally compelled its surrender.

Unfortunately for Otho, he allowed himself to be persuaded to retire to the south bank of the Po at Brixellum, where as commander-in-chief he could communicate with all his scattered forces, and he left the main operation to Suetonius and two other generals. This was fatal ; everything depended on prompt action, and a committee is never prompt ; Otho's generals quarrelled, delayed, and finally, marching straight for Cremona, blundered on the Vitellians who were ready and waiting for them. It was a soldiers' battle, and, though the Othonians fought bravely, they were driven back to their camp with great loss, and surrendered next day (16 April).

Death of Otho. Otho, however, was far from beaten. His men had shown that they could hold their own against the famous German legionaries ; many of them had not come into action at all and were full of confidence. His supporters, also outside Italy, were only beginning to arrive. He could have prolonged the war indefinitely and with good prospect of ultimate success. The Praetorian Prefect Firmus begged him not to ' desert his loyal army ', and the soldiers echoed the prayer. But Otho refused to enter on a struggle that would certainly be long and bloody ; his life, he said, was not so valuable that he should expose to danger men so brave and devoted. He urged his friends to make their peace with Vitellius, and destroyed all papers that could compromise them. Then, after calming a riot in camp, directed against those whom the soldiers suspected of treachery, among them especially Verginius, he slept quietly till dawn,

---

[1] Th reading in Tac. *Hist.* ii. 40, is uncertain, If the troops of Otho were making for the confluence of the Po and the Adda, that point may be taken to be seven miles west of Cremona, cf. Henderson, *ib.* pp. 340 f.

and then killed himself (17 April). His death, like his life, was typical of the Roman nobles of his time. Holding, as they did, most of life a thing to be lived without principle, they were prepared to throw it away as of no particular importance; suicide was a natural refuge for misfortune. But there must have been some special charm in Otho to excite the devotion he did; some of his men killed themselves close by his funeral pyre, and their example was followed in other places.[1] Otho was in his thirty-seventh year.

Vitellius as Emperor. Vitellius had already been Emperor to his own partisans for nearly four months; he held his position almost to the end of the year, though of course not undisputed. He is not the worst of the twelve Caesars, but he certainly was the meanest. He had in his favour high birth and a creditable record as proconsul of Africa under Claudius; but at Rome he had been the most shameless of flatterers.[2] He was, if we may use the phrase, hoisted on to the throne by Caecina and Valens, and he used his position only to gratify the lowest of passions, gluttony; the one contribution of his own to Roman life was the invention of a dish (' the Shield of Minerva ' he called it) so enormous that no potter could mould it, and it had to be cast in silver. He is said to have spent while Emperor 900,000,000 sesterces on his bestial appetite.

Hence his reign is quite unimportant except as marking another stage in the militarization of the Empire; he allowed his men, as they marched through Italy, to plunder as they pleased, and he was with difficulty prevented from shocking Rome's most cherished traditions by entering it wearing his general's war cloak. He also raised the number of the Praetorian cohorts to sixteen, and filled the places of Otho's men, who were honourably dismissed, by his own veterans of the German armies. The respect he showed to the Senate by attending it, and by refusing the names of ' Caesar ' and ' Augustus ', went for nothing in view of his conduct and of

[1] Bacon in his Essay on ' Death ' (*Ess.* II) quotes this as one of his illustrations to show that ' fear of death ' is mastered by other passions, however weak.

[2] He paid court to Messalina by stealing and kissing her shoe, and to Nero by insisting that he should show in public his prowess as a singer.

the shameless way in which his subordinates Caecina and Valens abused their power.

It should be added that at first he showed himself merciful to Otho's partisans, e.g. to his brother Titianus ; before the end of his brief reign, however, he was following the example of his predecessors in executing wealthy nobles on suspicion.

Vespasian Claims the Throne. But already, even before he had reached Rome, a rival had arisen to dispute his position. Vespasian was vindicating the majesty of the Empire by his victorious campaign against the rebel Jews (p. 142). On hearing of the death of Otho, he had administered to his soldiers the oath of allegiance to Vitellius, but it was received in sullen silence, and the leading men in the East suggested to him that he should claim the Empire for himself ; Licinius Mucianus, the Governor of Syria, and Tiberius Alexander, the Jewish Prefect of Egypt, were foremost in this. At first Vespasian hesitated ; in past Roman history the champions of the East, except Sulla, had not been successful, and the legions of Germany had a formidable reputation ; but at length he yielded to the enthusiasm of his troops, and made a new departure in Imperial history by dating his regnal years from the day (1 July) when the legions of Egypt swore allegiance to him. There was no longer a pretence of waiting for the Senate's action.

Vespasian had on his side a great superiority in numbers and in wealth ; Vitellius, however, would have been hard to displace had he exerted himself at all. But, as Tacitus [1] says of him later, he was ' like a sluggish animal, which, if fed, lies torpid ' ; ' past, present and future alike he dismissed from his mind '. He left all to his subordinates, and of these Valens more than equalled his master in vice, while Caecina was preparing to play the traitor. His legionaries were ruining alike their bodies and their discipline by indulgence in the pleasures of the capital, though it must be added that, when the final struggle came, they fought as bravely as ever.

The Struggle with Vespasian. Vespasian, while assuming the aggressive, provided for Roman interests in the East. He left Titus to besiege Jerusalem and himself secured

[1] *Hist.* iii. 36.

Egypt, all-important for the corn-supply of Rome, while Mucianus advanced westward, gathering the legions of the provinces to advance with him. The plan seems to have been to reduce Italy slowly by cutting off the corn-supply, and to wait till all the forces of the East were gathered for a united attack by way of Aquileia. But the issue was forced more quickly than the leaders had at first planned. A council of war was held at Poetovio, and, though the governors of the three Danubian provinces were either absent or un-willing to move, some of their subordinates took the matter into their own hands, and, relying on the eagerness of the Danubian armies and their jealousy of the Vitellian legions from the Rhine, pressed on to attack at once. The three leaders were Cornelius Fuscus, Procurator of Pannonia, Arrius Varus, a senior centurion, who had served under Corbulo, and, above all, Antonius Primus, commander of Galba's new legion, the Seventh.

Primus and Varus advanced at once on Aquileia some 150 miles away, and seizing it pushed on and secured the market town of Forum Alieni (probably Legnano) on the Adige. This strategy was risky in the extreme ; the enemy were much superior in numbers, and could easily have crushed Antonius' force as it straggled down through the Julian Alps. But Caecina, who had advanced to meet him, simply occupied the line of the Adige, and even there allowed the bridge-end to be seized. He was already in communication with the Flavian leaders, and with the commander of the fleet at Ravenna, Lucilius Bassus ; both had arranged to transfer their allegiance and declare for Vespasian. Bassus succeeded in carrying the sailors with him, but Caecina's men, loyal to their unworthy Emperor, put their equally unworthy commander in chains. Valens, who should have supported the army in Cisalpine Gaul, delayed, and finally, hearing of the desertion of the fleet, turned aside from the decisive field of action and took ship for Transalpine Gaul, probably intending to raise reinforcements ; if this was his intention, it completely failed, and he was made prisoner.

Second Battle of Bedriacum. So far Antonius Primus had carried all before him ; the leaderless Vitellians therefore determined to fall back on Cremona, and to join their comrades there. They crossed the Po at Hostilia, and marching a hundred miles in four days, they arrived at Cremona in time to relieve the garrison, which, after a hard struggle on the old battlefield of Bedriacum, had been driven back on the city. The united Vitellian army resolved to attack Antonius at once, and a desperate night-battle ensued; it was a struggle of legion against legion rather than between two leaders, a gigantic gladiatorial struggle fought out to the death. The feelings of the soldiers for good and for ill are well illustrated by a story in Tacitus; he records how in the darkness a son killed his father, fighting on the opposite side; then recognizing him, and overcome with shame, he proceeded to bury the body, protesting that the guilt was that of the State, not his own; the feeling of pity spread; 'men cursed the cruellest of wars', and 'none the less they butchered and spoiled kinsmen and brothers; they called it a crime, and committed it'.[1]

Finally the Vitellians gave way, and took refuge in Cremona, which the Flavians carried after a hard struggle. Then followed a horror almost without parallel in Roman history: a Roman colony was sacked by Roman troops; every form of cruelty or lust was displayed; it was an anticipation of the Spanish Fury at Antwerp or of the Sack of Magdeburg.

The Surrender of Vitellius. The whole of the North of Italy was now in the power of the Flavians, but Vitellius still had Rome and the country south and south-west of the Apennines. However he did nothing, and his officers were eager to make their peace with Vespasian, though the common soldiers still were loyal to their Emperor. So Antonius was allowed to cross the Apennines without opposition.

Negotiations were then opened through Sabinus, the Urban Prefect, a brother of Vespasian; he had been appointed to this office under Otho, and continued in it by Vitellius, for he was a man of the highest character and 'no mean parts . . . distinguished both at home and abroad'.[2] Among those who took part in the discussions was Silius Italicus, the

[1] Tac. *Hist.* iii. 25; cf. Henderson, *ib.* pp. 198 f.
[2] *Hist.* iii. 75; his only fault was that he was 'sermonis nimius'!

Epic poet. Vitellius finally consented to retire into Campania with a lavish pension, and it seemed as if the year of civil war was to end peaceably. But it was not to be ; once more the soldiers took the matter into their own hands, and attacked Sabinus on the Capitol. With his Urban Cohorts he defended it desperately, and in the fighting the famous Temple of Jupiter Capitolinus, ' The Pledge of Empire ', was burned (19 December). Tacitus lays especial stress on this, and all over the Western world its destruction was looked upon as an omen that Rome's dominion was coming to an end. Sabinus finally was captured and murdered, and Vitellius was compelled to withdraw his resignation.

The Flavians then advanced at once, eager for revenge, and Rome was taken after a horrible struggle in which Vitellius' German veterans died fighting desperately, while horror was added to the scene because the citizens of Rome went on with their business and their pleasures as usual, with bloodshed all round them. There could be no better illustration of the futility of the Roman mob ; they were worthless, and the strength of the Empire, moral and physical, was in Italy, in the provinces and, above all, in the army. Vitellius was caught and murdered, and his few remaining partisans surrendered. There were, however, only a few executions. Mucianus and Domitian, Vespasian's younger son, the heads of the Flavian party, were masters of Rome, but Vespasian himself did not arrive till October (A.D. 70).

The year 69 had seen three Emperors chosen, and three meeting violent deaths ; it had seen the common soldiers out of hand everywhere, and the Roman Empire seemed to be breaking up. The dualism of East and West had declared itself, and also the still more serious tendency for each provincial army to make its own Emperor. It was the glory of Vespasian that he so repaired the ruins of civil strife, and so reorganized the sound elements, military and civil, of the Roman people, that the year of disaster proved not the beginning of the end, but rather the beginning of the best period of government which Western Europe has ever known.

Rebellion in Judaea, A.D. 66–70. It will be remembered that, when the call came to Vespasian to make a bid for the

Empire, he was conducting a campaign against the Jews. For in A.D. 66 a rebellion blazed out among the Jews which was to lead to the supreme crisis in the history of this troubled people. A brief account has already been given of Augustus' dealings with the Jews, and reference has been made to Caligula's treatment of them and to Claudius' reversion to earlier policy in setting up Herod Agrippa as King of Judaea in A.D. 41 (Acts xii.). On the death of Herod in A.D. 44 Judaea again became a Roman province, governed by a procurator of equestrian rank.[1] The procurator now had his head-quarters in Jerusalem instead of in Caesarea, but the control of the Temple was given to Herod of Chalcis, brother of Agrippa I, and on his death to his son Agrippa II (Acts xxv.).

The immediate cause of the rebellion of A.D. 66 was rioting in Caesarea and Jerusalem, which occurred, it is said, on the same day. A decision had been made by Burrus, Nero's minister, that the Jews of Caesarea were not entitled to citizenship. In tumult they left the city, but when ordered to return by Gessius Florus, the governor, they were cut down by the Greek inhabitants as they entered the city. In Jerusalem the power of the patriotic party, the Zealots, had of late been increasing, and their leader Eleazar, son of the high priest Ananias, forbade Gentiles to make offerings, as they had hitherto been allowed, within the outer court of the Temple. The Moderate Party tried to restrain him ; a conflict took place ; Roman troops were called in, but were besieged in King Agrippa's palace where they finally capitulated ; in spite of promises of safety they were all killed. Meantime the Governor of Syria, whose duty it was to suppress any serious trouble in Judaea, marched on Jerusalem, but was repulsed with loss. Then Nero, who was in Greece at the time, appointed Mucianus to be Governor of Syria, and ordered Vespasian to suppress the Jewish rebellion which had now spread to Samaria and Galilee.

Vespasian in Judaea. With three legions, auxiliaries and the help of the native kings of Nabataea and Commagene, Vespasian moved from Ptolemais, where he had collected his army, into Galilee (Spring, A.D. 67). In the campaign

---

[1] Felix, A.D. 52–60 ; Festus, A.D. 60–62.

of this year he occupied Galilee, reducing Iotapata, its main stronghold, after a stubborn siege. Here the Jewish commander was Josephus, the historian, who was a leader of the Moderate Party ; after the siege he identified himself with the Roman cause and became Vespasian's client. In the next year much territory beyond Jordan was overrun, and finally Samaria and Idumaea. Vespasian's troops were about to converge on Jerusalem when news of Nero's death arrived ; and Vespasian, who was holding an ' extraordinary ' command, preferred to wait for fresh instructions from the new Emperor. His own accession to power postponed operations still further ; it was left for Titus, his elder son, to crush the rebellion in A.D. 70.

The Siege of Jerusalem. In the interval given by Vespasian's suspension of the campaign Jerusalem, crowded with fugitives, became the scene of the wildest disorder. The Zealots were in control, but their party was divided by jealousy. When Titus appeared under the walls of the city, they settled to some extent their differences ; but, even so, two parties remained, one led by Simon, son of Gioras, who held the upper city, the so-called Hill of Sion, while John of Gischala occupied the Temple.

The situation of Jerusalem, raised high on rocks and difficult of approach, makes it in any case a city difficult to storm. But its natural strength had been increased by the fortifications which the Jews hastily completed. Before the city could be taken two walls had to be stormed, and the defences of the Temple, the Tower of Antonia and the defences of the Hill of Sion overthrown. The siege was one of the most stubborn in history, and for an account of it we are indebted to Josephus. The first wall was held for many weeks ; at last it fell, and, when the Jewish leaders would not accept the favourable terms which Titus offered, he surrounded the city and cut off supplies. The second wall and the Tower of Antonia were stormed, and many of the inhabitants were allowed to pass out unmolested. But the extremists with many followers remained within the Temple, which Titus exerted all his efforts to spare. But the defenders themselves profaned the Holy of Holies, and finally the

Temple was burned to the ground, in defiance of Titus' orders, Josephus says. Still the stubbornness of the Jews was not broken ; they held out in the upper city, till they were compelled by famine to surrender or kill themselves. The leaders escaped by subterranean passages cut in the limestone cliffs, but at last hunger compelled them to give themselves up. Thousands of Jews perished by sword, fire or famine, and thousands were sold into slavery. Vespasian and Titus celebrated a triumph, though they disdained the title 'Judaicus'. After Titus' death an arch was put up in his honour, and among its sculptures may still be seen the seven-branched candlestick of the Temple which, though carried off by the priests, fell into the hands of the Romans after the siege.

Thus came about the 'abomination of desolation' which had such far-reaching results for Jews and Christians alike. Judaea became a province again, and the Tenth Legion built its camp on the ruins of Jerusalem.

CHAPTER X

THE GERMAN FRONTIER FROM THE DEATH OF AUGUSTUS TO A.D. 70

*T*HE *Elbe-Danube Frontier Given Up.* The defeat of Varus was indeed one of the 'decisive battles of the world', for it convinced the wiser Romans that further expansion of the Empire was impossible, and it also gave the bolder and more patriotic of the Germans confidence that successful resistance to Rome was possible. How nearly Rome had succeeded in absorbing the western half of Germany can be seen from the pages of Tacitus ; after the defeat of Varus, she still had allies, or at any rate friends, beyond the Rhine, the Chauci on the north coast, and later the Hermunduri in Central Germany, and even in the leading patriotic tribe, the Cherusci, Segestes, the father-in-law of the patriot Arminius, was a Roman partisan, and the hero's brother Flavus was a devoted Roman 'auxiliary'. The famous scene between the brothers on the banks of the Weser is significant ; Arminius taunted Flavus with being a

10

poorly-paid subject, and his brother in reply proudly pointed to the military honours he had won in the imperial service —the highest prize a soldier could hope for. This attraction of the Roman army was one of the foundations of Roman power ; the devotion of Gurkhas and Sikhs to the British Raj, strong as it is, has only part of the same attraction ; for the Roman auxiliary became on his discharge a Roman citizen, and so part of that military nation that he had been proud to serve.

Augustus and Tiberius were well aware of this division of feeling in Germany, and knew that the Roman legions, if properly handled, were invincible in the field. But they also knew from the experience of the Pannonian Rebellion (p. 60) how imperfectly secured the new provinces on the Danube were, and that to conquer and in addition to hold the vast region between Rhine and Elbe would mean a great extension of the Roman standing army, the burdens of which, financial and other, were already as much as the State could bear. Hence there can be no doubt that Augustus had Germany especially in his mind when he recommended to his successors the policy of ' keeping the empire within limits ',[1] a policy which Tiberius accepted as a 'rule of empire' ('praeceptum').[2]

The Forward Policy of Germanicus. But for the moment, on the death of Augustus, the policy of aggression was resumed. It might be fairly argued that the Germans needed a lesson, to show them that the Romans were still formidable, and the ' friendly ' Germans, like Segestes, probably asked for assistance. Moreover, the mutinies in the Rhine army showed how dangerous to discipline long inactivity might be, especially with new troops, who coveted the excitement and the glory of a campaign while without experience of its dangers and hardships.

The main reason for action, however, was in all probability the character of Germanicus. He was young and conscious of his ability as a commander, which he certainly over-estimated, and it was natural that he should wish to take up again, and if possible to complete, the work which his father Drusus had so well begun. And, loyal as he undoubtedly

[1] Tac. *Ann.* i. 11.   [2] Tac. *Agric.* 13.

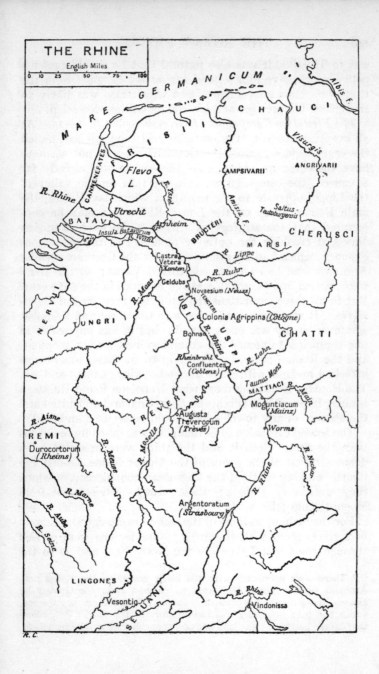

was to Tiberius, it was also natural that he should prefer a policy which gave him a good reason for escaping from the Emperor's close surveillance, and which also was likely to strengthen his prestige and his claims to the succession.

The First Two Campaigns of Germanicus, A.D. 14–15. At all events, as soon as the mutinies had been quelled, he led the eager legions against the Germans, who do not seem to have suspected an attack. As the season was already far advanced, the campaign was a mere raid up the valley of the Lippe, opposite to the mouth of which lay Vetera, the main Roman camp on the Lower Rhine. It may be conjectured that the strategy of this and the next campaign aimed at crushing the outlying members of the great confederacy, which had been formed under the Cheruscan leader Arminius, and had recently destroyed Varus ; so the Marsi were harried first (A.D. 14), and the Bructeri in the next year. But in all three campaigns the same features present themselves. It was easy to advance into Germany and to defeat whatever enemy was encountered ; but it was impossible in one campaign to secure the ground gained for the moment, and the Roman army, in returning to its base, was always attacked, and met with grave disasters twice (A.D. 15 and 16). The Romans found Germany what Napoleon found Russia, a country impossible to subdue because of natural difficulties and the absence of any towns which could be secured and held.

The second campaign of Germanicus was much more serious than the first. Both it and the third were preceded by a demonstration of the army of the Upper Rhine against the Chatti, who lay south of the Cheruscan confederacy, of which they were very jealous : these attacks were made from Moguntiacum (the modern Mainz).

For the main operations of the second campaign the Roman fleet co-operated with the army ; four legions were carried through the Great Lakes [1] to the North Sea, and so to the

---

[1] These were connected with the lower course of the Rhine near Arnheim by the Fossa Drusiana, which had been constructed by Drusus, the father of Germanicus. In the thirteenth century the sea, which had been gradually encroaching, formed the Zuider Zee, where the ' lakes ' had been ; the land has now (1931) been partially recovered.

mouth of the Amisia (Ems), where two land columns joined them, somewhere on the lower course of that river. The first object of this strategy was to secure the alliance of the Chauci and the Angrivarii, the coast tribes : then the whole army turned back and wasted the territory of the Bructeri. As a symbol of Roman victory, the scene of Varus' disaster in the Teutoberg Forest was visited, and the remains of his luckless army buried. But the main operation of the year, the attack on the Cherusci, seems to have met with but limited success, and part of the army under Caecina was all but overwhelmed by Arminius on its way back to the Rhine. It was only the firmness of its leader that saved it from the fate of Varus and his three legions ; Tacitus' account [1] of the struggle at the Long Bridges is a brilliant picture of the difficulties [2] of regular troops fighting an enemy on his own ground, and of the way in which discipline, if it holds, can snatch safety out of a desperate crisis.

The main army under Germanicus was almost equally unfortunate. The march of two legions homewards along the coast seemed easy, but the Romans were unfamiliar with the uncertain tides of the North Sea ; it was the season of the equinox, and the flood tide, with the north wind behind it, caught the army on the sea marshes. Though the loss of life seems to have been small, the destruction of stores was immense, and Tacitus draws especial attention to the fact that the whole of the Western provinces, even Gaul and Spain, were called upon to help make good the losses.

The Third Campaign, A.D. 16. Germanicus, however, had gained a kind of victory in the field, and fearing to be superseded made a great effort to obtain a decision in the next year. He enormously increased his fleet, and transported his army without difficulty to the mouth of the Amisia. He then advanced to the Visurgis (Weser), and, after forcing a crossing not without some loss, he brought Arminius to a

[1] Tac. *Ann.* i. 63 f.

[2] The disaster to General Braddock at Fort Duquesne in 1755, when Washington first saw service, and of the British Army in the Khyber in 1842 may be compared.

pitched battle at a place called Idistaviso.[1] Here, and again as they marched on towards the Elbe, the Romans gained two bloody victories, thanks mainly to their superiority in equipment ; but Arminius escaped with a wound, and the spirit of the Germans was unbroken. Even the success that had been gained was largely discounted by the disaster that befell the fleet on its return voyage, when it was caught in a storm and suffered terrible losses of men and material.[2]

The Forward Policy Abandoned. Tacitus, to whom Germanicus is a faultless hero and a commander to be compared with Alexander the Great, claims that one more campaign would have crushed German resistance. But Arminius' influence was as great as ever ; he deserves the title which his countrymen give him, ' the liberator of Germany ', for he had taught his countrymen that the Romans were not invincible, and, while he lived, they would never have yielded. The triumph (26 May, A.D. 17) by which Germanicus was tempted home may have been earned by successes in the field, but it was German bravery aided by the difficulties of German warfare, and not the envy of Tiberius (as Tacitus suggests), which robbed the prince of the title of ' Conqueror of Germany '. The Emperor acted from a wise policy ; he knew Germany well, and he reminded his eager nephew that he himself had accomplished more in ' his nine campaigns ' by ' diplomacy than by force '. He knew that the Germans might be safely left to quarrel among themselves, or, if we may use the phrase of another great German ' liberator ', Bismarck, ' to stew in their own juice '.

And the events that followed justified the prediction ; first

---

[1] Tacitus is called by Mommsen ' the most unmilitary of historians ', but his account of these two battles is confirmed by recent archaeological research. The site of the first battle was north of the Weser near Minden, and commanded an early track which ran towards the Elbe, the Roman objective ; after forcing this, Germanicus still found his left flank threatened, and turned north-east to the boundary of the Cherusci and the Angrivarii ; the boundary wall, described by Tacitus as forming the strength of the Germans' second position, can still be traced near the village of Leese.

[2] A brief fragment describing the storm survives from the works of Albinovanus Pedo, one of Germanicus' officers.

North and South Germany quarrelled,[1] and Arminius with his Cherusci drove the great King of the Suevi, Maroboduus, back into his own kingdom, that of the Marcomanni in Bohemia, from which he was soon expelled ; he died a fugitive in Italy. The fate of Arminius, though more glorious, was not very different ; he was accused by his own countrymen of aiming at the kingship and was murdered.

Rome also used on the Rhine the policy which she had developed in the East, and sought to win over her barbarian neighbours by giving them princes educated at Rome in Roman ideas. When the Cherusci, once Rome's deadliest enemies, having lost their other chiefs in civil strife, appealed to Claudius for the one surviving member of the family of their old leader Arminius, he sent them Italicus, the son of the ' auxiliary ' Flavus, who had been brought up in Italy. He was received with enthusiasm at first, but soon offended his countrymen by his Roman upbringing, and in the civil wars that ensued the power of his tribe was still further weakened. It was with good reason that Tacitus prayed two generations later that ' the tribes (of Germany) might continue, if not to love the Romans, at least to hate each other, since, when the destiny of Empire is driving us onwards, Fortune can give us nothing better than disunion among our enemies '.[2] This is a truly significant forecast of the coming danger which three centuries later was to overwhelm the Roman Empire.

It was not only that there were no more campaigns or advances into Central Germany ; the Roman forts also beyond the Middle Rhine from north of Mainz to north of Cologne were abandoned,[3] and even Roman trade here was stopped. The Romans protected themselves from invasion by keeping a wide strip of the right bank of the Rhine uninhabited [4] ; Mommsen compares it to the glacis of a fortress,

[1] So the Chatti were always quarrelling with their neighbours, the Cherusci (Tac. *Ann*. xii. 28) and the Hermunduri (in A.D. 58) (*ibid*. xiii. 57). [2] *Germ*. 33.

[3] Of these the chief was Aliso, on the river Lippe, up whose course lay the usual line of the Romans.

[4] A somewhat similar policy on a much greater scale is seen in the provision of the Treaty of Versailles, which demilitarizes the strip of Germany on the right bank of the Rhine.

stripped bare for purposes of defence. This deserted land was used for pasturage of the herds which supplied with food the army of the Lower Rhine. When the Frisii attempted to occupy it in the reign of Nero (A.D. 57), they were driven out, and a similar fate befell the Ampsivarii in the next year, in spite of the appeal made by their chief Boiocalus to his fifty years of loyalty to Rome.

The Lower Rhine Frontier under Tiberius. But it was only on the Middle Rhine that this policy was maintained; on the Lower Rhine, where the river turns westward and flows by various channels into the North Sea, the Roman Empire extended northward over what is now Holland. The Batavi, the most warlike tribe in this part, had submitted to Drusus without a struggle; they lived in the Island of the Rhine, which stretches nearly from Antwerp to Leyden and Utrecht. They paid no tribute, but furnished the best 'auxiliaries' in the Roman army, one thousand cavalry and nine thousand infantry, as well as the Imperial Palace Guard in Rome. Beyond them the Cannenefates in North Holland, and the Frisii in the modern Friesland, were in the same position, and furnished troops; the Frisii also paid some tribute in kind—in the form of hides. The Roman influence here was based on the power of their fleet; commanding the abundant water-ways, they had not the difficulties of transport which prevailed everywhere else in North Germany, and their wise policy of using the warlike tribes to fight for them did the rest; it was the policy by which Pitt turned the Scotch Highlanders into loyal and splendid soldiers, but it had its dangers, as was shown at the end of Nero's reign (p. 113).

Towards the close of the reign of Tiberius the Frisii revolted (A.D. 28), owing to the injustice of the hide-collectors, and they were allowed to remain for a time independent; the old Emperor had lost his vigour, and was suspicious of all his provincial governors.

Corbulo in Germany. In the reign of Claudius, however, Corbulo reduced them again to submission (A.D. 47), planted a Roman garrison among them, and civilized them by giving them allotments of land and by introducing urban institutions. At the same time he checked the raids of the Chauci, who, under the lead of Gannascus, were plundering the coasts of the North Sea in their light vessels and extending their ravages even to Gaul. It was a distant anticipation of the raids of the Northmen, which were later to contribute so much to the breakdown of Western civilization. Gannascus was a Roman deserter who, like Arminius, had learned the weak points of the Empire while serving as an auxiliary. Corbulo caused him to be assassinated by his own countrymen, restored discipline in the Roman army, and was preparing to reduce the Chauci beyond the Visurgis, when Claudius peremptorily recalled him. He obeyed with the characteristic remark, ' How happy of old time were the Roman generals '. After this there seems to have been peace in Northern Germany. Tacitus says that the generals had learned that distinction was most easily won by keeping things quiet But the Roman armies continued their civilizing influence ; the great mole for controlling the stream of the Rhine, diverting its waters into the northern channel, so as to make the ' Island ' at once more accessible on the south and more defensible on the north, was completed, and the ambitious scheme of uniting the Upper Saône with the Upper Moselle and so completing the water communication between North and South Gaul, was only given up because of the jealousy of the Governor of Gallia Belgica.

Roman Settlements on the Middle Rhine. The change of policy on the Middle Rhine is marked by the change in the encampments. The frontier had become a defensive one ; the four legions were no longer concentrated for offence in two great camps, but were placed one at Bonn, twenty miles above Cologne, one at Novaesium (Neuss), twenty-two miles below Cologne, and two at Vetera (Xanten), thirty-five miles further down. These camps became more permanent, as their remains show ; stone took the place of earthworks ; but still, as Tacitus says, Roman conservatism prevailed in part, and they were constructed as if they were to be bases for aggressive campaigns rather than for defence.[1] These were the military posts ; the great centre of Roman civilizing activity was Cologne, which in its name still bears witness

[1] *Hist.* iv. 23.

to the fact that it was the first Roman 'colony' on the Rhine. The Ubii, who from Caesar's time had been friends of Rome, were for protection transplanted by Agrippa (38 B.C.) to the left bank ; it was here that the worship of Rome and Augustus had been set up. Claudius, in honour of his wife Agrippina, who had been born there, made them a 'colony' (A.D. 50) (cf. p. 93). Rome's methods are admirably illustrated here—her acquisition of native allies on the spot, her policy of transplanting, and her gradual grant of privileges.

Roman Frontier Policy in Upper Germany. But Rome's frontier policy on the Upper Rhine was quite different from that on the middle course of the river. From the time of Germanicus onwards, the armies of the Lower and the Upper Rhine were kept apart. The line of division was a little stream near Rheinbrohl, the Vinxt ; this was afterwards the frontier between the elector-archbishops of Trèves and Cologne. It seems to have been chosen because it was the boundary of the territories of the Ubii and the Treveri, according to Rome's usual policy of recognizing native tribal divisions.

Of the four legions of the Upper Rhine, two were at Moguntiacum (Mainz), one at Argentoratum (Strasbourg), and one at Vindonissa (Windisch, not far from Basle). These were all on the left bank of the Rhine ; but here, even after the withdrawal of Germanicus, Rome kept some hold on the right bank. The fort built on Mt. Taunus by Drusus the elder and restored by Germanicus was probably given up for a time, but Rome still held the plain between the river Main and the Taunus, where the hot springs of the modern Wiesbaden attracted her. This was the southern part of the territory of the Mattiaci, who extended as far north as the Lahn, and who were by the end of the first century all brought under Roman rule. Here the Romans were in collision with the Chatti, against whom in A.D. 41 Galba, the later Emperor, gained some successes ; but it is unlikely that Rome extended her power far beyond the Rhine here before the time of the Flavians (p. 192).

Further south, in the valley of the Neckar, the way was also prepared for further advance, though here, too, the actual conquest came later. This region between the upper waters of the Danube and the Rhine from Basle to Mainz had once been occupied by the Helvetii ; when they moved into Switzerland, the country seems to have had no settled tribes for some time ; the Romans, south of the Danube, in Raetia, were able to prevent permanent occupation by tribes, but, following a policy different from that in Lower Germany, they allowed refugees from Gaul and elsewhere to squat on the deserted land.   Hence here, too, advance was easy under the Flavians, when the territory received the name of Agri Decumates.

Causes of the Great Rebellion of A.D. 69.   How great was the Roman confidence in the security of their defensive policy on the German frontier may be gathered from the fact that, as time went on, the forces on it were weakened.   Two veteran legions were drawn off by Claudius for the invasion of Britain (p. 277), and their places were taken by two new legions, and a third veteran legion was borrowed by Corbulo for his campaigns in the East.   Important detachments (*vexillationes*), too, were withdrawn by Nero at the close of his reign for his expedition to the East.   Further, the strength of the Rhine armies was still more depleted by the march of Valens and Caecina to Italy in support of Vitellius.

The causes of this rebellion, or as it should also be called, mutiny, were various ; some of these were general, some peculiar to the occasion.   The first of the general causes was no doubt the feeling that the hour of Rome's greatness was past.   However wise the policy of non-aggression may have been, it certainly left an impression of weakness among the barbarians, and though the scandals and the cruelties of Nero's rule in Rome were little known among the provincials, yet at least enough was heard of them to make their leaders think that Rome was degenerate ; and the soldiers had lost all enthusiasm for an Emperor who never showed himself among them.   It was therefore not accidental that Vindex, under cover of the plea of ' restoring the Republic ', headed a national movement in Gaul in the year before the mutiny broke out on the Rhine, and that later Civilis, at the height of his success, hoped for the co-operation of the northern Gauls, who dreamed of setting up a ' Gallic Empire '.

And this national feeling found dangerous expression in

the jealousy felt and shown by the ' Auxiliaries ' towards the legions. Recruited as they were from non-Roman sources, though generally armed and trained like Romans, they were indignant that they had to serve longer and received lower pay, while they considered themselves, not without reason, to be equally brave and efficient with the Roman troops. A good example of this jealousy was the feeling of the Batavian *auxilia* towards the XIVth Legion, to which they were attached ; so troublesome were they in the Vitellian advance on Italy, that they were sent back to Germany.

These causes for trouble were general and had existed for some time. They were brought to a head in A.D. 69 by the weakening of the Roman Rhine armies, spoken of above, and by the fact that the Romans themselves were divided ; the officers of the legions were very largely for Vespasian, the men were devoted to Vitellius. Hence there was mutual suspicion, and action was paralysed.

The man to take advantage of this opportunity was the Batavian leader, Julius Civilis. He had private wrongs to revenge, for he had twice been in danger of his life [1] on charges of conspiring against Rome, though he had been pardoned. He claimed friendship with Vespasian, and was actually urged by the Flavian leader, Antonius Primus, to stir up trouble in Germany, in order to prevent Vitellius drawing support thence. But he was also a German patriot, and knew how to move his countrymen by eloquent appeals to their superstition and their national feeling. Not the least interesting feature in the strange career of Civilis is his connection with the prophetess Veleda, for whom booty and prisoners for sacrifice were reserved after his victories.

Rebellion of Civilis, A.D. 69. The immediate occasion of the rising was the attempt of the Romans to raise recruits for Vitellius among the Batavi ; resistance to compulsory service is a frequent beginning of trouble. Civilis and his Batavians were joined by the Cannenefates, and they successfully repulsed the Roman attack on the Island. He was soon joined by the eight Batavian cohorts, returned from Italy, and made his army swear the oath to Vespasian. The

[1] Tac. *Hist.* iv. 13.

Roman garrison in Vetera, however, defied him and was blockaded ; the rest of Lower Germany was lost.

Hordeonius Flaccus, the Governor of Upper Germany, advanced to relieve the besieged camp. But he was old and in bad health, and, as a partisan of Vespasian, he was hated by his men. In the end he was murdered by them, and the command passed to Dillius Vocula, the one Roman commander who showed any ability or energy at this time. Vetera meanwhile, though undermanned and badly fortified, held out bravely against Civilis, who, towards the close of A.D. 69, threw off the mask of being a partisan of Vespasian, appealed to the independent Germans beyond the Rhine, and concerted a rebellion in Gaul with the Gallic chiefs, Classicus and Tutor of the Treveri, and Sabinus of the Lingones ; all of them bore the name of Julius and were in the Roman service.[1] They did not desert at once, but waited their opportunity till early in A.D. 70.

Vocula had succeeded towards the close of the previous year in relieving Vetera, but, miscalculating his strength, he did not withdraw all the troops from the camp ; he contented himself with strengthening its defences and provisioning it. Civilis attacked it again, and Vocula's second attempt to relieve it was foiled by the treachery of the Gallic leaders just spoken of. Some of his own officers and men, too, were bribed to go over to the enemy,[2] and he himself was murdered. The two legions, the Ist and the XVIth, then took the oath of allegiance to the Gallic Empire. Even then the heroic garrison of Vetera held out, though almost starving, and the camp was only taken by their voluntary surrender ; they stipulated that their lives should be spared, but that they should swear allegiance to the new Gallic Empire. The terms, however, were not kept ; the Germans fell on them as they marched away, and they were all murdered.

The story of the siege of Vetera is pathetically like that of Cawnpore in 1857 ; there is the same desperate but successful resistance against overwhelming odds, the same waiting in

[1] Sabinus prided himself on being a great-grandson of the Emperor of Gaul, Julius Caesar.
[2] Tac. *Hist.* iv. 57 well calls this ' flagitium incognitum '.

vain for relief which just fails to arrive, the same bravery, and the same treacherous end.

Causes of the Failure of the Rebellion. Rome's power on the Rhine seemed to be at an end. Her armies either were destroyed or had gone over to the enemy. All the Roman forts except Moguntiacum and Vindonissa were destroyed, and Colonia, the Roman colony among the Ubii, had to secure itself by submission ; it was with difficulty saved by Civilis from the hatred of the independent Germans of the right bank, headed by the Tencteri, who wished to destroy it as the ' bulwark of slavery '.

But the success of the revolt was already in peril. The Gauls, who saw in the burning of the Capitol (Dec. A.D. 69) a sign that the Roman dominion was at an end, dreamed of a new Gallic Empire ; but Civilis himself declined to swear allegiance to it ; he was well aware that the hostility of Gaul against Germany was at least as great as against Rome. And the Gauls themselves were not united; the Sequani, who had been on the national side in A.D. 68, and who had then supported Vindex, now defeated Sabinus [1] and the Lingones, and those Gallic tribes which had revolted were already quarrelling among themselves which was to be leader in the new empire, though it had not yet been won. The Gallic leaders wasted their time in enjoying their triumphs and in minor operations, without attempting to secure the passes of the Alps, beyond which Rome was already preparing her armies to restore her authority.

The Suppression of the Revolt. Eight legions were gathered to crush the rebels. One army under Annius Gallus reduced the region of the Upper Rhine, while Petilius Cerealis, famous afterwards in Britain, proceeded to reduce Gaul and the Lower Rhine.

Already, before he arrived, the Remi, ever the friends of Rome, had persuaded the Gallic tribes which had so far re-

---

[1] Sabinus abandoned the struggle at once, and hid himself in an underground chamber for ten years, while the report was given out that he was dead. The story of the devotion of his wife Epponina is one of the most romantic in classical history (Plutarch, *Amat.* c. 25). He was finally discovered and executed by Vespasian.

mained neutral not to join the rebels; and Cerealis certainly secured his success as much by wise diplomacy as by force of arms. He allowed the two deserting legions to return to their allegiance, and succeeded in persuading his own legions to receive them as comrades; he proudly showed the Gauls, who offered to assist him, that he could do without them, and, as Tacitus says, they were 'proniores ad officia quod spernebantur '.[1] He won over even the leading rebel tribes, the Treveri and the Lingones, by his famous speech, setting forth the blessings of Roman rule and the need of Gaul for protection against Germany.[2] He refused to allow his legionaries to sack the town of the Treveri, and after a hard struggle he repulsed Civilis and his allies who attacked him there. Then the rebellion rapidly collapsed. Civilis seems to have tried to make his peace with Rome, but the story of Tacitus in the *Histories* breaks off with his meeting with Cerealis on an island on the Rhine, and what happened to him is unknown.

Results of the Rebellion. More important than the fate of any individual or community were the general results of the rebellion. First, changes were made in the organization of the Roman army in which certain defects had made themselves very apparent. These changes will be described on a later page (p. 162). Secondly, the Romans by their wise policy of mercy secured the allegiance of the Gauls and of the Germans on the left bank, and Roman dominion here was henceforth safe. The Rhine was secured as the boundary of Roman power, even as Julius Caesar had planned. Henceforth, at any rate in the first and second centuries, the fighting with the barbarians is on the Danube rather than on the Rhine, which has remained ever since as a European landmark, furiously disputed from century to century, but never obliterated. And, though it is still a 'German river', and is likely to remain so, yet there is a marked difference between

[1] *Hist.* iv. 71.

[2] *Ibid.* 73-4. The speech is the finest possible statement of the principles of the Roman Empire and of the blessings it conferred on the world. Cerealis begins 'numquam facundiam exercui ', as so many speakers have done and do, but we can hardly believe that a speech so apt and so successful is the invention of the historian.

its two banks. Perhaps the finest Roman remains on the north of the Alps are those of Trèves, and the Germans of the Rhine valley, though retaining their language and remaining fully German, have been differentiated from those further east. It can hardly be an accident that the power of the Catholic Church has always been so strong in this part, both politically in the Middle Ages and in the creed of the population now.

But no part of Germany was ever Romanized as Gaul was. Roman trade with Northern Europe, so far as it existed, went rather over the Danube from Carnuntum to the valley of the Vistula, or to some small extent by sea to the mouths of the German rivers ; it did not go across the Middle Rhine, and Roman coins are rarely found in Central Germany. The towns in Germany—Cologne is an exception—which date back to Roman times, grew originally out of the *canabae*, the settlements attached to the legionary camps. Even the country houses seem to be placed on so regular a plan as to suggest that they were the results of land distributions to retired veterans, e.g., in the Wetterau and in parts of the Rhine valley.

Rome to Germany meant military force, not as to France a unifying and civilizing process.

CHAPTER XI

THE PRINCIPATES OF VESPASIAN, A.D. 69–79, AND TITUS, A.D. 79–81

ORIGIN and Character of Vespasian. Titus Flavius Vespasianus, the first of the Flavian Emperors, was sixty-one years old when he rode into Rome as Emperor. He came of a humble origin which prompted contemptuous comparison with the Julii and the Claudii, with Galba, Otho and Vitellius. His grandfather was a native of Reate, a little town in the Sabine hills, who had seen service as a centurion before becoming a collector of debts ; his father was first a tax-gatherer and later carried on the business of a money-lender among the Helvetii. Close to

Reate, too, Vespasian was born, and for his birthplace he always retained the greatest affection. No one would have supposed that from this family a new dynasty of Emperors would spring, though after the event men were quick to remember signs and omens foretelling it. The *gens Flavia*, says Suetonius, gave strength to an Empire that was tottering ; the *gens* could boast no history, but it was 'reipublicae nequaquam poenitenda'.[1]

Vespasian received some education ; he could write and speak Greek. He had seen military service in Thrace and Germany, in Britain in the reign of Claudius and in Judaea under Nero. He married Domitilla and had three children, Titus, the destroyer of Jerusalem, Domitian, who was present at the burning of the Capitol (p. 142) and was later Emperor, and a daughter Domitilla.

In appearance he was solidly built, with a short neck and coarse features and small eyes. In intellect he was not brilliant, but he possessed a pungent, if not always refined, wit. ' His merit ', says Gibbon, ' was useful rather than shining.' But his judgment was shrewd ; he had an eye for the best solution of a problem, and the tenacity necessary to put it into effect. Ability of this kind was more needful at the time in which he came to power than any brilliance of constructive skill. He penetrated into the causes of the disorder of the year A.D. 68–69 and was far-sighted in discovering its remedy.

The Purpose of his Reforms. He saw that the lessons to be learned from so much bloodshed and anarchy were political and military. Nero had neglected to keep in touch with the army ; every Emperor henceforth, not excepting the philosopher Marcus Aurelius, is careful to know and to be known by his army. Further, the peace and security of the West had been endangered ; the Western provinces had become increasingly Romanized ; their trade was growing, industries were springing up, Latin culture was spreading. Were the provinces unworthy of consideration in the counsels of the State ? Such another year of confusion would rend the Empire in pieces and destroy the Principate, which would command

[1] Suet. *Vesp.* I. Cf. *Eutrop.* vii. 19. ' Princeps (Vespasian) obscure quidem natus, sed optimis comparandus.'

neither respect nor power ; and the main cause would be that there was no recognized theory and no agreement as to the method by which one Emperor was to be succeeded by the next.

Vespasian's reforms were dictated in the main by two simple motives ; he worked first to place the Principate on the broader and therefore firmer basis of the goodwill of the provinces ; secondly, to establish some principle of succession. To carry out these aims he was forced to devote his attention to most departments of the political and military organization of the Empire.

The Army. No other course was open to Vespasian but to disband three of the disloyal legions of Germany[1] ; indeed their very names ceased to have a place in the army list. Two new legions were at once enrolled, and a third in A.D. 82. The fourth of the disloyal legions—the Twenty-second, commanded by Vocula—was spared and still remained in camp at Vetera ; but its composition was changed. Vespasian did not depart from Augustus' system of permanent camps ; legions were still posted in important points in Germany and there is no evidence that they were frequently moved.

An important change, however, was made with regard to the local auxiliary regiments. Their use had been recommended by several considerations ; they were inexpensive to raise and to maintain ; they possessed a knowledge of the country and were invaluable as scouts and light-armed troops. But the dangers involved in their use had become clear in the revolt of Civilis. Henceforth these clan-regiments never serve in the country of their origin. On the German frontier under Vespasian there are found Africans, Thracians, Spaniards, Damascenes, Aquitanians and others ; while the regiments raised in Germany might be sent as far as Britain or Dacia or Pannonia. It is possible, too, that *auxilia* were less rigidly composed of troops coming from one tribe or locality ; at any rate they are never again guilty of ' nationalist ' ambitions.

---

[1] This is the traditional view ; recently, however, it has been suggested that legio I was amalgamated with VII Galbiana to make VII Gemina, and IIII Macedonica and XVI Gallica were re-formed in the new IIII and XVI Flaviae (*J.R.S.* xviii. (1928), p. 58).

Again, there is some reason to believe that the legions tended to include fewer Italian recruits than before [1] ; service in the army had not attracted the best material of the Italian towns, and for the future the Western provinces supplied the greater proportion of the soldiers. To Spain, in particular, Vespasian granted many privileges, as will be seen, and it is reasonable to suppose that he demanded some return in the nature of recruits for the legions.

Finance. One of the Emperor's first cares was the restoration of the finances of the State. At the beginning of his reign he announced that 4,000,000,000 sesterces were needed to put the State once more on its feet.[2] Such was the cost of Nero's extravagance and a year of civil war ; the frontier defences, too, had to be put in order again, and the damage in Rome and Italy repaired. And so in A.D. 73 Vespasian assumed the censorship and held a census. He restored taxes remitted by Galba and he increased the tribute payable by the provinces, in some cases even doubling it. He is said to have stooped to the most discreditable methods of raising money, even to the sale of offices, but there is little reason to believe this last charge. At the same time he regulated carefully all expenditure and in the interests of economy he reorganized the administration ; in particular, he made changes in the management of the lands owned both by the State and by the Emperor, all of which he placed under imperial control. To such measures is due his reputation for ' parsimonia ', recorded by Suetonius and echoed by Gibbon— ' strict and even sordid parsimony '. Yet much economy was imperative if the Empire was to survive, and for his thriftiness and wise management Vespasian deserves all credit. So successful was he that he was able to spend money on the rebuilding and adornment of Rome, and he left a full treasury at his death. Even Suetonius admits that ' male partis optime usus est '.[3]

---

[1] Mommsen, *Ges. Schr.* vi. p. 36, and Rostovtzeff, *Social and Economic History*, p. 590, n. 8, take the view that Italians ceased to be recruited. H. M. Parker, *The Roman Legions*, p. 178, considers this too sweeping a statement.

[2] Suet. *Vesp.* 16.   [3] *Ibid.*

Buildings. The most important works for which Vespasian was responsible were (i) the temple to Capitoline Jupiter, destroyed in the struggle between the Flavian and the Vitellian parties; the rebuilding was not finished till the time of Domitian; (ii) a temple to Peace (A.D. 75), a goddess for whom Vespasian showed special veneration. The most famous of his buildings was (iii) the Colosseum, a vast amphitheatre between the Caelian and the Esquiline hills, which was begun by Vespasian and finished by Titus or Domitian. It was designed to hold 87,000 spectators, and its ruins may still be seen. Not only was Rome, the city, rising again from the dust in which she had been laid, but the very buildings were to be the token of the new life to which the Empire was called; ' Roma resurgens ' was the legend on some of the coins of Vespasian, and it aptly expresses the significance of his reign.

Political and Social Changes. Army reforms, financial stability, Rome rebuilt—these are among the least of Vespasian's achievements. The fame of his rule rests rather on (i) the change from diarchy to monarchy which he initiated, (ii) the new social conditions dating from his reign, (iii) his interest in the provinces and his liberal treatment of them; in this he set an example which was followed by every Emperor for at least the next hundred years.

The Diarchy Abandoned. The fiction of the diarchy had been wearing somewhat thin, for the successors of Augustus had not the patience, even if they had the skill, to keep up the pretence of a partnership between Princeps and Senate. Further, one of the partners, the Senate, had decreased in numbers as it had deteriorated in character; the persecutions of Tiberius, Caligula and Nero,[1] together with the losses of the civil wars, had wiped out whole families of the old aristocracy. It was easier, therefore, for Vespasian to fling aside the remaining concealments and to reveal the Principate as autocracy undisguised.

Vespasian held the consulship each year of his reign with the exception of the years A.D. 73 and 78. This was a reversal of the policy of the Julio-Claudian Emperors who held the office rarely. Augustus had seen that the tenure of the

[1] Cf. Tac. *Ann.* iii. 55, ' caedibus saevitum et magnitudo famae exitio'.

highest magistracy made him unpopular with the Senate, and since 23 B.C. he had held it only twice. Vespasian, however, not only held the office himself, but in his reign he caused his son Titus to be appointed no less than six times. But more significant still is Vespasian's use of the censorship. In Republican days this was a magistracy of great power and dignity, for the censors took charge of the roll of the Senate ; they could give and take away membership, and could exercise a general control over the morals of the State (*regimen morum*). When Sulla legislated to make the Senate supreme, this was the office which he tried to render powerless ; conversely, Vespasian, wishing to control the Senate, found the censorship the most useful weapon to his hand. Augustus refused the office, though he had on occasion taken ' censorial power ' ; Claudius in his love for ancient forms and dignities had made himself censor, but it was a step unpopular in aristocratic circles. The Flavian Emperors had no scruple in the matter, and Vespasian set the example by holding the office from A.D. 73 to the end of his reign.

Change in the Character of the Nobility. By virtue of his censorial powers he revised the roll of the Senate and admitted new members. He chose them, however, from a new class —the municipal aristocracy of Italy and the Western provinces.[1] The *municipia* had long been training men in local government and had sent others to seek a career in the ranks of the equites ; in both ways they had performed a valuable service to the State, and in return the doors of the Senate were thrown open to them. Thus Vespasian completed the process, begun by Julius Caesar and continued by Claudius,[2] of making the Senate represent the provinces. In its results the policy was justified, for this new class provided the material for the good government of the next century. It owed its existence to the Emperor, and was therefore more likely to respect his wishes ; this feeling of loyalty, together with the absence of traditional prejudices, made it an excellent source for the supply of devoted public servants. The old

[1] Suet. *Vesp*. 9. ' Amplissimos ordines exhaustos varia caede . . . supplevit . . . honestissimo Italicorum et provincialium allecto.'
[2] Tac. *Ann*. xi. 23.

families, then, were dwindling away ; at the Emperor's command a new aristocracy came into being ; the diarchy was almost dead.

The Social Effects. No less striking than the political significance of the change are its social effects. By drawing the new nobility from the middle classes Vespasian went some distance in setting a new standard of life in the capital. The new senators had less money to spend and fewer tastes to gratify ; ' in senatum . . . domesticam parsimoniam intulerunt '.[1] Since they owed their position to the Emperor, they were ready to follow his lead in matters social as well as political. Vespasian himself was a man of simple habits ; coming from a small hill town, he was appalled at the tradition of luxury and licence predominant in senatorial and imperial circles. With him as example a reaction set in ; ostentation became bad form and morals became purer. Society became healthier, for everywhere new blood was obtaining power and recognition.

Reconstruction of Spain.[2] No province received greater attention from Vespasian than Spain, and none was worthier of it. Here Roman civilization had been steadily increasing, particularly in Baetica, and the new Emperor was quick to recognize the importance of the province, and was statesman enough to see what was owing to it. To the whole peninsula he gave Latin rights and all that they implied. By those rights the larger communities throughout Spain were empowered to organize themselves as Roman *municipia*. The larger villages became towns, attracting to themselves an increased population from the neighbouring hamlets ; more than fifty new towns were thus created. Besides this the older townships were reorganized—' urbes renovatae cultu egregio '[3] : we know that over three hundred and fifty municipal charters were authorized under Vespasian, though many were not actually issued till Domitian's reign. We possess two lengthy fragments of two such charters, issued for the towns of Malaca and Salpensa, and to them we owe much of our information about the municipal organization of the

---

[1] Tac. *Ann.* iii. 55.

[2] This paragraph is largely derived from articles by Prof. McElderry in *J.R.S.* viii. (1918) and ix. (1919).   [3] Victor, *Caes.* ix. 8.

early Empire (p. 342). Here it is enough to say that by Latin rights the door was opened to the full Roman franchise ; Latin became the recognized official language throughout the province, and therefore tended to be used in trade and everyday intercourse ; Roman customs penetrated into remote corners, and Roman institutions were copied in every small township. The Spaniards felt that they were in some measure being taken into partnership with the ruling race.

Besides bestowing political privilege, Vespasian took other steps to secure the welfare of Spain. Roads were built to link up the new towns and to facilitate trade ; boundaries were regulated and taxes adjusted. Agriculture and industry prospered ; oil, wine, wheat and esparto grass were exported in large quantities. But more important was the output from the mines of lead, tin, copper, silver and gold : ' what Peru and Mexico were to Medieval Spain, Spain was herself to the Roman world '. It is very probable that Vespasian in his anxiety to fill the imperial treasury in some way reorganized the administration of the mines. Two important fragments of bronze tablets give us some idea of the organization of the mining village of Vipasca at this time. The mine was in imperial ownership, but was leased out to a company—*conductores*—who paid royalties to the extent of half the ore produced. Both free and slave labour were employed. In this *lex metalli* there are clauses regulating the conditions of life and labour which were to be provided for the workers by the *conductores*. Baths, laundries, shoemakers, barbers had to be supplied for the village, while schoolmasters were encouraged by being given exemption from tax. Safeguards against exploitation and overcharges are not forgotten ; indeed the whole document shows the extreme care with which the government considered the well-being of the miners.

Finally the crown was placed on the work of civilization in Spain by the establishment of the imperial worship at Corduba in Baetica, where a temple was built to ' Rome and Augustus ' and an annual festival founded. The cult had already spread in the more northerly districts earlier in the century ; but the southern district, that is to say the more

Romanized, now laid aside its scruples and accepted Caesar-worship as 'a symbol of unity and a test of loyalty' to the Imperial system.

Reorganization of the Eastern Frontier. The wars of Nero in the East had led to no great change in the system of frontier defence. The safety of this Eastern frontier from Zeugma to the Black Sea (about 300 miles) depended on the good-will of the vassal princes of Commagene and Lesser Armenia ; between these two states lay the procuratorial province of Cappadocia, unarmed except for local troops. If a hostile attack were directed against any point of this long line, the legions would have to be summoned from Syria, as had happened in the campaigns of Corbulo. Vespasian was not satisfied. In A.D. 72 he deposed the princes of Commagene and Lesser Armenia. Commagene was added to the province of Syria. The governor of Syria was now made responsible for the defence of Zeugma and Samosata, at both of which places there were important crossings over the Euphrates into Northern Mesopotamia. He was relieved, however, of the care of maintaining order in Judaea, for this troublesome country was now placed under the control of a legate in charge of a legion (legio X Fretensis) garrisoned at Jerusalem. Lesser Armenia and Cappadocia were annexed to the area admin-istered by the Governor of Galatia (an arrangement which continued to Trajan's reign), and both countries received legionary troops. In Cappadocia the XII Fulminata (and perhaps the XVI Flavia firma) went into permanent quarters at Melitene, where there was another famous ford across the river, while in Lesser Armenia the XV Apollinaris at Satala guarded northern Asia Minor from the menace of the Cauca-sian tribes, especially the Alans, who were already threatening the trouble which they later gave. Thus at last the Eastern frontier was made secure, not by the precarious loyalty of native princes, but by the strength of legionary camps.[1]

---

[1] B. W. Henderson, *Five Roman Emperors*, p. 60, believes that the XVI Flavia firma was stationed at Samosata ; but this is doubtful. See *J.R.S.* xvii. (1927), p. 121. The camp at Satala cannot with cer-tainty be attributed to Vespasian ; it may have been built by Trajan or Hadrian.

Titus as Consort. Vespasian was fully aware, as has been said, that one of the main weaknesses of the Principate lay in the lack of any theory of succession. He took particular care, therefore, to mark out Titus as his successor.[1] He made him his consort in the Empire. For this there was the precedent of Augustus and Tiberius, Galba and Piso. But more important privileges were granted to Titus than had been granted to Tiberius or Piso. Not only was he invested with the proconsular imperium and tribunician power, but he was also appointed Prefect of the Praetorian Guard.[2] It will be remembered that this powerful office had already constituted a grave danger to the Principate, a danger which Vespasian hoped to remove by conferring the office on his son. In addition, Titus was generally his father's colleague in the consulship[3] and in the censorship. Thus Vespasian closely associated Titus with his own position. It is suggested by Suetonius that Titus rendered his father valuable assistance in the duties of State. This may be so, but there is little doubt that Vespasian's motive in this partnership was to secure the succession for his son, and he did not fail. His relations with his other son, Domitian, will be referred to later (p. 175).

Opposition to Vespasian. Though Vespasian's policy at home and abroad shows that he possessed a broad and liberal outlook, it met with much opposition. Julius Caesar and Claudius had encountered severe criticism and secret ridicule when they extended political privilege to provincials, and the same hostility had to be faced by Vespasian. The remnants of the old aristocracy felt that their monopoly of privilege was being destroyed, and they resented being made to sit side by side in the Senate House with new patricians of obscure family and no tradition. Also, there still remained a few nobles who in spite of the unmistakable signs of the times threw longing glances back to the Republic. Prominent

[1] Cf. his saying, ' Either my son shall succeed me or no other ' (Suet. *Vesp.* 25).
[2] According to Suet. *Titus*, 6, Titus conducted himself in this office ' aliquanto incivilius et violentius '.
[3] Every year of Vespasian's reign except A.D. 73 and 78.

among these was Helvidius Priscus, the son-in-law of Paetus Thrasea, notorious in the reign of Nero (p. 111). Though he held office he refused to co-operate in working the constitution as now established; he greeted Vespasian in public as an equal, and published a propagandist pamphlet, entitled *In Praise of Cato*. Vespasian banished him, and then issued orders for his death, which later he tried unsuccessfully to avert. He also expelled from Rome the numerous vagrant philosophers, Stoic and Cynic; only Musonius Rufus the Stoic was spared; in his opinions he was not so virulent as the rest, some of whom continued to pour forth their invectives from their lonely places of exile. The Emperor was urged to silence them once for all; ' I will not kill a dog that barks at me ', he said.

But there was more than mere noisy barking in the diatribes and lectures of these philosophers; otherwise they would have been ignored by Vespasian, who was not anxious to proceed to extreme measures; the necessity of pronouncing sentence of death always gave him sorrow.[1] It is probable that there were many who denounced not the Principate itself—for at this time only a few fanatics seriously believed that the Republic could be restored—but the principle of hereditary succession which Vespasian was endeavouring to establish. They were obsessed by the Stoic ideal of Kingship, namely, the rule of the best man chosen from an aristocracy of the educated; these would be his friends and his counsellors, and on his death they would elect the best of themselves to succeed him. This was propaganda which Vespasian was not likely to tolerate; he condemned, says Suetonius, no innocent person, in spite of the fact that plots were constantly formed against him; of these, however, we have little knowledge.[2] But such a theory of the Principate exerted increasing influence, as we shall see later (p. 232).

Death of Vespasian. For ten years Vespasian as Emperor served the State well; he died at the age of sixty-nine (A.D. 79). His grim humour served him to the last. ' Methinks

[1] Suet. *Vesp.* 15.
[2] See Dio, lxvi. 16, for the plots of Marcellus, a consular, and Caecina Alienus, the old Vitellian general.

I am becoming a god,' he exclaimed as the first pains of his illness seized him. He was in Campania, whence he travelled to his farm at his native Reate, the cradle of his race, in which nothing had been changed.[1] There to the end he attended to State business. On his couch he was giving audience when he felt the approach of death. He struggled to his feet. 'An Emperor should die standing,' he cried, and fell back into the arms of his attendants. Titus succeeded to the Empire.

THE REIGN OF TITUS

Early Life. Born in A.D. 39 [2] close to Septizonium in a small and dingy room, which in Suetonius' time was still shown to visitors as the birthplace of an Emperor, Titus was educated at the palace with Britannicus as his companion. He saw military service in Germany and Britain, before accompanying his father to Judaea. Here he fell in love with Berenice, the sister of Agrippa, who returned with him on his triumphal return to Rome. Public feeling, however, proved too strong against a Jewess as lover of the Emperor's consort, and Titus was compelled to send her away from Rome, 'invitus invitam '.

Accession and Character. On the death of Vespasian Titus took his place without opposition. He had been marked out for the honour in no uncertain way (p. 169), and with the memory of the civil wars still fresh in their memory most men were no doubt thankful that there was a successor ready to hand. Nor was the new Emperor unpopular; he had won the affection of the legions in the East; he was handsome and well endowed with charm of manner and with intelligence.[3] At the same time there may have been a strain of cruelty or harshness beneath his outward graces, and some men divined that, like Nero, he would begin well and end badly. But his brief reign is little more than a record of his extravagant

[1] Suet. *Vesp.* 2, ' locum incunabulorum assidue frequentavit, manente villa qualis fuerat olim'.   [2] Or A.D. 37.

[3] Suet. *Titus*, 3, 'in puero statim corporis animique dotes exsplenduerunt magisque ac magis deinceps per aetatis gradus'. Among other accomplishments he could equal his shorthand writers in speed, and could imitate any signature !

expenditure on games and shows, while two calamities, a fire and an eruption, helped him to gratify his natural generosity, and so to increase the popularity which he anxiously sought.

Buildings, Games and Shows. The great amphitheatre, the Colosseum, begun by Vespasian, was finished and dedicated in this reign or early in the next. Close by, the so-called Thermae of Titus were built and their completion was celebrated by games and shows on the most stupendous scale. In such matters, says Suetonius, Titus was studious to gratify not his own but the people's taste ; at any rate gladiatorial combats and the slaughter of all manner of wild beasts were not enough. A naval battle was contrived in the flooded theatre, and pretended Corcyraeans and Corinthians enacted again the battle-scenes of Thucydides' narrative. Among the vast audience tickets were scattered which entitled the bearers to receive gold, horses, mules, food and even slaves from the Emperor's treasury.

Fire in Rome ; Eruption of Vesuvius. Some part, however, of Titus' expenditure was better justified. In A.D. 80 a pestilence broke out in Rome, and a great fire raged for three days, destroying the new temple of Jupiter Capitolinus and damaging other public buildings, among them the Pantheon and the Thermae of Agrippa ; there was some loss of life and many private houses were burnt. The Emperor vowed that none should suffer but himself ; he sold imperial furniture to relieve the suffering and to restore the buildings. In A.D. 79 occurred the famous eruption of Vesuvius, when Pompeii and Herculaneum and other parts of Campania were buried beneath the lava, to reveal to us after patient excavation a vivid picture of Greek life in a Campanian city. Of the eruption itself we have a wonderful description given by Pliny the Younger in two letters [1] which he sent to Tacitus, hoping that they would contain information useful for the history of his own times which he was writing. The first letter describes how his uncle, Pliny the Elder, who commanded the fleet at Misenum, met his death in the eruption. Compelling curiosity made him cross the Bay of Naples to examine more closely a cloud of strange shape which hung

[1] *Ep.* vi. 16, 20. Dio's account is very fanciful.

over the mountain's summit. Even as he approached the shore, ashes and red-hot stones fell upon the vessel; undismayed he reached a friend's villa at Stabiae where he restored confidence to the panic-stricken servants and with amazing calmness prepared to spend the night. But the storm of ashes increased, and repeated earthquakes drove the party from the house; in the open the fumes became suffocating, and, when day returned, his body was found on the shore uninjured. The second letter, less interesting perhaps, gives the younger Pliny's account of the eruption as he saw it from safety in Misenum.

For the relief of distress and suffering Titus took every measure he could. He appointed a commission of distinguished men for the purpose—*curatores reipublicae restituendae*—and placed resources at their disposal; he showed, says his biographer, not only the anxiety due from an Emperor, but also the sympathetic feeling of a father.

Titus' Waste of Public Money. Titus' generosity found a field not only in shows and schemes of public assistance, but also in excessive open-handedness to his friends. 'No one should leave the Emperor's presence disappointed,' he is reported to have said. Recollecting one evening that he had bestowed no gift, 'My friends,' he said, 'I have lost this day,' a saying which Suetonius says became deservedly famous. But public funds could ill afford such extravagance; the money accumulated by Vespasian's economy was wasted, and, as we shall see, Domitian was driven to plunder the rich families to make amends for his brother's recklessness. Titus might earn his title as 'amor ac deliciae generis humani', but it was well for the Empire that his reign was so brief.

His Death. Titus' health had long been feeble. He had tried every remedy suggested by doctor or priest without result. He bitterly lamented his bodily weakness, and protested to the gods that he did not deserve to die. But no treatment and no prayer availed, and in September A.D. 81 he died in his forty-second year at Reate after a brief reign of two years and two months. He left no son; he had made it clear, however, that Domitian was to succeed him, and no one disputed the succession.

BEFORE Titus had drawn his last breath, Domitian was riding in haste to Rome to claim the Empire. Arriving there he offered to the Praetorians the same donative which his brother had bestowed on them. The Praetorians at once declared him Emperor, and from that day—the 13th September, A.D. 81—he dated his tribunician years and his reign.

The Bias of our Authorities against Domitian. No Emperor, not even Nero, has fared worse at the hands of our literary authorities than Domitian. The bitter eloquence of Tacitus' masterpiece, the *Agricola*, the rhetoric of Pliny, the invective of the Christian Church combine to give us a gruesome picture of his tyranny and to rob him of whatever merit he may have possessed. Tacitus' doctrinaire hatred of the Empire is reinforced by a blind championship of his father-in-law Agricola, who had been prevented, Tacitus thought, from reaching still greater military glory by the crafty jealousy of the Emperor. Pliny the Younger, adorning his consular oration in praise of Trajan with every extravagance, spares no pains in condemning Domitian in order to heighten the contrast with his successors. Yet Pliny owed his career to Domitian and received more than one kindness from him. The reasons for the Christians' hatred will be touched on in another chapter. Thus the hostile tradition has been perpetuated through the ages; it may on the whole be just, but recent research has done much to suggest that Domitian was by no means unworthy of imperial power, and one recent writer goes so far as to call him ' the greatest of the Flavians '. For he seems to have taken his position seriously; while he had perhaps an exaggerated notion of his own dignity, recent investigation would suggest that he really had at heart the welfare of Rome, Italy and the provinces, and that he had a keen insight into the problems of government and the needs of that ' vast bulk of Empire which ', in Galba's words as given by Tacitus, ' could not be kept in equilibrium without someone to guide it '.

Domitian's Earlier Life and Character. The circumstances
of Domitian's earlier life will in part explain his character;
the parallel between him and Tiberius is obvious to us, and
Domitian, too, seems to have felt some sympathy with his
predecessor, whose ' Acta ' were his favourite reading. As a
boy and a young man, he was possessed of an ambitious
nature which had been allowed to find no outlet. Before
Vespasian reached Rome, Domitian had received honour as
his father's representative; from that time he had been
given no opportunity to exercise influence. He found himself the son of the Emperor, but without power, and he retired
in sulky disappointment to his Alban villa, whence he saw
Titus, his brother, receiving honour and privilege as the
Emperor's consort. He begged for a command in the East
and was refused. Meantime he received mere external
honours—the laurel wreath and membership of sacred colleges
and consulships. When Vespasian died, Domitian perhaps
hoped to become the consul of his brother; again he was
disappointed, and his jealousy, even hatred, of his brother
increased. Yet Titus seems to have intended Domitian to
succeed him, for he proposed that Julia, his daughter, should
marry his brother. But two reasons prevented this : Domitian
himself had religious scruples on the matter of marriage
between uncle and niece, though such union had received
the sanction of the Emperor Claudius ; secondly, he seems
to have felt a real affection for his mistress Domitia, daughter
of Nero's general Corbulo, whom later he married. For
twelve years, then, Domitian had to be content with the
semblance of power ; he consoled himself with poetry and
literature, and improved his archery in which his skill was
wonderful. Meantime his ambition smouldered below the
surface ; and, revealing itself now and then, it gave rise,
doubtless, to the stories told by his biographer of plots against
the life and authority of his father and brother. Thus was
a naturally cruel and imperious nature soured in early years.
Vespasian had perhaps good reason for distrusting his son,
yet perhaps it would have been wise to give him a military
training in the provinces. Neither Nero nor Domitian, the
two most hated among the early Emperors, gained experience

in provincial administration before coming to power. Domitian had the Flavian gifts of practical intelligence and power of organization; it is possible that the discipline of a camp might have exercised profound influence on his character.

The End of the Diarchy. The reign of Domitian marks an important stage in the development of the Principate. The movement from diarchy to monarchy, which was begun by the later Julio-Claudians and accelerated by the first of the Flavians, was practically completed by Domitian. The imperial power henceforth was sheer absolutism. Yet the next five Emperors are among the best in the whole series; their moderate use of absolute power may be due partly no doubt to the weakening of the opposition, but partly also to the fact that their power was now revealed and was recognized as absolute.

Domitian's Offices. There was no time when the Emperor did not hold supreme military power; Domitian's innovations must be sought in the sphere of politics, and curiously enough, of religion. His attitude to the chief offices of State shows his contempt for the diarchy. For the first eight years of his reign he was consul each year, though he generally laid down the office after a fortnight and never held it after 1 May; towards the end of his reign he seems not to have held it so frequently. In his lifetime he was seventeen times consul, more often, that is, than any previous Emperor. Yet, though Domitian, as consul, generally gave his name to the year, ample opportunity was left to the aristocratic class to hold this office, which still conferred distinction. In fact, in the use of the consulship Domitian did not go very much further than Vespasian. But in the use of the censorship he went much further; Vespasian had held this office for several years, but he regarded it as a yearly office. Domitian became censor in September A.D. 85, and in the same year announced his intention of holding the office for life as *censor perpetuus*. Thus he made his control over entry into the senatorial class complete. But he used the censor's powers for other purposes also; his attempt to reform religion and morals by virtue of his powers as censor and as Pontifex

Maximus is one of the most curious features in his puzzling reign.

Domitian as Religious and Moral Reformer. Domitian approached the duties of these two offices in much the same spirit as Augustus ; not only was the city of Rome to be adorned with temples of a dignity worthy of the imperial capital, but also the morals and religious ceremonies of its citizens were to be restored to their former purity and grandeur. Temples of Jupiter Capitolinus and Jupiter Custos, of Janus and Castor and Apollo were rebuilt, and in particular the worship of Minerva, whom Domitian regarded as his own protecting deity, was encouraged. At the same time the spread of the Oriental cults was checked, though an exception was made in the interest of Isis, whom Domitian himself worshipped ; it was in the dress of a votary of this goddess that Domitian escaped in the storming of the Capitol, and perhaps in gratitude he allowed her cult to continue unhindered. In A.D. 88 the Secular Games were held, and commemorated on coins of the time ; they had already been celebrated by Augustus in 17 B.C. and again by Claudius in A.D. 47, though their founder had declared in solemn formula ' that no one had already seen them nor should see them again '.[1] It was due to his belief in the influence of religion on the State that Domitian punished with death three Vestal virgins who were guilty of unchastity ; he allowed them to choose their manner of death. A little later Cornelia, another Vestal who had been acquitted, was found guilty, and was punished by Domitian *more maiorum*, that is, she was buried alive in the Campus Sceleratus.[2] In the interest of morals and marriage Domitian revived certain regulations of the *leges Iuliae* of Augustus, and many men and women of noble family were condemned under them.

---

[1] ' Quos nec spectasset quisquam nec spectaturus esset ' (Suet *Claud.* 21).

[2] Suetonius seems to have no doubt about her guilt (*Dom.* 8) ; Pliny expends his indignation not on the barbarity of the penalty, but on the fact that Domitian tried the case in his Alban Villa instead of in the Regia, the official house of the Pontifex Maximus (Plin. *Ep.* iv. 11. 6). The custom was originally due to hesitation to kill one who was dedicated to the gods.

In the interest of family life he refused to accept legacies from testators who left children. He tried to check the immorality of theatrical shows, and he prohibited the publication of libellous pamphlets against men and women of rank. Also, he made some contribution to the series of measures passed in this century to prevent the cruel treatment of slaves.

The Title ' Dominus et Deus '. Domitian's autocratic use of censorial powers naturally embittered the noble families whose manner of life he presumed to correct. But bitterness was increased to hatred when the Emperor, whose mother, it was remembered, for a long time had not even Roman citizenship, suffered himself to be saluted as ' Dominus et Deus '. The title *Dominus*, which implied that all men were his subjects, he refused at first to accept in public, though the poets Statius and Martial frequently apply it to him. As for the title *Deus*, to a man of Domitian's temperament the acceptance of it naturally followed from the cult of the Emperors, which was well established. Vespasian and Titus, Flavia Domitilla, the daughter of Vespasian, and Domitian's own son had been deified at death ; Domitian, finding himself so closely related to so many *divi*, did not refuse the honour in his lifetime. Finally, the complete title *Dominus et Deus*, though not officially conferred, became customary ; the Emperor began an official letter with the phrase ' dominus et deus noster sic fieri iussit ', and henceforth in writing and in speech it became the normal mode of addressing him.

Domitian and the Senate ; Encroachment on Senatorial Functions. Vespasian, as has been seen, possessed a shrewd practical sense, and he passed on this gift to his son. The Flavian dynasty may have re-shaped the Principate on more monarchical lines, but the changes which were made were generally dictated by a desire for greater efficiency. Domitian, no less than his father, was anxious to organize and to administer the Empire well ; his work on the frontiers and his care for Rome, Italy and the provinces are evidence, as will be seen, of this aim. But his attempts to secure better administration brought him into conflict with the senatorial order which in theory shared with him the executive functions in the State. Vespasian, finding the Senate deficient in

numbers and capacity, tried to put new strength into it.
Domitian, utterly lacking his father's patience, determined
to ignore it, except in so far as he found individual senators
competent and loyal. At the beginning of his reign he
repressed mercilessly the activities of the *delatores* in the
belief that 'qui non castigat delatores irritat'. He was
asked to go further and to promise that he would put no
senator to death. Titus had acted on this principle, though
his brief reign made it easy for him ; but Domitian was not
the man to play so lightly into the hands of treason, and he
refused. Thus he increased the hostility of the Senate. He
appeared occasionally at its meetings, and at first seemed
anxious to win its approval ; but he gave offence by attending
in his triumphal robe and by voting first when a division was
taken. He deprived the Senate of the revenues of the aqueducts ; since, however, the fiscus paid the expenses of their
upkeep, there was some measure of justice in the change.
But he insulted the Senate mortally by giving membership of
the judicial *consilium* to certain representatives of the equestrian class. This meant that an eques might sit in judgment
on a senator, and senatorial feeling was naturally outraged.

Praefectus Urbi and Praefectus Praetorio. During the
first years at least of his reign Domitian availed himself of
men of experience and capacity, many of whom had served
Vespasian also ; 'Domitian was bad himself,' says a late
historian, 'but he had good friends.'[1] Pegasus, the famous
jurist, who had held several provincial posts, became Praefectus urbi under Vespasian and was retained in office by
Domitian. He was succeeded by Rutilius Gallicus whose
career was similar, and later by T. Aurelius Fulvus, grandfather of the Emperor Antoninus Pius ; all three were men of
humble origin.[2] The position of Praefectus urbi grew in
importance under the Flavians, and was filled henceforth by
an eminent lawyer able to fulfil its judicial duties, which now

---

[1] Hist. Aug. *Alex. Severi Vita*, 65.

[2] For Rutilius Gallicus, see Statius, *Silvae*, i. 4. 68, 'genus ipse suis
permissaque retro nobilitas'. The poem celebrates his restoration
to health, and gives an outline of the duties of the praefectus urbi
at this time.

extended beyond the walls of Rome. On the other hand, it was not to the Emperor's interest to increase the power of the Praefectus praetorio, who commanded the garrison in Rome. Vespasian for safety's sake entrusted the office to Titus; Domitian divided its duties between two knights whom he frequently changed.

The Growing Importance of the Knights. Besides being admitted to the Emperor's *consilium*, knights were increasingly employed in the great secretaryships of State— *a libellis, ab epistulis, a cognitionibus, a rationibus*—though freedmen did not cease to serve in this capacity. Domitian thus took an important step (though the idea was not new) [1] in transforming duties which originally were performed by members of the Emperor's household into the great and distinguished offices which they became. In this reign Titinius Capito was *ab epistulis*, and Pliny, whose friend he was, describes him as one of the great ornaments of literature at this time—'ipsarum denique literarum iam senescentium reductor ac reformator'.[2] The secretary, however, who is best known to us is Claudius, the father of the Claudius Etruscus to whom Statius addresses a poem of consolation on the death of his father.[3] As a freedman he held office under Claudius, and retained it till the time of Domitian. Vespasian raised him to equestrian rank; under Domitian he fell into disgrace for a reason unknown to us [4]; he was exiled, but later allowed to live in Campania.

Rebuilding of Rome. After Augustus no Emperor spent more thought or money on the rebuilding of Rome. The damage done by the fire in Nero's reign had not yet been fully repaired, and under Titus a conflagration had injured many of the public buildings on the Capitoline Hill and in the Campus Martius. To set his name to monuments and temples appealed to Domitian's love of self-display and he set to work to rebuild Rome on a lavish scale. Only a few of his buildings may be given here. The temple of Jupiter

---

[1] Vitellius began this change.   [2] Plin. *Ep.* i. 17; viii. 12.

[3] *Silvae*, iii. 3.

[4] *Ibid.* 154, 'seu tarda situ, rebusque exhausta senectus/erravit, seu blanda diu Fortuna regressum/maluit'.

Capitolinus cost according to Plutarch more than 12,000
talents ; the gates and roof were of gold, and it was adorned
with great Corinthian pillars of Pentelic marble, and shrines
of Jupiter Conservator and Jupiter Custos were built within
its precincts. Many years were spent on the building of a
vast palace on the Palatine Hill which was finished about
A.D. 92. ' Fessis vix culmina prendas visibus ' ; Statius and
Martial give an exaggerated description of it, and in spite
of its magnificence regard it as unworthy of its owner.[1] A
temple to Vespasian and Titus was dedicated about A.D. 87 ;
the Curia was rebuilt, and in its midst was set a huge equestrian statue of the Emperor in honour of his victories on
the Danube ; ' nec veris maiora putes ', says Statius, who
devotes the first of his *Silvae* to describing it and singing the
Emperor's praises. The Colosseum begun by Vespasian was
finished, perhaps, in this reign and the famous Arch of
Titus was erected by Domitian to record the destruction of
Jerusalem by his brother in A.D. 71. Statues of the Emperor
were placed in great numbers throughout the streets of Rome,
till they became a jest ; on one of them, says Suetonius,[2] a
daring hand wrote in Greek, ' Enough ! '

The Capitoline Games; Popular Amusements. No doubt
imitating the ' Neroneia ', Domitian founded the Capitoline
Games, first held in A.D. 86 and intended to be held every
five years. For the purpose he built in the Campus Martius
an Odeum in which musical and literary competitions took
place, and a Stadium and a circus for athletic contests.
Poets, orators, musicians and athletes were attracted to this
festival from long distances, and those who received from
the hand of the Emperor the oak-wreath which was the
badge of victory became famous throughout the Empire.
For the populace amusements of other kinds were also provided—distributions of food and gifts, chariot races, mimic
battles and sea-fights ; no expenditure of money or life was
spared to keep the people amused and contented. At the
same time Domitian spent in *congiaria* far less money than
was spent by his successors.

[1] Martial, viii. 36 ; Statius, *Silvae*, iv. 2. 18–31.
[2] Suet. *Dom.* 13.

Domitian's Care for Italy and the Provinces. The economic
condition of Italy must receive treatment in another chapter,
but mention may here be made of certain steps taken by the
Emperor in its interest. In the first place, he cancelled debts
due to the Treasury of over five years' standing. Next, he
renounced the claim of the State to the so-called *subseciva*.
These were plots of land which at the time of the foundation
of a colony had been unallotted either owing to their inconvenient shape or to the unattractive nature of the soil ;
by degrees they had been absorbed into existing holdings or
appropriated by new-comers. They belonged strictly to
the State, and Vespasian in his desire to fill the treasury had
proposed to sell them. This measure caused hardship to
their occupiers who regarded them as their own ; deputations
were sent to him to protest, and he delayed action. Titus
reasserted the State's claim. It was left for Domitian to
institute an inquiry, and finally to confirm the occupiers in
possession. By this one edict, says Frontinus, ' he freed the
whole of Italy from fear '.[1] Thirdly, towards the end of his
reign he repaired the Via Latina and built a new road to
Cumae from Sinuessa, where the Via Appia turns aside to
Capua. Statius devotes a whole poem to a description of
the building of this road, the Via Domitiana, which replaced
an older and a longer route.[2] An interesting experiment was
made also by Domitian in economic policy ; he tried to
reduce the cultivation of vines in Italy and the provinces
with a view to encouraging the growing of wheat ; but in
the last years of his reign he admitted failure and cancelled
his edict (p. 334).

With regard to the provinces, Suetonius says emphatically
that Domitian showed himself so diligent in supervising the
governors that they never showed themselves more loyal or
more just than in his reign. We know of many governors
of merit whom Domitian appointed, among them Iavolenus
Priscus, the lawyer, and Sextus Julius Frontinus. The
encouragement given to municipal life has already been

[1] *De Controv. Agr.* 54. Suet. *Dom.* 9.
[2] *Silvae*, iv. 3. 22, ' longos eximit ambitus ' ; and later (36), ' at nunc
quae solidum diem terebat/horarum via facta vix duarum '.

mentioned, and in this reign many provincials of note and ability began their careers which were to lead them to high positions ; under Domitian many of the consuls were of provincial origin—Trajan from Baetica, L. Licinius Sura from Tarraconensis, Marius Priscus from Spain, while Julius Quadratus, consul in A.D. 93 and governor of many provinces, was born at Pergamum. Attention was paid to the development of roads, particularly in the East, and to public works of many kinds.

In spite of good government, however, the provinces may have had their troubles ; a late historian says that revolts took place due to exactions of tribute by violent methods ; something at any rate is known of an expedition in A.D. 85 or 86 against the Nasamonians of Africa who revolted, it was said, for this reason, but little is to be inferred about the general state of Africa from the attitude of this wild tribe. Some momentary excitement was caused in the East by the appearance of a pretender to the Empire who claimed to be Nero himself ; but he was easily dealt with.[1] Speaking generally, it may be said that the provinces were happy under the rule of this Emperor, and regretted his murder.

The Revolt of Antonius. Much positive good therefore can be set down as due to the rule of Domitian. But his auto-cratic bearing gave much offence, and there were many plots against him, though they were not always easy to expose. 'Miserable is the lot of Emperors ', said Domitian himself, ' who only by their deaths can prove that their throne has been assailed.' Suspicious he always was ; but he was turned into a tyrant of calculating cruelty by the rebellion of L. Antonius Saturninus in A.D. 88–89.

Antonius was commander of the two legions—XIV Gemina Martia Victrix and XXI Rapax—stationed at Moguntiacum. A conspiracy had recently been suppressed in Rome with great severity, and Antonius perhaps wished to avail himself of the resulting fury and panic in senatorial circles in order to gratify his own hatred of the Emperor, who had presumed to rebuke him publicly for his depraved manner of life. He proclaimed himself Emperor. Now the Roman armies were

---

[1] Suet. *Nero*, 57 ; cf. Tac. *Hist.* ii. 8.

notoriously favourable to Domitian, but Antonius secured the services of his own two legions by a trick which scarcely increases his claim to our sympathy. He seized the savings-bank in which his legions had deposited their pay, recently increased by Domitian. He used the money to bribe the Chatti to take up arms in his cause, and his legions seem to have acquiesced in his rebellion as the best way of recovering their money. The other two legions of Upper Germany stationed at Vindonissa and Argentoratum (XI Claudia and VIII Augusta), remained loyal.

On hearing of the revolt Domitian at once sent orders to the Danube army and to the VII Gemina in Spain, commanded by Trajan, the future Emperor, to hurry to the scene of the revolt. He himself with some Praetorian Guards left Rome at the beginning of January A.D. 89. All three forces were too late. For Lucius Appius Maximus Norbanus, commander of four legions in Lower Germany, moved up the Rhine to deal with Antonius, who started from Moguntiacum to meet him. Meantime the Chatti had mustered on the bank of the Rhine, which they hoped to cross where and when they wished, since the river was frozen hard. Domitian's luck held better than the frost. The ice broke up on the day of the battle, the scene of which is unknown ; the Chatti were unable to cross, and Antonius was defeated and lost his life on the field.

Consequences of the Revolt. Domitian continued his journey to Mainz. He did not punish the disloyal legions, though one of them—the XXI Rapax—was transferred to Pannonia. The legions of Norbanus were honoured by the title ' pia fidelis Domitiana ', but the last of these words was dropped after Domitian's memory was officially condemned. Domitian ordered that no soldier should have more than 1,000 sesterces in the military chest. More important, he abolished ' double ' camps, that is to say, camps containing more than one legion, and he reorganized Upper and Lower Germany. Hitherto for civil purposes both divisions of Germany had been under the control of the governor of Gallia Belgica, though the legati of the armies had enjoyed military independence. Henceforth the legati of Upper and Lower Germany became civil

and military governors. In A.D. 90 Iavolenus Priscus became
consular legate of Upper Germany, and the choice of an
eminent lawyer probably signifies that in Domitian's view the
German frontier was unlikely to give trouble in future and
that the province was ripe for the development of civil life.

But the result of the rebellion on Domitian was disastrous ;
the remaining seven years of his reign, though marked by
the same efficiency in administration, were devoted to a
relentless persecution of all who incurred his suspicion.

The Reign of Terror. Domitian's anger was directed chiefly
against the nobles and the philosophers. He had no evidence,
however, as to who was implicated in Antonius' plot, for
Norbanus is said to have destroyed whatever papers he found
in the rebel's camp.[1] He resorted therefore to the use of
spies and *delatores*, whom earlier in his reign he had dis-
couraged. 'Slaves gave evidence against their masters,
freedmen against patrons, and those who had no enemy were
ruined by their friends.'[2] We know the names and histories
of many of the informers. Marcus Aquilius Regulus began
his dishonourable career in Nero's time ; left penniless at
his father's exile, he accumulated a large fortune and an
evil reputation by his successful prosecutions.[3] Another
delator was Catullus Messalinus, a blind member of a noble
family, who became one of Domitian's most dangerous
weapons.[4] Mettius Carus made a fine art of his profession,
and attempted to establish a monopoly in it. Fabricius
Veiento, though he cringed in front of Domitian,[5] was feared
by all who had anything to lose. In a powerful paragraph
Tacitus describes the terror and havoc which they caused
—' tot consularium caedes, tot nobilissimarum feminarum

[1] This story may be untrue, for it is told also of Martius Verus in
the reign of Marcus Aurelius (Dio, lxxi. 29).

[2] Tac. *Hist*. i. 2.

[3] Pliny hated him both as a *delator* and as an orator. He was called
' omnium bipedum nequissimus ' by Mettius Modestus (Plin. *Ep*. i.
5. 14). Senecio, parodying Cato's definition of an orator, said of him
' orator est vir malus dicendi imperitus '.

[4] Pliny, *Ep*. iv. 22. 5. 'A Domitiano non secus ac tela, quae et
ipsa caeca et improvida feruntur, in optimum quemque contorquebatur.'

[5] Juv. iv. 123.

exilia et fugas '.[1] The Senate dared not refuse to condemn its own members, for Domitian usually made a show of giving his victims a formal trial. The Senate was paralysed with terror ; ' Nero withdrew his eyes : he commanded his terrors, he did not watch them : it was chief part of our misery under Domitian to see and to be seen ; our sighs were recorded against us '.[1] . . . Dio believes that Agricola, who died in August A.D. 93, was poisoned by order of Domitian ; Tacitus professes ignorance, but suggests that the Emperor's freedmen took an unusual interest in Agricola's illness. The two victims whose deaths perhaps caused most horror were Flavius Sabinus and Flavius Clemens, both cousins of the Emperor. Sabinus was condemned for *maiestas*, and Clemens and his wife were both condemned on the charge of having embraced a foreign religion,[2] though no doubt suspicion of treason was the real motive. Professed Stoics were naturally suspect, and the Senate solemnly passed a decree expelling philosophers and astrologers from Italy, Epictetus and Dio Chrysostom among them. Herennius Senecio had written a pamphlet in praise of Helvidius Priscus, who had been put to death by Vespasian ; Mettius Carus was ready with the necessary information, and Senecio was condemned to death. Fannia, Thrasea's daughter and Priscus' widow, had furnished Senecio with some of the material for his panegyric, and was exiled for doing so. Arulenus Rusticus went to the same end for a similar pamphlet. A famous actor, Paris, was believed to be guilty of an intrigue with Domitia, the Emperor's wife ; she was divorced and subsequently pardoned ; Paris was murdered in the streets of Rome, and mourned by an admiring people.

Confiscations of Property. 'His virtues he turned into vices,' says Suetonius of Domitian, ' through poverty he became rapacious, through fear merciless.' He had never stinted money to provide games for the populace ; he had raised the pay of the soldiers ; his wars and his public works had cost much ; in spite of these expenses the public treasury was full. But confiscation of property was the best way to weaken the senatorial opposition. The riches of his victims

[1] Tac. *Agr*. 45.   [2] Which may have been Christianity (p. 305).

went to replenish his private purse ; and those who survived attempted to stave off death by ample legacy to the Emperor.[1] Wills were forged and witnesses were bribed. Laws of Augustus which prohibited that legacies should be left to the unmarried or the childless were revived and strictly applied. As in the case of death sentences, so in confiscation a semblance of legality was preserved : ' the State, which is based on the laws, was destroyed by the laws themselves '.[2] And to rapacity and murder Domitian added a cruel cynicism. In the course of a trial he invited the Senate to show its love for him ; it responded by condemning the accused men to be beaten to death. Domitian interposed ; he begged that they might at least be allowed to choose the manner of their death [3] ; ' thus all men will know that I was present at this meeting of the Senate '. An amazing story is told by Dio of his cold-blooded cruelty. ' Having once made a great feast for the citizens, he proposed to follow it up with an enter-tainment to a select number of the nobility. He fitted up an apartment all in black. The ceiling was black, the walls were black, the pavement was black, and upon it were ranged rows of bare stone seats, black also. The guests were intro-duced at night without their attendants, and each might see at the head of his couch a column placed, like a tombstone, on which his own name was graven, with the cresset lamp above it, such as is suspended in the tombs. Presently there entered a troop of native boys, blackened, who danced around with horrid movements, and then stood still before them. offering them the fragments of food which are commonly presented to the dead. The guests were paralysed with terror, expecting at every moment to be put to death : and the more, as the others maintained a deep silence, as though they were dead themselves, and Domitian spake of things pertaining to the state of the departed only.' [4] Such were the tales told when Dio wrote—a hundred years and more after Domitian's death. It is impossible to deny that in the last years of his reign Domitian was rapacious and cruel—' immanissima belua ', says Pliny ; but his rapacity was

---

[1] Tac. *Agr.* 43.   [2] Plin. *Pan.* 34.
[3] Suet. *Dom.* 11.   [4] Dio, lxvii. 9, Merivale's translation.

directed against his enemies of the senatorial class, and was not inspired by any necessity to fill an exhausted treasury ; indeed it is later made a charge against him that his 'avaritia' was superfluous and unnecessary.[1]

The Murder of Domitian. Finally Domitian put to death Epaphroditus, one of Nero's freedmen, on the ground, it is said, that he had helped Nero to kill himself. But Domitian may have had suspicions that he was meditating treason, and Dio gives a pathetic picture of the Emperor in his last months, ever consulting astrologers and reading into every prophecy a menace to his life and power. At last his own household felt themselves insecure ; Domitia is said to have found some notes written by her husband in which she was marked out for death. His own wife and his servants conspired against him ; Parthenius, a chamberlain, arranged the plot. He contrived that the Emperor should give audience to Stephanus, a steward to Domitilla and under accusation for embezzlement, who promised to reveal a conspiracy to him. Domitian, reclining upon a couch, received him, and was at once stabbed in the groin by a dagger hidden beneath a bandage which his attacker wore on his left arm, pretending that it had suffered injury. Domitian leaped to his feet and grappled resolutely, calling to a boy who was in the room to give him the dagger concealed under his pillow ; nothing but the hilt was there, so well had Stephanus taken his precautions. The struggle continued, till Parthenius' servants rushed in and the Emperor fell stabbed with seven wounds (18 September, A.D. 96). His corpse was carried out on a common bier by hired servants and cremated by Phyllis, his nurse ; his ashes she placed in the shrine of the Flavian family.

The Succession. Like his father before him Domitian gave much thought to the question of his successor. His son, born in A.D. 73, died young, and seventeen years later his hopes of an heir were disappointed.[2] He turned his thoughts to the two small boys of Flavius Clemens, his cousin, and Domitilla, and entrusted their education to Quintilian. But in A.D. 95 he killed their father, and we do not know what happened to the boys.

[1] See *J.R.S.* xx. (1), 1930, p. 55 *seqq.*   [2] Martial, v. 3.

But the conspirators had already decided upon a successor, and their choice, M. Cocceius Nerva, had expressed his willingness to accept the Empire. The Senate, some of whom may have been privy to the plot, were overjoyed at the ' tyrant's ' murder [1]; a decree abolished his memory, and orders were given that his statues should be broken in pieces and his name erased from all inscriptions. His death was accepted with indifference by the people ; the Praetorians, however, were enraged, and were with difficulty prevented from punishing the murderers and nominating an Emperor ; but they lacked leaders, for their two prefects had been induced to join the conspirators. In Syria and on the Danube there were threatened mutinies, which however came to nothing. The army as a whole sullenly acquiesced for the moment.[2] And so ' in the eight hundred and fiftieth year from the foundation of the city, in the consulship of Vetus and Valens, the State returned to a time of utmost prosperity, having the singular luck of being entrusted to good Emperors '.[3] But further research will probably show that Domitian, in spite of the many stories against him, deserves to be regarded as one of the most capable administrators who ever occupied the throne of the Caesars. His work on the Northern frontier, described in the next chapter, goes far to bear this out.

CHAPTER XIII

THE NORTHERN FRONTIER UNDER THE FLAVIANS AND TRAJAN'S DACIAN WARS

*A*NNEXATION *of the Agri Decumates, A.D. 73.* Under the Julio-Claudian Emperors the defences of the Upper Rhine had received slight attention (p. 154). The tribes on the upper stretches of the Rhine and the Danube had given little trouble, and the Romans had been content to leave them unprovoked while the problems of the Lower Rhine and Britain claimed their attention and their armies.

---

[1] Plin. *Pan.* 52.
[2] Its acquiescence is strange ; perhaps a generous donative (unrecorded) is the explanation. [3] Eutrop. viii. 1.

With the victory of Vespasian the danger from the Rhine
seemed to have passed away, and the opportunity was taken
to reorganize the frontier system between the upper courses
of the two rivers.

The work done by the Flavian Emperors in these regions
was of the greatest importance, though it is only lately that
this has been realized. The literary authorities tell us
nothing ; the writers of the day were not likely to celebrate
the achievements, military or otherwise, of a Flavian Emperor.
What we know of the Flavian work on Rhine or Danube is
due to long and patient study of archaeological evidence.

A glance at the map will show one obvious feature of the
northern frontier. The Rhine after flowing west from Lake
Constance for about 70 miles turns sharply north and makes
with the Danube a triangle of territory which includes what
is now the Black Forest. This territory, which the Romans
called the Agri Decumates or Decumani (a name of which
no satisfactory explanation has been given), was thinly
inhabited ; no one knew to whom it belonged ; it was, as
Tacitus says, 'dubiae possessionis solum'.[1] In A.D. 73
Vespasian sent a force to annex it. We do not know his
motive ; he may have wished to straighten out the frontier
for strategic reasons, and to join up by roads the Rhine and
the Danube defences ; he may have wished to find a new
source of revenue, or land for his veterans. Nor do we know
any details about the advance ; an inscription tells us that
the legate of Upper Germany, Cornelius Clemens, was in charge,
and there may have been some little fighting. Slowly the
frontier was pushed forward ; fortresses were planted to be
replaced by others as Roman influence spread further north
towards the sources of the Neckar ; and where soldiers were
stationed, civil communities in time sprang up. How far the
advance had reached by the time of Vespasian's death it is
impossible to say ; perhaps a line drawn from Strasbourg
to Lake Constance will give some indication, but it must be
made to curve north somewhat so as to include Rottweil,
for here a centre of Caesar-worship was early established ;
and it is possible that the Vespasianic frontier included Baden,

[1] *Germ.* 29.

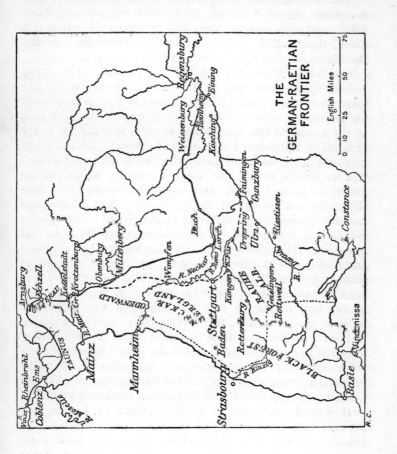

THE
GERMAN-RAETIAN
FRONTIER

English Miles
0 10 25 50 75

close to the Rhine, and Geislingen, east of the Neckar, joining up with the Danube as far north as Günzburg.

Simultaneous with this advance on the south an advance was made east of the Rhine between Strasbourg and Mannheim ; outposts and fortresses can be traced the whole way along, though they were abandoned as Domitian absorbed the Neckarbergland and the Odenwald.

Domitian's Expedition against the Chatti, A.D. 83–4. Domitian's ambition was to show himself to the world as a victorious general, and opportunity was not long delayed after his accession. The Chatti, a wild German tribe [1] dwelling in the forests of the Taunus region, were well known to the Romans in the past. From this tribe Roman soldiers taken prisoners in the defeat of Varus were recovered by a vigorous Roman general in A.D. 50 ; even so recently as A.D. 69 the Chatti, in company with other warlike tribes, had laid siege to the Roman military station of Moguntiacum (Mainz) and had withdrawn unmolested with their plunder. But now at last in A.D. 83 the Roman Government gave them its full attention. The tribe was already in arms and had attacked and burnt some Roman outposts on the German bank of the Rhine, opposite Moguntiacum, where Roman influence was steadily penetrating. Domitian started in person for the Rhine, but, hoping to take the tribesmen unprepared, he let it be known that he was leaving Rome to hold a census in Gaul ; at the same time he sent a bribe to the Cherusci intended to induce them to attack the Chatti, who were their neighbours and ancient enemies. Meantime at Mainz he gathered a strong army composed of the four legions of Upper Germany (I Adjutrix and XIV Gemina stationed at Mainz, VIII Augusta at Strasbourg, XI Claudia at Vindonissa), together with some praetorian cohorts ; a considerable force was sent also from Britain (certainly from the IX Hispana and perhaps from all four legions), and this weakening of the troops in Britain may have been the reason for Agricola's abandonment of his design to overrun Caledonia (p. 285).

Of the details of the campaign little is known ; such fragments of information as we have are derived chiefly from the

[1] *Germ.* 30.

Strategemeta of Sextus Julius Frontinus, who probably served as a general in it. Enough to say that Domitian slowly pushed back the Chatti into the forests of the Taunus, till at last they broke up and disappeared into the wilder country behind them. Then it was that the Emperor traced a new frontier line of 120 miles—' limitibus per centum viginti milia passuum actis '—though where precisely these miles are to be measured is uncertain. Perhaps a line from Rheinbrohl round the north of the Taunus and south to Kesselstadt will indicate what Frontinus meant, though Domitian's work of extending the frontier by no means ended here. At any rate forts were built in the newly acquired territory and joined by roads to Mainz where the legions were stationed, ready to bring help to any point of the new frontier which might be threatened. Thus was Roman civilization established on the right bank of the Rhine.

Domitian's Triumph : Purpose of the Expedition. In the autumn of A.D. 85 Domitian returned to Rome. In the last two years he had been hailed as Imperator five times ; and now he celebrated a triumph with lavish expenditure on games and shows. He took the title of ' Germanicus ', and coins were struck bearing the legend ' Germania capta '. The authors of the time do little justice to Domitian's work on the Rhine. His war against the Chatti was probably not merely a punitive expedition against a troublesome tribe, but was dictated by a desire to safeguard the growing civil life on the right bank of the Rhine (p.155), and to straighten out the frontier between the Rhine and the Danube. These aims are suggested to us by the organization of the conquered territory which took place in his reign and later, and which is in harmony, as will be seen when the Danube frontier is discussed, with the general policy of Domitian and his successors in this region. But the literary evidence has little to say on questions of policy, and Tacitus could hardly be expected to laud the military exploits of an Emperor who had done so great an injury, as he thought, to his hero Agricola.

Voyage of the Usipi. But if Tacitus ignores the broader aspects of the expedition, he gives an account of an episode which is not without interest. Close to the Chatti lay a small

13

German tribe of the name of Usipi ; in A.D. 82 or 83 [1] the Romans levied a contingent of auxiliary troops from this tribe and sent them to Agricola in Britain. Stationed on the coast of Cumberland and pining for their native land, they fell upon their guards and seized three vessels ; putting to sea they were driven round the north of Scotland and through the North Sea, till finally after dreadful sufferings they were thrown up on the coast of Holland and sold as slaves in Rome, where they told the story of their adventures.

The 'Limes Germanicus', from Rheinbrohl to the River Main. [2] After the expedition of A.D. 83–84 against the Chatti the way lay open for the reorganization of the frontier on the Upper Rhine. As has been said, Domitian established a line of forts from Rheinbrohl round the Wetterau to Kesselstadt on the Main. The forts were constructed of earth, and wooden watch-towers were placed at intervals. As the frontier was pushed forward, the forts left in the rear were rebuilt of stone and a carefully constructed system of defence was elaborated. In the time of Hadrian an outer line was pushed forward between Echzell and Gross-Krotzenburg ; as a result some of the forts were evacuated and became towns. Along the whole of this sector, from Rheinbrohl to the Main, Hadrian built a wooden palisade which was replaced some time in the third century by the so-called Pfahlgraben, an earthen wall and a ditch.

The Odenwald-Neckar Section ; the 'Inner Line'. From Kesselstadt to Miltenberg the course of the Main marks the frontier as established by Domitian. By this advance from the Rhine to the Main the district of the Odenwald was included in Roman territory, and Domitian's conquests in the Wetterau were joined up with Vespasian's annexations east of Mannheim and with the Agri Decumates. The next step was the extension of the frontier from Obenburg, near Miltenberg, to the river Neckar at Wimpfen. Then the course

---

[1] The date is uncertain and is closely connected with another uncertain date, the arrival of Agricola, A.D. 77 or 78. Tac. *Agr.* 28.

[2] The following account of the German, Raetian and Danube frontiers is a summary of B. W. Henderson's treatment of the subject in his *Five Roman Emperors*.

of the river was followed as far as Köngen. From Köngen, up the Fils to Urspring and so to Faimingen, on the Danube, a line was planned by Domitian, and on it wooden watch-towers were placed. A few forts were built in Domitianic times ; a palisade was erected by Hadrian.

Thus the whole of Vespasian's annexations were absorbed by Domitian's advance. As we shall see, troops had been stationed by Claudius along the south bank of the Danube, and Vespasian had advanced as far as Rottweil or Geislingen. But the fort at Rottenburg on the Neckar is Domitianic, and the whole district of the Rauhe Alb had not been penetrated till his time. His work, therefore, contributed much towards the straightening of the frontier between the two rivers.

From the Main to Lorch ; the ' Outer Line '. It will be convenient here to anticipate the reigns of Emperors not yet reached in the narrative chapters. During the reigns of Nerva, Trajan and Hadrian the frontier traced by Domitian remained substantially the same. In the reign of Antoninus Pius an important advance was made. In A.D. 140 there had been a serious revolt in Britain ; as a punishment auxiliary contingents of Britons were levied and they were posted on the ' Inner line ' and set to work building stone forts in the Odenwald. The veteran auxiliaries stationed on this sector were moved forward to a new line ; and, thus enclosing the British *auxilia*, they had the double task of guarding the frontier and ensuring the loyalty of the newly raised contingents of Britons.

The ' Outer line ', occupied about A.D. 155, ran in an almost straight course, ignoring geographical features, from Obenburg to Lorch ; a palisade stretched from fort to fort. For some years both the inner and outer lines were garrisoned ; about A.D. 180 the inner line was evacuated, and its forts became towns. But the legionary stations were never advanced ; they remained fixed at Mainz and Strasbourg, and the advanced posts were held by *auxilia*.

Finally, in the third century the Pfahlgraben replaced the palisade with more massive structure, running for some 200 miles along the German frontier from Lorch. But it did not do duty long : soon after the middle of the third century the barbarian pressure increased, and there were fewer troops to resist it. The Roman frontier fell back to the Rhine.

The 'Limes Raeticus'. In Augustus' reign it was convenient to regard the Danube as the boundary of Raetia, but little was done to protect it. Under Claudius small earthen forts were planted along the southern bank from Risstissen to Eining. These defences were strengthened by Vespasian, under whom a fort was built at Regensburg (Castra Regina), the head-quarters of the III Italica legion in the reign of Marcus Aurelius. Until Flavian times no attempt was made to occupy land across the river.

But, as has been seen, under Domitian a new boundary was made from Köngen to Faimingen, and some attempt was made even in Flavian times to cross the river lower down ; Vespasian stationed troops at Kösching, and Weissenburg may have been occupied by Domitian. Further, it is possible that towards the end of Domitian's reign a line of small forts may have been planted from Lorch to Buch and on to Weissenburg and Eining, but more probably the activity of Trajan and Hadrian is to be seen here. Some time in the reign of Antoninus Pius a stone wall eight feet high was built joining up these forts ; this wall—known as the Teufelsmauer—stretching from Lorch to Eining, represents the most northerly limit which Rome fixed as the Raetian frontier. Thus, for a short time, a continuous rampart—earthen from the Wetterau to Lorch, stone from Lorch to Eining—marked the German-Raetian frontier. But when the advanced German line was given up, the Raetian wall could no longer be maintained. Thus the Rhine and the Danube once more became the limit of Roman power, as in Julio-Claudian times.

The Danube Frontier. The attention which the Flavians devoted to the German-Raetian frontier had good results ; for the Romans experienced little trouble from this quarter during the second century, and four legions sufficed for its defence. That serious danger threatened further east became clear in Vespasian's reign. The features in the history of the Lower Danube frontier during the next hundred and fifty years are briefly these : (i) the growing restlessness of the peoples north of the river, (ii) the movement of legionary

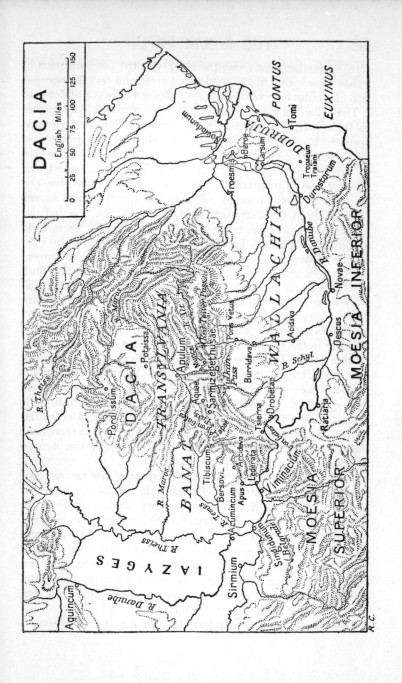

DACIA

English Miles

0   25   50   75   100 125 150

PONTUS EUXINUS

DOBRUDJA

Tomi

Troesmis

Tropaeum Traiani

Beroe

Carsum

Durostorum

WALLACHIA

R. Danube

Novae

Acidava

R. Schyl

Oescus

Burridava

Pons Vetus

Romula

Pelendava

MOESIA INFERIOR

Ratiaria

Drobetae

Tsierna

DACIA

R. Thess

Pordissum

Potaissa

TRANSYLVANIA

Apulum

R. Aluta

Aquae

Salinae

Tabae

Germizara

Sarmizegethusae

Ad Mediam

Tapae

Ad Aquas

R. Maros

BANAT

Tibiscum

Bersovi.

Apus

Actiava

Lederata

R. Temes

Viminacium

Singidunum

Belgrade

MOESIA

SUPERIOR

R. Tibiscus

R. Theiss

Acumincum

R. Tenes

Sirmium

R. Danube

IAZYGES

Aquincum

R.C.

stations further east along the river, (iii) the concentration of legion after legion in the threatened area, and (iv) the occupation of territory north of the river to form a bulwark of defence.

The tribes beyond the river were many, and they varied in their attitude to the Roman power. The Hermunduri, opposite Raetia, were friendly ; the Marcomanni, north-east of Regensburg, were already well known to the Romans (p. 52). Opposite Carnuntum lay the Quadi, a German tribe, as were the Marcomanni ; they were destined to give the Romans no little trouble. Far to the north of the Lower Danube, from the Carpathians to the Black Sea, roamed the Sarmatians—a vague term used by the Romans to include a number of tribes. In A.D. 69 a horde of them broke into Moesia and were destroyed. Two of the Sarmatian tribes, the Iazyges, who lived in the area between the Danube and, the Theiss, and the Roxolani, played a prominent part in the warfare on this frontier. Further east along the river was Dacia, inhabited by a number of loosely-knit tribes, not uncivilized and of different stock from the Sarmatians. Already in the reigns of Augustus and Tiberius they had sent raiding parties into Moesia, and under Nero a large number had been transplanted south of the Danube. But more recently they had given no trouble, being absorbed in their own quarrels. From the turmoil arose a single nation of Dacians under the leadership of a powerful king, Decebalus. In A.D. 69 raids were made into Moesia and were repulsed ; but soon after Domitian came to the throne, the danger assumed more alarming proportions.

Vespasian's Legionary Camps. Vespasian saw the need of strengthening the Danube defences. He rebuilt the Claudian fort at Carnuntum and planted another garrison close by at Vindobona (Vienna). Viminacium held two legions up to the time when Domitian prohibited double camps. At Ratiaria and Oescus Vespasian established legions which had hitherto been stationed in Dalmatia. Singidunum probably became a camp in the time of Trajan. Thus the tendency is for the legions to be moved eastwards, and Vespasian must be given the credit for seeing the need for this.

Domitian's Wars on the Danube. In A.D. 85 the Dacians

crossed into Moesia, penetrating far south and killing the governor of the province, Oppius Sabinus. During the eight years of spasmodic fighting which followed, the Dacians were joined by other tribes. Domitian himself made three visits to the frontier, one of them lasting eight months,[1] but the main task of restoring security was entrusted to his generals.

On the outbreak of the war Domitian went to Moesia, taking with him Cornelius Fuscus, the Praetorian Prefect, whom he placed in charge of operations.   By A.D. 87, Fuscus had cleared Moesia and had advanced into Dacia, marching probably by way of the Red Tower Pass (p. 201). He was driven back across the Wallachian plain and pursued across the Danube ; his army was annihilated and he himself killed (at Adamklissi in the Dobruja ?).[2]   The next force sent by the Romans was more successful ; Tettius Julianus with a stronger army crossed at Viminacium and at Tapae routed the enemy, inflicting so severe a loss that Decebalus sued for peace, A.D. 89.

The Emperor agreed to peace, for another danger threatened. Marcomanni, Quadi and Sarmatians appeared on the Pannonian frontier. Domitian,[3] therefore, made peace with Decebalus and sent through the king's territory a force, under C. Velius Rufus, to attack the invaders on the flank. The enterprise was apparently successful.

The Terms of Peace.   Besides agreeing to Rufus' march through his country Decebalus surrendered all his Roman prisoners.   Domitian on his side recognized his title to be King of Dacia, on condition that the crown should be regarded as having been conferred by Rome.   Domitian also agreed to lend to the king a number of Roman engineers and to make him an annual subsidy in money.   The poets celebrate Domitian's victory ; but it is difficult to regard the terms as anything but ignominious to Rome.   Though the Emperor took the title of ' Germanicus ' after his wars with the Chatti, he refused the title ' Dacicus '.

Again in A.D. 92 an attack was made on Pannonia by the Suebian Marcomanni and Quadi, who destroyed a Roman

[1] Martial, ix. 31.

[2] But cf. Juv. iv. 111, 112 and see note at the end of this chapter.

[3] Anxiety about Saturninus (p. 183) was another reason.

legion stationed in the province. Domitian spent eight months on the frontier ; he contented himself with clearing the province without taking reprisals. In Nerva's reign, too, there seems to have been fighting in this region. It was not till the time of Trajan that it was realized that the best means of protecting the Lower Danube frontier was to annex territory over the river. Domitian, however, strengthened the military defences ; a camp was built at Aquincum to watch the Sarmatians, and others at Novae, Durostorum and Troesmis to guard the Lower Danube. Moesia was divided into two provinces, Upper and Lower, each under a consular governor. For some ten years there was peace on the Dacian frontier. When hostilities were resumed, it was the Emperor Trajan who took the initiative.

The Cause of Trajan's Dacian Wars. The peace which Domitian concluded with Decebalus, King of the Dacians, was not likely to be of long duration. Its terms, as has been seen, did not lend great glory to Rome, and they provided no security for the tranquillity of the frontier. Of this Trajan was well aware ; the first winter of his reign was spent on the Danube, where he learned of the growing activity of the Dacian king.[1] For Decebalus was busy strengthening his defences and fortifying the few passes which led to his capital, Sarmizegethusae, and Trajan therefore decided to take the initiative in attack. An army was gathered from the legions of Moesia and Pannonia, reinforced by praetorians and auxiliaries, and in the spring of A.D. 101 was ready to begin the invasion of Dacia under the Emperor's leadership.

The Country of the Dacians. After passing Aquincum (Buda-Pesth) the Danube flows about 150 miles in a line from north to south ; it then turns almost due east, and after another 70 miles or so is joined by the river Theiss, which for its last 150 miles has also flowed in a southerly direction. In the oblong tract of land so enclosed by the rivers lived the Iazyges, a hardy race of horsemen. The river Theiss forms the western boundary of Dacia, which, speaking roughly, is intersected from east to west by the river Maros, which joins the Theiss, and by the south-western chain of the Transylvanian

[1] Dio, lxviii. 6,

Alps ; from the Alps many rivers flow in a southerly direction through the Wallachian plain to join the lower reaches
of the Danube, which forms the southern boundary of Dacia.
Wallachia was no doubt regarded by the Dacians as their own ;
but they dwelt chiefly north of the mountains, where their
walled capital, Sarmizegethusae, was situated. The approach
to this city from the south was difficult ; the passes were few
and arduous, but two of them were used by Trajan and must
be noted. The western approach was by the Iron Gate Pass,
to which two routes led ; the first started from Viminacium,
crossed the Danube at Lederata and followed the valley of a
small river to Apus, thence by Arcidava and Bersovia to
Tibiscum ; the second started at Tsierna and struck north to
Tibiscum ; here the two routes joined, and due east of Tibiscum lay, first, Tapae, then the Iron Gate Pass, then Sarmizegethusae. The eastern approach followed up the river
Aluta (Alt), which flows into the Danube near Oescus, through
the Alps by way of the Red Tower Pass to Cedonia ; here
turning west it led to Apulum, and hence to Aquae and
Sarmizegethusae.

That Trajan chose the western approach in A.D. 101 is
revealed by the brief fragment which is all that remains of
his ' Commentaries ' on the Dacian Wars, ' inde Bersobim,
deinde Aix(im) processimus '. Such hazardous reconstruction of the wars as can be attempted must rely on the
excerptor of Dio, who gives only the incidents which appealed
to him, and on the sculptures of the column which Trajan
erected, A.D. 113, in the forum at Rome which he built.[1]

Trajan's Column. The column which Trajan erected to
celebrate his Dacian victories stands 130 feet high ; and round
the entire surface runs a sculptured frieze [2] rising in spirals
towards the top ; on the summit stood a bronze statue of the
Emperor. The sculptures purport to give a pictorial account
of the wars ; men, women, horses, soldiers, boats, towns,

[1] And, of course, on inscriptions. The account of the Dacian Wars
here given is taken in the main from B. W. Henderson's *Five Roman
Emperors.*
[2] Average width, 60 centimetres ; wider at the top than at the
bottom.

harbours and rivers are all depicted. The scenery is indicated conventionally ; cities and ships are out of all proportion to the figures of the men in them : a wavy line shows the sea or a river (as in the arms of the city of Oxford), a tree stands for a forest. The interest of the sculptures naturally centres in the human figures of which there are said to be some 2,500. Every attention is given to detail ; it is possible, for example, to distinguish the allies of Decebalus by their arms and accoutrements, and to recognize different branches of the Roman army. At the same time the exact explanation of many scenes is not obvious, and many interpreters have tried to read their riddle with varying results.[1]

The First Dacian War. The Campaign of A.D. 101. Trajan mustered his troops at Viminacium on the Danube ; his aim was to reach the enemy's capital city, and his route lay by way of Bersovia and Λixis. The Column shows two pontoon bridges, doubtless at Lederata ; over one bridge march the praetorians, over the other the legionaries. The double bridge was probably to accelerate the crossing, though some interpreters think that the army was divided into two forces, one force crossing at Lederata and following the route which led by Bersovia, the other force crossing lower down the river at Drobetae, the whole army uniting again at Tibiscum. But such strategy is improbable. After offering the customary sacrifices and haranguing the troops Trajan pushed on into this little known country. His advance at first was slow ; he expected opposition, but encountered little. At Tapae the enemy was met in force, and the Column gives a spirited representation of a battle. Jupiter Tonans is shown hurling his thunderbolts at the Dacians ; the action was fought in a thunderstorm. The struggle was fierce, and the battle indecisive ; the sculptures do not suggest that Tapae was stormed, though Trajan was saluted as Imperator. Envoys approach, with what message we do not know ; soon after, men and women are shown slaying their cattle, lest they fall into the hands of the Romans. There was no submission. The Iron Gate Pass

[1] Conrad Cichorius in ' Die Reliefs der Traiansaüle ' gives the fullest and usually the best interpretation. Reference to the works of others may be found in Henderson's *Five Roman Emperors*.

was not forced ; winter was approaching and Trajan withdrew into winter quarters at Drobetae.

The Danube Bridge. The failure of this campaign strengthened Trajan's determination to annex some part of the Dacian land. In the winter of A.D. 101 he began his famous bridge over the Danube of which the remains are still visible at low water to-day. (The Column shows the bridge among the scenes of A.D. 106, but it must have taken some time to build, and one interpreter detects its beginning in a scene of winter, A.D. 101.) The site chosen was 6 miles below the famous gorge of the Danube known as the Iron Gate, where in A.D. 100, before the outbreak of war, Trajan had hewn a road in the face of the rock. Cassius Dio gives a long description of the bridge and expresses his admiration of it. It stood, he says with much exaggeration, on 20 piers of squared stone, 170 feet apart. The upper part was of wood, as the Column shows. As an architectural achievement the bridge, which was designed by Apollodorus of Damascus, was considered as among the greatest of Trajan's works.

The Raid of the Dacians and Roxolani. Trajan was not left undisturbed at Drobetae. In the country east of Dacia dwelt the Roxolani, a tribe of the Sarmatians, a race of fighters armed in chain mail, both horses and riders, and carrying long lances. To them Decebalus suggested a raid across the Danube in conjunction with his own Dacians. The Danube may have been frozen at the time, but in any case the tribes were accustomed to swimming across, in spite of their armour, and they now swarmed across into Lower Moesia, where the Roman garrison posts were widely separated. Trajan despatched some cavalry to deal with the Roxolani, while he himself sailed down the Danube perhaps as far as Oescus. The Romans attacked the raiders as they were returning to the river with laden wagons. A battle followed, vividly shown in the reliefs ; the Roman engines of war can be seen, and doctors attending to the wounded. It may be guessed that the Romans were victorious, for Trajan is shown congratulating his troops ; he receives some Dacian envoys and returns to Drobetae.

The Campaign of A.D. 102. Spring found Trajan's plans

already made. He had resolved to attempt the invasion of
Dacia by the eastern route. He strengthened his army by
sending for the I Minervia Legion from Pannonia, commanded
by his cousin Hadrian. We know of many other officers who
served in this year's fighting ; chief of them are Lucius
Licinius Sura, Trajan's second in command, Tiberius Claudius
Livianus, Prefect of the Praetorians, Marius Laberius Maximus,
whom we shall meet later, and Lusius Quietus, the Moor,
who had been in command of an Ala Maurorum under Domitian. He fell into disgrace with that Emperor and on the
outbreak of the Dacian War offered his services to Trajan ;
they were accepted.

From Drobetae the army marched east across the plain of
Wallachia, joining the river Aluta at Burridava and following
it as far as the Red Tower Pass. Decebalus had already sent
an embassy of ' Comati ', i.e. nobles of second rank, whom
Trajan refused to see. Later came some ' Pileati ', men of
noblest birth. Trajan bade Sura and Livianus return with
them and bear his orders to the king. But Decebalus refused
to listen. Trajan then turned his army westwards, ' climbing
the very heights ', as Dio says, till he came to the fortress at
Muncel. The fortress was stormed, thanks to the ' testudo ',
as the Column shows, and within it were found relics of
Fuscus' army. After another battle the Romans pressed
on to Aquae (the springs are shown in the Column), and here
Decebalus entered the Roman camp to make his submission
and to surrender his capital.

He agreed to give up his engines of war and his engineers,
and to receive no deserter from the Roman army. He
ceded part of Western Dacia (now known as the Banat) and
the Column shows the population evacuating this territory ;
peasants drive off their flocks, a father drags along a sulking
tired child, a mother carries her baby. The forts in this
territory were dismantled and Sarmizegethusae received a
Roman garrison. Such were the terms which Trajan imposed
and which Decebalus was ordered to petition the Senate to
grant. The Emperor returned home in the autumn of
A.D. 102 : he celebrated a triumph and took the title of
' Dacicus '.

The Second Dacian War, A.D. 105. But the peace did not last long. Decebalus was determined to renew the struggle, and neglected the conditions imposed on him. He welcomed Roman deserters and with their aid he renewed fortifications and manufactured arms. He raided the lands of the Iazyges, and there is some evidence that even in the first war he had been in communication with Pacorus, King of Parthia, to induce him to attack Rome simultaneously in the east.[1] By the spring of A.D. 105 he felt prepared to defy Trajan once more. He therefore persuaded Longinus, who was in command of the Roman garrison at Sarmizegethusae, to visit him, and on his arrival kept him in custody ; he then sent a message to Trajan demanding the restoration of the occupied territory in the Banat and payment of the expenses of the previous war. Trajan's reply was non-committal, for he wished neither to endanger Longinus nor to yield to the king. But Longinus found a way out of the dilemma. He obtained poison, sent a message to Trajan, and died ; for many years his name lived in the legends of Romanized Dacia. The king then poured his troops into Moesia.

Again the story must be deciphered with uncertainty from the Column, with a hint from the historian. Trajan left Rome in June for Ancona on the east coast of Italy ; thence he sailed by night to Iader on the Dalmatian coast. At Burnum he may have picked up a legion, the I Adjutrix ; he sailed from Salonae to Lissus whence he made his way up the valley of the Morava. Arrived in Moesia he relieved the Roman posts invested by the enemy, and, after the campaigning season was over, reached his bridge over the Danube, at the end of A.D. 105.[2]

From this point onwards the Column gives many picturesque scenes, though their value for any connected account of the fighting of A.D. 106 is little. Two forces seem to have made their way independently and to have united again at some point before the final siege of Sarmizegethusae. The sculptures show us the siege, which apparently was protracted ;

[1] Cf. the story of Callidromus in Pliny, *Ep.* x. 74.
[2] This reconstruction of Trajan's route is suggested by H. Stuart Jones.

Dacians are seen drinking poison rather than surrender; others succeed in escaping, Decebalus among them. The fugitives are pursued, even to the river Maros; strongholds are overthrown, and villages are on fire. At last Decebalus is overtaken and surrounded; he avoids punishment by stabbing himself with his sword. The last sculptures show the civilian men with their families and cattle driven off by the Roman soldiers to find new homes south of the Danube; the last figure is that of a goat nibbling at a tuft of grass.

Annexation and Settlement of Dacia. Trajan had determined to annex some portion of Dacia and to settle it as a Roman province. His reasons for this must be found in the military necessities of the frontier. The Danube had ceased to be an effective barrier defining the limit of the movements of the restless tribes on the north; if Moesia was to develop the urban life which Trajan encouraged, some guarantee for its security was needed. Dacia was to be a great bulwark thrown out into unfriendly territory. If a massed attack were made on it, and it were overrun, there would be time to defend the line of the river, where it was now possible indeed to reduce the number of garrison posts: Oescus and Ratiaria ceased to be camps. Further up the river, however, new camps were placed at Acumincum and Brigetio, and Pannonia was divided into two provinces. In Dacia itself the XIII Gemina was stationed, with head-quarters at Apulum. In actual fact, Dacia was unharmed for a hundred and fifty years, and beneath the protection which it afforded Roman territory south of the Danube reached hitherto unknown prosperity.

Nor did Dacia lose by the annexation. It was Romanized, and to this day the Roumanians, whatever their origin may be, proudly claim connexion with Rome, and Trajan's name lingers in folk-lore and story. Roman Dacia was probably smaller than Decebalus' kingdom; the rivers Theiss and Alt perhaps formed its western and eastern boundaries, while Porolissum may mark its northern boundary. From this tract thousands of the population were transported to the provinces south of the Danube where they could be kept under surveillance; in their room settlers chiefly from the eastern

Empire were planted. Roads were made, and their course is briefly described in the Peutinger Table; Sarmizegethusae became a colony with the title Ulpia Traiana; other cities grew up and were presently given the status of 'municipia'; Tsierna, Apulum and Porolissum became 'coloniae'. The provincial *concilium* met at Aquae, and later at Sarmizegethusae, where also the imperial cult was established. The salt mines and gold mines of the province were worked, miners being brought from Dalmatia for the purpose. As the work of colonization proceeded, local regiments of Dacians were recruited; they are found in many places in the Empire, and by the end of the second century Dacians became increasingly common in the army. It was always Rome's policy to turn her enemies into her staunch defenders.

NOTE.—In the Dobruja there are three 'monuments' which call for brief notice; all of them have been the subject of much discussion.

(i) At the village of Adamklissi there are the remains of a square 'altar' on which are inscribed the names of soldiers who perished in war. 'In memoriam fortissimorum virorum qui pro republica morte occubuerunt' is clear, but the name of the general is lost, and, though the names of about seventy soldiers can be read, the 'altar' obviously contained many more names. The 'altar', in Cichorius' view, is the mausoleum of Fuscus and his men who perished on this spot (p. 199). Others think it is a cenotaph, the place of Fuscus' death being unknown to us.

(ii) Close at hand is the Tropaeum Traiani, erected in A.D. 109, as is shown by the inscription which records its dedication to Mars Ultor. The circular mound of earth and stone which remains is about sixty feet high; originally it was encased with sculptures, which are now at Bukarest; they represent scenes of fighting with Dacians or Sarmatians and are curiously rude in execution. Cichorius holds that after some success against the Dacians Trajan built the trophy to Mars the Avenger, who avenged the defeat and death of Fuscus by the victories of Trajan. South-east of Novae Trajan founded a town to which he gave the name of Nicopolis.

(iii) From Tomi, on the Black Sea, a series of earthworks runs inland for a distance of some forty-five miles to join the Danube. These are interrupted in places by a stone wall obviously of later date. These works are often assigned to Hadrian.

But the interpretation of the monuments is much disputed. Mr. R. P. Longden, of Christ Church, Oxford, has kindly communicated the following theory: In A.D. 85 Oppius Sabinus perished during an invasion of Lower Moesia—possibly at Adamklissi. Domitian himself went to the province and Cornelius Fuscus succeeded in driving

the invaders back some distance. A wall (the greater earth wall)
was hurriedly built, A.D. 86, with thirty-five forts placed on an average
a mile apart. Behind this wall, and perhaps on the scene of Sabinus'
defeat, the cenotaph was built, also in A.D. 86. This was put up by
Cornelius Fuscus to those who had fallen with Sabinus, and possibly also
to those who fell in the victorious campaign. The Romans remained
penned behind their wall and the Dobruja was lost to them. The
ground was recovered in the late nineties, probably after Trajan's
accession ; after the Dacian Wars were over, the ' trophy ' was erected
(A.D. 109) beside the cenotaph of A.D. 86. It was the victories of Trajan
which first really wiped out the disaster of A.D. 85. The early successes
of Fuscus had only secured the defensive position and had been followed in A.D. 87 by an even greater disaster beyond the Danube.

CHAPTER XIV

THE PRINCIPATES OF NERVA, A.D. 96–98, AND
TRAJAN, A.D. 98–117

*T*HE *Character of Nerva's Rule.* The Senate had at
last secured an Emperor of its own choosing, and
there was little in Nerva's career or character which
was likely to make them repent. The son of a lawyer, he
had lived a life beyond criticism as a public servant. He
had held the consulship twice, in A.D. 71 and 92, and he came
to the throne at the age of sixty-two. There was no question, therefore, of the Senate being overriden by irresponsible
youth, or bullied by a successful general relying on the power
of his troops. Nor did the Emperor's personal character
give grounds for apprehension ; he was gentle in word and
act, anxious to avoid offence and to be at peace with all men.
Indeed his very forbearance provoked complaint ; it is bad
enough, murmured Fronto, a consul in Nerva's reign, ' to
have an Emperor under whom no one may do anything ; it
is worse to have an Emperor under whom everyone may do
everything '. This judgement is not quite fair to Nerva,
for more than once he showed himself firm, even courageous.
But the chief motive of his brief reign was conciliation ;
and some measure of success was achieved. Tacitus greeted
his accession with joy ; Nerva, he says, reconciled the Principate with freedom, ' res olim dissociabiles '. Such conciliation had its use ; it showed, if it were not apparent,

how foolish was the anachronism of Republican aspiration ; it soothed the Senate into good temper, and in doing so helped to make possible friendly relations between Emperor and Senate during the next eighty years. The Emperor, it is true, was no less autocratic in theory than Domitian was ; the proceedings of the Senate continued to be as futile as before ; but at the death of Domitian the senatorial party felt that they had won a victory—a victory paeaned in words by Tacitus and Pliny, but turned to little good account in fact.

Prosecution of Delators. As one of his first acts Nerva recalled all who had been exiled by Domitian and returned to them their confiscated property. He took stern measures against slaves or freedmen who had given information leading to the death or exile of their masters or patrons. Some senators wished him to go further and to lend his sanction to an orgy of prosecutions against *delatores* which threatened to break out. New-found freedom had intoxicated many with a lust for vengeance. ' All wished to prosecute all,' says Dio, and we may guess to what lengths this vindictive fury might have gone when we find that Pliny, the refined and gentle Pliny, was one of the most eager. The story may be briefly told. Publicius Certus had charged Helvidius Priscus with treason and carried through the prosecution with great acrimony. Domitian dead, Pliny was asked by Helvidius' family to punish his accuser. He agreed eagerly ; he saw, he says, a great and glorious opportunity to attack the guilty, avenge the miserable and advance himself. In the senate-house he delivered a carefully pre-pared oration full of the bitterest invective. There was some uproar, and the meeting was dissolved. But the Emperor refused permission for an actual indictment to be brought. Still, Pliny was satisfied ; his speech was published and Certus died some days after. So much for the Senate's newly-won freedom of speech, to be used by one of its best members ' to advance himself '. But Nerva emerges well from the incident ; he will allow no rankling resentment to disturb the restored peace of his reign. But he was less successful, as we shall see, in resisting the demands of the soldiers when they clamoured for vengeance.

Nerva's Relations with the Senate.   Nerva, then, attempted either to remedy or to bury the past.[1]   Naturally, his own relations with the Senate were friendly enough.   He promised to put to death no senator, and he kept his word, says Dio, even though plots were formed against him.   Impiety no longer became a charge to mask that of treason.   He consulted the prominent members of the nobility before venturing on any step.   When he appointed two commissions, one to purchase land for small-holdings, the other to explore methods of reducing public expenditure, he was careful to ask the Senate to nominate the members of the commissions.   He even went so far as to have a bill passed by the public assembly —an interesting revival, reminiscent of Claudius.   ' I have done nothing ', he said, ' which would prevent me from laying aside the imperial power, and safely retiring into private life.'

In spite of such studiously deferential treatment of the Senate at least one conspiracy was formed against him. Calpurnius Crassus, who vaunted his descent from the triumvir, took advantage of Nerva's mild rule to discover a hitherto concealed inability to serve an Emperor, who was, he said, no more than the ' first of the senators '.   The conspiracy came to nothing and its would-be ringleader was banished to Tarentum.

Measures in Favour of Italy.   It is in harmony with Nerva's character (or the necessities of his position) that he should have taken measures for the relief of poverty in Italy.   We have already seen that he distributed land to the needy ; to raise money for this purpose he is said to have sold much of the imperial property—furniture and jewels as well as villas and land.   He also released Italy from the charges of the *cursus publicus* and reduced the *vicesima hereditatum*.   But most famous of his measures is the establishment of the so-called *alimenta*, i.e. provision for the public maintenance of a certain number of poor children in Italy.   As will be seen later when the *alimenta* are described in detail (p. 334), the idea of such maintenance was not new, but Nerva first made it a charge upon public funds, and the plan was much developed

[1] Much of Domitian's legislation was retained, however.

by later Emperors. It must be remembered, however, that the Flavians were popular in Italy, and that Nerva could not afford to be less popular.

The Praetorians avenge Domitian. The soldiers, it has been said earlier (p. 189), grumbled at the accession of Nerva, but sullenly accepted it for the moment. But their discontent was not long kept in check. Casperius Aelianus, one of the Praetorian prefects under Domitian and retained in office by Nerva, bluntly demanded the punishment of Domitian's assassins. Nerva courageously refused, baring his throat to the swords of the soldiers. But the soldiers would take no refusal; they seized Stephanus and his accomplices, and put them to death. Nerva was powerless. Now, if not before, was revealed to him the weakness of his own position ; he was not a soldier and he had no hold upon the army which was the mainstay of the Principate. Thereupon he took his great decision, which was his main contribution to the history of the Empire.[1] He wrote a letter to M. Ulpius Traianus, governor of Upper Germany.

Career of Trajan and his Adoption. M. Ulpius Traianus, born at Italica near Seville, belonged to a family which had recently been made ' patrician ' by Vespasian. His father had held governorships in Asia and Syria, and in the latter province Trajan himself had served under his father. In Domitian's reign Trajan was praetor, and was later legatus of a legion in Spain, whence he had been summoned in haste to deal with the revolt of Antonius in A.D. 88 (p. 184). Three years later he was consul, and Nerva soon after coming to power sent him to Upper Germany as legate. He had shown himself a competent soldier, a loyal and skilful governor.

He was simple and unassuming, for all his handsome looks and successful career. He had no son. Such was the man to whom Nerva wrote offering adoption and a share in the imperial power. ' By thy darts may the Danai repent them of my tears,' he quoted, asking Trajan to lend his authority to quell the soldiers. The soldiers needed no controlling once they knew that Trajan was heir to the Empire.

[1] ' Reipublicae divina provisione consuluit Traianum adoptando ' (Eutrop. viii. 1).

Not waiting for an answer [1] Nerva went up into the temple of Jupiter on the Capitol and with every legal form and religious solemnity adopted Trajan as his son and consort ; ' simul filius, simul Caesar, mox imperator et consors tribuniciae potestatis '.[2] Three months later Nerva died, January, A.D. 98 ; he could rest content that neither senator nor soldier would dispute his choice of a successor. It is possible that the early adoption of a successor and Nerva's death shortly afterwards saved the Empire from another civil war.

Characteristics of Trajan's Reign ; the Evidence. The main characteristics of Trajan's reign are not hard to discover. Rome and Italy gained much from an Emperor who had their welfare and adornment much at heart ; the enmity of Emperor and Senate was replaced by a cordiality of relationship which is a welcome relief after three generations of suspicion. Abroad, the provinces were cared for as they only could be under a ruler so enlightened in ideals and so practical in administration. But to tactfulness as a ruler and to common-sense as an organizer, Trajan added also the power of leadership necessary to a successful general. Whether it was due to ambition or to the demands of circumstances, he carried through two campaigns in countries beyond the frontiers ; the Augustan ' limits of Empire ' did not restrain him. And as a man Trajan was just, gentle, easy of access, trusting and unaffected ; on him first of the Emperors a title was conferred to do honour to his personal character —' Optimus '—and the Senate of a later age could acclaim its Emperor with no greater compliment than ' Felicior Augusto, melior Traiano '.[3]

Yet for a reign of nineteen years the evidence is meagre in the extreme. Suetonius finished his lives of the Caesars with Domitian ; Tacitus has left nothing on Trajan's times ; the so-called Augustan History begins with the next Emperor, Hadrian ; Cassius Dio is preserved in excerpts ; Eutropius gives a summary which is little more than chapter headings. Pliny's Panegyric is undoubtedly useful, but deductions must be made from its extravagance ; his letters are invaluable,

---

[1] Plin. *Pan.* 9, 'eras imperator et esse te nesciebas'.
[2] *Ibid.* 8.   [3] Eutrop. viii. 5.

but cover only a corner of the field. In medieval legend little credence can be placed. And so the study of stones, inscribed and sculptured, is unusually important for this reign, and luckily Trajan made much use of stone.

Trajan on the Rhine and Danube. Trajan did not at once return to Rome on hearing the news of his adoption. He remained in Germany where he may have been given the general oversight of both provinces, Upper and Lower Germany. Nor did the news of his ' father's ' death, which was conveyed to him at Cologne by his cousin Hadrian, bring him to the capital ; he contented himself with writing to the Senate promising that no senator should suffer death at his hands. There was work of reorganization to be done on the Danube, though we are ill informed of its details. On the Pannonian frontier there had recently been trouble ; the Suebi, who evidently had not been decisively crushed by Domitian (p. 199), had again been defeated by the Pannonian legions in A.D. 97 and both Nerva and Trajan took the title of ' Germanicus '. In the winter of A.D. 98 Trajan himself visited this frontier to organize the defences ; it is possible that the peace concluded in A.D. 92 with the Dacians was in danger of being disturbed, and his presence, he thought, would check the restless energy of King Decebalus. Trajan was destined to return to the Danube very soon (p. 200), but in the spring of A.D. 99 he journeyed to Rome to make his first appearance there as Emperor.

In Rome. His arrival was greeted with the wildest enthusiasm. The sober Dio bears witness to this, while Pliny becomes ecstatic in his description of the Emperor's bearing and the impression which it made. ' What a glorious day ', a paraphrase of his ecstasy might run, ' was that on which you entered on foot the city which so longed for you. That you entered on foot was itself part of the glad miracle ; other Emperors were borne in, not on chariot drawn with milk-white steeds, but on the shoulders of men, to gratify their pride ; you stood above all only because of your higher stature ; your triumphal entry was a victory not over our forbearance, but over the arrogance of former princes. Neither age nor health nor sex kept the people back from feasting their eyes on so rare a sight. Boys learned to recognize you; young men pointed you out; old men marvelled at you, even the sick forgot their doctors' commands and crept forth to gain health and strength from the sight of you. Some declared that they had indeed lived and could die content, others that they had now the greater reason to wish for life. Every building was crowded, every spot which could give even a precarious foothold was occupied; the streets were thronged by crowds, through which you passed by a narrow avenue left for you amid the cheering multitude. You pleased all by greeting the Senate with a kiss, and every knight by name; but men's pleasure knew no bounds when they beheld you stepping through the press of the crowd unaccompanied and unguarded; on that first day you trusted your side to all.'[1] His wife Plotina too gave satisfaction by her humility; as she ascended the steps leading to the palace she turned to the crowd, ' I enter here ', she said, ' with the same feelings with which I should wish, if need be, to depart hence'; throughout his reign she shared her husband's popularity. Marciana, Trajan's sister, also lived at the palace, and Pliny says that the two imperial ladies equal in rank and fortune lived in perfect harmony with never a suspicion of rivalry.[2]

Trajan stayed two years in Rome before urgent duties summoned him to the northern frontier; in these two years he won the affection of Rome, Senate and people alike, and established his position so firmly that, though he was away from Rome for nearly half his reign, advantage was not taken of his absence. Of his measures during these two years we learn a good deal from Pliny's Panegyric; and, though they will be dealt with in detail when Trajan's domestic policy is discussed, a word or two on this speech of Pliny will not be out of place, if only to show the impression which Trajan so swiftly made.

Attitude of the Senate reflected in Pliny's Panegyric. Pliny was appointed consul suffectus for September A.D. 100. It was usual for the recipient of this honour to render thanks

[1] *Pan.* 22 ff.
[2] Though ' nihil est tam pronum ad simultates quam aemulatio, in feminis praesertim ' (*Pan.* 84).

to the Emperor in a brief speech in the Senate. Pliny profited
by the occasion to deliver a lengthy oration expressed in
terms of eloquent, not to say turgid, flattery ; but the speech
undoubtedly reflects the attitude of the senatorial party.
Trajan had punished the praetorians who forced Nerva to
avenge the murder of Domitian, and reduced the donative
which he offered them to one half of the sum given by his
adoptive father. He showed no mercy to the informers
who had terrorized the Senate — ' excidisti intestinum
malum '—and Pliny gives a vivid description of their punishment which he calls a ' pulchrum spectaculum ' ; they were
rounded up through the streets of Rome, and herded into
light boats hurriedly sought for the purpose ; they were
left to the mercy of wind and storm ; if any escaped to some
barren rocky island, he could there drag out such a life as
that to which he had in the past condemned many a senator.
Thus freedom of speech was restored, and Pliny dilates at
length on its benefits ; each member is free to give his view,
to dissent, and to offer to the service of the State his own
experience and judgement ; all are consulted, and the best
opinion, not the first, carries the day. So marked was the
Emperor's deference to the Senate that the Panegyric, though
rightly so named, seems in some places to adopt a tone even
of condescension ; the Senate had found a ruler after its own
heart ; it was gaining a sense of independence—' eadem Caesar
quae senatus probat improbatque '—and Trajan is bidden
to continue as he has begun.[1]

The Emperor listened presumably in patience to this
masterpiece of flattery. He derived some satisfaction from
the title ' Optimus '[2] which the Senate bestowed on him,
but far more no doubt from the restoration of harmony
between Senate and Emperor ; for he could now leave the
city with some degree of confidence that all would go well
while he was away on the northern frontier. His wars against
the Dacians have already been described (p. 200 ff.).

[1] *Pan.* 34, 35, 76.
[2] Pliny mentions this title, though Dio, lxviii. 23, seems to show
that it was not taken as an official title till A.D. 114. Yet an inscription
shows it in A.D. 112.

The Annexation of Arabia Petraea. In A.D. 106 Dacia became a Roman province. The same year saw the addition of another province to the Empire—Arabia Petraea. There was no provocation to war, and this province, unlike Dacia, was acquired with little resistance. The opportunity of annexation was presented by the death of the king of the Nabataeans. The recent history of the country may be briefly summarized. East of Jordan lay a strip of territory which belonged to King Agrippa II (Herod Agrippa). After the reign of Claudius his kingdom included Batanea, Trachonitis, and Abila, and it was further increased by Vespasian. When Agrippa died, his kingdom became part of Syria, either in A.D. 92 (or 93), or 100. To the north-east, east and south of this country was Arabia Petraea, which included on the north the city of Damascus, and on the south the Sinaitic peninsula and a tract of land east of the Red Sea as far south as Leuce Come. This was the kingdom of the Nabataeans ; their king had been reduced to the position of a client prince by Pompey and had continued such from then till Trajan's time. His people consisted of nomadic tribes loosely held together and living a precarious life on the desert ; but here and there towns flourished, made rich as centres of commerce. Malchus or Maliku, king of the Nabataeans, had assisted Vespasian when he invaded Palestine to crush the Jewish revolt. In 106 Dabel, Maliku's son, died, and Cornelius Palma, governor of Syria, was instructed to annex the country, Damascus and its immediate neighbourhood becoming part of Syria.

Under Roman rule Arabia flourished, and continued to flourish for three hundred years. The caravan routes were free from molestation, and along them the wares of the East poured to the great marts in the towns, Bostra, Gerasa, Philadelphia, Petra and others.[1] The remains of palaces, theatres, baths, temples and aqueducts attest the Romanization of the country. Bostra, under Roman rule, seems to have become more important than Petra, which was the capital of the kings. Bostra was the head-quarters of the

[1] Many of the places in this area have been made famous recently by T. E. Lawrence's *Revolt in the Desert*.

governor (*legatus pro praetore*) and of the legio III Cyrenaica, and later, under Alexander Severus, attained the status of a colony. Arabia Petraea, like Dacia, later furnished auxiliaries for the army.

Trajan's Administration. The Senate. As was suggested earlier, Trajan very quickly showed the Senate that he wished to keep on friendly terms with it, both politically and socially. He consulted it freely and even wrote letters to individual members of it, asking their advice. The Senate continued to exercise their juridical powers ; Pliny's letters contain much information, often rather wearisome, on the speeches delivered by counsel on either side, as for example, in the trial of Julius Bassus for extortion while governor of Bithynia.[1] Trajan politely sent home to the Senate despatches reporting the progress of his campaigns, and in settling terms with the enemy he was careful to make it clear that they were provisional until ratified by the Senate. This body responded by paying compliments to the Imperial prowess, and by deifying every member of his family. Yet in spite of this deference of manner and phrase Trajan was as much an autocrat as Domitian, and the Senate was fully conscious of its own position. Pliny, speaking about the Emperor's accessibility, continues with the words, ' Regimur quidem a te et subjecti tibi, sed quemadmodum legibus sumus ' ; but in spite of his rejoicings over the restoration of liberty he knows that in fact this liberty is somewhat meaningless.

Towards individual members of the Senate Trajan was natural and unaffected. ' You have been one of us,' says Pliny, ' you remember what you used to long for, and what you complained of when you were among us ; you now play your part as Emperor, yet you share your subjects' point of view.' So he hunted with his senatorial friends and dined with them unattended. He was warned, runs a story in Dio, that the loyalty of Licinius Sura was not above suspicion. Trajan called at his house uninvited, dismissed his own attendants and spent the evening there ; he entrusted himself to Sura's servants, even allowing his barber to shave

[1] *Ep.* iv. 9.

him. Next day he met the mischief-makers ; ' if Sura had wished to kill me, he would have done so yesterday '. Freedmen enjoyed no undue influence ; ' you realize ', says Pliny, ' that powerful freedmen are a chief sign of a powerless Emperor '.[1] Nor were slaves of individuals encouraged to reveal their masters' affairs. The fisc turned a deaf ear to those who were ready to give information which might benefit it,[2] and there was no longer obligation on the testator to remember the needs of an indigent Emperor ; life, children, property and reputation were again safe.

To the people Trajan was openhanded. His victories appealed to their imagination, for every conqueror appeals to the mob who take no share in his battles ; and the shows and games with which he celebrated his Dacian victories left nothing to be desired. His soldiers loved him. As he handed the sword of office to his Praetorian Prefect at the beginning of his reign, he bade him, ' Take this sword ; if I rule well, use it for me ; if ill, against me '. On the march and in battle he won their devotion ; he shared their toils and tended their comforts ; in one hard-fought battle we are told he was indefatigable, even tearing his tunic into strips to bind up his soldiers' wounds. For, whatever else he was (and he was much else), Trajan was a soldiers' Emperor.

The Forum of Trajan. In his efforts to make Rome a capital worthy of the Empire Trajan can be compared only with Augustus himself. His fame in this respect rests chiefly upon his new forum, which was as bold in plan as it was magnificent in appearance. The forum lay between the Capitoline and Quirinal hills, and much excavation was needed to obtain the necessary level space. Under the direction of Apollodorus, the builder of the Danube bridge, the Eastern shoulder of the Quirinal was cut back, buildings were cleared away and an area of roughly a hundred yards square was levelled. On this site were built the Basilica Ulpia, used as a lawcourt, and, connected to it, two libraries, one devoted to Latin works, the other to Greek. Round the forum a colonnade ran, into which entrance was given through Trajan's

[1] *Pan.* 88.

[2] ' Postquam non est cui suadeatur, qui suadeant non sunt ' (*Pan.* 41).

arch, leading from the forum of Augustus. The arch, adorned with sculptures, carried a statue of Trajan driven in a six-horse chariot, and on either side of the chariot were the statues of his generals ; in the centre of the square stood an equestrian statue of Trajan. Between the libraries the column bore aloft its spiral sculptured frieze, leading the eye to yet another statue of Trajan about 130 feet from the ground. No expense was spared ; the gilded horses flashed in the sunlight ; marbles of varied hue and richly veined relieved the brilliance of the white Attic marble of which the basilica was built, and, above all, the roofs rose in shining bronze, themselves surmounted by countless statues.[1]

The Welfare of Italy. Despite his campaigns Trajan seems to have been tireless in his care for Italy and the provinces. In Italy, harbours, roads, bridges, municipal finance, depopulation, ' alimenta ' all received his attention. At the Claudian harbour of Porto, opposite Ostia, Trajan excavated a new dock, and joined it to the sea by a channel two miles long ; and at Centumcellae in Etruria he improved the harbour.[2] He sailed, it will be remembered, from Ancona when he set forth for Dacia in A.D. 105, and some years later he reconstructed the harbour at his own expense. All over Italy inscriptions testify to his activity in the making of roads and bridges. His new Via Traiana ran from Beneventum to the port of Brundisium, which hitherto had not been easy of access ; at its point of departure the Emperor erected an arch which is still in a good state of preservation ; it was begun in A.D. 114 and was probably finished four years

---

[1] Both Domitian and Nerva seem to have done something towards clearing this area. The inscription on the base of the column says that it was erected by the Senate and people of Rome in A.D. 113 ' ad declarandum quantae altitudinis mons et locus tantis operibus sit egestus '. On Dio's authority this has been taken to mean that a spur of rock was cleared away, the excavations going down to a depth of 128 feet. Since, however, houses of the early Empire have been found under the foundations of the column, this view is given up. ' The least unsatisfactory explanation yet suggested is that " mons " refers to the extreme Eastern shoulder of the Quirinal, the Collis Latiaris, that was cut back so far that the height of the excavation was approximately 100 feet ' (Platner & Ashby, *Topographical Dictionary of Rome*, p. 238). [2] Plin. *Ep.* viii. 17.

later (p. 231). Many other roads he completed or repaired ; the Via Puteolana, begun by Nerva, Trajan finished ; he repaired the Via Salaria, and built bridges on the Via Latina, Via Appia and others ; and he strengthened the road running through the Pomptine marshes. In A.D. 109 he constructed the Aqua Traiana, which carried water to Rome from the hills of South Etruria 25 miles away. It is still in use. His efforts to repeople the deserted Roman Campagna may be more fitly described elsewhere (p. 338) ; it is enough here to say that he encouraged settlers in this region, and tried to check emigration from Italy ; he also extended Nerva's system of 'alimenta' and so indirectly aided Italian farming (p. 335).

In this reign a step was taken which is full of significance to the student of the Empire. Certain rights of local government had been granted to cities in Italy and to many in the provinces (p. 341) and among them was the right to control the financial administration of the city. Now Trajan was an efficient administrator with a keen eye for economy ; and these qualities he looked for in others also. When, therefore, he found that municipal magistrates were careless in their management of finance, spending more than they could afford and failing to balance their accounts, he appointed state officials—*curatores reipublicae* or *civitatis*—to control the finances and to check notoriously extravagant town councils. In Trajan's time such officials were seldom appointed for Italian towns, though we know of cases at Caere and Bergomum ; in the provinces they were more common. This encroachment by the central government on the powers of local authorities was undoubtedly in the interests of efficient administration, but efficiency may be dearly bought if independence and self-reliance are to be destroyed at the same time. And there is always the danger that such interference may become more frequent till bureaucracy becomes a tyranny, as was the case at Rome later. But luckily this day was far off, and Trajan cannot justly be charged with bringing it nearer. The fault lay rather with later Emperors who developed the bureaucracy and were in a position to see, but did not see, its evil results.

The Welfare of the Provinces. Trajan showed no less care for the provinces than for Italy. Most provinces can show many notable building works—bridges, aqueducts, roads—which were undertaken in his reign. But the happiness of the provincial did not depend on benefits such as these. Just government was even more important ; and in Trajan's reign, whenever a provincial governor was guilty of mis-government, he was promptly brought to trial. Pliny's letters give information about such trials. Mention has already been made of the *curatores* to control the finances of cities. But in the provinces Trajan was sometimes forced to resort to more sweeping methods. Two provinces in particular called for attention in this respect. In Achaia very many cities had been given the right to call themselves free cities—' liberae civitates ' ; one Emperor after another, through sheer reverence for the glorious past of such cities as Athens, Delphi and Sparta, had bestowed this privilege, which granted freedom from the control of the provincial governor. Yet some of these cities were hardly worthy of the privilege. Their affairs were in disorder ; through lack of energy, chaos and poverty were conspicuous ; the very streets resembled those of a deserted town. In A.D. 109 Trajan sent a certain Maximus to set their affairs in order—' ad ordinandum statum liberarum civitatum '.[1] No doubt there was some indig-nation in the cities, and even Roman admirers of Greek civilization felt some sympathy. Pliny at any rate wrote to Maximus and begged him to be tactful, to remember the ancient glory of these cities and not to rob them of the little that remained to them—the name of liberty. ' Remember the title of your office, and interpret to yourself its character and its importance—the regulation of the free cities. " To regulate " demands the sympathy of a citizen ; while what could be more precious than freedom ? Shame if destruction should take the place of regulation, and slavery that of freedom.'

[1] Later such officials were called *correctores* ; but since διορθωτής τῶν ἐλευθέρων πόλεων is attested for Trajan's time, and since διορθωτής seems to be a translation of *corrector*, it may be safe to call Maximus a *corrector*.

Pliny in Bithynia. The second province which needed supervision, not only of its free cities, which were not numerous, but of all its communities, was Bithynia. And the situation is not without humour : for the very man who wrote with such concern to Maximus was sent in A.D. III to Bithynia as 'legatus pro praetore provinciae Ponti et Bithyniae consulari potestate in eam provinciam ex senatusconsulto missus,'[1] that is to say, the province ceased to be senatorial and was placed under an imperial commissioner. The state of the province and Pliny's activities there are revealed to us by the correspondence between Trajan and Pliny, the tenth book of the Letters. Pliny had no experience of provincial administration, and he refers to the Emperor on topics which sometimes seem trivial, though he claims that Trajan had given him leave to consult him on doubtful points. Trajan answers with tireless patience and much shrewdness ; twice, however, he reminds his timid commissioner that he had been sent there for the very purpose of deciding such matters on the spot ; 'ego ideo prudentiam tuam elegi ut . . . ipse moderareris . . .'.[2] Some of the problems relate to public works, others to local government ; sometimes religious or financial matters call for elucidation. Is Pliny to build an aqueduct for Sinope or approve of the rebuilding of the theatre at Nicaea ? May he have the services of an engineer to drain a lake near Nicomedia ? The fee payable by supernumerary decurions varies in the several townships. Will Trajan make a general rule ? 'No ; local practice must be observed.' Apamea, a free city, has asked me to overhaul its finances. Shall I ? 'Certainly, since you have been invited ; it will not lose its privileges thereby.' Should condemned criminals be used as public slaves and receive wages ? May Nicomedia organize a fire-brigade, and Amisus friendly societies ? May I compel decurions to borrow public money, which is plentiful at the normal rate of 12 per cent. ? 'Put the rate low enough to attract voluntary borrowers ; use no compulsion ; such a course would be foreign to the spirit of our age.'   Certain ground, where your statue is set up, has been desecrated by burials. 'Allow no prosecution,

[1] Dess. 2927. Note the 'ex senatusconsulto.'   [2] x. 117. Cf. 32.

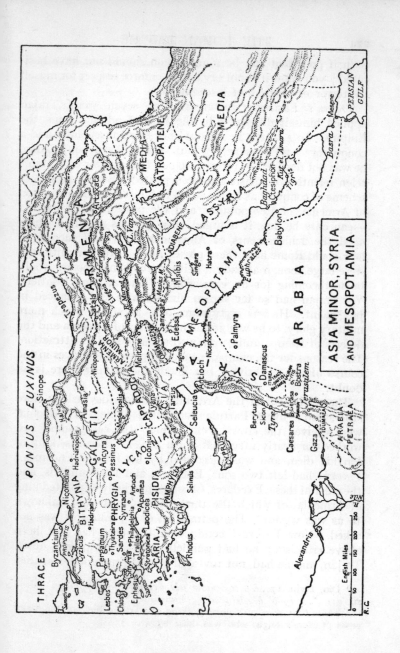

ASIA MINOR, SYRIA
AND MESOPOTAMIA

even if precedent can be found ; you should not have hesitated ; you know it is not my aim to enforce respect for myself
by terror or charges of lèse majesté.'

Trajan's Eastern Campaigns. For seven years Trajan
applied himself diligently to the task of administering the
Empire. In A.D. 113 he set out once more as a soldier and a
conqueror ; and after nearly four years of hard campaigning
he was not destined to return. Upon this chapter of Trajan's
reign relentless criticism has been poured. Such a grandiose
scheme of conquest as he proposed to himself—the annexation
of Armenia, of Mesopotamia and the possessions of Parthia
—can only be due, it is urged, to a reckless ambition which
aped the achievements of Alexander.[1] Even if successful,
how could Rome hold these possessions ? Her commitments
were large enough already ; neither troops nor money would
be forthcoming for an extension of her far-flung frontiers.
Yet Trajan had so far shown himself wise and balanced in
judgement. He was sixty years old—an age at which mere
military glory, to be won in the mountains of Armenia and the
deserts of Mesopotamia, may well seem to lose its attraction.
The reasons for the campaigns may suggest themselves in the
course of the narrative ; but about the pretext there is no
doubt.

The settlement of the Armenian problem devised by Nero
still stood ; by it Parthia nominated a king of Armenia,
who received the crown from Rome ; the compromise had
worked for nearly fifty years. In A.D. 110 Pacorus, king of
Parthia died, and was succeeded by his brother Chosroes.[2]
Pacorus had left two sons, Exedares and Parthamisiris, and
the elder of these, Exedares, Chosroes hurriedly appointed king
of Armenia, of which the throne for some reason unknown
to us was vacant. The permission of the Emperor was not
asked. Now Pacorus' conduct in the past had not been
above criticism ; he had publicly uttered complaints about
Trajan, and he had not revealed to the Emperor Decebalus'

---

[1] Dio, lxviii. 17 . . . πρόφασιν μὲν ὅτι μὴ τὸ διάδημα ὑπ' αὐτοῦ
εἰλήφει . . . τῇ δ' ἀληθείᾳ δόξης ἐπιθυμίᾳ.

[2] These were sons of Vologeses, king of Parthia, but not the Vologeses of Nero's reign, who was dead by A.D. 75.

overtures to him. Trajan chose to regard the appointment
of Exedares as an act of impertinence which called for punishment. He declared war on Parthia and embarked for Syria
in October A.D. 113. He was met at Athens by envoys
bearing an abject apology from Chosroes, who admitted that
Exedares as king was proving unacceptable to himself no
less than to Trajan, and begged that Parthamisiris might be
appointed to the Armenian throne. The Emperor's reply
was non-committal. He reached Antioch in January A.D. 114,
where he gave orders for the mustering of the Syrian legions.
He then held a meeting of the many petty kings of the neighbouring states. Not all obeyed the summons and some
regretted too late their refusal, in particular Abgarus, king of
Osroene, and Mannus, king of Arabia (Deserta).

In Armenia. In the spring of A.D. 114 Trajan led his army
into Armenia ; his objective was Elegeia, ten miles west
of Erzerum, which Corbulo had made his head-quarters.
He went by Samosata and Melitene to Satala, kings and
satraps meeting him with gifts as he travelled. At Satala
he held a great gathering of chieftains, who professed their
loyalty to him. Parthamisiris had meantime written to him
in all humbleness ; he laid aside the title of king which he
had used in a previous letter, and implored Trajan to grant
him an audience. Trajan ordered him to meet him at Elegeia.
Dio gives a vivid picture of the meeting of the Emperor
and the would-be king. Seated on a throne and surrounded
by troops Trajan received Parthamisiris, who humbly laid his
crown at the Emperor's feet. The soldiers cheered ; ' a
bloodless victory ', they cried, and saluted the Emperor. The
Parthian, thinking himself tricked and insulted, begged for
a private audience. Trajan granted it, promising nothing.
Next day, after an eloquent appeal by his suppliant, Trajan
clinched the matter ; Armenia, he declared, was now Roman
territory and would have a Roman ruler. Escorted by Roman
horsemen,[1] Parthamisiris fled from Elegeia, and Armenia
for the moment was placed under the control of the governor
of Cappadocia. Trajan returned to Antioch.[2]

---

[1] Later rumour said that he was slain by the escort.
[2] Presumably, though Dio does not say so.

15

Annexation of Mesopotamia. With Armenia secure on his flank Trajan ventured on the long march across the north of Mesopotamia as far as the Tigris. He crossed the Euphrates at Zeugma ; as he marched, he left garrisons at well-chosen points to safeguard his line of communication, while Lusius Quietus with his cavalry scoured the country in advance of the main column. As Trajan drew nearer to Edessa, the capital of Osroene, its King Abgarus, who had resisted the summons to Antioch, rapidly changed his policy ; he welcomed Trajan, entertained him royally and succeeded in winning his pardon. From Edessa the march continued to Nisibis, 150 miles away, and at this point Quietus was sent forward to seize Singara and to reconnoitre up to the Tigris, while some time or other Sentius, a centurion, was sent to bear a message to Mebarsapes, king of Media Adiabene, a vassal of Parthia. This king defied the Emperor, imprisoned Sentius, and was encouraged in his resistance by the support of Mannus and his Arabian troops. But Trajan had no time to deal with these defiant kings, for the year was coming to a close ; his army remained on the Tigris and he himself returned to Antioch. So far he had seen little of the enemy, nor was it surprising ; for Chosroes was engaged with his forces in resisting an insurrection led by Manisares, a vassal king perhaps, who had already announced to Trajan his readiness to revolt.

Campaign of A.D. 115 in Assyria and Parthia. While Trajan wintered at Antioch, there occurred, at the beginning of A.D. 115, the famous earthquake of which Dio gives a detailed, if exaggerated, description.[1] The tremors, he says, lasted for several days, and were accompanied by thunder and lightning ; thousands perished ; the whole Roman world suffered affliction, for Antioch was thronged with strangers on business or pleasure from every country. Trajan himself, it is said, narrowly escaped destruction ; a figure of greater than human stature led him forth to a place of safety. At any rate he survived to join his army at Nisibis in the spring of A.D. 115, where he had given orders that boats and wagons should be built during the winter, for there was little timber

[1] lxviii. 24 *sqq.*

on the banks of the Tigris itself. On his arrival the boats were transported to the river. Trajan's objective this year was the capital city of the Parthians, Ctesiphon, but before sailing down the river he thought it wisest to overrun Media Adiabene, whose king might cause trouble in his rear; besides Sentius was not to be forgotten. But Sentius was not resourceless; imprisoned at Adenustrae (the site of which is unknown) he managed to break loose from his chains, and releasing his fellow-captives he threw open the fortress to the approaching Romans. Trajan then moved down the river Tigris to Ctesiphon,[1] which he found already hurriedly evacuated by Chosroes (end of A.D. 115). The enemy's capital city was now in his hands, together with much treasure; and probably at this point he took the title 'Parthicus', and coins bearing the legend 'Parthia capta' acquainted the world of his success.

Still Trajan did not call a halt. He sailed downstream, past Kut el Amara and Basra, now famous in British history, to the Persian Gulf. Here, standing upon the shore, he sighted a vessel standing out to sea, bound for India: 'If I were still young', he said, 'I too at all costs would have sailed across against the Indians.' 'He counted Alexander happy,' says Dio. It is a pleasant anecdote. We may indeed wonder whether Trajan ever expressed such a regret; but Dio will not let him forget Alexander.

The Return Journey. By autumn of this year Trajan reached Babylon, where he sacrificed to Alexander in the very house in which, in June 323 B.C., that conqueror of the East had died. But vain regrets could not occupy him long—if at all—for here news reached him of insurrection in the north and the loss of many of his garrison posts, Edessa, Nisibis and Seleucia among them. Lusius Quietus was sent off at once and succeeded in reducing Nisibis, while two legionary commanders, Sextus Erucius Clarus and Tiberius Julius Alexander, destroyed Seleucia. Communications were thus restored.

---

[1] His route to Ctesiphon is a matter of dispute. Dio makes him come down the Euphrates to Babylon and transport his ships across the land to the Tigris. The Tigris seems the more direct approach from Media Adiabene. There is no evidence except Dio for the route.

Meantime Trajan crossed from the Euphrates to Ctesiphon, where further bad news awaited him. Chosroes' kinsman, brother or nephew, Sanatruces and his son Parthamaspates had collected an army and were bearing down upon the Romans. In this extremity Trajan resorted to bargaining ; if Parthamaspates would bring over his army to the Roman side, Trajan would bestow on him the crown of Parthia. The offer was accepted ; the two armies joined, and in a hard-fought battle they defeated Sanatruces' forces. Partha-maspates was duly crowned at Ctesiphon, only to be ejected when Trajan had departed. Thus surrendering Lower Mesopotamia, Trajan marched up the Tigris homewards. At Hatra he encountered opposition (late summer A.D. 116 ?) ; all the efforts of the Romans to storm the city failed ; there was little food and water ; at last the rain came, descending in torrents with violent hailstorms ; and, after it ceased, flies in swarms settled upon the food of the miserable assailants. The siege of Hatra was abandoned, and after a long and weary march Trajan with the remnants of his army at last reached Antioch (early A.D. 117 ?).

Purpose and Results of the Eastern Expedition. It is diffi-cult to believe that Trajan was impelled merely by a desire to emulate Alexander's conquests ; considerations both of frontier defence and of trade may have suggested the expedi-tion, though probably Trajan himself scarcely realized its difficulties. There is evidence that certain Caucasian tribes, in particular the Alans, were moving southwards, themselves pushed onwards by the migrations of the Huns to the north-east. In the reign of Marcus Aurelius they constituted a serious danger to Roman security in this region of the Empire, and it is not unlikely that Trajan hoped, by making an impression on the native chieftains, to protect the Roman frontier by a ring of petty states favourable to Rome ; the economy of this system always appealed to Roman Emperors. Thus the Armenian expedition may have had some justi-fication. As for Parthia, no demonstration of Roman power had been made since the time of Corbulo ; and it may be that the communication between Decebalus and Pacorus was but one piece of evidence of the growing hostility of the Eastern kingdom. There may have been economic motives, too. The annexation of Arabia had probably shown Trajan what sums could be diverted to the treasury in the shape of tolls and dues on merchandise passing along the trade routes from the East. Through Mesopotamia there were several well-known routes along which toll was paid as goods crossed successively the boundaries of many small kingdoms here. Fronto,[1] writing in the reign of Marcus Aurelius, says that at Babylon Trajan was busy fixing dues to be paid on camels and horses crossing the Tigris and Euphrates, and, isolated as this evidence is, it may give a hint that economic reasons in part dictated the expedition to Parthia. That these conquests were surrendered by the next Emperor is not proof that they ought never to have been undertaken (p. 235).

The Jewish Revolts. Though it was nearly fifty years since Titus had destroyed the Temple, the Jews of the Dispersion still nourished thoughts of murderous revenge ; even the generation which had not witnessed the destruction of Jerusalem was taught to hate the Romans and Greeks among whom it now dwelt. The conquest of Mesopotamia, whither many Jews had taken refuge, and Trajan's absence gave them an opportunity for revolt, and revolt spread from country to country. In Cyrene and Cyprus and Mesopotamia their fanatical fury blazed forth ; they massacred thousands, and ghastly accounts of their cruelties are recorded. The whole of Cyprus fell into the hands of the insurgents and the native population was exterminated ; from Cyrene, where so many were slain in the massacres and in the reprisals that the land was desolate for years, the revolt spread to Egypt, and the prefect, M. Rutilius Lupus, was besieged in Alexandria. Trajan sent Lusius Quietus to repress the rising in North Mesopotamia, and on his success appointed him governor of Judaea. In Cyprus the rebels were massacred by the Romans in their turn, under what general we do not know ; but we may well believe the Jewish writers who say that no mercy was shown.

Death of Trajan ; Career and Adoption of Hadrian. It was Trajan's intention to hurry on to Rome, for besides the Jewish rising revolts threatened from almost every quarter

---

[1] Naber, p. 202.

of the Roman world (p. 235). He had reached Selinus in
Cilicia, when paralysis struck him down, and, after lingering
for some few days, he died, probably on 8 August, A.D. 117.
But those few days were of tremendous significance to the
Empire ; for in them a successor was chosen. But how he
was chosen we are not certain.

Publius Aelianus Hadrianus was born at Italica in Spain in
A.D. January 76. Hadrian's grandfather had married Ulpia,
sister of Trajan's father ; thus Trajan and Hadrian were
cousins with a difference in age of twenty-two years. At the
age of ten Hadrian lost his father and passed under the
guardianship of his cousin, who at the time commanded
a legion in Spain, and of Acilius Attianus, a native of Italica,
and later Prefect of the Praetorians. Attianus took his
young ward to Rome to be educated ; here till the age of
fifteen he worked at the usual studies, in particular Greek
literature, and thus began that devotion to Hellenism which
he carried through his whole life. He returned for a year or
two to Spain, only to be recalled to Rome by Trajan, who,
childless himself, wished to show his affection for the promising boy and to help him to a political career. In A.D. 95
Hadrian was sent as military tribune to Aquincum, attached
to the II Adjutrix Legion, and in a short time he was
moved to Lower Moesia, whence he bore to Trajan in Upper
Germany the news of his adoption by Nerva. When Trajan
as Emperor travelled to Rome, Hadrian accompanied him,
and there he stayed till the Dacian Wars, marrying in A.D. 100
Vibia Sabina, a grand-niece of the Emperor. In the Dacian
Wars Hadrian's promotion was rapid, though not exceptionally
so ; he was quaestor in A.D. 101, and in A.D. 105 probably
received his first legionary command ; in A.D. 107 he was
governor of Lower Pannonia and in the next year consul. He
went with Trajan to the East in A.D. 113, but we know little
of his achievements here ; in A.D. 117 he was appointed
governor of Syria with his head-quarters at Antioch.

Such was the career of the man who on 8 August 117 received
a letter from the Emperor, written, so it was told, just before his death ; the letter declared Hadrian to be his adopted
son. On the 10th he received news of his ' father's ' death.

But scandal has also left its version of the adoption. The letters were forged, it is said, by Plotina, who had long been in love with Hadrian. She concealed the Emperor's death for a few days till her plans were made, and was helped by Attianus, Prefect of the Praetorians and Hadrian's guardian. Another story says that Roman officials were admitted to the darkened chamber in which Trajan lay, and believed that they heard the dying Emperor's bequest of the Empire to Hadrian ; but Trajan was already dead, and the words were uttered by a servant of Plotina. Of Plotina's love for Hadrian nothing more need be said, for it ill accords with what we know of her. Whether Trajan wrote the letter of adoption or not scarcely matters ; for though he never made Hadrian his consort in power, his attitude to him seems to suggest that he intended Hadrian to succeed him. If Plotina actually affixed his signature, it was in the best interests of the Empire.[1]

Summary of Trajan's Reign. The sculptures which adorn the arch at Beneventum summarize Trajan's achievements ; and by these scenes he would no doubt wish to be judged, for their general theme is the peace and prosperity created by his military victories. On the side of the arch facing Beneventum four main reliefs show Trajan received by the gods, received by the Romans, with his legionaries (perhaps he is making grants of land in his new colonies to them), and with his merchants and business men (at his new harbour at Porto ?). On the other side the victories of Trajan in the north and in the east are celebrated ; majestic figures of the provinces acknowledge his services to them. Beneath the arch, in the passage, one scene shows the Emperor doing sacrifice before he set out on his Eastern campaigns ; in the other parents

[1] The various stories are given in Dio, lxix. 1 ; *Vita Hadr.* ii. 6–10. It is likely that Trajan himself wished Hadrian to be his successor, but did not wish to dictate to the Senate. Hadrian probably disapproved of Trajan's military policy, and as a result there may have been some lack of sympathy between the two. Trajan's generals therefore would be anti-Hadrian, as the sequel shows (p. 236), while the court party, Plotina and Attianus, supported him. Trajan may have known of the existence of the parties and postponed open recognition of Hadrian as consort.

bring to the Emperor the children whom they may now bring up in confidence, thanks to his 'alimenta'. What is here claimed for Trajan is his due. Even though at his death trouble in various quarters (p. 235) seemed to threaten, it was largely by his victories that the peace which settled upon the Empire for the next fifty years was made possible; and Hadrian's diplomatic triumphs were largely due to the strong position in which Trajan left him. At the same time the burden of the wars bore heavily on the whole Empire; thousands of men were drawn away from Italy and the West and either perished or were settled in the new provinces to help forward the process of urbanization which Trajan held to be so important. As regards money, the wars were ruinous both to the Treasury and to the provinces on the borders of which they were fought; the movements of troops and the furnishing of supplies strained to the utmost the resources of the neighbouring districts. Yet Trajan was not blind to the needs of the Empire; his measures to secure good government in the provinces and financial stability in the cities disprove any suggestion of it. His work was unfinished, and Hadrian completed it.

CHAPTER XV

THE PRINCIPATE OF HADRIAN, A.D. 117–138

*T*HE *New Conception of the Position of Emperor.* In spite of obvious differences in individual character, the Emperors from Vespasian to M. Aurelius— Domitian by no means excepted—were animated by the same spirit of devotion to the Empire. The struggle between Emperor and Senate had indeed left the Emperor more powerful than ever; but, as a result partly of that struggle and partly of the character of the new aristocracy from which these Emperors were sprung, the main idea of the Augustan constitution was reasserted more strongly than ever, namely, that the Emperor is but the chief magistrate of the State. He bears its burden; on him as soldier and as administrator responsibility rests; to him senator and peasant, Italian and provincial look for their safety and their happiness, and they are ready to acknowledge him as god, as the chosen agent of Providence, if he can satisfy their needs. The Empire is now viewed as a whole ; the welfare of each province is seen to be necessary to that of all ; it is the Emperor's task to take this broad view. Except Domitian, every Emperor from Vespasian onwards had been trained in the service of the State as a commander of armies and as a governor of provinces ; and when the time came for him to administer the Empire as a unit, he could rely on the help of men who also were spending their energies in its service. This conception of the duty of the Emperor develops during the next fifty years till it finds its completest expression in Marcus Aurelius. It was, we may admit, an ideal worthy of the state which produced it ; it failed through many and complex causes, but the glory of its failure is the measure of its success.

Hadrian's Character ; a Problem. In character Hadrian is one of the most baffling and therefore one of the most interesting of Roman Emperors ; he was, as his biographer says, ' semper in omnibus varius ', and his biography confronts us with an assortment of mental and moral characteristics which seem to represent too much material to make up one mind.

He was, we are told, generous and large-hearted, yet crafty and suspicious, with a persistent streak of jealousy which urged him to cruelty. He was a skilful soldier, a sound administrator, a versifier, an art critic ; he painted and sang, and had a passion for hunting—' venando usque ad reprehensionem studiosus '. In travel his curiosity was insatiable. He was interested in religious observances ; he severely criticized an actor or a rhetorician and rewarded him ; he legislated in the interests of an old-fashioned morality, yet he was not a prude ; he wrote odes on the death of favourite horse and hound, and he climbed mountains to see the sunrise. He regarded membership of the Senate as the highest distinction which he could bestow, yet the Senate never really liked him. His character makes up in versatility what, at first sight, it seems to lack in singleness of purpose. It was too complex for most of his contemporaries to appreciate, and far too difficult for the compiler of a second-rate biography to understand; the modern historian, therefore, cannot be certain that he lays his emphasis correctly on the features which represent the real Hadrian.

Hadrian's Letter to the Senate; the Parthian Triumph. On the news of his adoption Hadrian wrote to the Senate. He asked for confirmation of his position as Emperor and pleaded that circumstances made it impossible for the Senate to be consulted beforehand. He promised to put no senator to death; he swore to place the service of the State before all else and begged that no title should be conferred on him unless he himself should desire it. Finally, he asked that divine honours should be granted to Trajan. Such a letter must have produced a good impression, but there was need for care, since Hadrian had no idea how Rome would receive the news of his accession. Attianus, Plotina and Matidia[1] hastened to Rome, bearing with them Trajan's ashes. The Senate conferred divine honours on Trajan, and the Parthian triumph for which Trajan was returning when death overtook him was celebrated, perhaps in October. Hadrian himself declined the honour of a triumph and Trajan's image rode in the triumphal car through the streets of Rome. The ashes of the dead Emperor were placed, it is said, in a golden urn which was enclosed within the pediment of his column.

In the city Attianus exerted all his influence on Hadrian's behalf, and, as will be seen later, it is probable that he encountered some opposition. At any rate in the first days of the reign he wrote to Hadrian warning him against three men who were likely to cause trouble; they were Baebius Macer, *praefectus urbi*, Laberius Maximus, the general of the Dacian wars, whom Trajan had exiled, and Gaius Calpurnius Crassus, who had previously shown disloyalty to Nerva and Trajan (p. 210). Hadrian took no action against them (though Crassus, attempting to escape from his place of exile, was slain 'without Hadrian's orders'); 'he showed an enthusiasm for clemency'; yet danger, not however from these sources, none the less threatened.

Mesopotamia Abandoned. Hadrian's Movements A.D. 117–18. *Disturbances on the Danube.* Meantime Hadrian had other

[1] Mother of Vibia Sabina, Hadrian's wife.

cares. The Jewish disturbances had only recently been suppressed ; in their turn ' the Moors were provocative, the Sarmatians were preparing invasion, the Britons could not be held under the Roman yoke '. Against the Moors Hadrian sent Marcius Turbo, his most trusted general. He then made his great decision ; he recalled his troops from the newly acquired territory on the Euphrates and thus renounced Rome's claim to dominion in Mesopotamia. Leaving Statilius Taurus as governor of Syria, he started in October from Antioch, the army accompanying him. Travelling by Tarsus, Ancyra, Juliopolis in Bithynia, he reached the coast and perhaps spent the winter at Nicomedia. Here news reached him of further disturbances on the Danube. North of the Danube mouth, the king of the Roxolani threatened trouble, while between Dacia and Pannonia, in the plains of the river Theiss, the Sarmatians were preparing an invasion. And so in the spring of A.D. 118 Hadrian travelled by road to the mouth of the Danube, at some point sending his army in advance into Moesia. He met the king of the Roxolani, who complained that the subsidy paid to him by Trajan had been reduced. The Emperor settled the matter satisfactorily and moved into Dacia. He grasped the situation quickly ; he summoned Turbo from Africa and put him in charge of Pannonia and Dacia, thus giving him powers superior to those of the two provincial governors. The Sarmatians were active in the district between the two provinces, and in giving Turbo this extraordinary command Hadrian wished to co-ordinate operations from the flanks and so to squeeze the Sarmatians out of the plains of the Theiss. In this Turbo was successful.

The Plot of the Four Consulars. At this point news reached Hadrian which brought him to Rome with all speed. He travelled direct by road to Aquileia and reached the city on 9 July, A.D. 118. A plot had been formed against his life ; the Senate, however, had discovered it, and before the Emperor's arrival had put to death the four ringleaders. The chief men concerned were Lusius Quietus, Avidius Nigrinus, Cornelius Palma and Publilius Celsus. Quietus might well harbour a grudge against Hadrian, for he had been passed over in the choice of a general to suppress the Moors ; his own compatriot Moorish troops had been transferred from his command elsewhere ; and so in retirement he nursed his resentment against the Emperor, who had cut short a career which under Trajan had promised so well. Of Nigrinus we know little ; Palma, who had annexed Petraea (p. 216), was a close friend of Trajan, and so too was Celsus. Hadrian strove to soothe the anger which the death of the four consulars aroused ; he professed his ignorance of the whole matter and repeated his promise to put no senator to death. Popular feeling he placated by gladiatorial shows which lasted six days and by lavish gifts of money ; it is clear that he took particular care to counteract the ugly rumours which went about to the effect that he himself had ordered the murders.

It is difficult to know what is behind the story of the four consulars, which is here told without the discrepancies present in the literary accounts. We may well believe that Hadrian's accession was not pleasing to the military party, which disapproved of his peace policy and saw with dismay his surrender of their conquests. Attianus probably was aware of the opposition of this party, and persuaded the Hadrianic majority in the Senate to take drastic measures. Whether there was a conspiracy, whether Attianus decided to forestall opposition which might become more active, whether Hadrian was in some way responsible for the deaths of the consulars are questions which cannot be decided. At any rate Hadrian deposed Attianus from the position of Praetorian prefect and presently gave him consular insignia and membership of the Senate ; and this, he said, was the greatest honour which he could give.

Hadrian's Travels. Hadrian spent many years of his reign in travelling about the Roman world ; there was probably no province which he did not visit, and several he visited twice. The motives for these travels were two—duty and pleasure ; it so happened that what duty compelled pleasure also suggested. The Emperor wished to know his Empire at first hand ; he wished to organize it on the basis of peace, and peace depended partly on the security of the frontiers and the efficiency of the army, partly on the welfare of the provincials.

To these matters Hadrian devoted his earnest attention. But also ' so eager was he for travel that he wished to see with his own eyes everything which he had read about the places of the earth '.[1] ' Omnium curiositatum explorator,' says Tertullian—peoples and customs, cities and mountains, art or religion, scenes made famous in history. There is no need to suggest that any other motive was at work ; it may be doubted whether Hadrian was consciously swayed by notions of cosmopolitanism or world unity, however much or little his travels may have contributed to these. He travelled, we are told, without pomp or display ; he covered long distances on foot, outstripping his travelling companions ; in snow or sunshine his head was unprotected. In Egypt and probably in Greece his wife, Sabina, accompanied him. Wherever he went, he was met with welcome, though in spite of his own simplicity his visits must have cost the cities much. In the east he was venerated as a god ; and there, too, more than in the west, titles were pressed upon him—' Restorer ', ' Benefactor ', ' Panhellenios ', ' Redeemer of the Universe ' and many others. Statues, temples and inscriptions commemorated his visits, and by their trail we can supplement the brief notes of his journeys given in the ancient writers.[2]

The First Journey. Hadrian left Rome some time in A.D. 121 for a protracted tour of the provinces ; he did not return till A.D. 125. His route was no doubt carefully planned in advance, but was modified frequently, as sudden emergencies demanded. He made first for Gaul and travelled about its districts, his generosity winning for him the title of ' Restitutor Galliae ' (on coins).[3] Hence he passed into Germany, probably from Lugdunum by way of Augusta Treverorum, on a tour of military inspection ; hence into Raetia and Noricum, his concern again being chiefly military defences and dispositions. In the spring of A.D. 122, he travelled up the Rhine to Holland, where the town of Forum Hadriani (Voorburg) bears witness

[1] Hist. Aug. *Vita Hadriani*, xvii. 8.

[2] The reconstruction of Hadrian's journeys has been attempted by Dürr, Weber, Henderson. Weber's scheme is here followed.

[3] At Apt his favourite hunter, Borysthenes, died and was given a memorial engraved with verses of Hadrian's own composition, still extant.

to his visit. Thence he crossed to Britain. The rising of the Brigantes which broke out in A.D. 117 had been quelled in A.D. 119–20, but the military defences of the island called for attention. His most famous monument is, of course, the wall which bears his name and which was no doubt planned by him (p. 288) ; he probably visited the legionary camps before returning to Gaul. Here news reached him of disturbances in Alexandria, and he hastened to Massilia ; but the trouble was quieted without his presence and he spent some time visiting the cities of Provence. Avignon was named after him Colonia Iulia Hadriana Avenio ; at Nîmes the news reached him of Plotina's death, and in honour of his mother he here built a basilica which should be ' a wonderful work '. From Provence his plans took him to Spain. Problems of local levies, road-building, temples, the flattery of local officials leave their records, though curiously his activities did not take him to Italica, his birthplace.[1] While he was in Spain, the Moors again rebelled. Hadrian made arrangements which led to their speedy repression, but it is improbable that he took the field in person. The winter was passed at Tarraco.

By the spring more serious news arrived ; the Parthians were preparing war. Hadrian sailed the length of the Mediterranean from Spain to Antioch, perhaps touching at Carthage. At some place on the Euphrates he interviewed the Parthian king ; as before with the king of the Roxolani, his presence was enough ; ' bellum . . Hadriani colloquio repressum est '.[2] All was now quiet on the eastern frontier, and Hadrian moved from Tarsus by way of Tyana and Ancyra to Bithynia. No doubt the camps of Cappadocia were visited en route. In Bithynia and Mysia he founded or refounded many cities— Stratonicea, Hadrianopolis, Hadriani close to Mount Olympus. At Troy he visited the tomb of Ajax ; at Nicomedia his generosity repaired the destruction caused by a recent earthquake. By Cyzicus, Pergamum, Smyrna he reached Ephesus, which he was to visit again later, for it attracted him greatly. Here he took ship ; he visited Rhodes and turned north to Samothrace, where he was perhaps initiated into the mysteries

[1] Dio, lxix. 10. ' Restitutor Hispaniae ' appears on coins.
[2] *Vita*, xii. 8.

of the Cabiri, for which the sacred isle was famed. A tour through Thrace brought him to the furthest frontiers of the Roman world, and in winter he settled the affairs of tribes and cities as far away as Panticapaeum, on the shores of the Tauric Bosporus ; by this he did much to ensure the peace of the eastern portion of the Danube frontier. From here, by Oescus and Drobetae, he travelled to Pannonia ; records of his interest in his troops and their camps remain (he even wrote an epitaph for a Batavian soldier, which still survives), and roads and new cities sprang up. Thence he turned south-east, and traversing Macedonia and Thessaly he came by Abae and Coronea to Athens, arriving in September A.D. 124.

Hadrian in Greece. For six months Athens became the centre from which Hadrian travelled to places of interest in the Peloponnese and elsewhere. Athens cast her spell on him, and he returned later on two occasions, spending in all some considerable time at a town which more than any other received his affectionate care. Some of his activities in Greece may be referred to without distinguishing whether they are to be dated to this or a subsequent visit.

Athens still prided herself on her ancient glories, and Hadrian flattered this harmless vanity. He consented to become archon and president of the Greater Dionysia, and actually fulfilled some of the duties of the office. He codified the ancient laws of Draco and Solon and later legislators. During his stay he assumed Greek dress and welcomed the society of philosophers and artists. His passion for building found ample scope ; he so extended the buildings of the town that outside the original boundary a new Athens arose, called Hadrianopolis. The two most important of the new buildings were temples to Zeus Panhellenios and Olympios. The former was built in connexion with the new Synod of Panhellenes, to which representatives from the Greek cities in Greece and Asia Minor were sent. There is no evidence, however, that this synod had any other than a sentimental significance. Panhellenic games were instituted and Hadrian assumed the title of ' Panhellenios '. The temple of Zeus Olympios was now completed ; it had been planned and begun centuries before by Pisistratus. From Athens Hadrian travelled to

Sparta, but no architectural remains bear witness to his presence. At Mantinea he visited the tomb of Epameinondas ; in this town he built a temple and at Corinth an aqueduct. He received complimentary decrees from the Amphictyonic Council at Delphi, and to the oracle he propounded the age-long riddle of Homer's birthplace. The religious rites at Eleusis piqued his curiosity, and he was granted initiation, proceeding to the second grade of ' epopt ' at a later visit.

Return to Rome. After an absence abroad of nearly five years Hadrian reached Rome in the summer or autumn of A.D. 125, having travelled by Nicopolis, Dyrrachium and Sicily. During the next year he remained in the capital ; in A.D. 127 he took a brief journey in Italy, doubtless to obtain first-hand information on administrative points which exercised him.

Hadrian's Journey to Africa ; Army Regulations. In the next year he visited the province of Africa. His object was primarily military, to inspect the army and examine the defences. He arrived at Carthage and travelled to Lambaesis, the new head-quarters of the Third Augustan legion, which for some years had been stationed at Theveste. On this famous legion with its auxiliaries the defence of Africa rested. Hadrian reviewed the troops, and watched their manœuvres ; by good fortune fragments of his speeches to some of the units still survive. They contain only praise—as is perhaps natural. A brief quotation may be given.

' To the First Pannonian Squadron.

' You were quick to obey orders and you manœuvred well over the whole ground. Your javelin-hurling was accurate and good, and that although the javelins were of a kind difficult to grasp. Your spear-throwing, too, was in many cases excellent, and the jumping was neat and lively. I would certainly have pointed out to you anything in which you fell short if I had noticed it—for example, if you had shown a tendency to overshoot your targets. But there has been no flaw of the kind. The whole of your exercises have been performed absolutely according to rule.' [1]

[1] The ' Allocutiones ' are given in Dessau 2487. The translation is taken from B. W. Henderson's *Hadrian*, p. 97.

Wherever Hadrian went he paid attention to military discipline. As a consequence of his peace policy there was a danger that the efficiency of the army might be impaired. By reviews and manœuvres he tried to keep it up to a high standard. He introduced modifications in tactics and training ; he reorganized the legion. Orders were issued on the minutest of details ; promotion was to be earned only by efficiency and length of service ; leave was to be granted sparingly ; officers' quarters were not to be too luxurious. The Emperor studied his men's interests, inquiring into their food, quarters and ' comforts '. Nothing escaped his attention, and in return he won the devotion of his troops and secured a disciplined and skilled army.

The Second Journey. The Emperor's restlessness and devotion to the needs of the provinces took him abroad again in A.D. 128 for a prolonged tour of the East ; he returned to Rome probably in A.D. 132–3. He stayed the winter in his favourite Athens, and crossed over to Ephesus in the spring. We know that he reconstructed the harbour, restrained the River Cayster within its banks and relieved famine by allowing the importation of corn from Egypt. From here he visited many places in Caria, Pamphylia, Phrygia and Cilicia, relieving distress at Tralles by a concession of corn which the rich officials paid for, visiting at Melissa (near Synnada) the tomb of Alcibiades and instituting a sacrifice there. For the benefits which he conferred on the Greek cities of Asia Minor he was hailed by the title of ' Panionios '. Summer found him at Antioch in Syria, and later in the year he went to Cappadocia, holding, at Samosata perhaps, a conference of local kings and rulers, and confirming by diplomatic methods their loyalty to Rome. The winter was passed at Antioch. In the spring he made for Coele-Syria ; we are told that he climbed Mount Casius to see the sun rise. He visited Palmyra and Bostra, where the Third Cyrenaica legion lay, and made his way by Philadelphia to Jerusalem. The city lay in ruins, witness to the fierce resistance offered to Titus. Hadrian now made a decision which was to have unforeseen consequences. He rebuilt the city ; he peopled it with Greeks, forbidding Jews to set foot in it. He gave it the status of a Roman colony

16

and the name of Aelia Capitolina. In all this there was deliberate intention. The destruction of the city was not enough, for even in ruins it could still appeal powerfully, perhaps more so, to the devotion of the worshippers of Jehovah ; a new worship, therefore, was to arise on the very site of the Temple—the worship of Jupiter and the Emperor.

From Judaea Hadrian travelled by the coast to Egypt, attracted, like Germanicus, by its monuments. At Pelusium he found the tomb of Pompey neglected and in disrepair, and he rebuilt it. At Alexandria he interested himself in the disputations and the salaries of the professors. Thence he sailed up the Nile. At Besa occurred an incident which profoundly moved him. A favourite page, Antinous, of whom he was very fond, fell overboard and was drowned. Hadrian deeply mourned his death. In his memory he founded an oracle of Antinous and built a city, called Antinoe, close to the scene of his death. The city was settled by Greco-Egyptian veterans, and was organized in tribes and demes named after the Emperor's family and Athenian cults and heroes. The ' Antinous-type ' exercised much influence on the art of the time, and his cult and mysteries were spread widely over the Eastern Mediterranean. At Thebes the Emperor and his wife heard the note of the Memnon statue, uttered, so it was said, to greet the rising sun, and on the left foot Balbilla, one of the Empress's ladies, scratched some lines of verse. In the Libyan desert Hadrian enjoyed some hunting, and returning to Alexandria sailed to Syria. His route now becomes uncertain. Probably by land he went to Pontus ; at Trapezus he reconstructed the harbour. Arrian in his report on the Black Sea, which he wrote at the Emperor's request, seems to imply that Hadrian had himself seen many of the places on the south and east coasts, but we cannot trace his movements. Hadrian returned to Athens, perhaps in the autumn of A.D. 131. From here he was summoned east by the success of the Jewish rebellion.

The Jewish Rebellion of A.D. 132. The Jews of the Dispersion had recently exhausted their strength in the rebellions at the end of Trajan's reign ; those in Judaea had remained quiet since the destruction of Jerusalem. Hadrian's studied insult to them in the founding of Aelia Capitolina lashed them to fury. Led by Simon, 'prince of Israel', and Akiba, a Rabbi of great learning, they sprang to arms. The governor of Judaea, Tineius Rufus, was unable to check the revolt ; and Gaius Publicius Marcellus made little headway against the guerilla tactics which the Jews knew so well how to employ. Hadrian then crossed to Antioch to observe the situation more closely, and summoned Julius Severus from Britain to direct operations. After a stubborn fight Bether, between Jerusalem and Bethlehem, the chief stronghold of the rebels, fell, and Rome took her vengeance. Captives were sold in thousands into slavery. Aelia Capitolina was built ; the Jews were excluded from it, though Palestinian Christians were given entry, and the church of Jerusalem flourished. The land changed its name to Syria Palaestina, and received as governor a consular legate in command of two legions.

Constitutional Changes. The Senate. Hadrian contributed more than any other Emperor from Vespasian to Marcus Aurelius to give to the Empire certain characteristics which it bore till the time of its decline. There is no reason to believe that he did so out of dissatisfaction with his own position or his relations with the other members of the constitution ; nor did he deliberately set out to lower the authority of the Senate. If the Senate did suffer loss, the changes which Hadrian made were only indirectly the cause. His attitude towards this body was always respectful and courteous. He apologized, it will be remembered, for taking the Principate without consulting it. He professed his hatred of previous Emperors who had detracted from its dignity, and he was himself punctilious in his attendance at meetings. He promised that he would punish senators only ' ex senatus sententia ' ; and to strengthen the Senate's authority as a court of law he refused to listen to appeals from its judgements. The supreme magistracy he was careful not to assume more than three times himself—a number which was equalled by many of his contemporaries. And in his private relations with individual members of the order he was simple and unaffected.

Hadrian's eye was everywhere ; he had a genius for detecting slackness or abuses ; his aim was efficiency, and there were few departments of state which were not affected by his passion for organization. When, however, organization is carried too far, freedom and self-reliance may be killed ; and Hadrian has been accused by some critics of initiating that bureaucracy which laid its heavy hand on the later Empire.

The Civil Service. The Equestrian Career. One of the most urgent problems which Hadrian had to face was that of the civil service. The early Emperors had done little more than extend the system used by Augustus, whose household provided the secretarial and administrative assistance which he needed. But by the second half of the first century the abuses of this system had become apparent ; freedmen gained an influence which reflected little credit on those who employed them. Vitellius, however, transferred some of the imperial posts to knights and Domitian shared some of the highest duties, such as *a libellis* and *ab epistulis*, between knights and freedmen.[1] But it was Hadrian who made it a rule that knights exclusively should hold these posts, and he made for the knights a purely civil career, even exempting some of them from the military service which had hitherto been a preliminary necessity for all appointments. The various other posts already referred to (p. 13) were, of course, still held by knights ; the Prefecture of the Praetorians was still the most important, and there is some evidence that under Hadrian this office gained greatly in prestige. Further, it was probably Hadrian who authorized for them the title *vir eminentissimus* to correspond with *vir clarissimus*, a title in use for senators. Certainly Marcus Aurelius gave it official recognition. There is little doubt that the equites deserved the increased importance which they gained and that the administration of the Empire became more efficient. But in the change the Senate may have seen an indirect encroachment on their own prestige.

Finance. In the regulation of finance Hadrian showed a shrewdness unaccompanied by parsimony and distinguished

[1] Tac. *Hist.* i. 58 and inscriptions prove the correctness of this. *Vit. Hadr.* xxii. 8 is therefore inaccurate.

by sound sense. He found that the resources of the Treasury
had been strained by Trajan's wars. Yet he was not grasping ;
he initiated no policy of confiscation, and at his accession
waived or reduced the *aurum coronarium*, the gift of money
which Italy and the provinces offered to a new Emperor.
Though he examined the public accounts as closely as a head
of a family his private expenses, he was never accused of
stinginess. He discovered that vast sums—900,000,000 HS.—
were owed to the Treasury ; the debts had accumulated for
years and had been carried forward as assets, though actually
they could not be recovered. Hadrian made a bonfire of the
records in Trajan's forum, A.D. 118. He commanded that
a general investigation of public accounts should be held
every fifteen years. The system of farming taxes was now
almost entirely abolished. The Flavians had made changes
in this direction, putting *procuratores* in place of companies
(*societates*) ; but Hadrian carried the changes still further.
To safeguard the interest of the fisc he set up new officials
called *advocati fisci*, who represented the Treasury in the law-
courts. The vast imperial estates were placed under a
procurator, who let them to middlemen—*conductores* ; these
exacted from the *coloni*, farming on the métayer system, contributions in kind and in forced labour. The management
of the estates became more efficient, but also the *coloni* felt
themselves protected ; they could appeal to the Emperor, and
an African inscription speaks of the Emperor's ' ceaseless
vigilance ' in their interest.

Legal Changes. Previous Emperors had already availed
themselves of the advice of an informal *consilium*[1] of senators.
Hadrian continued this council, but he gathered together also
a body of imperial *consiliarii*, composed of equites as well as
senators. Its duty was to advise him on points of law, and it
included therefore some of the most famous jurists of the
day, e.g. Iuventius Celsus and Salvius Iulianus. But it was
not a cabinet, and therefore the inclusion of knights could
not reasonably give offence to the Senate. To Hadrian was
also due a change which would seem to have been needed for
some time. To save litigants in Italy the expense of bringing

[1] See p. 10 note.

appeals to Rome and also to relieve the Emperor and city prefect of much work, he created four consular *iudices* whose duty it was to go on circuit, each in the district of Italy assigned to him. The judges, however, seem to have been discontinued soon, only to be revived, with certain changes, by Marcus Aurelius. But Hadrian's appointment of them helped to emphasize the need of another legal change which is the most famous reform of the early Empire.

The Codification of the Edict. In the time of the Republic the people was the sole source of law. But no law can fit every case ; it needs to be interpreted to suit particular circumstances. This interpretation was the work of the *praetor urbanus* in Rome, of the *praetor peregrinus* in Italy and of the proconsul in each province. Each of these magistrates issued at the beginning of his office his *edictum perpetuum*, i.e. he gave a summary of the principles of the law as he understood them ; this summary was *perpetuum*, i.e. it held good for his term of office, and by his interpretation of it he constantly added to it. But the *edictum* was not as arbitrary as it sounds, for (i) each magistrate generally took over complete the *edictum* of his predecessor, (ii) behind it there was always the law which remained unalterable and which the magistrate's interpretations were trying to make clearer. By the time of the Empire this mass of interpretative material was very large and of great importance.

With the establishment of the Empire the source of law, hitherto the people, changed ; the interpretative function of the magistrates remained. The sources of law now were (i) the Emperor, by his *responsa, edicta, decreta* ; (ii) the Senate, by its *senatusconsulta*, which, however, needed the approval of the Emperor before they became law ; (iii) the *responsa* of certain jurists licensed by the Emperor. In the last years of the Republic leading lawyers gave opinions on the merits of points put before them by clients. Their opinion carried weight, but no legal validity. Augustus selected a number of such jurists of consular rank and gave their *responsa* validity which the magistrate was bound to acknowledge.

Thus the Emperor was in control of the sources of new law, with the exception of the *edictum perpetuum*. Hadrian took the great step of reducing the *edictum* to a uniform system of universal binding force ; henceforth the magistrates could not alter the code ; they had to accept it and administer it as a whole ; nor could they add to it. The code was, of course, constantly being added to, but the additions now originated from one of the sources controlled by the Emperor. The magistrate ceased to be a law-maker.

Salvius Iulianus, Compiler of the Code. For the gigantic task of codification Hadrian selected Salvius Iulianus. Born at a small village, Pupput, on the coast of Africa, Julian came to Rome to study law under Iavolenus Priscus. There his exceptional knowledge of the law attracted Hadrian's attention, and, while he was still quaestor, he was entrusted with his great work, at a date unknown to us ; he finished it by A.D. 129. Though in the next two reigns he was a provincial governor, he found time to write a large number of books on law, and his influence on the development of Roman law lasted for centuries. For not the least valuable result of the codification was the impulse given to legal studies. Commentaries and Digests follow one another in voluminous progress, and within the next hundred years are to be found some of the greatest names of Roman jurisprudence, Paul and Marcellus and, greatest of all, Papinian and Ulpian.

The Effect of Hadrian's Reforms. The whole trend of Hadrian's reforms is in the direction of centralization with a view to efficiency. There is little doubt that efficiency did result ; the Emperor was now furnished with a civil service which could recruit men of brains and family and offer them a career. The Senate no doubt felt that the rise of the equites diminished its prestige, but actually its functions were not encroached on. In law, finance, administration the grip of the Emperor became tighter, but no one could say that the Empire suffered. ' Dum veritati consulitur, libertas corrumpebatur ' says Tacitus of an earlier age ; but neither *iudices* nor *curatores* nor *procuratores* necessarily meant the curtailment of liberty. If, later, the power of officials increased, the blame lies rather on those who hoped by the multiplication of bureaucrats to cure deep-seated ills. Hadrian attempted no radical change in the constitution ;

the developments which took place under him were really inherent in the system from its beginning.

Hadrian's Buildings. In the course of his travels Hadrian had built temples and monuments, roads, bridges and aqueducts in every province ; ' in almost every city ', says his biographer, ' Hadrian built something or founded public games '. He was fond of architecture and believed himself to have some ability in design. He designed a new temple of Venus and Rome, and sent the plans and drawings of the statues to Apollodorus, the architect ; the professional's criticism did not spare the amateur ; among other defects the statues were out of proportion ; ' if the goddesses wish to rise and leave their temple, they will not be able '. However the temple was built—presumably the plans were revised—on the Velian Hill and dedicated in A.D. 135 ; it commemorated Venus, as the ancestress of the Roman people, and the abiding genius of Roma Aeterna. It was destroyed before the ninth century. But three other buildings of Hadrian still remain, though much altered in their long history. Sometime before A.D. 125 he ' restored ' the Pantheon, built by Agrippa in 27 B.C. and burnt down in A.D. 80 ; but, since even the foundations of the existing building date from Hadrian's reign,[1] it is clear that the restoration is really a new construction, though Hadrian generously attributed it to Agrippa, as the inscription on the portico shows, ' M. Agrippa L.f. cos. tertium fecit.'

Towards the end of his reign Hadrian began the building of a great Mausoleum for himself ; it was finished in A.D. 139 by Antoninus, and in it were laid the bodies of the Antonine Emperors. Placed in the gardens of Nero on the right bank of the Tiber it was approached by a magnificent bridge— the Pons Aelius—built by Hadrian and finished in A.D. 134. This circular building was once encased in white marble, now long since stripped away ; it was surmounted by a colossal

[1] Platner and Ashby, *A Topographical Dictionary of Rome*, p. 383. This building with its portico and rotunda and interesting history is well known. In it Raphael was buried, in A.D. 1520 ; in 1625 Pope Urban VIII stripped away its bronze for cannon ; hence ' quod non fecerunt barbari, fecerunt Barberini '.

statue of Hadrian driving a four-horse chariot. In A.D. 590 above the building Pope Gregory beheld the Archangel Michael sheathing his flaming sword ; it was a sign that the wrath of God was appeased and that the plague which devastated the city would abate. And from that time the Mausoleum of Hadrian has been known as the Castle of St. Angelo.

Another building which may be briefly noticed is the Emperor's villa at Tibur. The villa, in one of the loveliest spots of Italy, was a country estate of about two and a half square miles ; beside the palace, set on a ridge between two streams flowing down to the Anio, there were other buildings —halls, corridors, colonnades and baths, a theatre and temples. For Hadrian with curious taste built replicas of what had pleased him in his travels—the Lyceum, the Academy, the Poicile, while the grounds were laid out to imitate, here, Thessalian Tempe, there, the Canopus of Alexandria ; within the villa Hadrian displayed his collections of works of art. Here, too, he could gratify those interests in literature, music, painting, mathematics which he had cherished throughout his long reign, and which helped to give his travels such fascination for him.

Hadrian's Interest in Art and Literature. Hadrian prided himself on having some taste in literature. There is no need to suspect that his interest in it was anything but genuine ; he was no poseur. Men of letters and artists received encouragement and reward at his hands. He was outspoken in his judgements. Favorinus, a learned man of the time, ventured to dispute the Emperor's use of a particular word, but presently owned that the Emperor was right. His friends asked him why he yielded ; ' The lord of thirty legions ', he laughed, ' must be allowed to know better.' Hadrian's taste was odd ; he preferred Ennius to Vergil, Cato to Caesar, Antimachus to Homer. He was fond of writing verses both in Greek and Latin, and several Latin epitaphs written by him are extant. One is written on his favourite horse Borysthenes, another on a Batavian soldier. Epigram seemed to attract him and he liked to cap one with another. The impression given by the remains of Hadrian's writing does not suggest that he can have exerted much influence on the literature of the day.

Yet it is difficult to be certain, for among them there are ' five lines of purest and most simple music of language, eternal alike for their simple fragile grace as for their sorrowful vain questioning into the unknown '.[1] They were uttered almost with the Emperor's last breath, when the death for which he yearned as a release from long-suffered pain was close at hand.

> Animula vagula blandula,
> Hospes comesque corporis,
> Quae nunc abibis in loca,
> Pallidula rigida nudula,
> Nec ut soles dabis iocos ?[2]

Plans for the Succession. The Emperor had no children, and, when in A.D. 135 or 136 he felt the slow wasting disease come upon him which was later to be his death, he turned his thoughts to the choice of a successor. In relationship Cn. Pedanius Fuscus stood closest. He was the grandson of Servianus, who had married Hadrian's sister, and was about eighteen years old, while Servianus was about ninety. Rumour played with both these names and no doubt much intrigue followed. All that is certain is that Hadrian put to death both Fuscus and Servianus. There may have been a plot, or Hadrian may have been demented by his pain ; we do not know. He then chose his heir, and, though there were men of distinction and ability, e.g. Aulus Platorius Nepos, whom he might have chosen, his choice fell on Lucius Ceionius Commodus Verus. Aelius Verus, as he was called after his adoption, had acquired a reputation as a lover of pleasure ; he was luxurious, good-natured, fond of literature. Hadrian adopted him and at once made him governor of Pannonia, where he seems to have acquitted himself with some credit. But his health was unsound, and in January A.D. 138 he died of consumption and was buried with imperial

---

[1] B. W. Henderson.

[2] ' Poor, pretty, fluttering soul, till now
In this kind body housed so safe,
To what strange realms departest thou—
A little, dim, chilled desolate waif ?
Ended—alas !—those comrade days,
And ended thy dear, merry ways.'

S. C. S.

magnificence in Hadrian's Mausoleum. Hadrian, therefore, had to make another choice of heir. At once he recommended to the Senate Titus Aurelius Fulvus Boionius Arrius Antoninus, a senator then aged fifty-one years, of blameless life ; a month later he adopted him as his son, bestowing proconsular imperium and tribunician power on him and so making him his consort in power. But the adoption was conditional. Antoninus must himself adopt two sons ; the first was Lucius, son of Aelius Verus Caesar and eleven years old ; the second was Marcus Annius Verus, aged sixteen, Antoninus' nephew, the future Emperor Marcus Aurelius.

It is difficult to give a reason for Hadrian's choice of Aelius Verus. The account which we have of him does not suggest that he would have made a good Emperor. Hadrian was fond of him, and presumably that is why he insisted that Antoninus should adopt the young Lucius, who at that age could scarcely give much indication of promise. On the other hand, in choosing Antoninus Hadrian showed judgement ; Antoninus held a predominant position in senatorial circles and as Emperor would be respected by all ; his policy, too, was likely to be a continuation of Hadrian's. Annius Verus, as will be seen later, had won Hadrian's affection, and there is every likelihood that this serious boy gave early promise of his strong character.

Hadrian's Death. Hadrian had but a few months to live ; his illness became worse ; in agony he prayed for the death which none would hasten for him ; yet, says Dio, he died daily. On 10 July, A.D. 138, at Baiae he breathed his last ; his ashes were brought to Rome and placed in his Mausoleum. With difficulty Antoninus obtained the title of Divus for Hadrian, but his persistence was successful and is one of the many explanations of his cognomen ' Pius '.

We are given no reason why the Senate should have been unwilling to give Hadrian divine honours. Some modern writers have believed that the Senate never liked him ; the murder of the four consulars and, recently, of Servianus, the recognition given to the equites, it is urged, produced a lasting hostility ; yet, if it had amounted to very much, he could scarcely have left Italy for years on end. Lack of sympathy was due rather to Hadrian's own personality, which was too complex to be easily understood.

The Dawn of the Age of the Antonines. When Hadrian died the world was at peace and was destined to be so for many years. Hadrian had made this his aim and he was successful. He had drawn the provinces closer and had given the Empire greater unity. He had helped backward districts, relieved agriculture, fostered town life. The legal code for which he was responsible became the foundation of later Roman law ; his civil service carried good government to the remotest places. The Golden Age of the Antonines was now to come, but the labours of Trajan and Hadrian alone made it possible.

CHAPTER XVI

THE PRINCIPATES OF ANTONINUS PIUS, A.D. 138–161, AND MARCUS AURELIUS, A.D. 161–180

*T*HE *Early Career of Antoninus.* T. Aurelius Fulvus Boionius Arrius Antoninus was fifty-one years old when he succeeded to the Empire. His family came from Nemausus (Nîmes). Antoninus himself was born at Lanuvium and educated at Lorium. His grandfather and father had been consulars, and he himself had held the usual offices and had been one of the four consular judges of Italy and proconsul of Asia. He married the sister of Aelius Verus, Annia Galeria Faustina ; his two sons died before his rise to power ; one of his two daughters, Faustina, he married to Marcus Aurelius, his adopted son, A.D. 145.[1]

The Reign of Antoninus. There is little to tell about the reign of Antoninus Pius. The historians leave us little information about important happenings either in Italy or the provinces ; this very lack of incident has been taken by

---

[1] According to *Vita Marci*, iv. 5, vi. 2, and *Vita Veri*, ii. 3, Hadrian wished Marcus to marry Lucius' sister, Fabia Ceionia, and Lucius to marry Faustina ; but cf. *Vita Marci*, xvi. 7. Since Hadrian wished Marcus to succeed him eventually, perhaps before Aelius' death he wished to betroth Marcus to Fabia, and after Antoninus' adoption to betroth him to Faustina.

some for a proof of the tranquillity of his times. Our sources are more concerned to describe the character of the man than to recount his acts. It may be said at once that no single rebuke is brought against him, except that in financial matters he was too thrifty ; apart from this criticism the ancient writers are in complete agreement as to his nobility of character. Even the Augustan History, which does not spare most other Emperors, sounds no discordant note. The letters of Fronto, fulsome in any case, cannot say enough in his praise ; the portrait given of him by Marcus Aurelius is a fine tribute to his influence over his young son, Aelius Aristides writes a probably sincere panegyric of the Antonine age and its author. There is no doubt that the good relations which Antoninus maintained with the Senate are in part responsible for the nature of the tradition about him ; but it is clear that his character made a great impression on his age. It is easier, therefore, to describe the man and his private life than to write a history of his reign. Since it is largely through the letters of Fronto and Marcus that we know with some intimacy the character of Antoninus, and since Marcus for over twenty years was closely associated with him, some account of Marcus himself will not be out of place here.

The Early Life of Marcus Aurelius. Marcus was born in A.D. 121 in Rome. His family came from Spain originally, and his grandfather had held the highest offices. While still a baby he lost his father and for a time lived in his grandfather's house in Rome, returning later to his mother's house on the Caelian Hill. His mother, Domitia Lucilla, an educated woman,[1] seems to have exercised great influence on her son, who speaks of her with much affection.[2] The boy was naturally studious, and we know something about his early education and much about his later rhetorical and philosophical studies ; he was taught at home by tutors ; chief among them was Fronto under whom he studied rhetoric, forsaking it later for philosophy to his tutor's great grief.

Marcus soon attracted the attention of Hadrian, who was struck by the boy's serious mind ;[3] among other marks of

---

[1] Fronto wrote to her in Greek.   She died in A.D. 156.   [2] *Medit.* i. 3.
[3] Playing upon the family name he called Marcus ' Verissimus '.

favour he gave him the privileges of knighthood, a most unusual honour for so young a boy. When Hadrian adopted Antoninus and Antoninus in turn adopted his nephew Marcus, Marcus went to live at his imperial grandfather's palace.[1] He left his own home, we are told, with sadness ; he seems already to have become aware of the burden of empire descending on him. Two years after the death of Hadrian, i.e. A.D. 140, Marcus became a member of Antoninus' household, and from that time a close and intimate friendship sprang up between father and son and Emperor and heir, which was cemented still further when in A.D. 145 Marcus married the younger Faustina, Antoninus' daughter.

Marcus was hurried from office to office with a view to occupying the position of consort as soon as possible. In A.D. 139 he held the quaestorship ; he was given the title of Caesar and thus marked out as heir to the Empire. In A.D. 140 he was consul with Antoninus as his colleague, and in A.D. 145 he held the consulship a second time. In the following year he was invested with the proconsular imperium and tribunician power, and thus became consort in the Empire at the age of twenty-five years.

It is noteworthy that Marcus received no military or administrative training in the provinces. He devoted himself to his studies and to the service of his father ; there was no time, says Dio, when he was not under instruction by tutors, and in the palace ' he was the slave of Antoninus '. To what extent he actually shared responsibility is uncertain [2] ; in a letter to Fronto, however, Marcus says that attendance at the law-courts takes up all his time, in another that he has just dictated thirty letters. Fronto congratulates him on a piece of literary work, composed though it was at a time when he was distracted by business-duties and letters to be answered throughout the provinces. In the palace Marcus won golden opinions ; his modest bearing, his simplicity of manner and his willingness endeared him to all.

The Private Life of Antoninus. Power came too late to

[1] ' Educatus est in Hadriani gremio.' *Vit. Marci*, iv. 1.

[2] *Vita Marci*, vi. 5. 'Cum formandus ad regendum statum reipublicae patris actibus interesset.'

Antoninus for it to make a great change in his character
or his manner of life. He continued to live on the same
easy terms of friendship as before his accession. Naturally
handsome, says his biographer, he was gentle, high-minded,
capable, generous, a good speaker and a lover of the country ;
he showed all these traits without carrying any to extremes
and without display. In particular, his simplicity impressed
his contemporaries. He dispensed as far as he could with
the formality and unnecessary pomp of the court.[1] He kept
the imperial freedmen under control. Much of the imperial
land and other property he sold, preferring to live upon his
own estates. His table was simply furnished ; he entertained
his friends freely and was a constant visitor at their houses.
He gathered round him men of letters and philosophers ;
Cornelius Fronto, Herodes Atticus, Junius Rusticus are perhaps the best known ; but the favour shown to such men
was probably rather in the interests of Marcus, for the Emperor
himself, though accomplished and particularly fond of drama,
took more pleasure in country pursuits, fishing and hunting.
He spent much of his time at Lorium, Lanuvium and Centumcellae, where he had villas, or at Naples and Baiae ; and
the letters of Marcus to Fronto give the most pleasing accounts
of the quiet and happy life which this devoted family led.
The letters deal chiefly with Marcus' own activities and in
particular his studies ; paraphrases of random passages will
show something of the way in which the day passed in the
imperial villas.

' I worked from three in the morning till eight ; at eight
I put on my slippers and walked about in front of my room
for an hour and enjoyed it.   I then put on my boots and cloak
—for that is how we have been commanded to present ourselves—and went off to say good morning to the Emperor.
Then we went hunting and did brave things ; I was told some
boars were killed, but I had no chance to see. Anyhow we
climbed a steep hill and reached home after mid-day. I
took off my boots and clothes and lay on my bed, reading
Cato's speech on Pulchra's property. . . . After reading the
speeches I wrote some miserable stuff worthy of the huntsmen

[1] ' Imperatorium fastigium in civilitatem deduxit.'   *Vita Pii*, vi. 4.

and vintagers whose din resounds through my room as I write. I seem to have caught cold; I don't know whether it is because I went out this morning in slippers or because I have written so badly. I shall pour the oil on my head and go to sleep, for I don't intend to put a drop into my lamp to-night; my riding and sneezing have tired me out.' [1]

'I slept late on account of my tiny cold which seems to bebetter. From five to seven o'clock I read some Cato "On Agriculture" and wrote a little, rather better than yesterday. I greeted my father and then attended to my throat, gargling with water and honey. . . . After lunch we all picked grapes hard; we got very hot and were very merry. At noon we returned home. I then had a long chat with my mother, while she was sitting above my couch. . . . Presently the gong sounded, a sign that my father was going to the bath. We dined in the oil-press room and were much entertained listening to the banter of the country people. And so back again; but, before turning over on my side to snore, I must give my dearest master an account of my day.' [2] Another letter describes a visit to Anagnia, a small town full of antiquities, shrines and curious customs, into which Marcus inquired diligently. Another describes how he was riding past a flock of sheep driven along a road, and overheard one shepherd warn the other to beware of the horsemen, for they were robbers; so Marcus set spurs to his horse, rode in among the sheep and scattered them in every direction.

Of Antoninus we have two descriptions written by Marcus himself; the shorter of the two may be quoted.[3] 'Do all things as a disciple of Antoninus,' he exhorts himself. 'Remember his perseverance in every rational act, his even temper everywhere, his piety, his calmness of expression, his gentleness, his contempt of empty fame, his eager grasp of affairs; how he would never dismiss anything till he had examined it through and through and understood it clearly; how patient he was with those who criticized him unfairly, though he never criticized them in return; how he never

[1] Naber, p. 68.   [2] Naber, p. 70.
[3] *Medit.* i. 16, vi. 30; the other may be found in Merivale.

hurried ; how he gave no hearing to slander, how acute a judge of character and act ; himself neither given to blame nor fear of men's opinion nor suspicion nor sophistry ; with what little he was satisfied—house, bed, food, servants ; how devoted to his work, how long-suffering, how firm and unvarying in his friendships. Remember his tolerance of those who outspokenly opposed his views, and his satisfaction when they made out the better case ; how god-fearing he was, yet not superstitious. Remember this, so that your last hour may come upon you, as upon him, with a conscience at rest.'

Antoninus and the Senate. In part the success of this reign was due to the good relation between the Emperor and the Senate, though it must be remembered that the Senate was very different in character and temper from that of the early Empire. Antoninus consulted his friends in everything, and gave an account of his actions in the Senate. He gave great satisfaction to this body when he restored to it the judicial administration of Italy by abolishing the four circuit judges appointed by Hadrian. It was his policy, says his biographer, to hand over to the Senate as much power as he would have wished it to have if he had himself remained a senator. At the same time he made no change which really increased its power ; the knights still occupied the important position given to them by Hadrian. On the other hand, the easy social relations between Antoninus and individual senators, the simplicity of his court, where powerful freedmen with favours to sell could obtain no footing, made him popular with the Senate as a whole. In later reigns, when the Senate wished to pay the highest compliment to an Emperor, it begged him to accept the name of ' Antoninus '.

Provincial Policy ; Finance. Antoninus showed the same broad sympathy with the provinces as Hadrian. The literary sources lay stress on the prosperity of the world under his rule and attribute it to his ready appreciation of the provincials' point of view. He undertook no progresses through the provinces, because, he said, they were a burden and expense to the cities visited. Antoninus preferred to stay at Rome or close to Rome, where he could receive dispatches

17

from the provinces and deal with them promptly. He retained able governors for some time in their posts, sometimes for seven or nine years, and the Praefectus praetorio, Gavius Maximus, held his office for twenty years. Procurators had injunctions to use no severity in the collection of taxes, and complaints against fiscal agents found a sympathetic hearing, for the Emperor made a point of mastering the details of imperial finance. It is interesting to find that at this era of the Empire certain sinecures had already found their way into the imperial service ; these the Emperor abolished.[1] Yet he could be generous with state funds when famine occurred ; when an earthquake destroyed cities in Asia Minor, he made liberal contributions towards the relief of the afflicted areas. He also spent money on public buildings. His biographer sums up his policy in the words ' opulentia sine reprehensione, parsimonia sine sordibus '.

We hear of one or two minor risings in Dacia and Mauretania, and a revolt in Egypt caused the Emperor to visit that country ; but it is clear that these troubles were not very serious.[2] There is general evidence that the provinces were happy ; a paraphrase of one or two passages from the Panegyric of Aelius Aristides will show a little of what one of Rome's admirers thought of her government.

' You have divided all who belong to your Empire into two classes ; the more civilized and powerful you have turned into citizens and made them of one race ; the rest remain subject to you. Neither the sea nor intervening lands debar men from citizenship, nor is Asia distinguished from Europe. All is open to all. No one worthy of office or trust is regarded as a stranger ; the whole commonwealth of the earth is governed by one good ruler, and each member of it resorts as it were to one common market place, to receive thence his rights. . . . Everywhere your rule is equal. . . . There is no distinction between island and continent, but, as though one land and one race, all obey in silence. Every ordinance and command is obeyed in a finger-flash ; it is enough for a thing

---

[1] And perhaps earned the adjective $\varkappa\upsilon\mu\iota\nu\sigma\pi\rho\iota\sigma\tau\eta\varsigma$, the one opprobrious epithet applied to him.

[2] Pausanias, viii. 43, gives a brief account of the wars of this reign.

to be decreed and it is done. The governors sent to the cities and the provinces are supreme in their sphere ; yet all render obedience ; the difference between them and their subjects is that they are the first to display the duty of obedience. You hold universal empire, but this is the distinguishing mark of your empire, that you rule over men who are free. . . . You alone has nature fitted to be rulers. The whole world keeps holiday ; the ancient burden of the sword has been laid aside and the world turns to every happiness. All strife is stilled ; there remains only the rivalry of cities, striving how each may be the fairest and most beautiful. Every city is full of gymnasia, fountains, porticoes, temples, workshops and schools. You do not stint your gifts to them ; never were they more blessed, thanks to your generosity extended to all alike. The cities are brilliant in their splendour and charm and the whole earth is adorned as it were a garden.'[1]

Foreign Relations. Hadrian's tactful frontier policy secured for his successor a period of almost unbroken peace. Our own island was the scene of the most vigorous fighting of this reign (p. 289). Important progress was made in the Germano-Raetian sector of the northern frontier (p. 195). In the East the city of Olbia had to be protected against raids by the Scythians, and the Alans of the Caucasus broke into Armenia. A letter from Antoninus to the Parthian king, we are told, dissuaded him from interfering in Armenian affairs. But there would probably be a different tale to tell if our authorities were not so miserably scanty, for an inscription shows that a certain Neratius Priscus was sent to Syria in command of some detachments of troops ' ob bellum Parthicum ' (probably A.D. 158).[2] Pius saw no doubt that a war was imminent, and perhaps Vologeses was one of the kings against whom Pius inveighed in the delirium in which he lay before his death. His biographer says that no one had such influence on foreign nations, for he always loved

---

[1] These passages contain much truth, in spite of all that can be said on the other side. Dio Chrysostom, e.g., is very scathing on the subject of the petty local jealousies of the Eastern cities.

[2] Dessau, I.L.S. 1076.

peace, so much so that the maxim of Scipio was often on his tongue, ' I prefer to preserve one citizen than to destroy a thousand of the enemy.' When the troubles of the next reign are borne in mind, it is difficult to resist the conclusion that, if Antoninus had shown a more vigorous policy, the disasters which followed his death need not have been so serious.

The Death of Antoninus. The intimate association of Emperor and adopted son, which had lasted for nearly twenty-two years, was brought to an end in A.D. 161 by the death of Antoninus at Lorium. He was seventy-four years old and his health had long been feeble. After three days' illness he felt his end approaching. He entrusted the state and his daughter to the care of Marcus ; he commanded that the statue of Fortune which always stood in the reigning Emperor's chamber should be taken to Marcus' room, and gave to the officer of the guard the watchword ' Aequanimitas ', thus summing up in his last conscious act his own life and the history of his reign.[1] For some time he lingered in delirium and died on 7 March, A.D. 161. His ashes were laid in the Mausoleum of Hadrian, and the temple which he had built to do honour to his wife was dedicated to them both—' Divo Antonino et Divae Faustinae '.

Accession of Marcus Aurelius ; Lucius Verus becomes Joint Emperor. Thus Marcus after his long apprenticeship succeeded to the Empire, compelled, says his Life, by the Senate. He immediately insisted that he should make Lucius, his ' brother ', his partner, investing him with the same powers as he himself held and honouring him with the title Augustus. ' From that time they began to rule jointly.'[2]

The figure of Lucius Verus, no less than that of his father Aelius, is surrounded with uncertainty. Seven years younger than Marcus, he was brought up in the house of Antoninus, sharing the simple healthy life of the imperial family, but never admitted, as Marcus was, to the confidence of the Emperor, nor undertaking administrative duties, though he

---

[1] Or expressing the calm confidence with which he entrusted the Empire to his successor.

[2] *Vit. Marci,* vii. 6. ' Ex eo pariter coeperunt rempublicam regere.'

was made quaestor and consul. As a boy he was high-spirited and impulsive, no student, but capable of correspond-ing on literary matters. Marcus entertained much affection and some admiration for him, congratulating himself that he had such a brother 'who was able by his character to urge me to watch over myself, and by his respect and devotion to give me pleasure'.[1] The praises of Lucius are sung by Fronto and Aristides and by certain later writers. Yet others dwell on his irresponsibility and love of pleasure, and attribute to him the worst excesses of the debauchee. It is probable that these latter charges are exaggerated, and that Lucius, though lacking his brother's strength of character, was in himself not unattractive.

Again, just as it is difficult to know why Hadrian insisted that Lucius should be adopted together with Marcus, so it is uncertain why Marcus raised Lucius to equal power. He may have felt that his brother's chance of succession was at one time more favourable than his own, though it was defeated by the death of Aelius ; and it would be characteristic of the man to make amends by associating Lucius in the Empire with himself. Cassius Dio gives another reason ; Marcus, he says, was physically weak, while Lucius was robust, younger and more fitted for a soldier's life. There is little doubt that Marcus realized that the peaceful times of Antoninus were over ; yet, as it turned out, it was Marcus himself who eventu-ally made the better soldier, schooling himself to warfare and enduring the hardships of campaigns on the northern frontier.

For the innovation of a co-equal Emperor Marcus has been severely censured. It was a plan which would only succeed in the special case in which it originated ; Marcus was devoid of jealousy, and Lucius was likely to be satisfied with the dignity conferred on him without harbouring designs of sole power. But otherwise it was a precedent fraught with danger and destined to lead to civil war or the division of the Empire between the two Augusti. Both these results occurred in later times ; but it would be impossible to say that they would not have occurred, if Marcus had not given precedent for the rule of two Emperors.

[1] Mommsen deplores Marcus' inability to judge character.

Finance. The quiet reign of Antoninus might have been expected to give the Empire a chance of recovering from the tremendous expense of Trajan's wars and Hadrian's building. But his policy, though careful, does not seem to have filled the exchequer to overflowing. There were ample funds from which Marcus and Lucius on their accession gave a *congiarium* to the people and to the troops in Rome a handsome donative, consisting of five years' pay to the praetorians and two and a half years' pay to the urban cohorts. This was an unusually large sum to be spent in this way, but events caused Marcus to be more economical for the rest of his reign. For war and pestilence and famine caused enormous expense to the Treasury, and the financial resources of some of the largest cities were unequal to the demands made on them. Soon after coming to the throne Marcus was compelled to cancel debts to the fisc and aerarium, and he sold imperial treasures—gems, crystal, silks and so on ; and later he found it necessary, against his wish, to exact taxes and to call in loans ; and he had resort to the policy, so fatal later, of depreciating the currency. He was stingy, says the Life, in making grants of public money, ' quod laudi potius datur quam reprehensioni ' ; yet in time of need he came to the relief of individuals and towns, remitting taxes and making grants of corn and money to towns ruined by earthquake and perishing of famine. He scorned to accept information which might profit the fisc or to favour the fisc in courts of law. When the soldiers, after the victories of the Marcomannic war, clamoured for increased pay, he was staunch in refusal ; if they received more, it must come from the lifeblood of their parents and kindred ; the strength of the imperial power lay not in soldiers, but in God. Marcus showed greater courage in defiance of his soldiers than some of his more military predecessors.

The Senate. The Senate under Marcus Aurelius had no reason for complaint. He increased its prestige rather than its powers ; whatever new authority he gave was judicial rather than administrative. The Senate now heard appeals from the consul, and carried through inquiries which particularly affected the imperial interest. Marcus also delegated some of his judicial work to praetorians and consulars. If a senator were tried on a capital charge, he investigated it himself, and, if there was a case to go before a court, he excluded knights from all part in the trial. He attended the meetings of the Senate as regularly as he could, and, if he wished to propose a motion, he did so in person, even travelling from Campania for the purpose. He continued to consult the ' optimates ' on matters of military or administrative importance ; his personal relations with individual senators were of the happiest. Though he refused to promise not to put a senator to death, yet in fact he shrank from doing so, and after the rebellion of Avidius Cassius (p. 270), he besought the Senate to be merciful, for he did not wish his reign to be stained by the death of any senator. But the ranks of the order were thinned by war and plague, and the Emperor resorted with some freedom to ' adlection ', in which his choice was always dictated by close personal knowledge.

Law and Humanity ; Ius gentium. The reigns of Antoninus and Marcus Aurelius were marked by progress towards humanity and the embodiment of broader principles in law. Antoninus' gentle nature and the philosophical outlook of Marcus urged them in this direction. It would, however, be a mistake to assume that the philosopher on the throne was solely responsible for the maintained tendency towards humanity. Stoicism had claimed the allegiance of many of the most educated and thoughtful minds in the first two centuries. Early in the Empire it had associated itself with Republicanism ; in the second century it exerted its influence upon law instead of upon politics. The ideal of Stoicism was ' secundum Naturam vivere ' ; Nature had a code of laws which could be followed ; the ' ius naturale ' had been lost sight of ; and just as the ' ius civile ' was broadened by the growing recognition of ' ius gentium ' due to Rome's expansion, so ' ius gentium ', it was thought, was a faint copy of ' ius naturale ' which might in time be recovered. The influence of Stoicism on law was indirect and gradual ; whenever old law was revised or needed to be reinterpreted, it was done in a broad spirit by lawyers who often had the Stoic ideal before them. This reinterpretation was really of more effect than the individual legislative enactments even of the Stoic Emperor. Marcus himself was responsible for many regulations on a variety of matters—he alleviated the condition of slaves, he insisted that nets should be stretched under acrobats, he reduced the expenses which might be incurred in gladiatorial games, he made changes in the law of inheritance, and adjusted the incidence of certain taxes. But his influence was probably more powerful through his own judgements in cases brought before him, to which we are told he devoted much time and attention, and his decisions show sense and humanity without sentimentalism.

The Parthian War. The threat of a Parthian war, which had made itself apparent towards the end of Antoninus' reign, came to a head soon after Marcus' accession. Vologeses III [1] took advantage of the change of Emperor to reopen the old Armenian controversy. Early in A.D. 162 he sent an army under Osroes, his general, into Armenia to place the Arsacid Pacorus on the throne ; who occupied it at the time is uncertain. M. Sedatianus Severianus, the legate of Cappadocia, since Vespasian's time an armed province, was responsible for the security of Armenia ; accordingly he crossed the Euphrates and was defeated and slain at Elegeia. A Parthian attack was also made on Syria, where revolt had apparently been contemplated ; the legions of the province under L. Atidius Cornelianus were utterly undisciplined and fled at the first engagement.

Roman Preparations. At Rome Marcus was making his preparations for the war even before the news of these disasters reached him. Lucius Verus was given supreme command, ' consentiente senatu ' ; capable generals were appointed to his staff, and troops were mustered to replace the lost armies. Marcus' presence was urgently demanded in Rome by recent distress caused by Tiber floods and by famine ; Lucius, he thought, was more likely to make a soldier than himself, and his presence in the East, as at least nominal commander, might lessen the risk of a rival Emperor being proclaimed.

[1] He reigned A.D. 148–92 (Marquardt). Mommsen thinks a Vologeses IV should be assumed.

To replace Severianus in Cappadocia, Statius Priscus was recalled from Britain, and Iulius Verus was appointed to Syria. Sometime early in the war Avidius Cassius took in hand the eastern army, disciplining them much as Corbulo had done a century before ; it is uncertain whether he was governor of Syria [1] or whether he went as chief of Lucius' staff, independent of any provincial command.

Troops were brought from distant provinces. Since the time of Hadrian the practice of moving detachments rather than whole legions had become common, and in the wars of Marcus Aurelius this practice is very apparent. The legion was becoming a garrison rather than a mobile force, and the *vexillationes* became miniature independent legions. And in Marcus' reign, when troops were scarce and were badly needed to deal with simultaneous disturbances, the system had advantages ; but it is evidence of the inadequacy of the Roman army at the time. Thus in the course of the war legio I Minervia was moved to Cappadocia from Bonn,[2] legio II Adjutrix from Lower Pannonia, legio II Traiana from Egypt ; but detachments came also from Vindobona, Moesia, Lambaesis together with auxiliaries from Mauretania and elsewhere. Two new legions were levied in Italy [3] and even some of the free cities—e.g. Sparta and cities in Asia Minor —enrolled citizens and freedmen in volunteer regiments. The whole organization of the war, as far as it could be effected from a distance, rested on Marcus ; though he gave all credit to Lucius, he admitted after his death that the whole plan of campaign had been his own.[4]

Marcus accompanied his brother as far as Capua, whence Lucius went to the south-east of Italy, setting sail from Brundisium in the autumn of A.D. 162. He called at Corinth and at Athens, where he visited his friend Herodes Atticus and was initiated into the Eleusinian mysteries, and eventually reached Antioch. Of his conduct in this luxurious city our

[1] From A.D. 164 Mommsen thinks.
[2] A revolt of the Chatti was perhaps due to the removal of these troops.
[3] II and III Italica, stationed after the war in Raetia and Noricum.
[4] 'Omnia . . . disposuit Marcus et ordinavit.' *Vita Marci*, viii. 14.

sources have far more to say than of the war itself, of which it is therefore impossible to give a detailed account. The main work was probably done by Lucius' generals.[1] In A.D. 163 Statius Priscus destroyed Artaxata, the capital of Armenia, and founded Kainepolis to take its place. The title ' Armeniacus ' was taken by Lucius in A.D. 163 and by Marcus Aurelius in the following year, when the trouble was really ended by the installing of Sohaemus as king of Armenia.[2] In A.D. 164 the Romans claimed to have overrun Mesopotamia ; Osroene fell into their hands, and this victory marks the successful beginning of the campaign in Parthia itself. Apparently Lucius offered the Parthians peace, which was rejected. Then the Romans moved (in two columns ?) against Edessa and Nisibis, and by Nicephorium down the Euphrates valley ; Seleucia was burnt to the ground, and, perhaps towards the end of A.D. 165, Ctesiphon was captured. In the following year Roman troops penetrated into Media.

In A.D. 166 Lucius returned to Rome and near the end of the year both Emperors celebrated a triumph. Lucius took the title ' Armenaicus Parthicus Maximus Medicus ', and after much pressure Marcus also agreed to accept this title, though later he renounced it. The war had crushed the Parthians for the moment and had slightly enlarged Roman territory, giving the Romans a foothold on the East bank of the Euphrates. Osroene was governed by a Roman official, Edessa received Mannos Philoromaios as its king, Carrhae was placed under Roman protection ; the rest of the territory overrun was handed back to the Parthians. Thus in a very modified form Trajan's policy was accepted by Marcus.

Avidius Cassius, to whom the success of the war was largely due, was made governor of Syria (A.D. 169), and was given superior powers over the governors of Asia, Cappadocia, Egypt and perhaps still further. It was clear to Marcus that

[1] Fronto gives an elaborate description of the splendid example of physical endurance which Lucius set. Unfortunately he compares him with Trajan, to Trajan's disadvantage, and this somewhat shakes our trust in Fronto as reliable evidence.

[2] About this time Lucius returned to meet Lucilla, Marcus' daughter, who was being brought east by Faustina ; Lucilla had been betrothed to him on his accession, and the marriage took place at Ephesus.

unity of command was essential in the East, for conditions were by no means settled. There is evidence of a revolt of the Boucoloi, Egyptian peasants, which Avidius suppressed ; the Bastarnae and other tribes made raids into Asia Minor, and in A.D. 172 there was a serious threat of another Parthian war, which, however, came to nothing. But the appointment of Avidius Cassius to such a command was dangerous, as events proved.

The Plague. The troops returned to their stations at the end of A.D. 166. They returned apparently triumphant, but they were to inflict upon the West a disaster far more serious than upon the Parthians. They brought back with them a plague—smallpox or bubonic plague has been suggested—which ravaged not only the Eastern provinces but spread also to Italy and the West, carrying off a good proportion of the army and numbers of the civilian population. The plague, together with a famine which was already bearing heavily on Italy, severely reduced the population of the Empire, and some historians consider that it was one of the main causes contributing to the decline of the Roman Empire. However this may be, the loss of so many soldiers could ill be afforded, for grave dangers threatened within and without the frontiers.

The Germano-Sarmatian War. In the first year of Marcus' reign the unsettled state of the tribes on the Northern frontier had become apparent. With considerable skill a serious invasion had been delayed by the governors[1] of the Northern provinces, who used both arms and diplomacy. The cause of the unrest was certainly not provocation by the Romans, but rather pressure upon the frontier tribes caused by the shiftings of the peoples still further North. Hordes of Langobardi and Marcomanni crossed into Pannonia and begged for land ; the Roman governor drove them back across the Danube. At this time the Parthian war broke out and the defence of the Northern frontier was necessarily weakened by the withdrawal of troops. Probably before the conclusion

---

[1] Among others, Aufidius Victorinus, who repulsed a raid of the Chatti into Germany in A.D. 162 ; Claudius Pompeianus, a governor of Lower Pannonia ; Calpurnius Agricola in Dacia.

of the Eastern war, vast bands of Marcomanni, Quadi and Iazyges broke into Pannonia, Raetia, Noricum and Dacia; some of them penetrated as far as Opitergium, which they destroyed, and Aquileia, which they invested; others threatened Sarmizegethusae.

Such was the situation which confronted the Emperor. The army was diminished by disease, the people oppressed by famine and plague and hysterical with fright, the exchequer was well-nigh empty. The situation was met with a heroism and a skill which confounded those who mocked at their studious Emperor. To provide money Marcus sold the imperial treasures; legions or *vexillationes* were summoned from Palestine, Arabia, Egypt and Cappadocia. Orders were issued for the immediate strengthening of the cities which might otherwise fall into the hands of the barbarians, e.g., Salonae in Dalmatia, and Philippopolis in Thrace. Recruits were called for, a measure which required tact amid the general panic. Marcus and Lucius then marched north to Aquileia. The Quadi at once submitted and were allowed to retreat on condition that they surrendered the thousands of prisoners whom they had taken. And now Marcus, rejecting the advice of his brother to offer peace, determined to wage a war of extermination, which he soon had to carry on alone, for Lucius died in A.D. 169 at Altinum. He saw, first, that unity of command was necessary, for the various governors of provinces could not act in concert; secondly, that he must occupy Pannonia and so divide the tribes who might then be defeated separately; thirdly, that the north side of the Danube must be permanently occupied to protect Pannonia, Raetia and Noricum just as Dacia protected Moesia. Accordingly as supreme general he took up his head-quarters at Carnuntum in Pannonia. In Raetia and Noricum Tiberius Claudius Pompeianus, with his second in command, P. Helvius Pertinax, afterwards Emperor, routed the tribes and cleared the country so effectually that only the Iazyges and Marcomanni remained to be dealt with. After a bitter struggle, in which the Romans were often repulsed with the loss of army commanders,[1] a decisive defeat was inflicted on the

[1] E.g. M. Claudius Fronto and Marcus Macrinius Vindex.

Marcomanni and the Emperor assumed the title 'Germanicus'.[1] Still, the end was not in sight. The Quadi, taking advantage of the Emperor's absence, revolted under the leadership of a new king. Marcus, however, set a price on his head and he was surrendered. By A.D. 175 the Iazyges were crushed and Marcus took the title of 'Sarmaticus'.

Thus the immediate peril was averted. Marcus intended to organize at once two new provinces ;—Sarmatia, which would include the lands of the Iazyges to the west of Dacia, and Marcomannia, the district of Bohemia which Tiberius a century and a half earlier had proposed to annex when rebellion distracted him. Rebellion once more prevented the country from being Romanized, for in Syria Avidius Cassius was proclaimed Emperor, and Marcus must fight for his throne. He ordered the tribes to furnish contingents to the Roman army ; he ordered the Marcomanni and the Iazyges to leave the North bank of the Danube uninhabited to a depth of ten miles ; he placed garrisons in Marcomannia, and with his wife Faustina and his son Commodus he left for the East to engage with Cassius.

The Transplanting of Tribes. The incessant raids of the barbarians induced Marcus Aurelius to extend a practice for which there was already precedent in earlier reigns. Agrippa transferred to the left bank of the Rhine the tribe of Ubii ; they had remained faithful to Rome and had to a great extent accepted Roman ideals and manners ; their chief city was Oppidum Ubiorum (Cologne). In Augustus' reign also 40,000 Sugambri and Suebi were allowed to settle in Gaul, and with Roman permission 50,000 Dacians had migrated to Thrace. Under Claudius and Nero there were similar movements, but it was Marcus Aurelius who adopted

---

[1] The so-called 'miraculous victory' must be placed in the year A.D. 174. According to the story (Dio, lxxi. 8) a thunderstorm, which occurred during a battle, relieved the Roman army parched with thirst and threw the Quadi into confusion. Christian writers attribute the storm and the victory to the prayers of the Christian soldiers : Eusebius speaks of one legion as being composed of Christians ; and Christian tradition called it 'the Thundering Legion'. But Fulminata was in use in Augustus' time : and it is doubtful whether at this time a Christian legion was possible.

the plan on an extended scale.[1] In the Northern provinces
there were large areas of thinly populated land ; here great
numbers of Marcomanni, Quadi and other tribes were settled,
particularly in Dacia, Pannonia, Moesia and Germany, and
even in Italy at Ravenna. Some of the barbarians received
the same status as the provincials by whom they were absorbed ; the majority, however, were ' dediticii ', compelled
to remain on the lands which they tilled, and to protect
them from attack. This was the beginning of the ' colonate ',
which in a later age developed into serfdom. The barbarians
who were settled at Ravenna caused much disturbance
in trying to obtain the city for themselves ; they were
removed elsewhere and Marcus made no further settlements
in Italy.

The intentions lying behind the policy of transplanting
are clear. i. It tended to reduce the pressure of tribes on the
frontier. Tribes who had been friendly to Rome during the
wars were given the land which they desired within the
borders of the Empire ; hostile tribes were removed en masse
and reduced to the position of ' dediticii '. ii. From the
point of view of defence the intention was that the transplanted tribes, after absorbing something of Roman civilization, should themselves furnish recruits to the army ; the
barbarian was to keep out the barbarian. Both purposes
failed. There were always new hordes ready to swoop down
on the frontier ; in the third century Alamanni, Goths and
Vandals replaced the Marcomanni and Iazyges. Again the
Romanization of the transplanted tribes could not be the
work of a moment, but circumstances would not wait for the
process of Romanization to go far enough. The army became
increasingly barbarian in nature ; a Germanized army and
strong Germanic elements in the Northern provinces made
the final triumph of the invaders all the easier (p. 363).

The Revolt of Avidius Cassius, A.D. 175. Avidius Cassius
had used his extraordinary power to good advantage in
maintaining order in the East. He had made himself very
popular in Syria, particularly with the Antiochenes ; he was

[1] 'Infinitos ex gentibus in Romano solo collocavit.' *Vita Marci*
xxiv. 3.

himself a native of Cyrrhus. When a rumour gained ground that Marcus was dead, Cassius proclaimed himself Emperor, receiving the support of the governor of Egypt; Cappadocia, however, was held to its loyalty by Martius Verus. Marcus Aurelius travelled through Italy to the seat of the rebellion, receiving on his way the good wishes of the Senate, who proclaimed Cassius a public enemy. But he arrived too late. Cassius had been murdered by his officers when they learned that the rumour of Marcus' death was false, and Marcus was robbed of the chance of defeating and forgiving his rival. His wife and children, however, were spared; letters implicating Cassius' fellow-conspirators were burnt unread.

The Death of Faustina. Marcus visited Egypt and Syria, laying light punishment on the rebel towns. On these travels his wife accompanied him; she had already been with him on the Danube, where she was called ' Mater Castrorum '. At Halala, a small village near the Taurus range, she died. Marcus' grief was very great. He asked the Senate to grant divine honours to her, and in her memory he founded a charity for poor girls in Italy (p. 336). The character of Faustina has fared ill at the hands of writers of a later age, who accused her of infidelity to her husband and of complicity in the rebellion of Avidius Cassius, whom she had promised to marry; these stories may safely be rejected.

Return of Marcus to Rome. Commodus as Consort. On his way back to Rome Marcus visited many towns of the East. In many of them he showed his interest in literature and philosophy; at Smyrna, for example, he met the celebrated orator and philosopher Aristides; at Athens he listened to Adrian, whom he had appointed to the chair of rhetoric; here too he regulated the salaries of various professors; at Eleusis he was initiated into the mysteries. Returning to Rome he was pressed by the Senate to nominate his successor; he nominated his son Commodus as consul for the next year A.D. 177, and in the course of the year the tribunician power, the title ' Augustus ' and the office of Pontifex Maximus were bestowed on him. Thus he occupied the same position as Lucius had occupied at the beginning of the reign.

The Character of Commodus. Ancient and modern critics
have few reproaches to bring against Marcus as Emperor,
and have fastened upon his choice of Commodus as successor.
Commodus was the sole survivor of Marcus' sons; he was
carefully educated with a view to the responsibility which
would fall upon him. Cassius Dio [1] says that he was not
naturally vicious; ' indeed he was exceptionally innocent ';
his very simplicity made him easily influenced by his friends,
who played on his ignorance and cowardice and made of him
the finished tyrant and debauchee which he showed himself
in his reign. When he was taken into partnership in the
Empire, he was fifteen years old. Though he had shown
no conspicuous ability, he had shown no promise of his later
character. [2] Rather may Marcus be criticized for nominating so young a boy as his consort. But, again, he had
no reason to suspect that Commodus would be left as
sole Emperor so soon; hereditary succession was probably
the best way of avoiding civil war, and not even the
philosopher could forgo the claims of family. In a satire
written by Julian the Emperor, Marcus on his arrival
in heaven is reproached with having entrusted the Empire
to his son; he replies with Jupiter's words to Mars : ' Long
ago would I have smitten thee with my thunderbolt, if it
were not that I loved thee, because thou art my son.' Thus
we may acquit him, as the council of the gods also acquitted
him.

Return of Marcus to the Northern Frontier; His Death.
During the Emperor's absence his generals appear to have
dealt successfully with the tribes who had taken advantage
of Cassius' revolt to cause trouble once more. In A.D. 178,
however, no further headway could be made, and Marcus
determined to go again to the scene of war. The two Emperors
left Rome in the summer of this year. In the next eighteen
months Marcus vanquished again the Quadi and Marcomanni
and overran their lands completely. ' Si anno uno super-

---

[1] lxxii. 1. 1.
[2] Cf. Julian in ' The Caesars '. ' He was not bad ', Marcus is made
to say, ' when I entrusted the State to him.' Cf. Herodian, i. 7. 3;
i. 8. 3.

fuisset, provincias ex his fecisset.' Again bad luck attended the Empire ; on 17 March, A.D. 180, Marcus Aurelius died at Vindobona, worn out with the strain of campaigning ; he was the first Emperor to die at his post fighting the enemies of Rome. Once more the lands North of the Danube, for good or ill, escaped Roman dominion ; for Commodus, disregarding the counsel of his staff, made an unworthy peace with the enemy and hurried back to Rome to claim the Empire.

The Character of Marcus ; the ' Meditations '. The character of Marcus as Emperor perhaps stood higher in antiquity than in modern times. While he was campaigning on the Northern frontier, Marcus kept a note-book in which he jotted down, often in disconnected and ungrammatical Greek, his own inmost thoughts and musings. The books under the title of Εἰς Ἑαυτόν or ' Meditations ' have been known for some centuries and have directed attention rather upon his personal character than upon his activities as Emperor ; he is often regarded as too unpractical a moralist to have fulfilled his imperial duties well. Yet the sketch given in the foregoing pages suggests that his reign was one of ceaseless activity in which he was called on to face crisis after crisis ; and ancient writers, while loving to dwell on his personal character, do not forget to assess him as Emperor. He was a hard worker ; he attended carefully to all imperial duties, giving a minute care to details. He could handle men, says Cassius Dio [1] ; he could overlook mistakes : he did not fuss or punish unnecessarily, yet he knew how to give praise when it was due, and he used men for purposes which they could fulfil, realizing that they could not be moulded according to his wish. His temper was even and undisturbed by slander, and, though he was eager for his own reputation, he did not shrink from criticism. In spite of his weak health he forced himself as a soldier to endure hardship ; when the armies were hard pressed and many nobles fell, he was counselled to retire from the field and he refused. He was a just and moderate ruler, says another historian ; [2] alone of kings he showed forth philosophy not merely in words and

[1] lxxi. 34. 2–3.   [2] Herodian, i. 2. 3.

18

maxims ; in him the Stoic ideal reached its highest expression.
His fortune was not worthy of himself; ill-health and ill-
luck pursued him ; the amazing thing is that he was true to
himself.[1] His main interests were in philosophy and his
home ; he wanted affection and friendship, yet as Emperor
and philosopher he was lifted above men's heads. ' He is a
classical example of a man set to do work for which his tastes
unfitted him and doing it well.' ' Perhaps there is no greater
evidence of the power of human beings to subdue circumstances than this clear tranquil voice rising out of a cloud of
solitude and above the din of war.' [2] And so ' lent by the
gods, Marcus returned to the gods ', and Commodus, his
son and his ' misfortune ', succeeded to the Empire.[3]

The ' Meditations ' were written in camp on the Northern frontier.
They were not written for publication, but are rather the written
communings of Marcus with himself. The first book, which was
probably written last, is more connected in style than the others ; it
gives a summary of the debt which Marcus felt he owed to his father
and mother, teachers and friends for their influence on him. The
remaining eleven books contain musings on morality and philosophy.
They have been an inspiration to generations, and to men so different
as Renan and General Gordon. Marvellous as they are, they become
still more so when it is remembered that they are the thoughts, not
of a monk who had renounced the world, but of the man who by courage
and perseverance was striving to uphold a world which threatened to
collapse.

CHAPTER XVII

THE ROMAN CONQUEST OF BRITAIN

AUGUSTAN Policy towards Britain. Tacitus,[4] in one
of his untranslatable summings-up of history, says
' Julius Caesar seems rather to have drawn the attention of his successors to Britain than to have bequeathed it
to them ' ; that he seriously intended to conquer it is not
at all likely ; as in his two expeditions across the Rhine, so
in his two British campaigns, it is clear that he aimed only

[1] Dio, lxxi. 36. 3, 4.
[2] R. W. Livingstone in *The Mission of Greece*, p. 76.
[3] *Vita*, xviii. 2.   [4] *Agr.* 13.

Hadrian's Wall

English Miles

Bowness
Burgh-by-Sands
Carlisle (Luguvallium)
Birdoswald
Housesteads (Borcovicium)
Chesters (Cilurnum)
Wallsend (Segedunum)
Corbridge (Corstopitum)
Newcastle (Pons Aelius)

ROMAN BRITAIN

English Miles

Inchtuthille
Ardoch
Mumrills
Old Kilpatrick
Wall of Antoninus Pius
Trimontium
Hadrian's Wall
Corstopitum
Luguvallium (Carlisle)
Voreda
S. Shields
Chester-le-Street
Vinovia
BRIGANTES
Monapia
Overborrow
Lancaster
Malton
Isurium
Eburacum (York)
Bremetennacum
Mona
Manchester
Anavio
Deva (Chester)
Lindum (Lincoln)
ORDOVICES
CORNOVII
Derby
Ermine Street
Viroconium (Wroxeter)
Sabrina F.
Watling St.
Ratae (Leicester)
Fosse Street
ICENI
Venta Icenorum (Caistor St. Edmund)
DEMETAE
SILURES
DOBUNI
Glevum (Gloucester)
Verulamium (St. Albans)
TRINOVANTES
Camulodunum (Colchester)
Isca Silurum (Caerleon)
Venta Silurum
Corinium (Cirencester)
Aquae Sulis (Bath)
Londinium
Calleva Atrebatum (Silchester)
Venta Belgarum (Winchester)
BELGAE
CANTIUM
Durovernum (Canterbury)
Rutupiae
Portus Lemanae
DUMNONII
Isca Dumnoniorum (Exeter)
Regnum (Chichester)
Gessoriacum (Boulogne)
Vectis

R.C.

at keeping his army employed and ready for the final struggle that was bound to come in Gaul, while at the same time he gave warning that Rome would stand no interference from outside nations.

That Britain formed part of Augustus' scheme of Empire is also unlikely; he knew that diplomacy here could do the work of force, and in the Monumentum Ancyranum he rightly records the reception of two British refugee princes as an important act. It is true that he allowed his court-poets to conjure up before the eyes of Rome dreams of British conquest [1]; but nothing was done, and the dreams faded away: Strabo,[2] writing under Augustus, gives the official view that the conquest of Britain ' would not pay '.

Change of Policy under Claudius. This inactive policy was continued for nearly thirty years after Augustus' death, but meanwhile Roman influence in Britain was being quietly extended. Caesar, following the old Roman tradition, had formed an alliance with Cunobelinus [3] the ruler of the Trinobantes, the chief tribe in South-East Britain, and his coins, which have been found in at least ten counties, show a decidedly Roman type; he seems to have ruled for more than thirty years.

On his death, however, disputes as to the succession sent one at least of his sons as an exile to Rome, and the friendly reception of the fugitive there seems to have provoked to aggressive acts the British rulers who had expelled him. Claudius, also, here as elsewhere, was in favour of a spirited foreign policy, and coveted the title of ' extender of the Empire '.[4] No doubt too the supposed wealth of Britain tempted the Roman capitalists.

The Expedition of Aulus Plautius Silvanus, A.D. 43. The expedition now undertaken against Britain was organized on a great scale. Four of the best legions were withdrawn from

---

[1] Cf. Vergil, *Georgics*, iii. 25, and Horace, *Odes*, i. 35.

[2] Strabo, iv. 200.

[3] The Cymbeline of Shakespere. So Caesar calls the tribe, but the best MSS. of Tacitus give Trinovantes.

[4] This is expressly stated by Suetonius, and is confirmed by the allusions to ' prolatum imperium ultra Oceanum ' in Claudius' speech at Lugdunum (p. 93) and in contemporary epigrams.

their usual provinces, and two new ones were added to the Roman army list to meet the fresh demands on the military forces of the Empire. From the Upper German frontier came the Second and the Fourteenth legions (Augusta and Gemina Martia), from Lower Germany the Twentieth Valeria Victrix and the Ninth Hispana from Pannonia, together with *vexillationes* from the Eighth; two of these, the Second and the Twentieth, remained in Britain throughout the whole period of Roman rule. With auxiliaries the whole force may have been about 50,000 strong. The commander Aulus Plautius was one of the most distinguished Roman generals (he had been consul fourteen years before), and on his staff was Vespasian, who had won his position by good service, and now confirmed it by his exploits in this campaign.[1]

The whole geography of the invasion is uncertain; our only account, that of Cassius Dio, is vague in the extreme. It seems probable, however, that the expedition landed somewhere in Kent,[2] and pushed on, not without severe fighting when crossing the Medway, till it reached the Thames; here the Romans met with a check, and halted for some months for the Emperor himself to arrive with reinforcements. The passage of the river was then forced, and a rapid advance made on the capital of the Trinobantes, Camulodūnum, the modern Colchester; this was stormed, and then Claudius returned in triumph to Rome. He was, if Dio could be trusted, only sixteen days in Britain, but this is an impossibly short time.

Results of the First Campaigns. Aulus Plautius seems to have remained in Britain four years; when he was recalled in A.D. 47, he received the honour of an ovation, then for the last time given to one not a member of the Imperial house. Three other parts of Britain are mentioned as having been reduced in his time. The first of these, the dependent kingdom of the Regni (in Sussex round Chichester) may well have been secured while he was waiting for Claudius and reinforce-

---

[1] Tacitus says (*Agr.* 13) he was ' monstratus fatis ' in it.
[2] No doubt one of the places was Rutupiae (Richborough near Sandwich), where recent excavation has revealed the ditch of a large camp which is dated to the period of the invasion.

ments ; the name of its king Cogidubnus is known to us from the famous Goodwood inscription, now at Chichester, in which he is called ' Rex ' and ' Legatus Augusti in Britannia ', a very unusual title. The second and more important extension was over the kingdom of the Iceni in East Anglia, whose ruler, Prasutagus, also submitted voluntarily, retaining his territory as a Roman vassal. No doubt this submission was made after Claudius had returned to Rome. During this same period Vespasian had been pursuing a victorious career in the West ; we are definitely told that he ' conquered the Isle of Wight (Vectis), fought thirty battles, and subdued two powerful nations '.[1] It is not improbable that he pushed his success as far as the borders of Somerset, for a Roman ' pig of lead ' has been found in the Mendips, bearing the date of the ' ninth year of Claudius ', i.e. A.D. 50.

Ostorius Scapula. The Fosse. Ostorius Scapula, the successor of Plautius, set himself to secure the conquests already made. The great roads, based on London as their starting-point, began to stretch across the country south-west, north-west and north. Tacitus implies that Ostorius found the rivers Trent and Severn as the limit of Roman power.[2] So rapid a conquest seems extraordinary, but Roman trade and commerce for nearly a hundred years since the invasion of Caesar had prepared the way, and the geographical features of Britain are such that an invader, once established in the South-east and having forced the line of the Thames, finds little in the Midlands to hinder his advance.[3] The West and North of the island are very different in their features and cost the Romans much fighting : Rome's hold on them, as will be seen, was always much looser and was disputed again and again.

To guard the area already won Ostorius drew a line from

[1] Suet. *Vesp.* 4.

[2] *Ann.* xii. 31, reading ' cis Trisantonam et Sabrinam ', Dr. Henry Bradley's suggestion. Tacitus is our main authority for the next fifteen years ; unfortunately his books vii.–x., which described the first conquests, are lost.

[3] So after the Battle of Hastings, William the Conqueror met with serious resistance only in Exeter, Wales, and the counties north of the Humber.

South Devon to Lincoln. This line is now known as the Fosse or Foss-way, some 220 miles in length, though the modern road follows only part of the course of the ancient ' limes '. The fosse was a frontier and a road, drawn as straight as could be, though at the same time geographical features were carefully utilized.[1] On this line legionary forces were temporarily planted to keep out the Welsh tribes while Ostorius devoted his attention to the Iceni. With some trouble he disarmed the Iceni : he planted a colony of veterans at Camulodūnum, where the worship of the Emperor was also established. He was then free to attack the Welsh tribes.

The First Attacks on Wales, A.D. 48–61. His forward movements began with operations against the Ordovices in North Wales, and met with some success. In the regions north of the Humber the Brigantes, after giving some trouble, became Roman allies. With each advance the bare camps of the legionaries were moved forward, to Viroconium (Wroxeter) and eventually to Deva (Chester) and Lindum (Lincoln) Ostorius' main attack was then concentrated on the Silures in South Wales, who were now led by Caratācus (Caradoc), the last of the sons of Cunobelinus. The fighting pursued the usual course of campaigns in a difficult country. Roman discipline gained a victory in a pitched battle, and Caratācus was shortly afterwards betrayed by the Roman ally, Cartimandua, Queen of the Brigantes, and sent to Rome (A.D. 51). The scene [2] of his spirited appeal to the Emperor, which won him an honourable release, though he was kept interned in Italy, is one of the best-known in the history of the Principate.

But in Britain the struggle was continued with fluctuating success ; it was a war of extermination against the Silures, and in the end Ostorius died worn-out (A.D. 52). That the Romans had suffered severely may be judged from the fact that during the next eight years the two governors remained inactive.

[1] This view of the Fosse is taken from an article of great interest in *J.R.S.* xiv. (1924) p. 2, by R. G. Collingwood. He shows that the ' limes ' (frontier and road) was of temporary value : by the time of the ' Antonine Itinerary ' it had lost all importance and is not mentioned there.

[2] Tac. *Ann.* xii. 36–7.

The Campaigns of Suetonius Paulinus, A.D. 58–61. Suetonius Paulinus, who came to Britain in A.D. 58, was a soldier of a different kind. He aimed at breaking the stubborn resistance of the Britons by striking at their national religion in its special home, the island of Mona (Anglesey). The Romans from Caesar's time onwards had always found in the cult of Druidism the strongest element in Celtic nationality. Of Suetonius' preliminary operations we know nothing, but by the beginning of A.D. 60 or 61 he was on the shore of the Menai Straits and forced a passage, not without difficulty, for the Roman troops had supernatural terrors to overcome as well as the resistance of the enemy in a strong position. The victory, however, was complete, and Tacitus records with grim satisfaction (no doubt he had heard the story from veteran soldiers) how the altars of the Britons were found reeking with human sacrifices.

Causes of the Rebellion of Boudicca. But Suetonius in the moment of victory was recalled by the news that the province in his rear was in rebellion. The causes of this were the usual ones ; heavy exactions both by the Roman officials and by individual usurers [1] pressed hard on the Britons ; the regular taxation of an organized rule, even when moderate, is always resented by a more primitive people, accustomed only to the occasional, though often arbitrary, demands of their chiefs. And the veterans and the Roman traders who had poured into Britain had abused their power to ill-treat and insult the natives. The immediate cause of the revolt, however, which began among the Iceni, was the death of the old Roman ally Prasutagus. He had bequeathed his kingdom and property to the Emperor, hoping by this surrender to save some of it for his family. But the Roman lawyers applied the maxims of their law mercilessly to a state of civilization to which it was entirely foreign ; the chiefs of the Iceni, holding land by native tenure from the chief as head of the nation, found themselves mere tenants-at-will in the Roman sense, and were dispossessed of their lands by the new

[1] Scandal said that much of the enormous wealth of the philosopher Seneca had been lent at high interest to the Britons, and was now being called in suddenly.

owners.[1] And the king's own family were treated as slaves by the representatives of his Roman heir ; his queen Boudicca was scourged, and his daughters violated. It was this 'unutterable shame' that 'turned the coward's heart to steel, the sluggard's blood to flame,' and the Romans found themselves faced with a fury that they had not met in their first invasion. Camulodunum had never been fortified, and, after a brave resistance in the Temple of Claudius, hated by the Britons as the 'arx aeternae dominationis ', the Romans, men, women and children, were murdered with every kind of barbarian cruelty.

Unfortunately the Roman troops were all scattered. Petilius Cerialis, the commander of the Ninth Legion, hurrying down the line of the Ermine Street from Lincoln, was overwhelmed, and escaped with only his cavalry ; the officer in charge of the Second Legion near Isca refused to obey Suetonius' order to concentrate.[2] The commander-in-chief therefore had only his own men of the Fourteenth and Twentieth legions, and some of these he had to leave behind to guard his base. He, however, marched boldly down to meet the main army of the enemy, and reached London, which was already the largest town in the now civilized parts of Britain : but, unsupported as he was, he had not troops to defend it, and he was compelled to abandon it to the victorious barbarians ; 70,000 Romans are said to have perished in the sack which followed.[3] But Suetonius kept his courage ; he knew that a disciplined army, if it does not lose heart, may be a match for any number of unorganized forces. And so it proved ; falling back, probably along the line of Watling Street, towards his base, he tempted the pursuing enemy to

[1] This seems the natural explanation of the passage in *Ann.* xiv. 31, ' praecipui quique Icenorum, quasi cunctam regionem muneri accepissent (sc. Romani), avitis bonis exuuntur '. Similar hardships have been caused by the premature application of British law ; the lands of Highland chieftains, held by them as heads of their clans, were treated as if they were ordinary property, completely at the disposal of the chief.

[2] His choice was a difficult one, and he felt it his duty to guard his own front ; in the end, after the victory of Suetonius, he committed suicide from shame. His name was Postumus ; see Tac. *Ann.* xiv. 37.

[3] Traces of destruction by fire have been found frequently in the earliest strata of Roman London.

attack him on ground that he had chosen, where he could be neither surrounded nor outflanked, and gained a complete victory. Eighty thousand Britons are said to have fallen, and their leader Boudicca committed suicide. It is one of the curious chances of history that this barbarian queen is a striking figure at once in the narrative of Dio and in modern popular history, that she has the honour of a statue in the London which she sacked with such cruelty, and that she is credited in a well-known English poem with being the ancestress of the English nation, which had at most only a very partial descent from her people.

The victorious Romans were in no mood to show mercy, nor did they. Nero finally sent his own freedman, Polyclitus, to arrange a settlement, and Suetonius was recalled. His successors during the rest of the reign of Nero naturally adopted no active measures, and after that Emperor's death a distracted Roman world for two years had no time to think of conquest in distant Britain.

Roman Advance under Vespasian. But with the restoration of peace in the Empire and the reduction of the rebels in Gallia Belgica and on the Rhine, all was changed in Britain. It is difficult not to attribute the forward movement, which then was resumed, to a definite policy of conquest on the part of Vespasian. He knew Britain better than most Romans, and it is impossible that it was by a mere coincidence he sent to command there successively three of his best generals, Petilius Cerialis (71–4), Frontinus (74–6), and Agricola (77–84), the first and the third of whom at any rate had previously served in this province.

Petilius Cerialis extended the Roman province northward at least as far as Malton, possibly to York, and Frontinus [1] reduced at last the stubborn Silures in South Wales ; the legionary base under him was moved forward to Isca Silurum (Caerleon).[2]

---

[1] Frontinus apart from his distinction in the field is known to us from his books on Military Tactics and on Aqueducts, the latter our chief literary source of knowledge on the subject.

[2] Both in York (Eburacum) and at Caerleon excavation has established these dates ; Caerleon always remained chiefly a military centre, but York became a place of civil importance also.

The First Four Campaigns of Agricola, A.D. 77–80. The account of the campaigns of his successor, Agricola, is one of the most interesting pieces of Roman literature. Inspired by *pietas* for his father-in-law, Tacitus has drawn a masterly picture of a good Roman governor, a picture the interest of which is heightened by contrast with the account of Domitian, whom the historian paints as the worst of Emperors. Unfortunately the historical value of the treatise is not equal to its literary value ; in geography it is especially weak, and throughout there is an absence of definite facts.

The campaigns began in the autumn of A.D. 77 [1] with an attack on the Ordovices in North Wales, who were speedily reduced : this was followed up by the conquest of Mona.

In the following year Agricola broke new ground. Advancing north by the West Coast route, broadly speaking that of the London and North-Western Railway, he seems to have reached Carlisle (Luguvallium).

In A.D. 79 Agricola seems to have transferred his line of advance to the east of the Pennines, where the entrance to Scotland is easier. He certainly reached the line of the Forth and Clyde in the following year (A.D. 80), but how much of the advance was made in the first of these two years is disputed. [2] What is important to notice is that he carefully secured the ground won by establishing forts in well-chosen places and carefully provisioning them ; hence the natives failed in their endeavours to retake them, when the Roman legions withdrew to their base camps in the winter. [3]

[1] Some put the date of Agricola's first campaign in 78, and so alter by a year all the subsequent dates. For a full discussion of the point, cf. Anderson's excellent edition of Furneaux's *Agricola* (Oxford University Press, 1922), Appendix I ; this admirable little book shows how literary history can be explained and supplemented by the results of excavation.

[2] Tacitus (*Agr.* 22) says that in A.D. 79 Agricola reached the ' estuary ' of the ' Tanaus '. This river is variously identified as the Tyne, the Tweed, or the North Tyne at Dunbar. As Agricola reached the Forth in the next year, it seems probable that he had established the line of the Tweed in A.D. 79, and had pushed excursions beyond it, securing the ground next year.

[3] Several of these forts have been carefully explored, e.g., that of Trimontium (Newstead) on the Tweed, which is elaborately described in Curle's *A Roman Frontier Post*.

Agricola's Further Advance, A.D. 81–3. The movements of the next year, 81, are the most uncertain of all. The most probable theory is that Agricola, having reduced South-East Scotland, attempted to reduce the South-West.

Ireland also is mentioned as coming within the sphere of his plans at this time ; as usual the Romans had found an excuse for further aggression by receiving an exiled Irish prince. Agricola was sanguine enough to think that one legion with auxiliaries could conquer and hold the island (he little knew Ireland !). The theory that he actually tried to conquer it is wrong.

The last two campaigns are perhaps the most interesting ; at any rate Tacitus found them so, and lavishes his genius in describing movements which lead up to a brilliant battle-piece. He recognizes that the Forth and Clyde was a ' natural frontier ', but the ' bravery of the soldiers and the glory of the Roman name did not allow ' Agricola to acquiesce in it. The Romans now brought the fleet into co-operation with the army. It is clear from Tacitus' account that, after securing the line of the ' Isthmus ' by well-planted forts (several of which have been excavated[1]), the Roman armies advanced North-East, having the Ochils on their right and the Grampians on their left ; the strongly defended forts at Ardoch and Inchtuthil seem clearly to date from the time of Agricola. He succeeded in forcing the elusive enemy to a battle at Mons Graupius,[2] and gained a bloody victory ; Tacitus even speaks of Britain as ' thoroughly subdued '.[3] No doubt Agricola intended to move next year still further North-East up Strathmore, and, like the Emperor Severus later, to penetrate as far as Aberdeen. His fleet meantime had sailed round Britain, and had showed that it was an island.

[1] E.g. Barhill near Glasgow, Old Kilpatrick, Mumrills and elsewhere : see Collingwood, *Archaeology of Roman Britain,* p. 66.

[2] *Not* the Grampians. Where the Mons Graupius was we know almost as little as did Mr. Oldbuck (in Scott's *Antiquary*) ; all that we can say is that it must have been not far from Dunkeld.

[3] ' Perdomita '. It is noticeable that this statement comes in the Histories (i. 2) not in the Agricola, the narrative of which plainly contradicts it.

But if this was his intention, he was not allowed to carry it out ; Domitian, who had already allowed him an unusual extension of office, recalled him in A.D. 84, and the Highlands of Scotland were not penetrated by him or by any other Roman. The Emperor was wiser than the man on the spot in fixing the limits of the Roman Empire. In A.D. 86 the II Adjutrix, which had replaced the Fourteenth Legion in A.D. 71, was removed to the Danube. This suggests that the chief reason for the abandonment of the offensive against Scotland was the need for troops elsewhere.

Results of the Campaigns of Agricola. How far the posts planted by Agricola on the line of the Clyde and Forth, and beyond the Forth, were held, has been much disputed. But excavation now seems to have made it clear that the ground he had gained remained generally under Roman control until a date towards the end of the reign of Trajan. Agricola may not have been the brilliant general Tacitus describes, but he was undoubtedly a very capable tactician, a strategist with a fine eye for the features of the country in which he was operating, and a first-rate engineer. But his greatness as a civilian makes him no less important. He represented the best type of Roman governor, a type which we may fairly claim to have been a not uncommon one ; he was just as well as severe, he was courteous alike to his own people and to the natives, he knew how to praise as well as to command, and by every means he tried to win the people whom he ruled to Roman civilization, and he largely succeeded.

The results of his work, however, must be sketched later. Here it must suffice to say that Britain seems on the whole to have had peace for thirty years after his recall by Domitian.

CHAPTER XVIII

THE ROMAN OCCUPATION OF BRITAIN

SCANTINESS of Written Records in Second Century A.D. The thirty years that follow the recall of Agricola are an almost complete blank, so far as literary authorities are concerned. It seems probable that this absence of records corresponds to the actual facts, and that during this period the *Pax Romana* prevailed and Roman civilization was quietly advanced ; it was true for once that ' happy is the country that has no history '.

There is an almost equal absence of records for the sixty years that follow, but here certainly this is not due to the prevalence of peace. On the contrary we know that at any rate twice Roman authority was severely shaken, and that once at least Rome made a definite advance. The scanty written records have to be supplemented by the evidence of excavations.

Troubles under Hadrian. The most important piece of literary evidence is the rhetorical statement of Fronto, writing under Marcus Aurelius, that the Romans suffered in the time of Hadrian losses in Britain comparable to the terrible losses caused by the contemporary Jewish rebellion. This vague indication no doubt refers to the fact that the Ninth Legion, which had its head-quarters at York, seems to have disappeared from the army list at the end of Trajan's reign. The only parallel cases are the disappearance of the three legions destroyed with Varus (p. 53), and of the three legions which had disgraced themselves by accepting service with the Gallic Empire in A.D. 70 (p. 162).[1] The destruction of the Ninth Legion must have shaken for a time the whole power of Rome in Britain, at any rate north of the line of the Humber, and was no doubt the chief reason why Hadrian, early in his reign, visited Britain, and why the Sixth Legion was transferred thither at the same time. Spartianus in his Life of Hadrian says ' that he found many things to put right in Britain '. There is no doubt that Roman authority was restored as far as the line of the Tyne and Solway, and partially beyond ; but the construction of the great ' Roman Wall ' proves clearly that the Emperor drew a sharp line between Britain south of the Tyne and Solway line and the wilder country to the north. The ' Roman Wall ', the finest surviving piece of Roman work in England, and the finest Roman frontier boundary in any country, is, in its inception and probably in its completion, the work of Hadrian.

[1] The V Alaudae disappeared under Domitian.

The Stanegate-Vallum Frontier.[1] It is important to remember that neither the defence of the frontier nor the Wall itself was planned all at once ; the Romans felt their way to a solution of the problem.

The so-called Stanegate was a road made by Agricola ; it connected a number of forts placed between Corbridge and Carlisle ; some of the forts were of pre-Agricolan times, others were built by Agricola himself. The line of the Stanegate was probably regarded as a temporary frontier, much as the Fosse was, the temporary frontier drawn by Ostorius. At the beginning of Hadrian's reign it was planned to give this temporary frontier a more permanent character. The existing line of forts was to be the basis of a stronger system of defence ; North of the Stanegate a vallum, a ditch to mark the frontier, was dug and on the vallum new forts were placed.

The Vallum. The vallum was longer than the Stanegate. It began about five miles West of Newcastle (Pons Aelius), and from this point to Chesters it was unsupported by any previous system of forts. West from Chesters the vallum tends nearer and nearer to the Stanegate ; at two points they almost meet, but in any case they run on to Carlisle with never more than four miles distance between them, and in most places the distance is much less. The vallum was prolonged further West than the Stanegate, reaching as far as Dykesfield, which is to the West of Burgh-by-Sands.

The vallum is a ditch thirty feet wide and seven feet deep ; on each side is a mound about twenty feet from the ditch. Its purpose was merely to mark the frontier-line ; it was not a military work ; it could not possibly be defended. The whole defence rested on the soldiers in the forts, who would repel attack in the open. The new forts were not meant to bear the brunt of any invasion ; they were meant to house the soldiers securely ; the repelling of an attack would be done in the field.

---

[1] This account of the ' Wall ' is taken largely from R. G. Collingwood's *The Archaeology of Roman Britain* ; but in the interests of brevity certain points which really belong to hypothesis are here stated dogmatically.

Hadrian's Wall.   Hadrian visited Britain in A.D. 121 or 122, and ' it is tempting to conjecture that the Stanegate-vallum frontier had been constructed before his visit ', and that the addition of the Wall was the result of that visit ; there was only an interval of a year or two between the digging of the vallum and the beginning of the Wall. The need for the Stanegate-vallum frontier had been suggested by the serious revolt in A.D. 117–118 ; but evidently Hadrian was not satisfied.   He planned a military work to stretch from coast to coast on the North side of the vallum ; the actual details of construction were modified in the process of building.

At regular intervals the vallum was filled up and the mounds were levelled ; in this way level crossings were made, over which the soldiers carried stone for the Wall from the quarries to the South of the vallum.   The original plan envisaged a wall ten Roman feet broad from Newcastle to Carlisle ; but at Housesteads the crags were thought to be sufficient defence, and at Birdoswald a deep valley was considered to be fortified enough by a temporary Turf Wall. When the ten-foot foundations were laid, the plan was changed ; the Wall was to be continuous [1] ; it was to be henceforth only seven and a half feet wide, and it was to extend to Bowness on the West and to Wallsend on the East ; a few of the Stanegate-vallum forts could still be manned, but new forts also were built.

The Wall was built of dressed stones and its core was of concrete.   At every mile a milecastle was placed, a miniature fort about fifty-five by sixty-five feet, and between each milecastle two turrets thirteen feet square were built into the Wall at equal intervals to serve as signal stations.   The Wall was ' an elevated sentry-walk ' about thirteen feet high.   The milecastles held about a hundred men, and from the milecastles sentries patrolled along the top of the Wall.   The sentry was protected by a breastwork over which he had a clear line of vision to the bottom of a **V**-shaped trench on the North side of the Wall ; the nearer lip of the trench was about 18 feet away.[2]   No mound of earth was thrown up against

---

[1] I.e. it was to be built at Housesteads and was to replace the Turf Wall at Birdoswald.   [2] The ' berm ' varies considerably.

the South side of the Wall; the top was reached by ladders at the turrets. The purpose of the Wall, which was finished by A.D. 127, was not to stand a siege nor to resist a massed attack, but to prevent raids; even if the raiders broke through, a signal would be flashed to the nearest fort, troops would be sent out, and the Wall would prove a severe obstacle to raiders returning with their plunder.

Along the North Cumberland Coast, which was open to attack from across the estuary, the line of signal-stations and forts (though without the Wall) was continued from Bowness perhaps as far as St. Bees Head, and the forts, which corresponded to the milecastles of the Wall, were in touch with larger forts behind.

In spite of attack from time to time (notably under Severus, who effected considerable repairs) the Wall of Hadrian stood as a barrier against barbarism for three hundred years. It was held by about fifteen thousand auxiliaries. They came from all parts of the Empire, and some of the cohorts were on duty there throughout the whole period of the Wall's history.

The Antonine Wall. The same energy which built the Wall of Hadrian no doubt maintained quiet in Britain for a space; seventeen years later, A.D. 142–3, under Antoninus Pius Rome once more assumed the aggressive. The line of the Forth and Clyde was occupied by a new wall, this time a turf and clay wall. Lollius Urbicus, the Roman general, had with him detachments from all the three British legions and a certain number of auxiliaries, and from excavations, and especially from the inscriptions they have left, the nature of the wall can be reconstructed. Its nineteen forts were built in part on the sites of some of Agricola's forts; these had been ' selected with the eye of a master of the art of permanent defence '.[1] The whole length of the new wall was some 36 miles; it was complete by A.D. 143 and a great road was run from Corbridge behind the wall of Hadrian to near Edinburgh;

[1] G. Macdonald, ' The Building of the Antonine Wall ' (*J.R.S.* xi. (1921), pp. 1–24)—a most interesting account, based on the seventeen inscriptions that have been found. See Collingwood, *Archaeology of Roman Britain*, p. 82.

19

a similar road seems to have been planned on the West, but it was never completed, and no great camp is found in the South-West of Scotland, while the traces of small forts there are few and unimportant.

But if the Romans hoped to reduce to order the space between the two walls, or at least the Eastern part of it, they were miscalculating. A third and last rising of the Brigantes (about 155 B.C.) again shook Roman power [1] on both sides of Hadrian's Wall. The rebels to the South of it were reduced, and we hear of no more trouble from this tribe; but the region to the north of Hadrian's Wall (i.e., the South-East of Scotland) must have been very imperfectly conquered; no inscriptions from the reign of M. Aurelius (A.D. 161–80) have been found there, and it is probable that for a short time the Antonine wall was abandoned. When it was finally relinquished is uncertain; some great disaster befell it and its buildings were destroyed; early in the reign of Commodus there was a severe rising in Scotland and the wall may have been finally lost; but it is probable that the great disaster occurred in A.D. 197, when Clodius Albinus withdrew the troops in Britain to Gaul.[2] If the later date is accepted, the Wall was in any case lost for a short time about A.D. 180, and the title of 'Britannicus' assumed by Commodus might commemorate its recovery. Apart from the two campaigns of the Emperor Severus (A.D. 193–211), who pressed far beyond the wall of Antoninus and may even have reached the neighbourhood of Aberdeen, Rome had done with Scotland. On that country she had made little impression.

It remains to sketch what effects Rome produced on England or, more accurately, on the country south of Hadrian's Wall.

Contrast of the Military and the Civil Districts of Britain. The history of the two regions in Roman Britain (p. 278)

---

[1] Our only literary information about this comes from a most unlikely place: Pausanias (viii. 43) in his description of Arcadia, the centre state of the Peloponnese, gives a long digression on the wars of the pacific Antoninus Pius, who had a legendary Greek descent. See Haverfield in Mommsen's *Provinces*, i. 352.

[2] Cf. Collingwood, *op. cit.*, p. 85.

has been shown to be very different ; the South-East and the
Midlands were conquered easily and held without difficulty,
while the West and the North were reduced only after hard
struggles, repeated again and again. There is a similar contrast in the civilization which the different parts attained ;
in the North and West there are no towns and very few
villas ; the most remote villas are north-west of Aldborough
(15 miles north-west of York) and on the South coast of Wales.
On the other hand, it is in these parts that Roman military
remains are found, the base fortresses of the legions and the
small forts (*castella*) in the wilder regions beyond, guarding
the main roads and the most important strategic points.
The remains of well over a hundred of these, loosely called
' Roman camps ',[1] have been identified, though it is certain
that nothing like this number were held at the same time ;
the forts in Wales were largely given up under the Antonines,
and the auxiliaries who garrisoned them moved North into
Scotland. Under Severus troops were moved back into Wales,
but the country was thinly garrisoned till the fourth century
(p. 296).

In the peaceful districts, the remains of ' villas ' are
abundant, though very often little of them has been left,
while in these parts the few military remains either date
from the early period of conquest or are due to special circumstances.

These two kinds of remains must be described separately.

The Military Sphere. The base camps of the three legions
which held Britain were at Caerleon, Chester (probably transferred from Wroxeter), and York (transferred from Lincoln) ;
these fortresses were of some fifty or sixty acres in extent.
But the troops in them were ordinarily reserved for special

---

[1] The word ' camp ' is generally used, but is misleading ; the posts
garrisoned by the soldiers, whether large or small, were permanent,
and as time went on, were built of stone, instead of, as usual in the
first century, turf, or sometimes clay, and timber. Of course there
are also remains of temporary earthworks, used in field operations,
e.g., in Scotland, North of the Forth-Clyde line, and in Wales. In
Antonine times stone-built *castella* are less frequent ; there seems to
have been a reversion to the first-century method of earthworks.
See Collingwood, *op. cit.*, p. 47.

emergencies, either the suppression of serious risings or the building of fortifications further to the front.[1]

The ordinary hard work of defence was done by the auxiliaries, who were planted, as has been said, in bodies usually of some 500 or 1,000 men, over the regions where Rome's hold was less established ; their forts, varying in size from three to nine acres, were connected by roads, and close to the roads most of the fighting would take place. The lay-out of the big fortresses and of the advanced forts was much the same. They were square or oblong, with four gates, from which ran the four main streets, meeting in the centre, where stood the *Praetorium* or *Principia*, i.e. ' Headquarters '. Here, apart from the necessary offices, were kept the standards in the centre chamber at the back of the buildings, where was the shrine of the regiment. This building was almost always of stone ; near at hand were the quarters of the commander and of the officers. In the rest of the enclosure were the men's barracks, the store rooms, and granaries with a year's supply of corn, and, if there were cavalry, stables for the horses. In the larger fortresses there were also a hospital (*valetudinarium*) and workshops.

An almost invariable adjunct for any permanent post, great or small, was the bath-house, which was usually outside the walled enclosures. This seems to have served not only as a bath but also as a club-house for the soldiers, and, to judge from the frequency of altars to ' Fortune ' found among the remains, gambling was allowed and freely practised. Outside the legionary camps the civilian population which followed the troops was settled (*canabae*) ; and the smaller forts had little settlements attached to them in which the soldiers' wives lived.

The defences of the forts varied with their position and date. In some advanced regions, especially in Scotland, an elaborate system of ditches covers the front, and in one fort, Rough-Castle near Falkirk, there is a network of pits, which no doubt were originally armed with wooden spikes, like Caesar's ' lilia ' in his works at Alesia.

---

[1] E.g. on Hadrian's Wall and on the Antonine Wall the inscriptions record the work of detachments of all three legions.

The Romanized Parts of Britain. As has been seen (p. 277), the Romans took advantage of the British tribal divisions during their first advance in Britain, and these were also used for the government of the country, when it had been reduced. Here, as in Gaul, Rome followed her old policy, dating from the time of the Republic, of conciliating the chiefs and giving them administrative powers in a Roman form. Two inscriptions have been found, which mention the 'Tribal State', the governing body of which (the *ordo*) was no doubt made up of the leading men.[1] But these tribal authorities were less important than the similar ones in Gaul. The tribes there were larger and wealthier ; hence their names have survived in many modern French towns ; in England there were comparatively few towns, and only one, Canterbury, preserves in any form the tribal name. Whatever the cause, Roman civilization in Britain was but very partially urban.

Towns in Roman Britain. It was however the definite policy of the Empire, especially under and after Claudius, to encourage town life. Tacitus,[2] in a famous chapter, tells us how Agricola encouraged the Britons to build 'temples, market places, houses', with the result that they began to adopt Roman dress, and enjoy 'porticoes, baths[3] and elaborate banquets', the 'delenimenta vitiorum' as he bitterly remarks. 'Civilization', he goes on, was 'a part of submission' (he calls it 'slavery'), and he was right ; then as now a civilized race, holding down a more primitive one, makes its task easier by introducing the comforts and attractions of its own life, which its subjects are only too ready to enjoy.

But Britain was a poor country, and under Rome, as in every later age, at any rate till our own day, the English

[1] The best known records a decree of the *ordo*, 'respub. civit. Silurum ', for a monument to a Roman governor in the third century A.D. (cf. Haverfield, *Roman Occupation of Britain*, pp. 184 ff.). A similar monument was found at Wroxeter in 1924, mentioning the 'state of the Cornovii ' ; it was dedicated to Hadrian in A.D. 130 (*J.R.S.* xiv. (1924), p. 244).

[2] *Agr.* 21.

[3] The elaborate but unfinished bath, uncovered at Wroxeter in 1928, may well be the result of Agricola's encouragement of Roman ways.

countryside has had a strong attraction, even for the wealthy and the comfortable ; hence the Roman towns in England were, as has been said, few and comparatively unimportant ; there is a great contrast between them and the towns of Gaul or the Rhine Valley in the number of inscriptions found. There were only four colonies, Camulodunum, Glevum, Lindum, and Eboracum, and of these the last two were military settlements before they received colonial status.[1] Besides these there was only one *municipium*, Verulamium (St. Albans), dating from the time of Claudius.

But the number of towns without definite organization was very considerable ; some of these were probably Roman in origin, but this was the exception. Londinium, the largest of Roman towns in Britain, seems to date only from the time of Claudius,[2] although, as Tacitus tells, a Roman population of 70,000 perished there in the great rebellion. The larger towns were laid out in streets which intersected one another at right angles, though within the ' insulae ' the development of shops and houses might be irregular ; the smaller towns had no plan, consisting of a group of houses placed haphazard. A large part of the Romanized population lived outside the towns in villages, and ' villas ',[3] to use the technical word, are frequent in many parts of the country, e.g. in Somerset nearly seventy examples have been noted, and almost as many in Hampshire and the Isle of Wight. The larger number of these date from the third and early fourth centuries, the period when Roman Britain was most prosperous.

Extent of Romanization. How far the people of Britain were Romanized is much disputed. But the evidence of

---

[1] Gloucester under Nerva, York at an uncertain date before A.D. 237.

[2] The advantages of position which have made London throughout its history the greatest English town were too great to be taken advantage of before England became part of a European system ; they were not suited for the unimportant inter-tribal intercourse of pre-Roman times. See *Royal Commission on Historical Monuments* : *Roman London*, Vol. 3.

[3] The word is used loosely for isolated dwellings in the country, and embraces alike the home of a big landed proprietor (e.g. that at North Leigh, near Oxford) and the farm house. For the distribution of villas, see the Ordnance Survey Map of Roman Britain, 2nd ed.

inscriptions, scanty as it is, yet so far as it goes, seems to show that Latin was the language even of the hand workers, who used it for mere casual scrawls.[1] Very likely many of the natives still talked Celtic, but, if they wrote it, specimens have not come down to us.

While the shapes of the houses are not of a Mediterranean but of a Celtic type, such as was required by the greater rigours of a Northern climate, their fittings and ornaments, so far as they have survived, are Italian : the decorations are imitations of the classic patterns, and the table-ware is largely imported,[2] though the cooking-pots are made in Britain by imitation. The usual result of an imported civilization came to pass in Britain ; fabrics became neater but more conventionalized, and the individual art of the native workman died out ; the Briton preferred the dull imported products of his Roman master (which mass-production no doubt made cheaper), just as British machine-spun fabrics have displaced the native weavings of India and China. It was only in occasional art products that the native British genius survived, e.g., in the ' dragon brooches ' with their brilliant colouring (these brooches, however, disappear in the second century), or in vigorous though primitive pieces of sculpture, such as the head of the Gorgon from the pediment of a temple at Bath, or the Corbridge lion. In view of the Roman character of the remains, we can accept the evidence of Plutarch that Greek grammarians were teaching in Britain in the first century A.D., and of Juvenal that British lawyers were trained by schoolmasters from Gaul. But Roman Britain has left us no literature.

[1] For examples, cf. Haverfield's *Romanization of Britain*, pp. 24 ff., e.g., a rude brick shows the word ' puellam ', probably part of an amatory sentence ; ' Austalis dibus xiii vagatur sibi cotidim ' (' has been going off on his own every day this fortnight ', Collingwood) is a criticism of a London workman.

[2] The so-called ' Samian ' ware is found almost everywhere, made first in Italy at Arretium, and then, from the first century onwards, in Gaul, which ousted the Italian potters from the trade. There were of course many local fabrics, e.g. the so-called ' Castor ' ware, made near Peterborough, with its ' returning spirals ' and spirited copying of nature.

Prosperity of Britain in the Third and Fourth Centuries A.D.
Britain then in its civilized parts seems to have been fairly
Romanized, and in the third and fourth centuries A.D. was
one of the more prosperous parts of the Empire. It was able
in the time of Constantine to send skilled artisans to Gaul,
and to export corn and cloth. But Roman civilization
was soon to perish; by the end of the third century
forts [1] began to be erected in the South-East of Britain to
protect it against the Northern pirates, who, however, do
not become really troublesome till about 350. About A.D.
270 a Celtic invasion from Ireland began; that this was
formidable in the fourth century, can be seen from the
rebuilding of old Roman forts which had been given up
during the times of peace (e.g. at Segontium—i.e. Carnarvon),
and the building of new forts, e.g. at Cardiff.[2] In the year
A.D. 367 hordes of Picts and Scots swept over England,
reaching even to London and Kent. Theodosius restored
peace and rebuilt the defences. Prosperity might have
followed, but successive claimants to the Empire needed
troops, and Britain was left undefended. The Roman
troops were finally withdrawn from Wales about A.D.
400, and from Britain, if we may trust the accepted date,
in 410. But, as Mommsen says, 'It was not Britain that
broke loose from the Empire, but the Empire that gave up
Britain '.

After this withdrawal we have a century of obscurity, of
which we know nothing. Gildas' account (written about
A.D. 540) is full of the gravest inaccuracies. We can only say
that a sort of Roman-British civilization, preserved mainly by
the Church, survived in Wales and Cornwall, but that in
England as a whole Romanization died out; the Latin-
speaking inhabitants were absorbed by the English invaders,
or were driven West into Wales, to fall back from their
acquired to their native civilization.

[1] These apparently took the place of the *Classis Britannica*, which
was suppressed after the rising of Carausius (about 280). The forts
of the ' Saxon Shore ', i.e. the South-East of Britain, are distinguished
by their high thick walls, in which there are few entrances; they
become something like mediaeval castles.

[2] The walls are ten feet thick, and have recently been restored.

CHAPTER XIX

CHRISTIANITY AND THE ROMAN GOVERNMENT

'THEN returned they unto Jerusalem from the Mount called Olivet, which is from Jerusalem a sabbath day's journey. And when they were come in, they went up into an upper room. . . . The number of names together were about an hundred and twenty.'[1] Such was the beginning of the Christian church. Nearly three hundred years later Constantine, Emperor of Rome, placed the sign of the Cross upon the shields of his soldiers.

Christianity ceases to be a Sect of Judaism. For a short time after the Crucifixion (A.D. 29?), the little company of disciples continued to observe the Jewish law.[2] Outwardly they were Jews, worshipping in the Temple ; in their hearts they held the faith that their Master was alive and would come again to establish the Kingdom of God. The small band of Christians grew from 120 to 3,000 and then to 5,000.[3] Many Jews had come from various parts of the Empire to Jerusalem for the feast of Pentecost, and among them many conversions were made. This was of profound importance for the history of Christianity. For these Jews, living outside Palestine, did not share the rigid exclusiveness of the strict Jew living under the shadow of the Temple ; their horizon was widened and their outlook was more liberal, and some at least of them, who became converts, believed that the new religion must shake itself free from the bonds of Judaism if it was to become of universal appeal. Their first spokesman, Stephen, was the first martyr of the Church ; but it should be remembered that it was before the Jewish tribunal, the Sanhedrin, that he was tried as a heretic Jew, and that he was stoned by staunch defenders of the Jewish law (A.D. 33).

Now followed systematic persecution of the leaders of the new faith, which was driven into Samaria and Judaea and as far afield as Syrian Antioch. Persecution followed them still ; messengers were sent from Jerusalem to stir up trouble against the fugitives in the synagogues; on this errand

[1] Acts i. 15.   [2] ii. 46.   [3] ii. 41 ; iv. 4.

Saul was sent to Damascus. None the less the Gospel was preached wherever the fugitives went, at first to none save Jews[1] ; soon, however, Gentiles were baptized, first, the despised Samaritan, then the Ethiopian and the Roman centurion Cornelius ; finally ' men of Cyprus and Cyrene, when they were come to Antioch, spake unto the Greeks '. At Antioch the believers were for the first time called Christians—a term of ridicule bestowed by the populace.

Thus Christianity won its first victory ; it was not to be confined to one nation.

But problems remained ; was the Jewish Christian to lay aside every item of his Judaism ? how much of Jewish custom must the Gentile Christian accept ? There is no need to tell again the story of the conference of St. Paul and Barnabas with the church at Jerusalem, A.D. 49. Christianity here won its second victory ; as long as Gentile converts showed by their life that their conversion was sincere, they were exempted from Jewish customs and rites.[2] Henceforth the Apostle of the Gentiles could carry forth a Gospel emancipated from Judaism, though throughout his work the antagonism of Judaisers met him at every turn.

St. Paul's Journeys. This is not the place in which to describe the missionary journeys of St. Paul. But certain familiar points may be noticed which are of importance for the present purpose.

i. St. Paul used well-established routes of commerce and communication, and visited places which were centres of Greek culture and Roman administration. No doubt there were settlements of Jews in such places, and St. Paul made a practice of preaching first in the synagogues. But his message was also for the Gentiles, and, if Christianity was to become universal, such centres were the most important places of attack.

ii. Few of his converts came from any but the humblest of social grades.

iii. Whenever his activities created disturbance, it was

[1] Acts xi. 19.

[2] This interpretation of Acts xv. 2 sqq. is held by many modern scholars ; see, e.g., A. F. Blunt's edition of ' The Acts '.

CHRISTIANITY

due either to the opposition and false charges of his Jewish opponents or to the anger of those who were threatened with commercial loss, as at Philippi and Ephesus.[1] It is possible, too, though we do not hear of it in the Acts, that some of the disturbances were caused by the social effects of the new religion, for example, divisions and estrangements in families caused by the conversion of individual members.

iv. The journeys were made possible only by the *pax Romana*, while a ready means of communication was afforded by the *koine*, the Hellenistic Greek dialect, which was so widely spread over the Mediterranean, particularly on its Eastern side. St. Paul's safety was often guarded by Roman officials themselves, who, in doing so, believed that they were protecting a Jewish sectary from the ill-treatment of fanatical persecutors. Gallio, Claudius Lysias, Antonius Felix, Porcius Festus[2] believed that the case brought before them consisted of ' questions concerning your own religion ' and acted accordingly ; it was only because St. Paul, when accused of treason, had appealed to Caesar that Festus did not dismiss the accusations entirely ; for, as he saw, the real point at issue was not one of treason but of religious observance.

The distinction between Christianity and Judaism realized by the people. Thus Christianity began by being a sect of Judaism. Little by little it emancipated itself, and its fiercest foes for a time were the Jews themselves. Meantime the Roman governors made no distinction, and, with the aim of keeping the peace between quarrelsome Jews, they gave to Christianity the protection which it needed. Such at any rate, as far as we know, was the official attitude till A.D. 64.

But the populace in various centres knew better. It, too, no less than the Roman government, was familiar with the practices of Jews, and, unlike the Roman government, it vented its hatred accordingly. But in time it learnt that in its midst there was something which seemed more dangerous and contemptible than Judaism, something which through its ' odium humani generis ' was definitely anti-social. This charge was first formulated against Christianity

[1] Acts xvi. 19 ; xix. 24.
[2] xviii. 12 ; xxi. 37 ; xxiv. 1–7 ; xxv. 14 sqq.

in the time of Nero ; but it is clear that the unpopularity
of the Christians had gradually grown in the preceding years,
and that it had some semblance of justification.

Odium humani generis.[1] The very ardour with which the
new Christian communities accepted the faith betrayed
them into excesses of feeling and behaviour which earned
for them the hatred of the mob. In a world which was
everywhere craving for some new religion to satisfy its needs,
Christianity, because of its origin, could at first appeal only
to the lower social orders. Yet Christianity proclaimed
social equality (or might give the impression of doing so),
and in the minds of its opponents this was identified with
social revolution. Communism upset family relations and
interfered with the rights of the 'paterfamilias', and the
growing tendency towards celibacy caused resentment.
Further, Christianity proclaimed the early return of Christ
to judge the world ; the fiery language of prophecy was taken
literally by the mob as predicting the overthrow of paganism
and the final conflagration of the world, from which Christian
believers would be rescued into immortal life. The con-
sciousness that they were somehow 'set apart' betrayed
the Christians into a narrow exclusiveness which rapidly
developed into intolerance. With fanatical zeal they gloried
in the impending catastrophe, and in later years deliberately
provoked hostility to obtain the crown of martyrdom. Public
opinion retaliated ; the exclusiveness of the Christians, it was
said, was a mask to hide the revolting and immoral practices
commanded by their religion. In no age was the opposition
of the Church and the world clearer. Society and the government showed to religion in general a tolerance which has had
no parallel since ; yet because of its beliefs Christianity
answered tolerance by intolerance. It was inevitable that it
should be so ; strong in the faith that the existing organization was soon to perish, the Christians refused to co-operate
with it. To take part in religious festival, even passively, to
take an oath, to shoulder civic responsibilities, to serve in the
army were inconsistent with their religion. The Christian
held aloof, and his aloofness seemed like the pride of conscious

[1] Tac. *Ann.* xv. 44.

superiority. Yet the pagan provincial was proud of the Empire and proud of his civic life ; the non-co-operation of the Christian, if it should spread, would plunge Roman civilization into the destruction foretold in his gloomy prophecies ; and the Roman world valued its civilization.

Such was the common view held about Christians in the second century ; but already by the time of Nero it was taking shape.

The Attitude of the Government towards Religion. In Republican days the State had found it necessary to take notice of the strange religions which settled in Rome and Italy ; in 188 B.C. it had driven out the worship of Bacchus. But in the two centuries which followed, the hold of the national religion was much weakened and many Oriental cults had taken root in Rome. The State, even if it had wished, could not have destroyed them, for the governing classes were attracted by their fascination. The cult of Isis, for example, met with some opposition in the first century B.C., but it finally triumphed when the triumvirs built temples to Serapis and Isis in 43 B.C. Henceforth Rome showed toleration to any religion which would satisfy two conditions : first, it must not be dangerous to public morals or to the political and social organization of the time ; secondly, it must extend to other religions, including the religion of the State, as much toleration as it itself received. The religions of the day found it not difficult to satisfy these conditions —indeed the Roman policy tended to purge the Oriental cults of some of their grossest features ; they were not concerned with political or social questions ; no devotee of them dreamed of imposing his god on anyone else; he was perfectly willing, as inscriptions show, to identify one deity with another or to pray in comprehensive formula to all at once.

The Misunderstanding between Christianity and the Government. Christianity alone failed to satisfy these conditions, as reports from provincial governors to the central authority made clear. Morally, it was reported to be corrupt ; in this the government was misinformed, for the simplicity and purity of the early Christian communities cannot be denied ;

indeed their purer conception of morals may in part explain their aloofness from the world in which they saw so much that was revolting. Socially it was dangerous, for it preached equality to the lowest orders ; politically it was intolerable, for it set up a state within a state and substituted a new loyalty for that of Rome, and taught exclusiveness. Now the unity of the Empire was an ideal very dear to the Romans, and the worship of Rome and Augustus embodied that ideal. Other religions found it no hardship to conform to the State's demands in this respect ; the Jews alone were exempt individually, but the yearly sacrifice in the Temple on behalf of the Emperor was held to be sufficient conformity on the part of this curious and privileged faith ; and after the destruction of the Temple the contribution hitherto paid by Jews to its upkeep was diverted to that of Jupiter at Rome. After the time of Nero, perhaps in Domitian's reign, the test of Caesar worship (i.e. of Rome and the reigning Emperor) began to be imposed on Christians ; and hence arose the great misunderstanding between them and the State. To the government Caesar worship was a test of political loyalty ; to the Christian every act which promoted the interests of the State contributed to the support of idolatry and sacrilege. One side thought in terms of politics, the other in terms of religion ; each started from such fundamentally opposite points of view that neither could understand the other.

Christianity in Rome. We do not know when Christianity first came to Rome ; by the time of Claudius there was already established there the nucleus of a Christian Church, which by A.D. 57 held a very high place in the estimation of the Christian communities. Clement, Bishop of Rome, A.D. 92–101, who was related to the Flavian family, was probably a disciple of St. Peter. The Jewish members of the Church at Rome were no doubt expelled by Claudius when he drove out the Jews,[1] and no doubt they returned very soon : among them were Aquila and Priscilla. That there were also many Gentile Christians in Rome is suggested by St. Paul's letter

---

[1] 'Iudaeos impulsore Chresto assidue tumultuantes Roma expulit.' Suet. *Claud.* 25 ; whether there is here a reference to Christianity is disputed.

to the Romans (A.D. 57),[1] and the majority of these were of the lower orders. We may well believe that during his two years of easy imprisonment (A.D. 60–62) St. Paul greatly enlarged the Church. Yet we know of one woman of high position. In A.D. 57 Pomponia Graecina, the wife of a Roman general, was tried before a court consisting of her own family as being ' superstitionis externae rea '.[2] She was acquitted, probably because her religion was not distinguished from Judaism, which was not at that time forbidden.

The Neronian Persecution. In A.D. 64 the great fire occurred in Rome, of which mention has already been made. That the minds of Christians were occupied with thoughts of a final conflagration of the city was already known to the police. ' Correpti qui fatebantur ' ; these famous words of Tacitus have provoked much discussion ; here they are held to imply that ' to have predicted the fiery destruction of Rome with evident longing for it was sufficient in Nero's eyes to establish their guilt as authors of the actual fire or at any rate as enemies of society '.[3] Henceforth ' the Name ' is charge enough ; for at last the government is convinced of the danger inherent in the beliefs of the Christians. Those who perished as incendiaries were few ; those who perished for ' the Name ' were more numerous, and among them tradition includes St. Peter.

The Basis of the Persecution. It is of more importance to discover the basis of the persecution than to describe its horrors. The trial was held either before Nero or before the *praefectus urbi* ; in other words, it was held before a magistrate who by virtue of his general power of *coercitio* (police powers) could pass judgement on all bandits, robbers, fanatics who disturbed public security. And for the first two centuries this was the basis on which persecutions rested. Hence the extent, degree and duration of a persecution depended upon the interpretation which a magistrate, whether at

---

[1] The date preferred by Edmundson, *The Church in Rome in the First Century*. Rom. xvi. 3–16.   [2] Tac. *Ann.* xiii. 32.
[3] Note that ' confession ' precedes ' arrest ' ; ' confession ' of what ? Can ' fateor ' used in this way mean ' confession ' or ' profession ' of Christianity ?

Rome or in the provinces, might place upon his powers of *coercitio*. There was no general edict condemning Christianity ; it was a police matter within the discretion of the magistrate. Persecution, therefore, during this and the next century was possible on various grounds—incendiarism, treason, magic, ' religio illicita '—but these charges were not specified individually ; ' the Name ' itself as implying something which ought to be suppressed on all or any of the above grounds was sufficient charge, for those who professed it were regarded as wicked and undesirable ; ' odium humani generis ' sums up their offences.

The so-called Persecution by Domitian. The Neronian persecution did not last ; it provoked the impassioned denunciation of the writer of the Apocalypse, but as a whole the Christian Church, so far as we have evidence, was untroubled and grew in peace for twenty-five years. Then occurred the ' second persecution ' with Domitian as author, whom later Christian tradition has made a rival to Nero as the enemy of the Church. But there was no general persecution, merely ' a series of isolated acts directed chiefly against a few influential persons, including members of his own family '.[1]

The tax imposed on the Jews for the upkeep of the temple of Jupiter has been mentioned. Domitian, in need of money, discovered that a large number of people ' living the Jewish way of life ' had evaded payment. He determined to exact it ruthlessly from Jews by birth. But he was also ' a moral and religious reformer ' (p. 177). Those, therefore, who were not Jews but had adopted Jewish customs by choice were to be punished, and under this category no doubt fell the Christians, who, though not connected with a synagogue, seemed to be protecting themselves behind the privileges granted to real Jews by birth. Dio says that ' many were charged with atheism ', and no doubt many Christians suffered ; but we have clear knowledge of three only, and in these cases the underlying motive may have

[1] Edmundson, *The Church in Rome in the First Century*, p. 168. The theory of an extensive Domitianic persecution has rested chiefly on a late date for the Apocalypse ; modern criticism now prefers a date about A.D. 70.

been political. They were Flavius Clemens (a cousin of the Emperor) and his wife Domitilla, and Acilius Glabrio. Clemens and Glabrio were executed, Domitilla was banished. Dio states that they were charged with ' impiety and a Jewish life ', but it is well known that he studiously refrains from mentioning Christianity ; that all three were Christians is placed beyond all reasonable doubt by the evidence of the catacombs. Yet it should be remembered that Domitian was childless, and therefore Clemens and his sons were the heirs to the Empire, while Suetonius says that Glabrio was condemned as ' molitor rerum novarum '. Thus ' atheism ', i.e. Christianity, may have been only an excuse for their removal. But, whatever the truth, it is clear that Christianity was now ascending to the highest levels of Roman society, claiming even the family of the Emperor, and that there was nothing even approaching a general persecution.

The Correspondence of Pliny and Trajan. By far the most famous episode in the early history of the relations between Christianity and the Roman government is the correspondence of Pliny the Younger, governor of Bithynia, who wrote to the Emperor for guidance.[1] It should be observed that, if there had been any general edict against Christianity, even the timid Pliny would not have needed or ventured to ask advice on the treatment of Christians. Pliny had been sent as special commissioner to deal with a difficult province ; under these special circumstances, he asks, how was he to interpret his powers of *coercitio* with regard to the Christians, for he had had no previous experience of their crimes or the punishment due to them or the procedure to be followed ? Yet it is sufficiently clear that he was familiar with the ordinary procedure. A number of people were brought to him ' tanquam Christiani '. He asked them whether they were Christians ; they admitted it ; he asked the same question a second and a third time ; on receiving the same answer he ordered their execution. So far all was normal. But Pliny discovered that the Christians in Bithynia were very numerous, and anonymous charges were brought against a large number of persons. On examination many denied that they were

[1] Plin. *Ep.* x. 96, 97.

20

Christians, others said that they had long ceased to be such, and they complied with Pliny's demand that they should worship the statue of the Emperor as a test of their loyalty. The remainder of Pliny's letter may be interpreted thus. ' In popular belief Christians are guilty of immoral and murderous practices ; to have renounced Christianity does not automatically free a man from the guilt of having taken part in these practices. Accordingly I determined to find out what these people really believe and do. I learnt that they met at stated times for a religious service ; an oath was taken binding members to refrain from theft, robbery, dishonesty and immorality ; they also took part in a religious meal of a perfectly harmless nature. The torture of two slave-women revealed nothing else. It seems to me, therefore, that a lenient view of the case may be taken, and that recantation should be followed by complete pardon. Am I right ? Further, hitherto " the Name " has been sufficient charge. But I could discover nothing more than " an absurd and excessive superstition ". Is it " the Name " or the crimes involved in " the Name "—" flagitia cohaerentia nomini "—which deserve punishment ? Is distinction to be made for sex or age ? ' Pliny is obviously dissatisfied with the vagueness, the intentional vagueness, of the existing procedure.

Trajan's Reply. To Pliny's long and hesitating letter Trajan replied briefly. ' You have followed the correct procedure in sifting the cases of the Christians who have been brought before you. For no definite rule of general application can be laid down. There is no need to hunt them out ; if they are brought before you and proved guilty, they are to be punished ; at the same time, if they deny that they are Christians and demonstrate this in act, that is, by offering supplication to our gods, then they may obtain pardon by recantation, whatever suspicion they may have incurred in the past. Anonymous charges are not to be entertained in any accusation at all ; they are a very bad precedent, and do not suit the spirit of our age.'

Thus no direct answer is given to some of Pliny's questions which hinted at leniency, nor is he relieved of responsibility by being given a clear-cut rule. The vagueness still persists, and Pliny, like other provincial governors, must use his discretion. ' The Name ' continues to be a charge, and convicted Christians must be executed. Yet Pliny need not round up the Christians ; such a campaign of extermination would cause more disturbance of the peace than their continued existence. In the case of those who recanted, the past was to be forgotten. Trajan's decision was a compromise ; as supreme magistrate he could not tolerate the disloyalty to the State implied in Christianity, nor could he as a statesman proceed to extreme measures against a religion which he saw was not a real danger. The Roman attitude, therefore, as shown by this expression of it, was far from intentionally hostile. Christians had much more to fear from the hatred of the populace, particularly in the Eastern towns, which, when excited by some event, almost compelled the government to be consistent and to proceed against those who were in theory its enemies. ' If the Tiber floods the city or the Nile refuses to rise or the sky withholds its rain or disasters occur—earthquake or famine or pestilence—the cry is raised at once " Christianos ad leonem ".' [1]

Christianity in the Second Century. By the second century the attitude of more educated Christians had changed. The immediate coming of Christ had lost its hold upon their imaginations ; the denunciation of apocalypse gave place to the reasoned pleading of apology ; the Christian writers strove to show the Emperors that their faith was not dangerous, and the letters of Bishops to their churches frequently urge that martyrdom for ' the Name ' was not to be wantonly courted. Thus Aristides [2] presented an Apology to Hadrian in Athens. A few years later (A.D. 140) Justin Martyr, a presbyter at Rome, addressed his Apology to Antoninus Pius, and at the end of the century the fierce Tertullian, of Africa, and Minucius Felix wrote their defences with the same purpose, though in very different styles. [3] But the Roman government maintained its attitude. During the second

[1] Tertullian, *Apology*, 40.

[2] Not the Aristides referred to on p. 258.

[3] Melito, Bishop of Sardis in the time of Marcus Aurelius, also wrote an Apology.

century, as during the first, there was no general persecution. When Christians were martyred, as e.g. Ignatius, Bishop of Antioch, or Polycarp, Bishop of Smyrna, it was due in general to spasmodic outbursts of popular fury, intensified, as against Ignatius, by the ' obstinatio ' with which they sought the crown of martyrdom.

The Rescript of Hadrian. Probably in A.D. 123, Hadrian wrote to Minicius Fundanus, governor of Asia, in reply to a query addressed to him by the previous governor. The gist of the rescript is this : ' Christians may be unpopular, but their unpopularity is not to prejudice their trial. Charges brought must be proved conclusively ; prosecutors bringing false charges must be punished with severer penalties.' ' The Name ' is still an offence, but injustice must not be done. It should be observed that this rescript like that of Trajan was addressed to the governor of an Eastern province, where fanaticism was particularly rife. Hadrian, then, inaugurated no new policy, though indirectly he protected the Christians, and no trustworthy evidence attributes any execution to his reign, save that of Telesporus, Bishop of Rome. Under Antoninus Pius we know of three Christians who were put to death, the most noteworthy being the aged Polycarp, Bishop of Smyrna. ' Eighty and six years have I served Him and He never did me wrong ; and how can I now blaspheme my King who has saved me ? '

Marcus Aurelius as Persecutor. It is one of the curiosities of history that Marcus Aurelius, who of all men in the early centuries of our era most resembled in character the Christian ideal, was ranked by later Christian tradition as one of the severest persecutors of the Church ; in modern times, if he is acquitted of the charge of cruelty, he is reproached with indifference in not modifying the existing attitude of the law towards the Christians ; in his reign at any rate, it is urged, some improvement in their lot might have been expected. Neither charge can be substantiated.

The chief persecutions of his reign may be mentioned. At Rome Justin, who had already addressed an Apology to Antoninus and had remained free from arrest, was brought to trial before the City Prefect, probably on the accusation of a personal enemy. If the account which we have of the trial may be believed, it shows, first, the unwillingness of Junius Rusticus, the prefect, to convict, secondly the proud glory of Justin in his trial. Justin and his six companions were put to death. We hear of the trial of three Christians at Pergamum ; and in Africa, at Madaura and Scili, the first Christian blood shed in this province was shed in the reign of Marcus, or immediately after his death.

Another famous episode belongs to this reign. At Lugdunum and Vienna the mob set upon the Christians with uncontrolled fury, and the most prominent members of both churches were arrested. Their slaves accused their masters of the worst crimes with which Christians were credited. Before the Roman magistrate the only charge was that they were Christians. Some of the prisoners were Roman citizens, and the governor wrote to the Emperor, in camp on the Northern frontier, to ascertain the procedure to be adopted towards them and towards the few who had recanted. Marcus[1] answered that pardon was to follow recantation, citizens were to be beheaded, the rest were to be thrown to the wild beasts of the arena. The victims were in number forty-eight ; among others the fifteen-year-old slave-girl Blandina showed the utmost heroism in the face of torture and death.

Certain points may be noted. There was no change of policy ; the law followed its normal course. But it is possible that collisions between the government and the Christians were more frequent in the reign of Marcus Aurelius. For this there were good reasons. Christianity was spreading in the Western provinces, and the populace was beginning to show the same hatred of it as had long been common in the East. Further, the reign of Marcus was a time of general anxiety ; disasters followed one another—famine, plague, earthquake and the fear of invasion. We may remember

[1] In the *Meditations* of Marcus the following passages seem to glance at Christianity : i. 6 ; iii. 16 ; vii. 68 ; viii. 48, 51 ; and xi. 3, where ὡς οἱ χριστιανοί is probably a gloss. A letter from Antoninus and Marcus to the κοινόν of Asia, containing a command that ' if anyone perseveres in bringing such a person into trouble as being such, let the person charged be acquitted even if the charge be made out and let the prosecutor be put on trial ', seems too indulgent to be authentic.

Tertullian's complaint that every disaster was visited on the unfortunate Christians. The law therefore remained the same ; but in this reign it so happened that for special reasons it was more often invoked.

In the first two centuries, therefore, persecution was desultory, spasmodic and largely dependent on the discretion of the magistrate. The government adopted half-measures, and half-measures, so far from suppressing Christianity, rather afforded a stimulus for its growth. For the Christian Church grew rapidly ; its branches multiplied and organization took more definite form.

Of the later history of Christianity in the Empire we cannot here speak ; Commodus, partly owing to the influence of his mistress Marcia, showed himself indulgent ; in the third century persecution took a new and severer form.

CHAPTER XX

ECONOMIC CONDITIONS IN THE EARLY EMPIRE

'IT has needed the good fortune and the self-discipline of eight hundred years to weld together this structure which cannot be torn asunder without the ruin of those who do so. Wherefore, love and cherish this peace and this city of Rome, which conquerors and conquered alike have the right to enjoy.' [1]

The Pax Romana was the gift of Augustus, enjoyed for more than two hundred years by the Roman world. The struggles of rival Emperors at times caused a ripple on the smooth surface of Roman peace, but the greater part of the Empire remained undisturbed. It is only of recent years that the amazing prosperity of the Empire has begun to be apparent to us ; the condition of the provinces at various periods is being carefully studied, and thanks to the labours of archaeologists and the witness of thousands of inscriptions a clearer picture of life under the Empire is taking shape. The two chapters which follow can attempt to do little more than

[1] Tac. *Hist.* iv. 74. The words of Cerealis to the Treveri and Lingones.

draw attention to some of the main features of the Pax Romana; they may roughly be divided into two types, economic and social, though it will be difficult always to maintain the distinction.

From the very earliest times of which we have knowledge the trader was busy on the shores of the Mediterranean; he carried his wares from harbour to harbour, running many risks, but apparently reaping his reward in spite of them. Phoenicians, Greeks, Carthaginians, Romans held in turn supremacy as the merchants of the Mediterranean. But they traded under many disadvantages; the various states to which the shores of the sea belonged were often at war; piracy was rife, particularly in the Eastern seas, and markets were precarious; there was no common currency and no universal law. Yet in spite of the obstacles commercial intercourse flourished; enterprise is of the essence of successful trade.

Augustus restored peace to the world, and he and his successors developed a new theory of Rome's relations to her provinces. Piracy was in great measure suppressed; war within the Empire was henceforth rare; frontiers were guarded. In every province Roman administration secured good order and the peaceful development of its resources; life and property were safe, protected by the embracing arms of Roman law. As the Romanization of backward lands progressed, Latin and Greek became more widely spread as the medium of communication; the imperial Mint provided a standard currency, and Roman coins are found from Ireland to China. Trade will always find routes for itself, but the great roads built primarily for the easy movement of troops facilitated also the movement of goods and made transport safe. The restoration of a strong central government pleased no one more than the traders of every nationality, and as a result of the Pax Romana the first two centuries witnessed the economic development of the known world; prosperity reigned in lands which are to-day desolate and barren.

At times the State deliberately aided commercial enterprise. No tariffs favoured Italy at the expense of the pro-

vinces ; roads were built by the Emperors with the intention
of opening up promising districts ; ships and troops were
dispatched to important points in the interest of the traders.
' The might of the Roman Empire ', says the elder Pliny,
' has made the world the possession of all ; who would deny
that human life has profited by the exchange of goods and a
common partnership in the blessings of peace ? ' [1]

It will be convenient in this chapter, first, to take a hurried
view of the Empire within the limits of its frontiers, and to
ask how much of the world Rome knew beyond those frontiers,[2] and then to describe in somewhat more detail certain
aspects of the economic life of Italy.

I. *Trade and Communication.* We must not take too mean
a view of the commerce of the first two centuries. During the
greater part of the year the sea was alive with vessels, some
coasting from place to place, others taking long voyages to
distant markets. Rich men invested their capital in commercial companies, which had their agencies at the busy
ports. Raw material was transported by sea or land to be
manufactured elsewhere. The technique of one factory
was carefully watched by the craftsmen of another, and in
some industries, as e.g. glass and pottery, we can trace the
fortunes of rival centres of production. Skilled workers,
who could organize production to suit a particular market,
were in demand, and no trouble or expense was spared to
obtain them. Increased numbers of merchant vessels were
needed ; the guilds of shipwrights and carpenters have left
plentiful witness of themselves in the inscriptions found at
large ports. New harbours were built to take the increased
shipping, and in capacious warehouses at the dockside the
varied produce of East and West was stored.

Certain features of Roman trade may be indicated, though
it must be remembered that such general statements cannot
be more than rough guides.

[1] ' Quis enim non communicato orbe terrarum maiestate Roman
imperii profecisse vitam putet commercio rerum et societate festae
pacis ? ' (Plin. *N.H.* xiv. 2).

[2] In the sections which follow use has been made of *The Trade
Routes and Commerce of the Roman Empire*, by M. P. Charlesworth,
and *The Ancient Explorers*, by M. Cary and E. H. Warmington.

i. In the Eastern half of the Mediterranean trade and industry had been organized long before the Romans penetrated so far ; the Western provinces on the other hand were new and unexploited. Hence the West produced the raw material—minerals, hides, wool, animals, agricultural produce—while the East exported manufactured goods. Further, the long-civilized Eastern provinces supplied the markets of the West with the luxuries in food and dress which the newer Western civilization was now demanding with unsatisfied insistence. These provinces, too, were the channel of communication with that little known further East, India and China, whence came a supply of costly goods—silk, ivory, perfumes, jewels, etc.—which the rich could afford. Hence there was a perpetual movement of coined money eastwards, and in a later period the scarcity of coin in the West gave rise to serious economic crises.

ii. At the end of the Republic Roman merchants had themselves carried their enterprise into distant lands. Under the Empire, though the Roman merchant is still to be found, the bulk of the trade seems to have been in the hands of Greek and Syrian merchants ; no doubt much Roman capital was behind them. Further, Greek and Asiatic craftsmen were the best ; they flocked in great numbers westwards and were employed in the new factories of Italy, Spain and Gaul. Trade, then, was a chief cause of that extraordinary mingling of nationalities of which more will be said later.

iii. The government, being a consumer of certain goods on a vast scale, was directly interested in their production. Gold and silver and copper were needed for the currency, iron, lead and leather for the army, stone for roads, marble for public buildings, corn for the people of Rome. The State, therefore, was intimately concerned in the production of these things, and mines and quarries and vast tracts of agricultural and pasture land were owned by the Emperor or were under imperial control.

iv. To gain some idea of the conditions of trade we must think ourselves back to the days before steam-power and wireless communication. Voyages were rarely attempted in the depth of winter, but for the greater part of the year sailings from the great ports were fairly regular and a traveller could generally rely on a passage. On the matter of speed of communication our information is scanty ; naturally the record times tend to be quoted. The imperial post service, used for government purposes, aimed at certainty rather than speed ; [1] fifty Roman miles a day on land represents its normal rate, but in emergency a merchant could no doubt send a special messenger at greater speed. Normal communication, however, was much slower. The voyage from Rome to Alexandria took about three weeks, from Rome to Berytus about a month, from Ostia to Gades ten days, from Rome to Tarraco four days. About a year was allowed for a voyage to India and back, with ample time for turning round the cargo.

Egypt. We may begin our brief survey with Alexandria, the most important trade centre of the Mediterranean. On the north she was in communication with every main seaport ; on the south and east routes of commerce converged upon her—the Nile, the waterways from the Red Sea and caravan routes from Arabia, Palestine and Syria ; they made her the chief centre of exchange between East and West. A canal route ran from the Delta to Arsinoe and Clysmon ; a caravan route from Coptos, which could be reached by a two-days' voyage up the Nile, led through a break in the mountains to Myos Hormos on the Red Sea ; another route led to Berenice, also on the Red Sea, and a third to Syene, Philae and Ethiopia. Alexandria was well fitted to receive water-borne traffic from the interior, for she had three harbours, one of which was reserved for the inland trade. We shall see in a moment with what countries the ports of the west shore of the Red Sea traded ; the eastern side never attracted as much traffic, since the petty princes of the Arabians levied toll on goods passing through and were not

---

[1] See *J.R.S.* xv. (1925) (i.), p. 60.

Times taken by imperial couriers are : Mainz to Cologne, 108 Roman miles, 12–14 hours ; Rheims to Rome, 1,440 Roman miles, 9 days ; these are exceptionally fast rates. Rome to Alexandria (via Aquileia, Sirmium, Byzantium, Antioch, Alexandria), 3,100 miles, 63 days ; Limyra (Lycia) to Rome by sea, about 1,800 miles, 36 days.

always friendly. But the major proportion of goods handled in Alexandria came from Egypt itself. Twenty million bushels of corn passed over the quays each year to be shipped to Rome, besides quantities of other cereals for the general trade ; building stone, porphyry and granite were quarried in the mountains east of the Nile, and gold and silver were mined near Syene. Quantities of raw material were sent to Alexandria to be worked up, for the town, besides being a port, was a centre of industry on a large scale. Leather, wool, flax and, from the further East, silk, cotton and ivory were manufactured in factories which were so much an imperial monopoly that little room was left for private enterprise. The manufactured articles found their way over the Mediterranean, and in particular the export of linen, papyrus and glass was enormous.

The Further East. There is no clear evidence that the Greeks in Seleucid times reached India in their commercial ventures. With the dawn of the Empire the Egyptian Greeks turned their attention to the commerce of the Erythraean Sea, i.e. the modern Arabian Sea. At first they crept along the southern coast of Arabia, past Arabia Eudaimon (Aden) and on to Makran till they reached the mouth of the Indus, paying toll as they passed to Arabian and Parthian overlords. In the reign of Tiberius a certain Hippalus formed some idea of the position and shape of India, and relying on the monsoon pushed across from South Arabia to the Indus. Later voyagers gained courage, till eventually after A.D. 50 traders cut across from Aden to Muziris (Cranganore), a famous port on the south-west coast of India ; Strabo says that in one year 120 ships would leave Myos Hormos for India.

During the rule of the Flavian Emperors the demand for the luxuries of the East sent traders still further afield. Zanzibar, on the east coast of Africa, was reached and its cinnamon duly sent back to the Mediterranean. The interior of Ceylon was visited, and here large numbers of Roman coins are still dug up. The Ganges was reached, and finally, under Hadrian, the direct voyage from Ceylon to Malay was made across the Bay of Bengal. The credit for this is due to a certain Alexander, who also ventured through the straits of Malacca to

Cattigara in the Gulf of Tongking. Thus contact with the Chinese was established; in A.D. 166 a commercial mission was sent from Marcus Aurelius to the Chinese Emperor, of which mention is made in Chinese records. Direct intercourse with China had long been wished for, but the land route had hitherto been made difficult by Parthia. But at times when Roman influence in the East was paramount the overland silk-route became better known, and about A.D. 120 agents were sent by an enterprising merchant, Maes by name,[1] from the Persian Gulf to Merv and the Oxus ; they met the Seres at some point to the east of Kashgar, and later Miran was reached. When conditions were favourable, Bactrians and Indians reached Asia Minor by this route as far as Merv, continuing their land journey by the Euphrates and so eliminating the voyage up the Red Sea.

The sea-borne trade with India and China brought, besides silk, rare woods, teak and ebony, ivory, cotton, jewels and what was specially prized, pepper ; to India was taken tin, lead, wine, glass, and much coin found its way there. After the time of Marcus Aurelius trade with India fell away, though the Byzantine Empire still used the land route to Kashgar.

Antioch in *Syria* may be regarded as the third city of the Empire. Not only was it the chief city of a most important province, but also as a commercial centre it, too, like Alexandria, was a meeting-place of the Eastern and Western worlds, and was famous for its wealth and luxury. Its port Seleucia received the Western traffic, and the coastal traders of Asia Minor, Syria and Egypt ; on land Antioch was served by many important routes. To Egypt the road led by the Orontes to Heliopolis and the Upper Jordan valley, and across the plain of Esdraelon and the ranges of Ephraim and Carmel to Gaza ; on the East, routes of unknown antiquity led to Damascus and over the desert to the oasis of Palmyra, a city which, though outside the province, was much influenced by Rome ; to Palmyra came the merchandise of Mesopotamia and, indirectly, of India and China ; from Antioch to Babylon

---

[1] Maes reported the fact that silk was not a vegetable product, but was spun by a caterpillar.

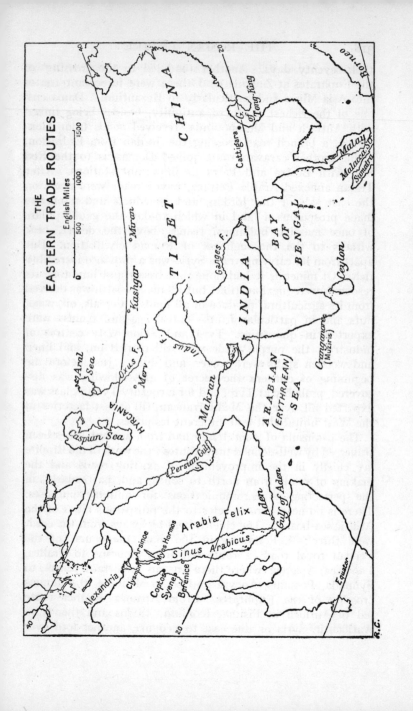

THE
EASTERN TRADE ROUTES

English Miles

0   500   1000   1500

BORNEO

CHINA

G. of Tong-King

Cattigara

Malay

Sumatra

Molacca Str.

TIBET

Ganges F.

Kashgar

°Miran

BAY
OF
BENGAL

Ceylon

INDIA

Crangamore
(Muziris)

Aral
Sea

Oxus F.

°Merv

Indus F.

Makran

HYRCANIA

ARABIAN
(ERYTHRAEAN)
SEA

Caspian Sea

Persian Gulf

Arabia Felix

Gulf of Aden

Aden

Alexandria

Clysma Arsinoe
°Myos Hormos

Sinus Arabicus

Coptos
Syene°
Berenice

Equator

R.C.

took seventy days. Another road led to the crossing of the Euphrates at Zeugma, and there were important routes into Asia Minor and particularly to Byzantium. Damascus, one of the richest marts of antiquity, besides being linked with Antioch and Mesopotamia, received goods from Alexandria, a branch road crossing the Jordan from Esdraelon, while another caravan route joined Damascus to the Red Sea, with Bostra and Petra as important stations. After Trajan annexed Arabia Petraea, paved roads were made on the east side of the Jordan, and aqueducts and reservoirs made prosperous a land in which to-day the gaunt pillars of once massive buildings, rising above the desert, bear witness to the thoroughness of Roman civilization. But apart from its carrying trade Syria was a province incredibly rich. Of minerals it had none ; in basalt and limestone its resources were inexhaustible, but its main wealth was derived from its agricultural produce of all kinds. Cereals, oil, wine, nuts and in particular fruits—dates, figs and plums—were exported in quantities. Tyre and Sidon were centres of industry ; the purple trade was still carried on, and linen and woollen stuffs were woven and dyed. Just before the beginning of our era the secret of glass-blowing was discovered, probably at Tyre, and for a century Tyrian glass was exported all over the Mediterranean, till at last factories in the West imitated it and undercut its prices.

The peninsula of *Asia Minor* had from ancient times been traversed by well-defined trade routes ; the work of the Empire lay chiefly in the improvement of existing roads and the making of roads from north to south, and, particularly, in the perfecting of communications for military purposes. There is no need here to refer to the prosperous cities of the Asiatic sea-board. The chief inland highways from the coast were three :—i. Following in the main the course of the Persian royal road, a route led from Ephesus to Tralles, Laodicea, Apamea, where there was an important centre, to Synnada, Pessinus, Ancyra and so to Melitene, the famous crossing of the Euphrates. From Apamea another route led to Antioch in Pisidia, Iconium, Tarsus and thence to Antioch in Syria or due east to Zeugma, another ford over

the Euphrates. ii. Further north an ancient highway, starting from Smyrna, followed the Hermus valley to Sardis and
thence went to Pessinus, Ancyra, Megalopolis, where a fork
gave the alternative of Melitene or Satala. Tradition says
that wares from India reached Europe by this route, which
continued to the Caspian Sea, the Oxus and Northern Bac-
tria. Still further north the chief road stretched from
Nicomedia to Amasea. After the reign of Nero, when the
eastern frontier was ' armed ', roads from Satala to Melitene
and southwards were important for military purposes, and
the northern roads were strengthened to give easy means of
transport for the reinforcements from the Pannonian legions
by way of Byzantium. By the end of the first century, too,
trade with the Caucasian lands had increased. The chief
route from north to south was from Sinope to Tarsus, through
the Cilician Gates.[1]

Of the varied resources of Asia Minor it is impossible to
give any idea in a brief paragraph. Every kind of agricultural
produce was conveyed down to the harbours. In the south
saffron and ointments and gums were made from plants, and
canvas from goats' hair ;[2] in the Roman province of Asia
wool and purple cloth ;[3] in Pontus fruits and nuts, honey and
delicacies from the fisheries of the Black Sea—these are a few
of the main exports. Phrygia and Caria were famous for
their marble, but metals were not mined in any quantities
during Roman times.

From the earliest days of Greek colonization trading
stations had been planted on the shores of the *Black Sea*.
This trade continued into Roman times, and in the second
century probably became more important ; Hadrian commissioned Arrian to survey its coasts ; and the Black Sea
fleet repressed the activities of piratical tribes. But at the
end of the reign of Marcus Aurelius the migration of inland
peoples tended to unsettle the tribes close to the sea ; security
became less assured and trade decreased.

Greece played little part in the commerce of the Empire.

[1] The Bagdad Railway makes its way through the range of mountains to the north of Cilicia by way of the Cilician Gates.
[2] Cf. St. Paul at Tarsus.   [3] Cf. Lydia of Thyatira.

Some of its quarries were still worked; a little wine and honey were exported, and Corinth retained its position as a distributing centre. But neglect seems to have been the main feature of that unfortunate land. Enterprising Greeks found openings as craftsmen, traders, masons, potters, doctors, teachers and officials in any country but their own, and, if we may believe Dio Chrysostom, whole tracts of country lay desolate, for better soil could be found elsewhere. Industry —particularly weaving and dyeing—survived half-heartedly in some districts, notably at Patrae; but, on the whole, Greece, in spite of the efforts of Hadrian and Herodes Atticus, presents a sorry spectacle in this period.

Before imperial times land communication between Italy and the *Northern Provinces* had depended chiefly on the Via Aurelia, the coast road to Genoa, on the west, and a road from Bononia to Aquileia on the east. But after Augustus' pacification of the Alpine tribes, routes over the mountains themselves became practicable. Mediolanum was a centre of roads leading over the Alps, which were crossed by the Mont Genèvre, the Great St. Bernard and the Little St. Bernard passes. By the first pass Arelate and Valentia could be reached; the second, by Augusta Praetoria and Vindonissa, was the main highway to the Rhine; the third led to Vienna and Lugdunum, whence roads radiated to all parts of Gaul. From Aquileia important roads led to the Danube towns and to the east—one by Siscia and Viminacium to Byzantium, another to Dyrrhachium where it met the Via Egnatia to Thessalonica, another due north to Virunum and the Danube, another north-east to Poetovio and Carnuntum, Aquincum and other stations on the Danube.

The northern provinces had few manufactures; their wealth lay in minerals, timber, animals for the arena, and hides; in return for these they imported manufactured goods, clothes, pottery and luxuries. On the northern frontier, and beyond, the Syrian trader has left witness of himself, though here the Treveran merchant proved a severe competitor. The legionary camps attracted dealers, and in time, as peace flourished and roads improved, a busy trade throve in the Danube lands. The old amber traffic with the Baltic was renewed, attracting merchants of every nationality to the frontier stations ; the elder Pliny records the expedition of a Roman knight who started from Carnuntum and reached the Baltic Coast after traversing 600 miles ; and coins have been found in Northern Germany. But, though Rome valued the mineral resources of these provinces, her interest in them was chiefly military.

Of the divisions of *Gaul* Narbonensis was the most productive. The valleys provided good pasturage, and oil, wine, hams and wool were exported to Italy from Massilia, Narbo and Arelate. Good roads linked up the province with Spain and Italy and also with Lugdunum, the centre of the road system of the whole of Gaul. The Rhone and the Atax carried down freights from the interior ; the numerous inscriptions of the guilds of shipwrights, carpenters, rivermen and others testify to the busy trade carried on along the waterways. Indeed Gaul was particularly fortunate in navigable rivers—e.g. the Garumna, Arar, Dubis, Mosella, Sequana ; and it was safer and quicker to transport goods from Britain to the Mediterranean on the Gallic waterways than to convey them by sea. The other divisions of Gaul, though less fertile, made their contributions ; the olive and the vine did not grow freely in the colder climate ; wool was their main export, and they eagerly imported wine and oil and the produce of more favoured countries. Of gold and silver Gaul produced little ; Britain easily outbid her. On the other hand, flourishing potteries grew up at Lezoux, La Graufesenque and elsewhere, and even as far north as Rheinzabern (Tabernae Rhenanae) in the Rhine valley ; hundreds of furnaces have been found and the signatures of thousands of potters are known. During the early part of the first century the earthenware of Arretium was imported into Gaul, but soon the Gallic factories produced in such quantities that they captured the trade of the Western Mediterranean and their ware was actually imported into Italy. Glass also was manufactured in large quantities, particularly in Normandy, and had a wide distribution in Gaul, Germany and Britain.

With *Britain* there was considerable trade even before

21

Claudius' occupation of the island. The main lines of communication were the mouths of the Garonne, Loire and Seine : traffic also went down the Rhine and coasted along the channel to Portus Itius, where it made the crossing. Gessoriacum (Boulogne), besides being a port, was also the station of the Roman fleet. The main articles of export from Britain were corn, wool, hides, slaves, baskets, hunting-dogs and oysters ; tin does not seem to have been plentiful, but lead was exported in quantities. There were also industries—weaving, pottery, iron-working—but these probably did little more than supply local needs.

The Romans long before the Empire were well aware of the resources of *Spain*, but it was only during imperial times, and particularly under the Flavians, that its mineral wealth was fully exploited. Augustus by his foundations—e.g. Caesar Augusta, Asturica Augusta, Lucus Augusti, Emerita —did much to open up the Western and Northern regions ; the roads connecting such places surrounded Spain with main lines of communication, which were connected with the interior districts by later Emperors ; in particular the North-Western area, with its port Brigantium, was well served with roads for the transport of minerals. Caesar Augusta was the starting-point of the main roads ; a road round the peninsula ran by Valentia, New Carthage, Malaca, Gades, Olisipo, Bracara, Brigantium, Asturica and so back to Caesar Augusta, whence also an important route cut across to Emerita.

Of the fertility of the Spanish valleys Roman writers can scarcely say enough in praise. Both in crops and in herds the country was prolific, and its export of corn, oil and wool was enormous. The industries of Spain were not so developed as those of Gaul. But undoubtedly it was its mineral wealth that made Spain so valuable to the Empire. Gold and silver were mined in Lusitania, Gallaecia and Asturica, and at New Carthage there were silver mines, worked by the Carthaginians and still productive. Before the lead of Britain became a serious rival, Spanish lead from Baebelo, in the north, and New Carthage easily held the market. Iron, tin and ' minium ' (vermilion) were also obtained. So important were the mines to the government that by the second century they were all under the control of an imperial *procurator metallorum*, and were worked either direct by the State or were leased to *conductores*. An important inscription shows us the terms on which a copper mine was leased at Vipasca (Aljustrel) in South Portugal. The State regulated to the minutest detail the life of the mining village which sprang up round the mine, and on the whole it may be said that it protected the health and happiness of the miners employed, who were free men and slaves. Inscriptions show that the mines and quarries throughout all the provinces were as a rule controlled by state officials.

The profound influence of Rome on *Africa* is only now being discovered. Districts which are now desert were once productive, thanks to the Roman thoroughness of irrigation. Cities with their amphitheatres, baths and temples, now at last uncovered, rose amid fields rich in corn and olives. Mauretania, the least fertile area, produced some vines and its hills gave pasturage for flocks of sheep. Timber, too, particularly ebony and citrus wood, was exported for furniture-making. On the coast the purple trade was still active. Though there were roads connecting the main places, the absence of legionary troops in this part accounts for their comparative neglect ; further, commercially Mauretania was more closely in touch with Spain than with senatorial Africa, and most of the transport was by sea. Numidia was not developed till the time of the Empire ; it was richer than Mauretania and its marble was famous. But it was the province of Africa proconsularis which really justified the proverbial fertility of Africa in Roman times. Corn, vines, olives, fruit-trees, nuts, herds of horses and donkeys, cattle and flocks of sheep—for these it was noted. On the coast the industry of fish-curing and pickling throve. The main ports were Carthage and Utica, but soon the whole coast was dotted with trading villages and a busy traffic plied along it, while such ports as Hippo Regius, Hadrumetum, Tacape and Oea handled the millions of bushels of corn needed for Rome. Inland there were busy centres of trade, which had grown in importance as the camps had developed into cities. The province was connected with Egypt by a road through Cyrene, though doubtless the sea-route was more used.

So hasty a survey will not have failed if it suggests that throughout the Empire there was ceaseless movement of men and goods. Nationality proved no hindrance ; tariffs offered no barrier ; what one country lacked was supplied by another. The boundaries which formerly separated countries lost much of their meaning except for administrative purposes. Travel was easy and commercial intercourse meant also the exchange of ideas. The Gaul, the Syrian, the African and the Dacian shared a common heritage ; the world was growing smaller ; the Empire became one, though it still sheltered much diversity. Though trade co-extensive with the Empire could not have grown up apart from the idea of the Empire as a political unity, it did much to draw closer the bonds of Empire and was at once a result and a cause of its unity.

II. We may now turn to Italy and consider her economic condition during the first two centuries.

The two centuries preceding the Empire had witnessed clearly marked changes in the condition of Italy, changes due in most part to the rapid acquisition of provinces. The Punic Wars had drained the country-side of men ; the casualties had been heavy ; large tracts of land—two million acres, according to modern calculation—lay idle or were devastated by the enemy ; and outside the stricken area labour was difficult to obtain. Those who survived the wars either had not the courage to go back to a ruined farm or preferred the lucrative opportunities opened up in the provinces or the attractions of town life. The destruction of Carthage, insisted on by those of the aristocracy who had the development of Roman commerce at heart, had great effect on the theory and practice of farming in Italy and threw markets open to Italian industry. The big estates in Italy, many of them formed out of *ager publicus* which was lying idle, demanded labour, and labour was not to be had. The Carthaginian system of farming large estates by slave-labour was familiar to the Romans, and the recent wars had given them an almost unlimited supply of slaves. But slave-labour was not really suitable for skilled farming, and therefore *latifundia* were mainly composed of grasslands, over which ranged herds of cattle tended by slaves. None the less such was the shortage of labour that the attempt was made to use slave-labour on arable lands, for the owner-farmers of small estates had decreased in numbers. It is true that Sulla, the triumvirs and Octavian had planted out thousands of veterans on small plots of land appropriated from their enemies, and this tended to break up big estates ; but the soldier made a bad farmer, and he often drifted back to the city. Meantime wealth poured into Italy, brought by individuals or paid to the conquering city in the form of tribute. The ' new rich ' bought land, the possession of which at once gave a standing in society, but they were not concerned to make it pay, and residential estates became increasingly common. The Carthaginian harvests were diverted to Rome and the distribution of cheap corn became frequent ; its effects on Italian agriculture will be considered below. Meantime industry prospered, for the markets of the world were now available.

The civil wars had to some extent dislocated commerce and made security of tenure precarious. None could guess what the future held. Octavian's victory, therefore, was hailed with joy by all concerned in agriculture or trade. Peace was to bring untold blessings. Yet his victory brought hardship to some. The veterans had to be satisfied ; and for his soldiers Augustus spent six million sesterces in buying land round towns which had resisted him in his early struggle to power ; owners or occupiers were ejected, among them Vergil's blind father, who was driven from his little farm at Mantua, near Cremona : ' barbarus has segetes ? ' Not every case of dispossession had so happy a sequel.[1]

Latifundia. The *ager publicus* had been acquired by the State partly as the result of conquest during Rome's expansion in Italy, partly as the result of confiscations after the Second Punic War. It lay chiefly in the uplands of the south of Italy, in Lucania and Apulia. The capitalist turned large tracts of it to his own use, and in time use meant to him

[1] See *Eclogues*, i. and ix.

possession. It may be urged that by making it productive the capitalist was doing the State a service. Here was one cause of the *latifundia*. Secondly, aristocratic families, who were forbidden to engage in commerce, invested their capital in land ; and, in the state of the land market resulting from the depopulation of the country-side and the confusion of the civil wars, there was a tendency for them to enlarge their estates. But the large estate paid best if it specialized in some particular form of production, while, if production was to be on a large scale, a good market close at hand was necessary. Hence large estates of this type were only possible in localities where a good market was available. Thirdly, the area for miles round Rome was appropriated for the parks and country houses of nobles who wished to be within easy reach of Rome ; they did not, of course, attempt to make their land profitable.

Thus the large estates must not be regarded as being scattered uniformly over Italy ; they were possible only under certain economic conditions.

The Effect of Imported Corn. It has been said above that the harvests of Carthage were diverted to the city of Rome to feed its growing population. Sixty million bushels were imported each year in the time of Augustus. We may, therefore, ask two questions :—Was Italy unable to raise enough corn to feed its population ? or did cheap corn ruin Italian farmers, in particular those who farmed on a small scale, by depriving them of their best market ? Italy was never a corn-producing country comparable with Africa or Egypt. Its cornlands produced enough to provide for local needs and to send a surplus to the country towns close at hand. But it would be a mistake to assume that corn was sent from remote parts of Italy to Rome ; the cost of transport alone prevented this. When Rome was a small city, the surrounding country supplied her needs ; as the population grew, reaching the figure of nearly a million,[1] and as the area round Rome became appropriated for country houses and for market gardens raising vegetables for the capital, she drew the additional supplies which she needed not from Italy,

[1] Beloch's figure.

which would have been prohibitive in cost, but from over-seas ; Egypt and Africa were nearer to her than the fertile Po valley. Nor, even if land-transport had been cheap, would the amount of corn actually imported have sufficed to feed more than the merest fraction of the Italian population. The growing of corn in Italy, therefore, was still a necessity.

Labour on the Large Estates. So far, then, we assume *lati-fundia* for grazing in certain districts, residential estates, particularly round Rome in Campania and Etruria, and, scattered throughout Italy, large estates producing corn, vine, olives close to a market. The whole area of Italy is by no means yet accounted for ; but we may pause for a moment to consider the nature of the labour on the large estates.

When slaves were brought into Italy in thousands after the wars in the East, a ready solution seemed to have presented itself to the Italian capitalist. Land was cheap and so now was labour ; the larger the scale on which he operated the greater his chance of success. And so he bought hundreds of slaves ; he put them to work on ranch or farm ; he treated them abominably, finding it cheaper to replace them when worn out than to care for them during life. Such was the solution of the labour problem ; for a time it seemed satisfactory to the landowner, and the evils of the system continued unabated till the later years of the Republic.

But from the beginning of the Empire it is possible to detect a change, which becomes more marked in the course of the first century. Slave-labour began to find less favour with agriculturists. This is accounted for not by humanitarian reasons (though these exerted increasing influence) ; rather (i) slaves were becoming scarcer as war grew rarer, (ii) the fallacy in slave-labour became apparent; it was not a cheap but an expensive way of farming. Thus the old *latifundia* tend to decrease, and the *colonus*, whether free or freed, becomes more common.

Columella, writing in the time of Nero, makes clear the expensiveness of slave-labour, which he diagnoses as the main cause of the change in agricultural conditions. The system aimed at extracting work from an unwilling worker ; supervision was wasteful and costly ; the hardier type of slave was necessary for field work, but he was less intelligent ; loss through death or ill-health meant loss of capital ; the difference in the cost of maintenance of the poor free man and the slave was not great. To increase efficiency inducements had to be offered—wages, private property, family life, cottages, a small holding—but this meant that the position of the slave approximated to that of the free man, and the system was obviously costly. The tenant-farmer grew in numbers and importance ; though he may have had a few slaves working for him, they had their cottages, and their lot was very different from that of former times. On the uplands the old system perhaps survived here and there, certainly till the time of Claudius, though the *ergastulum* is rarely met with. In other words, slave-labour was found to be profitable only on pasture lands, and this fact alone tended to prevent the extension of *latifundia*, in the Republican sense, beyond certain areas.

The Small Property. So far much of Italy remains unaccounted for ; and here small farms of moderate size continued to flourish. The large estate needed a good market close at hand ; in many parts of Italy there was no such market. The small country towns could not absorb a large surplus of any single commodity ; their population consisted largely of owners of large and small farms and plots—*agelli* —skilled craftsmen, artisans and shopkeepers. In such districts there was little specialization of production. The growing of corn, therefore, for home needs was necessary ; the surplus, which was intentionally small, except perhaps in the Po valley where there were towns to consume it, satisfied the limited local market. In such localities the small farm was the rule. Horace's farm, worked by eight slaves, the rest of the land being let to five tenants, was typical of those of central Italy, while the Campanian farms, owned by men who lived on them, were about the same size. And the old Roman love of the land was still strong ; ex-centurions, retired civil servants, freedmen who had made money in trade bought land which in Augustus' time was cheap, though the demand tended to make it dearer.

The prospects, therefore, of Italian agriculture were not hopeless. In the first century and the first half of the second century ' Italy was one of the best cultivated lands of the Empire '.[1] Whatever changes took place in its prosperity were due to developments over which agriculture itself had no control (p. 332).

Italian Industry. Some writers on economic conditions in the ancient world have held that the ' self-sufficiency ' of the household was a distinguishing feature. By this they mean that by far the greater proportion of food, clothing, furniture and utensils was made on the farm itself. Now, while undoubtedly in early times the farm to a great extent had to supply its own needs—though there probably never was a time when exchange did not take place—the skilled craftsman producing manufactured goods played an important part in ancient economy. Opposed to ' house-economy ' is the system of specialized production for extensive markets—in other words, the factory system. The Roman Empire can show examples of such specialization ; but it would be a mistake to assume either rigid house-economy or a developed specialization either in agriculture or industry.

We must imagine Italy at the end of the Republic as a land studded with small country towns and villages ; on the southern coast were the Greek cities of some size ; on the main roads and in the Po valley were other towns, often colonies ; on the west coast there were famous places, Ostia, Puteoli, Capua, Pompeii, Naples and resorts such as Baiae. In the majority of these towns we must imagine craftsmen working in their shops with an apprentice or a slave or two ; they undertook work to order, and they travelled out to farms to perform jobs which the farmer could not do for himself. The smith at his forge, the cobbler at his last supplied local needs. On some farms implements—baskets, nets, etc.— were manufactured, and undoubtedly spinning maids plied their tasks in big households even under the Empire. If the village grew into a town, craftsmen worked on a larger scale, employing more hands and satisfying the increased demand ; but their products did not spread beyond the town

[1] Rostovtzeff.

and its immediate neighbourhood. Thus, for a large proportion of Italy we must assume (i) free craftsmen owning or renting their shops and working either by themselves or with a few apprentices or slaves, (ii) freedmen who set up in industry for themselves, (iii) freedmen or even slaves financed by their patrons or masters, to whom they paid a percentage of the profits.

The Industry and Trade of Pompeii. The excavation of Pompeii has thrown much light on the economic condition of a small town in the middle of the first century, and, though it was not representative of all towns of Italy, being a seaport with some trade connections, its economy differed little from that of the inland towns. The commonest feature of industrial life here was the small workroom and shop open to the street ; here the craftsman worked, and around him his wares were displayed. Such a shop was really part of a house, but was unconnected with it ; the house was built round a central courtyard, and its frontage on the street was let off to traders and artisans. But, as the shopkeeper's business expanded, he might be well enough off to possess the whole house himself ; then the shops would be connected with his house and more rooms would be used as workrooms or storerooms. The manufacturer or trader of Pompeii does not seem to have minded combining his house with his shop ; he may have aimed at becoming a local magistrate ; but, though his house was adorned with frescoes and objects of art, within its area were also the dyeing vats or the bakehouses which gave him his profits. The most centralized business was perhaps that of baking ; one bakery which was found contained ovens which would hold over 2,000 loaves, but it is clear that the owner cannot have held a monopoly in a town of 25,000 inhabitants. Wine and oil came direct to the shops from the producer. Much spinning and weaving was still done in the household, and the cloth woven at home was sent to the fullers to be bleached and finished, and the fullers of Pompeii developed their business on a comparatively large scale. Of Pompeii, however, it may be said that no business expanded to such an extent as to demand larger accommodation than the ordinary house could give. Few products reached outside markets, though the jars of *garum*,[1] packed by Umbricius Scaurus who seems to have done a brisk business, have been found at Rome.

It is clear, then, that the consumer and the producer were much nearer than in modern times ; the shopkeeper was often the manufacturer also, and there was little of the elaborate organization of modern distributing trades.

Industry on a Large Scale. Elsewhere, however, particular circumstances favoured the growth of ' big industry '.

At Arretium, Puteoli and Modena extensive potteries sprang up, enjoying their greatest activity from about 30 B.C. to A.D. 20. For some reason—the discovery of the trade secret of the paste or the influence of a master designer has been suggested—they commanded a large market, their ware being shipped to all parts of the western Mediterranean. Hundreds of slaves were employed in producing this red-glazed pottery, commonly known as ' Samian ' ware. In metal-work conditions varied ; the skilled working of gold and silver and jewels hardly called for mass production, and the working of iron was chiefly in the hands of local *ferrarii* and *cultrarii*, though there seems to have been some concentration at Puteoli. But work in bronze and copper was undertaken on a large scale at Capua, thousands of workmen being employed and their manufactures being exported even to Germany and Britain, while many of the bronze statues, lampstands and tables found at Pompeii were probably made at Capua. Again, when the secret of glass-blowing was discovered, certain Greek manufacturers settled at Rome to exploit the market there. Judging by the quantities of ware found at Rome, their factories must have been extensive. But it is in the making of bricks and tiles that the factory system can be seen at its best. The industry was regarded as a part of agriculture, and, since it was therefore respectable for an aristocrat, it attracted capital. The names of Asinius Pollio and indeed Cicero himself have been found on tiles. The fire of Rome gave an impetus to the industry, which throve chiefly in the neighbourhood of the Tiber. Domitius Afer, for example, came to Rome in the reign of Tiberius as a

---

[1] A kind of fish-paste.

poor man ; his stamp on bricks has been found in many different buildings in Rome ; his heirs added yard after yard, and the business eventually passed by inheritance to the mother of Marcus Aurelius and so into imperial possession. So, too, the Pansian factory—' officina Pansiana '—close to Ariminum passed into imperial possession ; its ware was transported as far afield as Dalmatia and Istria. But again special circumstances were necessary for production on a large scale—suitable clay and a good market ; further, the brickyards round Rome seem to have used the Tiber as a means of carrying their goods cheaply to the city and to Ostia.

No Single Formula Describes Italian Conditions. It is impossible, therefore, to describe Italian agriculture or industry in any comprehensive formula. The methods of agriculture varied, naturally, according to the soil and the play of economic forces. Pliny the Elder in a famous phrase asserts ' Latifundia perdidere Italiam, iam vero et provincias '. Yet his own evidence bears witness that Italy was not ruined, and, when he wishes to praise the prosperity of Southern Gaul, he describes her as ' Italy rather than a province '. In industry, again, the scale of production varied ; the inscriptions of the humblest craftsman, the profits of the magnate suggest that industry offered at least a livelihood to those engaged in it. For the first half-century of our era there was no general economic depression in Italy.

The Development of the Provinces. But towards the end of the first century changes of great moment to Italy had taken place. The civilizing of the western provinces had proceeded rapidly ; their resources were worked ; the growth of towns provided markets to absorb the increased production ; communications were improved. The western provinces, therefore, not only supplied themselves with goods which they had previously imported, but also captured markets dominated hitherto by Italian merchants ; and they even exported produce to Rome. The provinces, then, became less dependent on Italy for capital, skill and goods, and Italy felt the effect.

The Effect on Italy. An interesting symptom of the change

may be seen in the decline of Puteoli and the rise of Ostia. At the beginning of the Empire Puteoli was the busiest port in Italy; trading vessels put in there because they could pick up cargoes of wine, oil and manufactured goods, which Ostia, the port of Rome, never a manufacturing city, could not supply. But, as Italian exports became less in demand and Rome itself called for larger imports, Ostia replaced Puteoli as Italy's chief port. The *stationes*—trading agencies—moved to Ostia, which, though it had received the cornships, had not greatly attracted the private merchant. Claudius realized the importance of Ostia, as has been seen above (p. 89), and his works there were carried on by Trajan. Excavation has revealed the extensive *horrea*—warehouses—which lined the dockside and bear witness to the enormous traffic of goods; while inscriptions show the numerous *stationes*, the colleges of dock-porters and other workmen: in this port every nationality and every religion met.

The emancipation of the provinces decreased the demand for Italian exports; imports into Italy had to be paid for in money, and, as less wealth came into Italy by trade, the purchasing power of the middle classes and the country population deteriorated, and the small landowner found himself deficient of capital.

Yet money came into Italy in other ways. Provincial families, ennobled by office or enriched by a career in government service, naturally tended to take up residence nearer the capital of the Empire; indeed it was desirable that members of the new nobility should identify themselves with Italy, and the Emperors—notably Trajan—insisted that senators should possess a certain amount of land in Italy. Such families, therefore, bought estates with capital which had been acquired in the provinces. In the changed circumstances the small landowner found it harder to make a living; he was embarrassed for lack of capital. Hence a feature of this period is the growth of the tenant-farmer, both free and freed. Large estates, therefore, may have increased in number, but they were not the *latifundia* worked by gangs of slaves familiar under the Republic. Italian agriculture prospered.

Domitian and the Growing of Vines. Another sign of the times is afforded by an order issued by Domitian. In 91 B.C. a bad harvest was accompanied by a good vintage, and in the following year there seems to have been a general shortage of corn. Over-production of corn, Domitian felt, was impossible, and already the provincial vineyards were covering too many acres. He ordered, therefore, that no new vineyard should be planted in Italy or the provinces, and that the existing provincial vineyards should be reduced by half. Naturally, there were protests ; they secured some modification of the decree, but it was enforced in Africa, and to some extent in Northern and Central Gaul and in part of Spain. Thus the export wine-trade of Italy was assisted. But such favouritism of Italy was rare in imperial policy.

The Alimenta. It has been said above that the small farmer, who still existed in numbers, was embarrassed for lack of capital, while the new nobility invested money in Italian land. These statements may be illustrated (i) by the institution of the ' alimenta ', (ii) by a brief reference to Pliny's farms.

Some time in the reign of Claudius or Nero [1] a certain Procula set up a memorial to her father, T. Helvius Basila, a public servant ; on it there is a brief record of the generosity which he showed towards his native town, Atina in Latium. He gave to it a capital sum of 400,000 sesterces on the understanding that the interest should be devoted to the provision of free corn for the children of the town and a gift of 1,000 sesterces to each child on coming of age. In such public spirit there was nothing exceptional (p. 344). The Emperor Nerva [2] enlarged the idea, and instituted a state system of maintenance grants, ' alimenta ', for the children of poor parents in Italy ; but he ingeniously combined with it a plan for advancing public money to farmers on the security of their farms. The scheme may be explained thus :—A farmer

---

[1] Dessau's dating, I.L.S. 977.

[2] Aurelius Victor, *Epit.* 12, ' puellas puerosque natos parentibus egestosis sumptu publico per Italiae oppida ali iussit '. Coins of Nerva show ' Tutela Italiae S C ', and Nerva, seated, extends his right hand to a figure representing Italy ; between them a boy and a girl.

who wished for capital to develop his land reported to the fisc that his farm was worth, say, £1,200 ; the fisc advanced him one-twelfth of this, namely £100 ; the farmer paid to his municipality annual interest at (probably) 5 per cent., i.e. £5 ; the municipality applied the £5 to the maintenance of poor children ; if it were not paid by the farmer, the town could seize the land pledged as guarantee. Thus the farmer obtained a loan from the state, and the price he paid for it was spent by the town in maintenance grants.

Our information about the ' alimenta ' is derived chiefly from two inscriptions. The first inscription, dated A.D. 103, in Trajan's reign, relates to Veleia, a town in the Po valley. It shows the sum lent, the value of the farms and the number of children maintained ; from its evidence it is clear (i) that the small farmer was by no means extinct, (ii) that there was little tendency in the uplands, where these farms were situated, for the large estate to absorb the smaller ; on the contrary, there was competition to secure the smallest parcel of land. The second inscription, dated A.D. 101, relates to the Ligures Baebiani, near Beneventum, but it provides less information and need not detain us.

The significance of the alimentary institutions has been variously assessed ; some commentators see in them philanthropy on a large scale without inferring the decay of Italy ; others regard them as a conscious attempt to repopulate the country-side.[1] Without assuming that the rural areas were becoming desolate, which as a general statement is untrue, we may take it that in the country towns there was some distress owing to the decreased purchasing power of the middle classes. But the provision of capital for farmers is probably quite as important an aspect of the institution. The picture of healthy and well-fed children, however, appealed more to contemporary imagination, as it does now, and coins

---

[1] ' It might be enough to see and to applaud simply that traditional Roman sense of the duty of benevolence, even though this imperial philanthropy took the easy, perhaps uneconomic, form of doles to parents ' : B. W. Henderson, *Five Roman Emperors*, p. 220. See also p. 228, ' Was it not rather that innate Roman devotion to the State, that pietas instinct in him from the beginning ? '

and sculptures of several reigns celebrate the imperial solicitude
for the youth of Italy. For the scheme, modestly started by
Nerva, who contemplated grants for 5,000 children, was enlarged by the Emperors from Trajan to Marcus Aurelius.
Antoninus founded a special endowment in memory of his
wife Faustina, and Marcus Aurelius did the same.

The administration of the system throughout Italy was
entrusted to a *praefectus alimentorum*, of senatorial rank.
Beneath him were *procuratores* of equestrian rank, both in the
central administration at Rome and in the districts of Italy.
' Alimenta ' instituted at places in the neighbourhood of the
great roads were placed under the supervision of the *curatores*
of these roads.

Just as the State apparently imitated private example,
so in turn it invited imitation. Rich men in the townships
established similar endowments ; that of Pliny the Younger
is perhaps the best known,[1] but inscriptions provide other
examples not only in Italy, but in Spain and Numidia.

Pliny's Farming. Pliny is a good example of the new
imperial nobility of Flavian and Antonine times. He belonged to one of the leading families of Comum, where he had
an estate inherited from his mother. He acquired an estate
also at Tifernum in Etruria, and built himself a country-
house at Laurentum, in Latium. In perhaps a dozen of his
letters he gives us glimpses of his own estates and incidentally
of the condition of Roman agriculture. But it must be
remembered that Pliny, a kindly man of letters, was not
himself a farmer of experience, though he relied on his estates
for his income.[2] In one of his letters he complains that the
capital value of land which he contemplated buying adjacent
to his own had fallen. Should he buy ? The land itself was
good enough, but it had been mismanaged ; the tenants
were short of money and in arrears ; rents had gone down and
new tenants were difficult to find (which may have been due
to the bad name the land had gained under mismanagement).
He was ready to find the purchase price, even by borrowing
from his mother-in-law ; evidently there was no great risk in
buying land. Indeed, when he wished to provide an income

[1] *Ep.* vii. 18.   [2] iii. 19.

for his old nurse, the best plan, he considered, was to buy
her a farm, so that she might live on the rent of it. ' When
I gave it to her, it was worth 100,000 sesterces ; but rents
have gone down and it is worth less now ; under your care '
—he writes to a friend who had taken a lease of it—' it will
recover.' There is no complaint here or in any other letter
about the infertility of the soil. Pliny's complaint concerns
rather the difficulty which the tenants found in paying their
rent, which, kindly landlord as he was, he frequently reduced
for them.[1] His estates were chiefly let to *coloni* on a five
years' lease, though at Tifernum he placed a bailiff in charge
of one farm retained in his own hands for his amusement.
Yet this estate brought him in rents an income of 300,000
sesterces per annum.

Pliny's letters, in spite of their grumbles, do not suggest
the depopulation of Italy or the bankruptcy of Italian farming. ' On the upper Tiber ', he says, ' you may still find the
grandfathers and great-grandfathers of the young people still
living ; you are constantly hearing old stories and tales of the
past, so that when you set foot there you may fancy that
you have been born in another century.' [2] And Pliny was a
rich man ; it is true that he had a little capital out at interest,
but the bulk of his income came from his land. And, though
he was generous to his tenants, generous even to the contractors who bought his hanging crop of grapes and were
disappointed in the yield when the vintage came, yet he lived
comfortably and had surplus enough to gratify his generous
nature ; we know that in various benefactions he gave away
over 4,000,000 sesterces ; and that does not complete the
tale.

Summary. We may sum up briefly as follows :—The
development of the provinces robbed Italy of her position
as a leading export country ; her industry declined and her
purchasing power as a whole diminished. She had ceased
to be the economic centre of the world. The opportunities of
wealth in the provinces attracted enterprising Italians ; and
government service took them far afield. Emigration from
Italy was a necessary consequence, which Nerva attempted

[1] *Ep*. ix. 37. [2] v. 6. 6.

22

to stop by new settlements in Italy, and Trajan by a general prohibition. Meantime Italian land was changing hands ; the old aristocracy had disappeared ; a new nobility took its place and invested capital in Italian lands, partly because it was naturally drawn to Rome and Italy, partly because Trajan insisted that senators should so invest their money. The new landowners had made their way in the provinces ; they consisted chiefly of the new imperial nobility created by the Emperor or of freedmen and others who had grown rich in trade. The land which they owned was farmed not by the old system of slave-gangs, which was now uneconomic and obsolete, but by *coloni* both free and freed ; *latifundia* therefore had changed its meaning. At the same time small farmers owning their farms still existed.

Some Features of the Second Century. The long and arduous wars in which Trajan engaged made possible the peaceful reign of Hadrian and the Antonines ; yet there is little doubt that they placed a heavy financial burden on the Empire. Hadrian found the finances in a grave condition, and his first act was to remit the *aurum coronarium* and to cancel debts to the fiscus and the aerarium. The upkeep of the army was a burden on cities and individuals, more particularly in the areas close to the seat of the war ; for Roman policy demanded that the billeting of troops, the provision of food and supplies should in great measure fall on the townships. Indeed, the State demanded more and more from communities and individuals. Hence the cry for the remission of taxes.

It is surprising that the Empire, despite its wealth, should feel the burden of war so acutely. It is perhaps a warning that we should not overestimate its resources. On the other hand, the machinery for the collection of taxes may have broken down, and Hadrian's reorganization of the civil service may have aimed in part at more efficient methods of gathering in the revenue. At any rate, Hadrian saw the need for the consolidation of his Empire ; if the Mediterranean lands were to become one state, the economic basis on which that state rested must be secure, and therefore progress in the lands already organized as provinces, rather than further expansion beyond the frontiers, was the most urgent need.

And so Hadrian devoted his life to the provinces, and his plan for ensuring their progress was to develop their agriculture and industry, to encourage a vigorous middle class and to promote city life.

After Trajan the limits of Empire were never again widened ; in other words, there were no new markets to be seized and no new provinces to be developed. The industry and commerce of the Empire must be in the main self-contained, for the barbarians of the North could take little in the way of goods. Therefore, if industry was to thrive, the purchasing power of the Mediterranean lands must increase. And so Hadrian encouraged the growth of a vigorous producing class. On the uncultivated imperial estates in Africa he settled tenants ; on condition that they cultivated olives and fruit trees, he gave them the right to hand on their land to their heirs. And elsewhere, in Attica, Macedonia and Asia, he pursued the same aim of increasing the number of small landowners ; he also let out the imperial mines in small concessions to individuals. On the creation of a class of hard-working farmers and producers depended the further development of the provinces. Again, on the development of the provinces depended the growth of city communities. To the Romans the city stood for civilization, culture and commerce ; it raised the standard of life for a portion of the population and created a middle class, which, as the Emperors saw, was the real hope of the Empire. And, as we have seen, cities sprang up wherever Hadrian went.

The Antonines. Yet Hadrian's activities were not without expense to the Empire. His journeys had laid on the cities through which he passed the burden of entertaining his staff and gratifying his passion for building. Under his reorganization the civil service cost more. And so the reign of Antoninus is marked by much imperial economy. Antoninus refused to take long tours through the provinces out of consideration for the finances of the cities. His own court life was as simple as possible ; imperial estates and even furniture were sold to put money into the fisc.

Yet when Marcus succeeded to the throne, he found it necessary to cancel debts to the State once more ; evidently

the Antonine peace was not entirely prosperous.   And within
a few years the Empire was smitten by plague brought from
the East by the army.   Famine followed and in some areas
the population suffered incredibly.   A year or two later the
wars with the barbarians were bravely carried through ;   the
quality of the army was as good as ever.   Yet Marcus was hard
pressed for money ;   he dared not increase the taxes of the
already over-burdened cities.   Industry and agriculture had
alike suffered ;   the townships, in spite of their magnificent
buildings, could find no ready money for the wars ;   the
demands of the State had already exhausted their resources.
Yet the State must have more money ;   the final step was
taken by Caracalla in A.D. 212, when he granted Roman
citizenship to the Roman world, and so made the provincials
liable for the taxes hitherto paid only by Roman citizens.[1]

CHAPTER XXI

SOME ASPECTS OF SOCIAL LIFE UNDER THE EMPIRE

ROME'S Willingness to Extend Privilege.   The History
of the Republic makes it clear that in rising from a
city-state to a Mediterranean power Rome owed her
success in large measure to her power of incorporating the
conquered lands within her own political life.   So successful
was this policy that by the end of the Republic she had
made full Roman citizenship or some portion of its rights a
distinction and a reward which communities or individuals
were glad to win.   But these privileges were not lightly
bestowed ;   the community must reach a certain standard
of civilization and responsibility before receiving rights which
would place it on a level with the sovereign city ;   hence in the
provinces there is a series of degrees of privilege and self-
government.   For to the Romans civilization reached its
highest point in a city-community controlling its own local
affairs, yet remaining a member of a larger whole, the Empire ;
and the basis of Roman provincial policy was the encourage-

[1] See p. 34.   He wished in particular to extend the incidence of
the *vicesima hereditatum* which he doubled.

ment of city-life. Such conditions, it was thought, provided the best life for the individual and the community. It was not a new ideal, but Rome succeeded in reconciling it, as Athens had not, with the idea of Empire. Whether eventually she carried the urbanization of the Empire too far is a matter of dispute ; but at any rate in the first two centuries urban life achieved unparalleled success ; there is little trace of the decay and paralysis which later seized on the municipalities of the Empire.

It is impossible here to give an account of the stages in the extension of Roman privilege under the Republic, or to enter into details about the status of *colonia* and *municipium*.[1] The policy of Julius Caesar was all in favour of comprehensiveness. He sent out many citizen colonies, he gave the full franchise to the Transpadanes and to Gades, and he admitted Gauls to the Senate. The cities receiving incorporation into Roman privileges were granted a charter in which the terms of their constitution were set out ; one of such charters is contained in the so-called Lex Iulia Municipalis, passed by Julius Caesar in 45 B.C., which some scholars have regarded as providing a typical or model charter. Other charters, or fragments of them, give us valuable information about the varied types of self-governing cities.[2] Two points stand out clearly in the relations between Rome and the city-communities. First, Rome showed the greatest respect for local customs and traditional offices and names, in spite of the fact that municipal self-government tended to be modelled on one type ; in the East old forms lingered on for centuries : in the West, where the cities often had no traditions, uniformity of type was greater. Secondly, the cities were proud to share in the privileges granted by Rome, and copied, even to the minutest detail of form and ceremony, the methods by which the ruling city was governed.

Municipal Government. The municipal charter insisted on the recognition of three elements in the government of the city. The plebs or populus, consisting of *cives* and resident aliens, annually elected the magistrates : the charters of

[1] See *The Companion to Latin Studies*, p. 366.
[2] Eleven municipal charters provide us with most of our information.

Malaca and Salpensa, in Spain, show the careful arrangements made for a free election by the people, while the *graffiti* of Pompeii show the popular feeling evoked by such elections. The chief magistrates were the *duoviri*, the counterpart of the consuls at Rome. Precise rules of eligibility are laid down in the ' Lex Iulia Municipalis ' and later charters. A candidate must be free-born, thirty years old,[1] of good character and record, and he must have fulfilled the minor offices to be mentioned presently. The procedure of nomination and election was similar to Roman practice. One of the *duoviri* presided at meetings of the popular assembly and the local Senate and had charge of public buildings, festivals and funds ; every five years a census was taken by the chief magistrates, who in the census year were called *quinquennales*. Under the Empire the *duoviri* no longer had powers of criminal jurisdiction, which were transferred, in Italy to the Praetorian or City Prefect, in the provinces to the governor, but civil cases involving sums up to a stated amount were within their competence. The duovirate was collegial, that is, each *duovir* could within limits veto the proposal of the other. The Emperor was often elected *duovir* without a colleague, in which case he was represented by a praefectus. The chief magistracy from early days involved no small financial burden ; a fee was payable on taking up office, and public opinion demanded generous expenditure on games and festivals.

Inferior to the duovirs there were two aediles who performed much the same functions as the aediles at Rome ; in some *municipia* duovirs and aediles formed one college of *quattuorviri*. The financial administration of the cities was in the hands of quaestors. Besides these magistrates there were also priests and flamens charged with the conduct of religious ceremonies.

The municipal counterpart of the Roman Senate was the *curia*, composed of *decuriones*, usually a hundred in number. The *ordo* was usually filled by ex-magistrates, but in any case a high property qualification and free birth were necessities. Every five years the *album* of *decuriones* was revised by the chief magistrates. The *curia* was consulted by the *duoviri*,

[1] Later reduced to twenty-five.

who were executive officers carrying out its wishes as regards finance, games and the general management of the town ; it also heard appeals from the judicial decisions of the *duoviri*. Various honours and privileges were accorded to the decurions, who in return made munificent gifts for the adornment or well-being of the city.

The Ordo Augustalium. Below the *curia* ranked the order of *Augustales*. The institution of this order was due to Augustus himself and was one of the most successful of his many strokes of genius. We shall see presently that one of the most amazing and important features of the social life of the early Empire was the rise of the freedman class. To attach this class to himself and to the new régime, to give it self-respect and a means of gratifying its ambitions, to divert some of its wealth into unselfish channels—for these purposes Augustus authorized the creation of an order of Augustales. Its first object was to provide for the cult of Rome and Augustus in the towns of Italy and the provinces, particularly the Western provinces. Officials known as *seviri* were elected for the purpose by the *curia*, regard being given to wealth but not to social origin or standing. After a year of office the *seviri* passed by decree of the *curia* into the *ordo Augustalium*.[1] Organized as a college, the Augustales had their own officers, club-houses, property and honours. They ranked in public esteem next to the decurions, and were made conspicuous by insignia and badges, by the purple-edged toga and by the *lictors* who attended them. Their servile birth debarred them from membership of the *curia* and from the magistracies, but they were happy in the enjoyment of local prestige. In this way the ex-slave achieved fame and popularity, expending money on works of public utility and in return receiving the *ornamenta* of the higher offices which he himself could never fill.[2]

[1] The system was not uniform in its beginnings, and there is much variation in the relation of *sevir* to *Augustalis*, as inscriptions show. Trimalchio was a *sevir Augustalis*, Petr. 30, the only place where the title occurs in Latin literature.

[2] Children of a freedman, born after his manumission, could hold local offices.

The Appeal of the Municipality. The service of the township evoked a public spirit which can show few parallels in later history. Men were proud of their membership of the Empire. At the same time the Empire was vast, almost too great for the imagination to lay hold of, and the posts in the imperial service were few ; yet loyalty and pride asked for some outlet and ambition needed some way of satisfying itself in a narrower sphere. The inscriptions show in countless numbers the pride with which the municipal offices were held ; epitaphs, laudatory inscriptions, memorials record these honours and dignities with careful precision. But the inscriptions bear no less full witness to the extraordinary power of this pride to call forth the generosity of the citizens, whether magistrates or not, whether rich or poor, free, freed or slave. Money was poured out for the public use ; roads, theatres, temples, baths and aqueducts were built at private expense ; schools were endowed, and professors' and doctors' salaries were paid ; legacies were left for the perpetual endowment of games or a festival or the distribution of food to poorer citizens. In the Greek East such munificence was no new thing, though under the Empire it increased enormously. But it was one of the achievements of the Empire that it established these *municipia*—self-governing communities claiming the devotion of their citizens—throughout the Western provinces, even on the confines of the Empire—on the fringe of the Sahara, in Germany and Dacia. The original inhabitants, fast absorbing Roman ideas, ex-soldiers recruited perhaps from the other side of the Mediterranean, traders, officials, newly created knights, slaves and freedmen—never before was there such a mixture of types and races fused together to make up a vigorous city life in hundreds of cities which were miniatures of Rome.

The Decline of the Municipalities. Yet the decay of municipal life, and why it came, is one of the most interesting and puzzling problems of Roman history. The very opportunities inherent in the system to some extent proved its downfall ; there seemed to be no limit set to the prosperous and happy communal life which it fostered. As a result, local pride was responsible for much extravagance in municipal finance ; one city vied with another in the brilliance of its material splendours. Such ruinous competition was particularly rife in the Eastern provinces, as the speeches of Dio Chrysostom and the letters of Pliny show. Municipal budgets failed to balance, and public opinion demanded still more generous expenditure on the part of the rich, who found the burdens laid upon them insupportable. Volunteers for office ceased to come forward, and a charter of so early a date as the reign of Domitian [1] contains a clause setting out procedure in case the supply of candidates should fail. In later centuries the rank of *curialis* was made hereditary and inalienable, to prevent evasion of the financial burdens which were made obligatory on it. The city became divided into two castes—those who compulsorily found the money, and those who as of right benefited by its expenditure. But in the first two centuries there was little serious decline in municipal life, though here and there symptoms may be seen. Cities which were unable to set their finances in order invited or were glad to receive the guidance of the central government ; the financial reorganization of the towns was part of Pliny's task as commissioner of Bithynia in A.D. III, and a year or two earlier Trajan sent Laberius Maximus to Achaia to set in order the finances of the free states there (p. 221). Such commissioners—*correctores*— with supervision of a large district became common in the third century (p. 363). But even in Pliny's time municipal finances not only in the provinces but in Italy also were liable to supervision by *curatores* ; these were appointed by the Emperor, temporarily and as need arose, to regulate the finance of a single town which was in difficulties through mismanagement. Later Emperors continued the appointment of *curatores*, and in this way the path was clear for the bureaucratic control of the cities which came to a head in the reign of Diocletian.

Slavery. It was said earlier that one of the most amazing features of the social life of the early Empire was the rise of the freedmen. To trace this rise we must first descend into slavery.

There is no need to recall here the merciless enslavement

[1] The *lex Malacitana.*

which followed upon every victorious war during the Republic, nor need we repeat the horrors of the slave-market and *ergastulum*. Under the Empire slavery still continued, but great changes took place. The wars of the Empire were not against civilized peoples but against barbarians ; there was not another Greece or Asia to be exploited, whence came most of the slaves in Republican times. The barbarian prisoners made bad slaves, fit only for the roughest of work on hill-ranches ; they were not in great demand. The East still supplied slaves, but they were enslaved not by war but by birth. The Roman Peace made slaves scarcer and dearer. It was necessary, therefore, to provide a reasonable family life for slaves ; under the Empire the *verna* becomes increasingly common. But this cost money, for the bringing up of slave-children from infancy increased their price. Thus there were economic reasons for the changes in the conditions of slavery. There were also social reasons. The fact that a family life was granted to slaves tended to improve their lot, but, further, slaves were given positions of responsibility not only in private houses, but also in offices, banks, shops and businesses. The Roman dislike of retail trade and of the routine of business still continued, and slaves, often more educated and versatile than their masters, performed much of this work. The *peculium*, or slave's private property, was earned in many ways—by perquisites, by profits on a shop financed originally by his master's capital, by commercial ventures, and in some cases by wages. The very complex law of the *peculium* shows to what extent the slave could enter into business relations with free men, while inscriptions reveal that this property often amounted to very considerable sums and might include land, property, ships, and rights of various kinds. Again, Augustus in starting his imperial civil service had employed his own slaves and freedmen in the inferior positions, and this tended to improve their status ; townships, commercial companies and the imperial government employed them in increasing numbers. The slave was allowed to belong to his *collegium*, which was a combination of a social and a burial club. Of course, cases of cruelty are all too frequent ; on the other hand, Pliny the

Younger was on good terms with his staff ; he treated them with indulgence, too great indulgence, he says, and in his attitude towards slaves Pliny was typical, as in many other respects, of the society of his day, which in simplicity and kindliness was very different from that of Julio-Claudian times.

And, when enlightened opinion set a new standard, law followed its lead. Under the Republic the power of the master was unlimited, but during the first two centuries increasingly stringent legislation was passed, due partly to increasing humanity and partly to Stoic influence. As early as A.D. 20 criminal slaves were tried by the same procedure as free men ; for those who were ill-treated there was a right of appeal, and by the second century innumerable regulations protected the slave's life, property and honour.

The institution of slavery perhaps could find its nearest approach to justification in the early Empire. It could be, and often was, a ' compulsory initiation into a higher culture '. To take a man from some backward race or country, to expose him to the influences of civilization, educating him and teaching him a craft or a profession, to turn him into a useful and independent member of society—these were the actual achievements of slavery in a multitude of cases. Was the process completed ? Did the compulsory initiation lead to citizenship ?

Manumission. A slave-owner had always possessed the power to manumit, or set free, his slaves at his own discretion. During the late Republic the practice of manumission raised the important question of the ' libertine ' vote, round which political problems of some importance centred. The civil wars with the resulting chaos had ruined many noble families which could no longer support expensive establishments ; their slaves were manumitted in large numbers, and it should be noted that manumission by a Roman citizen turned a slave into a Roman citizen. When Augustus restored security he found a problem difficult of solution ; the upper classes were decreasing, while the freedman class was increasing at a dangerous rate. We have already seen the social legislation by which he tried to encourage marriage in the upper strata

of society (p. 17). This was one approach to the problem ;
there was also another, namely, to check manumission. And
throughout the twenty-seven years during which Augustus
bravely attempted the almost impossible task of reforming
social and moral standards by legislation, he gave his attention
to the problems of the freedmen class.

His reforms marked an epoch and set the whole system of
slavery and manumission on a reasonable basis. Hitherto
marriage between free and freed was invalid : in the *lex Iulia*
of 18 B.C. such marriage is recognized as valid.[1] This concession was revolutionary ; the freedman class was no longer
to be dissociated from the great bulk of the free population.
The upper levels of society were to be rejuvenated from
below.

Manumission, therefore, gained a new importance ; and
safeguards were necessary. And so Augustus introduced
restrictions ; he was the first to attack the ancient principle
that manumission by a Roman citizen created a Roman
citizen. The *lex Fufia Caninia* limited the proportion of
slaves who could be manumitted by will. The *lex Aelia
Sentia* (A.D. 4) insisted that the manumitter must be twenty
years old and the slave thirty years old if Roman citizenship
was to result ; the manumission must be by will or must take
place in the presence of a Roman magistrate. If these conditions were not fulfilled, or if a slave were manumitted informally, i.e. by a letter or before witnesses, the freedman became
a Junian Latin—a status recognized by the *lex Iunia* of
Augustus' reign ; Junian Latins could not make a will or
receive a legacy and on their death their property reverted to
their patron. But a Junian Latin who married a woman of his
own or higher rank and had one or more children could
claim citizenship for his family, and formal manumission
could give this to him at any time. Thus there were varying
grades of freedom ; the best elements of the slave class,
Augustus intended, should emerge into freedom, and their
children could hold any office or magistracy in the *municipia*.

[1] Except when senatorial rank was involved. The concession is
attributed in *Dig.* xxiii. 2. 44. pr. to the *lex Iulia*, in *Dig.* xxiii. 2. 23
to the *lex Papia Poppaea* of A.D. 9.

The Imperial Freedmen. The political influence of the
freedmen holding the great secretaryships of state has already
been touched on (p. 88). The positions of power which
they occupied naturally gave opportunities for the amassing
of wealth, and men like Narcissus and Pallas were as unscrupulous in their cupidity as they were in their political schemes.
The administration of the provinces, appointments to official
posts, the leasing of rights and contracts in connexion with
public works gave ample opportunity for corruption. The
wealth of Pallas was proverbial, and it was further increased
by a decree of the subservient Senate which voted him (in
A.D. 52) the praetorian insignia, a sum of fifteen million
sesterces, and publicly gave thanks that the descendant of the
Arcadian kings had thought more of the public good than of his
own illustrious birth, and had allowed himself to be enrolled
among the servants of the Empire ; further a decree was
engraved in bronze to record ' the old-fashioned simplicity '
of the possessor of three hundred million sesterces.[1] Even
the best of the freedmen, men of ability, integrity and frugality
of life such as Abascantus, for example, or the father of Claudius Etruscus,[2] accumulated fortunes which enabled them
to build for themselves magnificent houses and to furnish
them with every costly rarity. The ostentatious display of
wealth was, indeed, natural in these men, for in the first years
of the Empire high social rank was closed to them. Yet by
degrees they forced their way in ; social exclusiveness gave
way to wealth and power ; Abascantus and the father of
Claudius Etruscus had married daughters of senatorial
families, and Felix, brother of Pallas and procurator of Judaea
where ' he exercised the dominion of a king with the spirit
of a slave ', had been ' the husband of three queens ',[3] and
was related by marriage to the Emperor Claudius. In the
second century the ascent to the highest social castes became
easier, and many senatorial families, had they cared, could
have traced themselves back to a servile origin at no remote
date.

[1] Tac. *Ann.* xii. 53. Plin. *Ep.* viii. 6, cf. vii. 29.
[2] For the careers of these freedmen, see Statius, *Silvae,* iii. 3. 43,
and v. 1. 75. [3] Suet. *Claud.* 28.

The Class of Freedmen. The two types of imperial freedman, the gross Pallas and the frugal Abascantus, find their
counterparts on a humbler plane. The romance of Petronius,
the 'Satiricon', of which the 'Cena Trimalchionis' is the
chief incident, gives us a realistic caricature of the worst type
of freedman. Trimalchio came to Italy from Asia as a slave-
boy in the reign of Augustus. He insinuated himself into the
favour of his master and mistress, and finally was left co-
heir to his master's property with the Emperor himself. He
invested his money in ships, and in spite of early disaster his
enterprises prospered and he bought land in Africa, Italy and
Sicily : so vast were his possessions that a gazette was regularly
issued reporting events occurring on his estates! But he
could afford to neglect matters somewhat now and to devote
himself to the enjoyment of his wealth, to the duties of a
sevir Augustalis and to the parading of his smattering of
literary culture. And the guests at his table were of like nature.
' See that fellow at the bottom o' the table there ? It seems
only yesterday he was carrying fuel on his back. Now he's
worth hard upon a million. How did he manage it ? Well,
they do say, but mind you I don't know for certain, that 'twas
a goblin hoard, real fairy treasure trove. A purse-proud
slave he is too. Not that I envy anyone, mark you, if God
gives him wealth. That other chap down there i' the lowest
seat hasn't feathered his nest so well. Just touched a million,
hesitated, then—crash ! Really not his own fault though,
and there's no better fellow living. His scoundrels of servants
robbed him. No good trusting to pot-luck with a friend
either ! It's a lonely road going down hill. A good honest
trade his was, too. Eh ? Oh ! yes, an undertaker. Feasted
his friends like a king. Those dinners—what a dream they
were ! ' [1] And so the account of the banquet proceeds, with
elaborate descriptions of the ridiculously extravagant dishes,
snatches of conversation and farcical incidents, and throughout
there runs a vulgarity, a parade of wealth and an unabashed
conviction of its power. The account is caricature, yet
caricature implies a basis of truth. The freedman had risen
rapidly to wealth ; in high social grades he saw luxury and

[1] The translation is taken from B. W. Henderson's *Nero*, p. 332.

extravagance, and he made the same vulgar use of his money and placed the same faith in it as has been seen in many a later day of rapid social change.

Juvenal and Martial and Petronius may sneer at the parvenu freedman, but a longer view suggests that 'the rise of the emancipated slave was not only inevitable, but that it was on the whole salutary and rich in promise for the future '.[1] This is the view suggested by the numerous inscriptions relating to freedmen. The majority of them, it is clear, lived in a humble way as artisans, shopkeepers and agents and craftsmen. By work and thrift they made a living, supported a family and had enough money to spend on simple amusements ; they owed to slavery whatever education or apprenticeship in a trade they had received, and many an epitaph shows the pride they felt alike in their craft and their independence. The majority remained in humble circumstances, and were content to do so, banding themselves together in ' colleges ' which had as the basis of association often a common trade or a common cult, but often also nothing else than a desire for fellowship.

The Colleges. The Roman people had always possessed a genius for association. The sacredness of the family, the clan and the tribe, the religious fraternities, the principle of collegiality so firmly established in constitutional usage— these are examples in Roman history of the strength of the group instinct ; and the Roman, in spite of his military genius, loved a committee. But towards the end of the Republic the State had frowned on ' meetings ' ; they were too great a danger to political peace. Augustus also held this view [2] ; all clubs or colleges—*sodalicia, collegia*—were prohibited, except certain religious societies made sacred by their antiquity or specially sanctioned by the Emperor ; and henceforth any new college must obtain the sanction of the State. But the instinct of association was too powerful. Some time in the first century A.D. more general permission was given for ' funerary colleges ' to enrol members, provided that they did not meet more than once a month, and in the second

---

[1] Dill, *Social Life at Rome*, p. 102.
[2] Cf. Trajan in Pliny, *Ep.* x. 34.

century colleges were allowed to receive legacies and to emancipate their slaves. It is clear that under the guise of a funerary club many other purposes—religious or social—may be served, and the rapid growth of colleges, their prosperity and wealth, show that the government interpreted its own rules somewhat broadly ; at the same time the activities of individual colleges were well known to the local police, who in case of need would always take action on the grounds of ' illegality '.[1]

The majority of the colleges, whatever other purposes they may have served, were burial clubs. Their first objects were to provide for the decent burial of their members, and to perpetuate their memory by an inscription on funeral urn or tombstone. The inscriptions bear witness to a stable and lasting family life and to much genuine affection, and the desire that the individual life may not pass away unremembered is pathetically insistent. Sometimes a small bequest is left to the college that a lamp may be kept burning in a shrine in memory of the dead or that the college may celebrate the birthday of the departed. By the Antonine age the activities of the colleges were at their fullest. Traders on the frontiers gathered themselves together in clubs to safeguard their interests and to find society ; artisans plying the same craft in the cities of Gaul, time-expired soldiers in Africa, boys and young men in the fashionable towns who were interested in the same sports and pleasures, slaves and men of the large households, devotees of this god or that goddess, sailors and dockporters, the warehousemen of Ostia, hawkers, gladiators and river-boatmen—*collegia* of all these and countless others are to be found in multitudes. We possess lists of members of some of the clubs, and the articles of association of one or two. The list of members sometimes contains the names of free men, freedmen and slaves in the same college, and those of inferior social rank sometimes occupy high positions in the management of the college. All was done in due order ; the constitution imitated that of the municipality ; officers were appointed, rules passed and recorded,

[1] Cf. Tac. *Ann.* xiv. 17, ' collegia quae contra leges instituerant dissoluta '.

dignities bestowed, banquets held and fines inflicted for bad behaviour. Men of wealth and influence were invited to become patrons of the college, and lent their name and gave their money to further its activities.

The college satisfied a need, as its wide diffusion suggests. Society was sharply divided into strata, and in the townships the privileges of position given by wealth or profession were jealously guarded. Certain trades were mean and socially ' impossible ', and those who pursued them felt themselves isolated amid the splendour and bustle of a large town. They were driven back upon their own resources, and they found satisfaction in the social pleasures provided by their colleges, which were modelled upon the institutions of a society which they themselves could not enter.

Religion in the Early Empire. One of the most interesting features of the Early Empire is the variety and richness of the forms which religion took in this age. Rome was not only the political but also the religious capital of the world —' sacrosancta civitas '.[1] Just as the Empire embraced within it the states which had once been independent, so it gathered together the religious thought and experience of the Mediterranean and the East. Systems and faiths which had once exercised their appeal within the restrictions of the philosophical school or the particular temple of a local god were now able to extend their range ; free movement of men within the Empire was accompanied naturally by the free movement of thought and ideas. Hence in every city a variety of religious faith and practice is to be found—survivals of the primitive faiths of the countryside, elaborate systems of cosmology, ascetic philosophical codes, vague and care free scepticism, Oriental religions accompanied by fanaticism and ecstasy, stately ritual handed down from time immemorial, cults from Thrace, Asia, Syria, Carthage, Persia, and the Italian village. Never were men so curious about the unseen ; and every kind of answer to questions about the universe, the gods and human destiny was answered in many ways to satisfy the educated and the uneducated alike. Crass superstition, magic and astrology were accepted in every grade of society, yet by their side pure

[1] Apul. *Met.* xi. 26.

23

faiths of undoubted spiritual appeal claimed multitudes of earnest believers. Rome was heir to the thought and faiths of the Mediterranean ; cults which for centuries had exercised merely a local influence came into the open and claimed universal dominion ; they jostled each other in competition, and in moving from mind to mind were modified and often purified ; in the Egyptian cults, for example, as presented in Italy, there is little trace of the animal gods of the Nile. The cults were willing to accommodate themselves to new surroundings, and their worshippers instinctively identified the god of one religion with the god of another ; ' syncretism ', as we shall see, is a feature of the age, and of great importance in the history of religion.

The Religion of the State. The pains which Augustus took to restore the old state religion were not wasted (p. 15) ; the religion of Numa [1] and the worship of Capitoline Jove as enshrined in the ritual and ceremonies of the State lasted as long as paganism itself, and proved far more powerful a foe to Christianity than the more attractive faiths which we shall speak of later. The State religion had little emotional appeal ; it originated among a race of farmers wrestling with nature for a living ; its deities were processes of nature rather than beings ; it strove to placate the ' numina '—' powers '— and to make them favourable, and this might be done by the correct piece of ritual correctly performed. Rome as a city-state struggling with her neighbours had consecrated this ritual of the fields, and she had emerged victorious, thanks to the character of the men she bred. Rome the conqueror of the Mediterranean had maintained the ritual, even though other gods had established themselves in the capital, and amid the disruption of the last century the ceremonies were still half-heartedly performed, though temples had fallen into dis-repair and unbelief was rife. Yet Augustus strove to resus-citate this old religion, with its precision of ritual and its spells. The sacred colleges were revived, among them those of the Titii and the Arvales fratres. The noblest families offered their sons as priests in the colleges ; Marcus Aurelius knew by heart the long ritual, often couched in archaic language

[1] Cf. the first chapter in Pater's *Marius the Epicurean.*

which few could in his time understand. The reformed religion was closely connected with the Principate ; the Arvales fratres offered prayers to Dea Dia for the welfare of the Emperor and celebrated with thanksgiving the chief days of his life. No matter who was Emperor the same prayers were offered ; the ' proceedings ' of the college which we possess show equally fervent prayers for all the Emperors of the year A.D. 69. ' The Emperor is dead, long live the Emperor ' is the spirit of their refrain.

It seems curious that such a religion could have been seriously restored. But a kind of ' archaism ' swept over the minds of many of the Romans ; it is seen clearly in the Emperor Claudius, but in the second century also interest in early Roman lore was very great. The explanation seems to be this. Augustus ' restored the republic ' ; it was manifest that in its plainest sense this was not true, but he did something even more important ; he saw that in her receptiveness to foreign thought and morality Rome was in danger of losing her own distinctiveness ; she was losing hold of the traditions which had built up Roman character and was sacrificing all stability and sense of continuity with the past. The restored religion, therefore, succeeded, not as religion but as a symbol of faith in the Roman êthos transmitted through the ages.[1] This faith was reaffirmed in another form in the worship of Rome and Augustus. It is true that the priests were under the control of the civil power, but in the early Roman religion civil and religious authorities were identical, and it was ' the apotheosis of the State ' which Augustus hoped to restore. And many educated minds agreed with this aim ; they held their own religious beliefs in private and were at liberty to do so, but they sympathized with the re-affirmation of Roman individuality.

The religion of Numa survived elsewhere, not in the ceremonies of the capital, but in the cottages of the peasants. Just as a real belief in fairies and ' little folk ' haunted the

[1] It might perhaps be urged that the restored religion, in so far as it expressed the ideas of continuity and direction, was not without some religious value in a world in which belief in Tyche was widespread.

countryside in spite of centuries of Christianity, so in those days the fear of the 'numina' lingered on by the side of more modern cults. But, naturally, rustic superstition has left little trace of itself in the literature.

The worship of Capitoline Jupiter had long been closely bound up with the life of the city, and the Augustan revival naturally extended to the cult of this god (p. 15) along with Juno and Minerva. The destruction of the Capitol in the civil wars of A.D. 69 was regarded as a calamity portending disaster ; Tacitus describes with some minuteness the ceremonies performed when the foundations of a new temple for these 'guardian deities of the Empire' were laid.[1] From the beginning of the Empire the worship of Jupiter gained new strength ; he became the most important of all the gods, and his cult spread far and wide over the new provinces. But it was not the Jupiter of the early Republic, as we shall see.

Movement towards Monotheism. The world was full of religions and new gods were easily made. Nevertheless there was a very definite movement towards monotheism, in thought, if not in religious practice. Philosophy had long ago moved beyond polytheism to monotheism or scepticism. When Helvidius Priscus performed the sacrifice of the 'suovetaurilia' in honour of Jupiter, Juno and Minerva,[2] he was not necessarily untrue to his Stoic belief in a single Universal Reason animating the world. The gods were aspects of the Divine principle, and for the masses 'expedit esse deos'. But in popular belief also there was a similar movement. Many of the cults, as we shall see, claimed for their deities universal dominion ; Magna Mater was 'queen of the earth'. Again, there were many points of similarity in the theology, rites and language, and there was a general readiness to borrow. Amid their conflicting claims the individual worshipper was at a loss, and he solved the problem by worshipping many gods and eventually identifying them. An inscription, typical of very many, records a dedication to 'Jupiter Optimus Maximus, Juno Regina, Minerva Sancta, the Sun Mithras, Hercules, Mars, Mercury, the Genius of the

---

[1] 'Praesides imperii deos', Tac. *Hist.* iv. 53.   [2] *Ibid.*

place, and all gods and goddesses '. In many cases the name of Jupiter is followed by an adjective which shows that he is identified with a god of oriental origin. One dedication is to Jupiter Optimus Maximus Aeternus, and Aeternus is an epithet of Jupiter Dolichenus, whose home was Commagene. Silvanus, the woodland god of early Roman religion, is known as ' castrensis ' and ' invictus ', epithets borrowed from the Persian cult of Mithras. Thus there was much syncretism, and this made eventually for monotheism, purer religion and the final reception of Christianity.

The Oriental Cults. The Mystery cults had a long history behind them, and were destined to last for centuries more. Orphism had its origin in the Dark Ages before Greek history begins ; and it lasted for two thousand years. The rites of Eleusis were celebrated for twelve centuries before they ceased at the end of the fourth century A.D. Magna Mater was worshipped in the fifth century in Greece and reigned till the fall of paganism, and Isis retained her popularity in the Graeco-Roman world for 800 years from the fourth century B.C. Besides these there were the cults of Adonis, Sabazios, Serapis, Aesculapius and others, of great antiquity. The Mystery religions had won their popularity in Greece largely through the appeal which they made to the individual as an individual and not as a citizen taking part in the religion of the State. In their best form they offered personal religion and a personal salvation which was not independent of moral effort ; in their worst form they offered magical release from reincarnation and a dangerous emotionalism often accompanied by immorality. They were directed to men and women alike, and they admitted no barrier of race or social standing. In the Roman Empire they won their popularity for the same reasons, and the government was not hostile (p. 301). Like Stoicism they recognized that all men were of divine origin ; unlike Stoicism they maintained the need of priestly intermediaries and the revelation given by initiation and sacrament for the realization of the divine relationship. Much of their appeal was also due to impressive ritual. In many cases ascetic preparation led the way to the supreme revelation in the temple of the deity. The preparation might extend

over many lives, but there is always a note of encouragement
and promise ; ' be of good cheer ' is found graven on the tomb-
stones of the Isiac votaries. In the meantime the initiate
was inspired to fight with faith the ' holy warfare ', and some
of the prayers which still survive suggest that the spiritual
effect of these religions was in many cases very great.

Mithraism. One of the most interesting of these cults is
the worship of Mithras. Its strength lay in its capacity to
embrace all creeds and philosophies in a single system which
satisfied the speculative and mystical tendencies of the age.
For the philosopher it brought the lore, astrological and cosmo-
logical, of the East, for the devotee a system of sacraments.
The cult came from Persia, it was modified by contact with
Babylon and spread over Asia Minor. Greek religion was
then laid under contribution, for Mithras now took human
form, and the famous scene of Mithras kneeling on the shoulder
of the bull, as he drove his dagger into its neck, became fixed
once for all ; sculptures of this scene have been found in
hundreds of Mithraic chapels from the Danube to the Solway
and from Asia to Africa. The sculptures show the stages of
the career of Mithras. Born in a cave he spent his boyhood
in the chase, training for the great achievement of his man-
hood, the pursuit and slaying of the bull. After his victory
he became reconciled with the Sun, and the love-feast seals
the reconciliation. Round these main ideas allegory after
allegory is woven. His birth is the dawn of a day, the beginning of a new era ; the cave is the vault of heaven or the
embracing arms of creation ; the sacrifice of the bull typifies
the everlasting struggle with evil and is an earnest of ultimate
victory ; the blood of the bull is the life-giving stream which
gives new birth to the soul. The sun is the symbol of infinite
goodness and light, the nearest that man can approach to
God himself. Till his victory Mithras has yet to prove
himself ; the love-feast symbolizes his acceptance by Infinite
Goodness.

Mithraism was particularly the cult of the Roman soldier,
and Mithraea have been found in numbers on the military
frontiers of the West ; but it also flourished in the sea-ports
and centres of commerce, brought thither by slaves and

traders. It was a man's religion ; it was not concerned with
dreamy fatalism but with struggle, and it appealed to the
soldier. It began to make its way into the West in Flavian
times, but by the third century it had undisputed sway and
was particularly marked out for attack by the fathers of the
Church.

CHAPTER XXII

CONCLUSION

TO indicate the debt of the Western provinces to
Romanization would not be an easy task. We may,
however, suggest some elements of that debt.
Imagine a Western provincial, of the middle classes, living
in a town about the end of the first century. He lived in a
city planned on Roman lines, self-governed according to the
Roman model. Public buildings, temples, baths, porticoes,
theatres and aqueducts showed architectural styles and building skill not native to his country and embodied for him
principles and ideas gathered from countless sources. The
festivals and games, the sevirate, the companionship of his
college, local elections satisfied his social and political interests ; imperial matters were probably too remote. In religion
he could choose as he wished from the various alternatives
offered ; he could worship the deities which had haunted his
native place from the distant past, or he could allow himself
to be fascinated by the ceremony of Eastern ritual. The
philosopher in the lecture-room or at the street corner would
cater for any speculative interests he might have and would
acquaint him with the precepts of Stoicism or any other
system. His own native language was still in use, though
Latin was fast replacing it. Latin opened to him the civilization of the day, and, if he added a smattering of Greek, he
had entry into the thought of the Mediterranean from its
early days. His son, going to a school endowed perhaps by
the generosity of some fellow-citizen, read the *Aeneid* of
Vergil, and he himself could buy the epigrams of Martial or the
latest writings of Tacitus at a reasonable price ; in any case

the 'acta diurna', published at Rome, reached him quickly and the imperial courier system linked up the city with the capital. His life and property were protected by Roman law ; in some places, if he brought an action in the courts, the native law of his land under Roman supervision might be the basis of the trial. In the market-place and on the harbour-quays he met men of alien nationality and strange tongue, summoned from their homes on a thousand different needs. The traders told him of strange countries and their produce ; in the shops he could buy their wares, imported from Italy or Asia or India. Legionaries and auxiliaries passed along the great roads : but, unless he lived in a garrison town or close to the frontier, he would seldom see the soldiers on whom he knew his peace depended—unless it were a governor's escort, or a veteran seeking retirement, or a draft of newly raised *auxilia* on their way to one of the great camps. The clothes he wore followed Roman fashion ; the wool from which they were made might come from another province, and for his womenfolk he could buy the silks and perfumes of the East. His table, furnished with Gallic pottery or Tyrian glass, could offer the delicacies of distant countries.

At almost every point of his life he was conscious of his debt to Rome, and to Rome of the Emperors he gave his allegiance. True, rumours reached him of luxury and depravity in the capital, but the tales of the scandalmongers could be discounted. To him the Emperor was the embodiment of whatever gave fullness to his life. Three or four generations ago his forbears were little removed from barbarians ; he himself might one day be a Roman citizen, heir to agelong traditions. Rome had wrought the change, and for him she was directed by other than human power ; therefore he venerated 'Rome and Augustus' and in doing so recognized the divine mission of Rome in history.

Yet the decline of the Empire is no less a fact than its earlier success. But why the Empire declined is a riddle of which the solution is not easy. Many of the symptoms of decay are obvious, and there is a temptation to diagnose as a cause what may be only a symptom. The economic collapse of the Empire, for example, is admitted, but this collapse is itself in need of explanation, nor is sufficient reason forthcoming to explain the intellectual and spiritual stagnation of the later Empire.

In the closing years of the reign of Marcus Aurelius the barbarian tribes of the North delivered the massed onslaught which they had long threatened. In the third century the fierceness and persistence of their attack was redoubled, and fresh waves of barbarians took the place of those who had been momentarily repulsed or had been admitted within the bounds of the Empire. In A.D. 213 Caracalla successfully resisted the Alamanni who now made their first appearance on the frontier ; in the middle of the third century the Franks overran Gaul and Spain, the Alamanni invaded Italy itself and were dislodged with difficulty, and the Rhine and the Danube once more became the frontier limits. A year or two earlier the Goths streamed into Thrace and Macedonia and at last were driven back by Aurelian (A.D. 270-75) ; the province of Dacia was left to them as their prey and they remained quiet for a century.

It is possible that Rome could have resisted these attacks with greater success and no loss of territory had it not been for a disaster which befell from another quarter. The army of Augustus was in numbers the smallest army consistent with the security of the Empire under normal conditions ; it was assumed that attack would come from only one quarter at a time. Nor was the army organized for rapid transport from one front to another, and in the second century it had become even less mobile, as was evident at the time of the double attack of the barbarians and the Parthians in the reign of Marcus Aurelius. When, therefore, a new and vigorous Persian Empire arose in A.D. 230 to take the place of the fallen Parthian kingdom, and when this new enemy carried war into the Eastern provinces of the Roman Empire, the existing Roman army was put to a very severe test ; it is a tribute to the brave resistance of the Empire that in A.D. 284, the date of the accession of Diocletian, the frontiers on the North and on the East were still intact.

This successful resistance is all the more remarkable if the history of the third century is borne in mind. When Commodus was murdered in A.D. 193, none could claim the Empire by hereditary right; civil war broke out, and Emperors, some capable, some worthless, were made (and often murdered) in rapid succession by the army. During the third century the problem of defence eclipsed all others; all purposes were subordinated to military needs and the army became supreme. But even a military Emperor could not hold together so vast an Empire threatened by danger at either extremity; the central control was weakened and there were movements of disintegration. The chief resistance to the Franks and Alamanni was made by Postumus, who was proclaimed by his troops Emperor of Gaul and held independent power for fifteen years (A.D. 258–73). In almost the same years the kingdom of Palmyra, which under its queen Zenobia overran Syria, Egypt and Asia Minor, kept the Persian advance in check. Both these movements of disruption were brought to an end by Aurelian (A.D. 270–5), who restored the unity of the Empire. It was marvellous that after the crises of the preceding century unity could be restored, and Diocletian (A.D. 284–305), understanding this, determined to reorganize the system of defence and of government with a view to preventing all risk of disintegration in the future.

But success had been bought at a tremendous price. Prosperity had made the upper classes unwilling to take up a military career; the equestrian career as early as Hadrian involved no military training. Yet officers to take responsible commands were necessary. Promotion from the ranks became increasingly common; the great commands were held by professional soldiers originally recruited on the frontiers, and the Emperors themselves in the third century were as a rule men who had risen from the ranks. Again, so great was the demand for men that no type of recruit could be refused; the barbarians settled within the frontiers were required to furnish men, and soon the barbarians from beyond willingly served for pay in the army of their enemy. The barbarization of the army is one of the main features of the later Empire; it was a gradual process and its gradualness helps to explain why the ultimate transference of the Western

Empire from the Romans to the barbarians took place almost unperceived.

The upkeep of an army which gained in power as the need for its upkeep became more urgent strained to the utmost the economic resources of the Empire. Early in the third century (A.D. 212) Caracalla bestowed the franchise on the majority of the inhabitants of the Empire. His chief aim was to make them liable to pay the taxes paid by Roman citizens ; at the same time the granting of the franchise reduced all members of the Empire to one level, and all were left equally powerless against a State which was becoming more and more imperious in its demands. The decurions of the cities were now required to guarantee the raising of a certain sum as taxes for the imperial treasury, and, when men naturally shrank from the office, they were compelled to undertake it. Municipal independence, which was heir to the freedom of the Greek city-state, was swallowed up by a bureaucratic Empire. The ' collegia ' of artisans and craftsmen, merchants and traders and others were now required to furnish services to the State. The continual depreciation of the currency eventually made it impossible to raise taxes in money ; the prices of the commonest articles of use rose to incredible heights; the State accepted payment of dues in kind or in services. Imperial officials were created in great numbers to extract what they could from a world already impoverished by civil war and high taxation. An army of barbarians and the grip of a bureaucratic government for the moment saved the unity of the Empire ; but the Empire with all its resources could not pay the cost of its salvation.

Yet, as Diocletian saw, the mobilizing of whatever energies and resources still remained for the service of an all-pervading government offered the only hope of survival ; his reforms, made possible by temporary quiet on the frontiers and observed in principle by his successors, gave the Empire a respite of a hundred years. The army was doubled in size and recruited largely from barbarians ; and landowners were compelled to furnish recruits. Two centuries before the army had been one of the civilizing influences of Rome ; now it was composed of men to whom Graeco-Roman civilization was unfamiliar, and legions were stationed in Italy, now reduced to the level of a province.   The civilian population was carefully organized according to its capacity to pay taxes ; rank with its duties became hereditary and no one could leave the class to which he was assigned.   The ' colonus ' was forbidden to leave his farm, for the State must be able to rely on a given amount of produce, and the ' colonate ', the hope of agriculture under the Early Empire, was corrupted into serfdom.   If the State was to control the minutest transactions of daily life, it was clear that one man was incapable of directing its manifold activities.   Diocletian therefore shared his power with Maximian ; he himself ruled the East, with his seat at Nicomedia, while Maximian ruled the West from Milan.   Later, two other governors with the title of Caesar were placed one in control of Gaul and Spain, the other in the Danube provinces. Diocletian intended that the Caesars should take over the position held by the Augusti, himself and Maximian, and so the problem of the succession would be solved.   The plan failed ; civil war followed, from which Constantine emerged as sole ruler in A.D. 324.   But the Empire was again divided at different times, till Theodosius (A.D. 378–95) once more asserted its unity, and his rule was as wide as that of Augustus. But his sons divided the Empire once more.   In the West the real power had long been passing into the hands of the military commanders, who were barbarians ; in A.D. 476 the last pretence was thrown aside, and a barbarian general ruled the West as the representative of the Eastern Emperor.   And, a little later, in the West barbarian kingdoms rose up in place of the Roman Empire and new nations came into being : in the East the Empire was to stand for another millennium ; both halves of the Roman Empire carried on in different ways the traditions of Greek and Roman civilization.

It seems, then, that there was ever growing danger beyond the frontiers and spasmodic civil war within, that the army besides increasing in size became barbarized and dominated the whole life of the Empire, which was utterly exhausted by the cost of imperial defence and bureaucratic organization, and thrown back upon primitive methods of life.   Yet the question remains why the Romans left the task of resisting the barbarians to the barbarians themselves. Had the Roman qualities of soldierly endurance and self-sacrifice vanished? Had the old Roman virtues lost their power?

The problem, in the last resort, reduces itself to one of moral and spiritual values. In the first two centuries Rome achieved the greater part of her task of civilizing the world. She gathered into a unity nations and tribes of every kind and at every stage of development. She gave them much and she received much. On the whole her influence was beneficial; can the same be said of theirs? In seeking to level up the nations was she herself dragged down? was Roman civilization spread too thinly over too vast an area? Was Roman character modified, even corrupted, by the characters of the nations which the Empire absorbed? or did the crossing of Eastern and Western race-types lead to racial degeneration and infect the vigorous Western stock with the decadence of the East, assuming that the East was decadent? Or, again, did she estimate too highly the benefits of material prosperity and so set a false standard for her subjects to emulate? or was her government too paternal? Did she do too much for her subjects and encourage a spirit of dependence?

In the answering of such questions lies the fascination of the study of the Roman Empire.

APPENDICES

I

CHIEF DATES

B.C.

63. Birth of Octavian. Consulship of Cicero. Pompey took Jerusalem.

53. Defeat and Death of Crassus at Carrhae.

44. Murder of Julius Caesar.

43. Octavian's first consulship.

42. Battles of Philippi. Birth of Tiberius.

38. Octavian married Livia.

36. Sacrosanctity of the tribunate conferred on Octavian.

33. Return of Octavian from Dalmatia for his second consulship.

31. Battle of Actium. Octavian consul from 31 to 23 B.C.

30. Octavian received *ius auxilii*. Annexation of Egypt.

29. Arrival of Octavian from Egypt. Expedition of M. Crassus against the Dacians successful.

28. Census held (4,063,000 citizens). *Lectio senatus.*

27. First form of the Principate : triumviral powers resigned : procons. imperium for ten years conferred : consulship held for seventh time ; title of ' Augustus ' conferred. Division of the provinces into senatorial and imperial.

27–24. Augustus in Gaul and Spain.

25. Marriage of Marcellus and Julia. Galatia became a province. Expedition to Arabia Felix. Reorganization of Africa ; appointment of Juba to Iol and Tingis.

23. Second Form of the Principate. Augustus received confirmation of proconsular imperium, the *tribunicia potestas* and special privileges. Death of Marcellus. Publication of the first three books of the *Odes* of Horace. (Augustus *trib. pot. i.*)

22. Conspiracy of Fannius Caepio and Licinius Murena. Augustus refused the dictatorship and perpetual censorship, but accepted *cura annonae.*

B.C.

22–19. Augustus in Greece and Asia Minor.

21. Agrippa *praefectus urbi* : he married Julia.

20. *Curatores viarum* appointed. Restoration of the ' Parthian standards '.

19. Cantabri defeated by Agrippa. Death of Vergil.

18. *Leges Iuliae.* Corn supply organized. Agrippa received procons. imperium and *trib. potestas.*

17. Augustus adopted his grandsons, Gaius and Lucius Caesar. *Ludi saeculares.*

16. Defeat of Lollius in Gaul. Subjugation of Alpine tribes and the Raetians.

15–13. Augustus in Gaul.

13. *Trib. potestas* of Agrippa renewed for five years. Tiberius consul. Agrippa in Pannonia. Horace published the fourth book of the *Odes.*

12. Death of Agrippa. Augustus became Pontifex Maximus.

12–9. Drusus in Germany (legatus of Tres Galliae). Tiberius in Pannonia.

11. Tiberius married Julia. Death of Octavia.

9. Tiberius received procons. imperium (?). Death of Drusus.

8. Census held (4,233,000 citizens). *Lectio senatus.* Tiberius in Germany. Deaths of Maecenas and Horace.

7. Triumph of Tiberius.

6. Tiberius invested with *trib. potestas.* He retired to Rhodes.

5. Augustus *consul xii* ; entry of Gaius Caesar into public life.

4. Death of Herod, King of Judaea. The Year of the Birth of Our Lord.

2. Augustus *consul xiii.* Entry of Lucius Caesar into public life. Augustus received title ' Pater Patriae '. Exile of Julia.

A.D.

2. *Consules suffecti* first appointed. Death of Lucius Caesar. Return of Tiberius from Rhodes.

4. Death of Gaius Caesar. Tiberius adopted by Augustus and invested with *trib. potestas* for ten years. Adoption of Germanicus by Tiberius. Tiberius sent to Germany.

6–9. Campaign against the Marcomanni. Rebellion in Pannonia and Dalmatia.

9. Defeat of Varus by Arminius. *Lex Papia Poppaea.*

13. Tiberius received *trib. potestas* and equal powers with Augustus.

A.D.

14. Census held (4,937,000 citizens). Death of Augustus. Germanicus in Germany. Accession of TIBERIUS. Revolt of the legions in Pannonia and Germany.

15. Revival of the laws of *Maiestas*. (Tiberius *trib. pot. xvii.*)

16. Accusation of Libo Drusus. Germanicus recalled from Germany; his triumph.

17. Rise of Sejanus. Germanicus in the East.

18. Tiberius *consul iii.*

19, 21, 26. Risings in Thrace.

19. Death of Germanicus.

19-24. War in Africa against Tacfarinas.

20. Condemnation of Piso.

21. Rebellion of Florus and Sacrovir in Gaul. Tiberius tended to withdraw from Rome to Capreae. *Consul iv.*

22. *Trib. potestas* conferred on Drusus.

23. Death of Drusus.

25. Trial of Cremutius Cordus.

26. Complete withdrawal of Tiberius.

28. Agrippina, daughter of Germanicus, married Domitius Ahenobarbus.

29. Death of Livia.

31. Execution of Sejanus. Tiberius *consul v.*

33. Agrippina, wife of Germanicus, put to death. Financial crisis in Rome.

35-36. L. Vitellius legate in Syria. Peace with Parthia.

37. Death of Tiberius. Accession of GAIUS. *Cos.*

39. Conspiracy against Gaius. *Cos. ii.*

40. Gaius in Gaul. Embassy of the Jews. *Cos. iii.*

41. *Cos. iv.* Murder of Gaius. Accession of CLAUDIUS. Exile of Seneca. Agrippa became King of Judaea.

42. Deaths of Paetus and Arria. *Cos. ii.* (*Cos. in* 37 A.D.)

43. Expedition of Claudius to Britain. *Cos. iii.*

44. Death of Herod Agrippa, King of Judaea.

47. *Ludi Saeculares.* Corbulo in Lower Germany. *Cos. iv.*

48. Execution of Messalina. Claudius censor.

49. Claudius married Agrippina. Death of Silanus. Seneca recalled.

50. Claudius adopted Nero. Capture of Caratacus by Ostorius Scapula.

51. Burrus appointed Prefect of Praetorians. Vologeses became King of Armenia. *Cos. v.*

53. Nero married Octavia.

24

370 THE ROMAN EMPIRE

A.D.

54. Death of Claudius. Accession of NERO. The Parthian War. Corbulo began his command in the East.

55. Death of Britannicus. Nero *cos.*

57. Advance of Corbulo into Armenia. *Cos. ii.*

58. Capture of Artaxata by Corbulo. Otho sent to Lusitania. Nero's finance proposals. *Cos. iii.*

59–61. Campaigns of Suetonius Paulinus in Britain.

59. Murder of Agrippina by Nero.

60. *Cos. iv.*

61. Rebellion of Boudicca. St. Paul in Rome about this date.

62. Nero married Poppaea Sabina. Death of Burrus. Ascendancy of Tigellinus. Disaster at Rhandeia.

63. Settlement of Armenian question.

64. Fire at Rome.

65. The Pisonian conspiracy. Deaths of Seneca, Lucan and Poppaea.

66. Submission of Tiridates. Nero in Greece.

66–70. The Jewish Rebellion.

67. Nero in Greece, which received 'immunity'. Death of Corbulo. Contemplated expedition against Caucasian tribes. Vespasian conducted the war against the Jews.

68. Revolt of Vindex. GALBA proclaimed Emperor. Death of Nero. *Cos. v.*

69. The Year of the Four Emperors. Galba, killed January 15. OTHO Emperor, killed himself April 17. VITELLIUS Emperor, died December 22. VESPASIAN proclaimed Emperor July 1. Revolt of Civilis in Germany. Dacian raids into Moesia.

70. Vespasian's march to Italy. Titus took Jerusalem. Vespasian *cos. ii.* Titus *cos.*

71. Triumph of Vespasian and Titus. *Cos. iii.* Domitian *cos.*

72. Vespasian *cos. iv.* Titus *cos. ii.*

73. Vespasian and Titus censors. Annexation of Agri Decumates. Domitian *cos. ii.*

74–79. Vespasian *cos. v–ix*, Titus *iii–vii.*

75–77. Domitian *cos. iii, iv, v.*

77 or 78. Arrival of Agricola in Britain.

79. Death of Vespasian. Accession of TITUS. Destruction of Herculaneum and Pompeii.

80. Fire at Rome. Titus *cos. viii.* Domitian *cos. vii.*

81. Death of Titus. Accession of DOMITIAN.

82. *Cos. viii,* to 88 *cos. xiv,* 90 *cos. xv,* 92 *cos. xvi,* 95 *cos. xvii.*

A.D.

83–84. Expedition against the Chatti. Domitian took title 'Germanicus'.

84 or 85. Recall of Agricola from Britain.

85. Domitian censor. Expedition against the Nasamones.

85–89. War against the Dacians.

88. *Ludi Saeculares.*

88–89. Rebellion of Saturninus.

92. Attack on Pannonia by Marcomanni, Quadi and Iazyges.

93. Death of Agricola.

95. Execution of Flavius Clemens.

96. Death of Domitian. Accession of NERVA. Trajan on the Northern Frontier.

97. Adoption of Trajan by Nerva. Both assumed the title 'Germanicus'.

98. Death of Nerva. Accession of TRAJAN. *Cos. ii.*

99. Arrival of Trajan in Rome.

100. Hadrian married Vibia Sabina. Trajan *cos. iii* (101 *cos. iv,* 103 *cos. v,* 112 *cos. vi*).

101–2. The First Dacian War. Trajan took title 'Dacicus'.

105–6. The Second Dacian War.

111. Pliny the Younger in Bithynia.

113. Trajan set out on his Eastern campaigns.

114. The title 'Optimus' conferred on Trajan.

116. Trajan took title 'Parthicus'.

117. Death of Trajan. Accession of HADRIAN. *Cos. ii* (108 *cos. i,* 119 *cos. iii*).

117–18. Hadrian on the Danube.

118. The Conspiracy of the Four Consulars.

121. Birth of Marcus Aurelius.

121–5. Hadrian's First Journey.

127. Hadrian's Italian journey.

128. African visit and beginning of Second Journey.

129. Completion of the Code by Salvius Julianus.

132. Rebellion of the Jews.

136. Adoption of Aelius Verus. *Cos.* (137 *cos. ii*).

138. Death of Verus. Adoption of Antoninus by Hadrian, and of Lucius Verus and Marcus Aurelius by Antoninus. Accession of ANTONINUS PIUS.

139. Antoninus *cos ii* (120 *cos.,* 140 *cos. iii,* 145 *cos. iv*).

140. M. Aurelius *cos.*

145. M. Aurelius *cos. ii.*

146. M. Aurelius received procons. imperium and became consort.

A.D.

154. L. Verus *cos.*

161. Death of Antoninus Pius. M. AURELIUS and LUCIUS VERUS Emperors. Pressure of Tribes on the N. Frontier. Langobardi and Marcomanni crossed into Pannonia. L. Verus *cos.* ii.

162–6. The Parthian War.

163. Destruction of Artaxata by Statius Priscus. Lucius Verus took title ' Armeniacus '.

165. Capture of Ctesiphon (?). Irruptions of Northern tribes as far as Aquileia. Lucius Verus took title ' Parthicus Maximus '.

166. Return of Lucius Verus to Rome. Return of troops. Outbreak of Plague. M. Aurelius took titles ' Parthicus Maximus ' and ' Medicus ' and ' Pater Patriae ', L. Verus ' Medicus ' and ' Pater Patriae '.

167. L. Verus *cos.* iii.

167–8. Marcus and Lucius went to the N. Frontier.

167–8 to 180. War with the Quadi and Iazyges.

169. Death of Lucius Verus

172. Threat of another Parthian War. M. Aurelius and Commodus took title ' Germanicus '.

175. Revolt of Avidius Cassius. M. Aurelius and Commodus took title ' Sarmaticus '.

176. Death of Faustina (?). Commodus became consort.

177. Commodus nominated as successor. *Cos.* (and in 179, 181, 183, 186, 190, 192).

178. M. Aurelius returned to the N. Frontier.

180. Death of M. Aurelius. Accession of COMMODUS as sole Emperor.

II

THE CHIEF PROVINCES OF THE EMPIRE IN A.D. 117.

SENATORIAL.

Consular.

Asia, 133 B.C.
Africa, 146 B.C.

Praetorian.

Baetica, conquered 197 B.C., separate
   prov. in 25 B.C.
Narbonensis, 120 B.C., Imp. in 27 B.C.,
   Sen. after 22 B.C.
Sicily, 241 B.C.
Macedonia, 146 B.C.; Imp. A.D. 15–44.
Achaea, 146 B.C.; Imp. A.D. 15–44.
Crete and Cyrene. Joined as a prov.
   in 27 B.C.
Cyprus, 27 B.C.; Imp. 27–22 B.C.
Bithynia, 74 B.C. Extended in 63
   and 7 B.C. Imp. after A.D. 135.

IMPERIAL.

Consular.

Tarraconensis, organized as prov.
   25 B.C.
Germania Superior, A.D. 17.
— Inferior, A.D. 17.
Britain, A.D. 43.
Pannonia, A.D. 10. Divided by Trajan.
Moesia, 29 B.C. or the reign of
   Claudius. Divided by Domitian.
Dacia, A.D. 107.
Dalmatia (formerly Illyricum). Sen.
   till 11 B.C.
Cappadocia, A.D. 17; procuratorial
   till Vespasian. See p. 168.
Syria, 64 B.C.

Praetorian.

Lusitania, separated from Hispania
   Ulterior in 27 or 25 B.C.
Lugdunensis ⎫
Belgica   ⎬ Became separate prov.
Aquitania ⎭ in A.D. 17.
Galatia, 25 B.C. See p. 168.
Cilicia, 64 B.C.
Arabia, A.D. 103.
Pamphylia and Lycia. Pamphylia,
   25 B.C.; Lycia, A.D. 43. Sen.
   after A.D. 135.
Judaea, procuratorial A.D. 6–41 and
   A.D. 44–70. After 70 became a
   separate prov., distinct from
   Syria under a praetorian legatus.

Procuratorial.

Raetia, 15 B.C., procur. up to A.D. 169:
   then praetorian.
Noricum *as* Raetia.
Thrace, A.D. 46.
Mauretania Tingitana, A.D. 40 or 42.
Mauretania Caesariensis, A.D. 40 or 42.
Sardinia and Corsica, 231 B.C., Sen.
   till A.D. 6, then Imp. Sen.
   under Nero. Imp. under Vespa-
   sian and after.
Alpes Maritimae, A.D. 14.
— Cottiae under Nero.
— Poeninae in existence in 2nd
   cent.

Egypt, 30 B.C., governed by a praefectus of equestrian rank.

Armenia, A.D. 114. Praetorian (?).
Mesopotamia, A.D. 115, abandoned
117, reconquered 165. Praet. (?).
Assyria, A.D. 115. Praet. (?).
Commagene, absorbed in Syria, A.D. 72.

A date standing by itself denotes the date of the creation of the
province.

THE SENATORIAL AND EQUESTRIAN CAREERS

THE SENATORIAL CAREER

THE *cursus honorum* appears on monuments in ascending or descending order of the offices held. But the consulship is still regarded as the crown of the career, and so is often taken out of its correct position and put immediately after the man's name. Priesthoods and religious offices also are treated separately. Further, though a career may be described in descending order of ranks held, i.e. the reverse of the chronological order, the appointments held by virtue of the same rank may be put chronologically. For each step in the career gave admission to appointments of which none or one or several might be held before the holder passed on to the next step.

Qualifications. i. senatorial birth,
or ii. the granting of the *Latus clavus*.

In both cases the possession of the senatorial census of 1,000,000 HS was necessary.

Posts held before the quaestorship:
a. vigintivirate, composed of
    xviri stlitibus iudicandis, members of the civil courts,
    iiiviri capitales, assistants to civil magistrates,
    iiiviri monetales, in charge of the mint of the Senate,
    ivviri viarum curandarum, in charge of the streets of Rome.
b. service as 'tribunus militum laticlavius'. After the Flavians this service was often of an administrative nature.
c. the position of 'sevir equitum Romanorum', i.e. head of one of the six squadrons of Roman knights. (Honorary and optional.)

The ordinary steps were quaestorship, praetorship, consulship, but the Emperor could exercise his power of 'adlectio' to place a man 'inter quaestorios', etc.

Quaestor. Minimum age, 25 years. Office for a year, 5 December to 4 December (provincial quaestors appointed in July). Twenty in number. Ten or eleven were assigned to the senatorial provinces.

This was the lowest office to give entry into the Senate.

quaestor pro praetore ; finance of senatorial provinces.
    „   urbanus ; the senatorial treasury.
    „   principis }link between Emperor, Senate
    „   consulum } and consuls.

Tribunus plebis (ten). {These were ranked as of the same degree. Office was for one year ; tribunate from 10 December, aedileship from 1 January.
Aedile (six).

This step was necessary for plebeians. But patricians omitted it, passing from quaestorship to praetorship, for the tribunate and the plebeian aedileship were closed to patricians.

Praetor. Minimum age, 30 years. Office for a year, from 1 January. Twelve in number.

praetor urbanus ; civil cases *inter cives*.
    „   peregrinus ; . . . . . involving peregrini.
    „   de fideicommissis.
    „   hastarius ; president of the centumviral court.
    „   aerarii (23 B.C.–A.D. 44), of the senatorial treasury.

Two years' interval. But after the praetorship none outside the Emperor's family could hope for the consulship for at least 10 to 12 years. During these years the ex-praetor held important ' praetorian ' posts :—

A. appointed by the Emperor,
    (i) legatus on the staff of a provincial governor.
    (ii) legatus legionis.
    (iii) legatus pro praetore exercitus qui in Africa est.
    (iv) legatus pro praetore of a non-military Caesarian province, e.g. Belgica.
    (v) praefectus aerarii Saturni (at certain times).
        „   „   militaris after A.D. 6.
    (vi) curatores viarum and operum publicorum (at certain times).
B. appointed by the Senate, by lot, proconsul of a senatorial province (except Asia and Africa). The Emperor had the right to exclude a name from the *sortitio*.

Consul. Minimum age, 33. Consuls were two in number and were—

A. ordinarii. They gave their name to the year. Office beginning on 1 January was for a year.

B. suffecti. Appointed on 9 January. They were appointed in pairs for 2, 3 or 4 months.

A second consulship was very uncommon.

Ex-consuls might pass on to the important ' consular ' posts :—

A. appointed by the Emperor,
>> (i) legatus of an armed imperial province, e.g. Britain or Syria. In spite of being an ex-consul such a governor was known as legatus Augusti pro praetore.
>> (ii) in Rome, curatores operum publicorum, etc.
>> (iii) praefectus urbi. This was the crown of the senatorial career.

B. appointed by the Senate,
>> proconsul of Africa.
>> proconsul of Asia.

An example of a senatorial career :—

P. Mummio P.f. Gal. Sisennae Rutiliano cos., auguri, procos. provinc. Asiae, legato Aug. pr. pr. Moesiae superioris, praef. aliment. per Aemiliam, praef. aer. Saturni, leg. leg. VI Victric., praetori, tr. pl., quaest., trib. leg. V Maced., Xviro stlitib. iudic., patrono municipii, cur. fani H.V., salio, Herculanii Augustales, l. d. s. c.[1] (*In dextro latere*) dedicata kal. Iun. Maximo et Orfito cos.[2] (*In sinistro*) curantibus P. Ragonio Saturnino et C. Marcio Marciano, q.[3] ordinis Augustalium Tiburtium. (Dess. 1101.)

A dedication to P. Mummius, Publii filius, Sisenna Rutilianus, of the Galerian tribe, by the Augustales of Tibur, who worshipped Hercules. The career is in descending order ; the consulship (cos) and the priesthood (augur) are taken out of their place, as is usual. Local honours, though perhaps latest in time, come last. Mummius was patron of the town of Tibur, curator of the shrine of Hercules Victor and held a priesthood (salio). He began his career as a member of the decemviri stlitibus iudicandis, i.e. in the civil courts ; he passed on to military service as tribune

---

[1] Loco dato (for the memorial) senatus consulto ; senatus is the local senate.

[2] A.D. 172.   [3] Quaestoribus, of the ordo.

of the Fifth Macedonian Legion ; he then became quaestor, then tribunus plebis, then praetor. His ' praetorian ' posts were legatus of the Sixth Victrix Legion, and prefect of the senatorial treasury. He then became consul, and his ' consular ' posts were :—prefect in charge of the ' alimenta ' in the districts on the Aemilian road, legatus Augusti pro praetore of Upper Moesia, and finally proconsul of Asia. (Praefecti alimentorum might be either praetorian or consular, so that his consulship might have come after his office as praef. aliment.)

The Equestrian Career

The necessary qualifications were (i) free birth, (ii) the equestrian census of 400,000 sesterces, (iii) inclusion in the roll of the equites ; this was dependent on the Emperor's approval.

Military offices provided a qualifying service. The *militiæ equestres* were (i) praefectus fabrum ; semi-military and not essential ; (ii) praefectus or tribunus of an auxiliary cohort or ala ; (iii) tribunus angusticlavius of a legion (angusticlavius is generally omitted in inscrr.). Other posts, e.g. praefectus castrorum, praepositus vexillationibus, are found, but they do not affect the career. The next step might be tribunus cohortis vigilum or urbanae or praetoriae. From Hadrian's time these preliminary military posts were not essential to the career.

From this point begins a series of administrative posts :—

(i) fiscal agents, e.g. procuratores Augusti, who held in imperial provinces the same position as quaestors in senatorial provv. ; procuratores a rationibus, procuratores vicesimae hereditatum, etc.

(ii) procuratores of imperial procuratorial provv.

(iii) procuratores of imperial departments at Rome, e.g. a libellis, ab epistulis, a rationibus ; in the early Empire these were held by freedmen, after Hadrian always by knights.

(iv) prefectures ; the most important of these were, in ascending order of rank, praefectus vehiculorum, classis, vigilum, annonae, Aegypti, praetorii.

Hadrian arranged the lower administrative posts in four classes according to the salaries attached. A. sexagenarii, 60,000 HS, e.g. advocatus fisci, subpraefectus classis, adiutores attached to the various departments. B. centenarii, 100,000 HS, procuratores alimentorum, aquarum, monetae, operum publicorum, etc. C. ducenarii, 200,000 HS, procurator provinciae, ab epistulis Graecis and Latinis, etc. D. trecenarii, 300,000 HS, procurator a rationibus.

In the second century, either in the reign of Hadrian or Marcus Aurelius, certain titles were recognized as belonging to the various posts ; the praefectus praetorio was known as vir eminentissimus, the other praefecti and the highest procuratores as viri perfectissimi, the lower procuratores as viri egregii : a knight without office was known as splendidus eques Romanus.

An example of an equestrian career :—

M. Petronio M.f. Quir. Honorato praef. coh. I Raetorum, trib. mil. leg. I Minerviae p. f., praef. alae Aug. p. f. Thrac., proc. monetae., proc. XX hered., proc. prov. Belg. et duar. Germaniar., proc. a ration. Aug., praef. annon., praef. Aegypti, pontif. minori, negotiatiatores (sic) oleari ex Baetica patrono. Curatoribus Cassio Fausto Caecilio Honorato. (Dess. 1340.)

The offices held are in ascending order.

The oil-merchants of Baetica to M. Petronius, Marci filius, Quirina tribu, Honoratus. His military posts were :—prefect of the First cohort of Raetians, military tribune of legio I Minervia pia fidelis, prefect of a squadron of Thracians attached to the (Eighth) Augustan legion. He then proceeded to financial and administrative posts .—the Mint, the collection of the vicesima hereditatum (the 5 per cent. tax), fiscal duties in Belgic Gaul and Germany, the position of a rationibus, prefect in charge of the corn supply and finally prefect of Egypt.

IV

THE TREASURIES

I. Aerarium (senatorial).

Managed under the Republic by quaestors ; 28–23 B.C. by prefects (of praetorian rank chosen by the Senate) ; 23 B.C.– A.D. 44 by praetors ; A.D. 44–56 by quaestors (Claudius' anti-quarianism) ; A.D. 56 and later by prefects of praetorian rank chosen by the Emperor.

Assisted by the Emperor—

i. four times with 150 million sesterces, *Mon. Anc.* 17.

ii. Augustus left it 40 million, Tac. *Ann.* i. 8 (but interpretation disputed).

iii. Nero gave 40 million, Tac. *Ann.* xiii. 31.

iv. Nero gave 60 million regularly, xv. 18 ; Furneaux thinks that this payment represents the cost of corn distribution, trans-ferred by Claudius or Nero from aerarium to fiscus ; Mommsen otherwise ; see Furneaux.

Received—

i. revenue from senatorial provinces, i.e. *tributum soli* and *tributum capitis.*

ii. *portoria* and customs from Italy ; but not *vicesima heredita-tum* or *centesima rerum venalium.*

iii. *bona damnatorum* and *caduca* (unclaimed legacies, which were numerous owing to the Lex Papia Poppaea ; but the Emperor frequently claimed them. Cf. Tac. *Ann.* vi. 2).

II. The fisc. Probably not centralized till Claudius' time, though Tacitus uses the term of earlier times.

Under *a rationibus,* a freedman until Hadrian ; a procurator in every imperial province and many minor officials, including freedmen and slaves ; also procurators of imperial estates situated in senatorial provinces. Received taxes of imperial provinces and confiscated property and *caduca.*

III. Aerarium militare. For pensions of soldiers ; set up by Augustus. Tac. *Ann.* i. 78. Received *centesima rerum venalium* and *quinta et vicesima mancipiorum venalium* and *vicesima hereditatum.* For complaints as to the way in which it was spent, see Tac.

379

Ann. i. 17, 'uligines paludum . . .' Administered by three prefects of praetorian rank.

IV. Patrimonium Caesaris. The private fortune of the Emperor as Emperor; received revenues of Egypt and of the imperial estates; passed to his successor.

V. Res privata. The strictly personal property of the Emperor. Differentiated from the *patrimonium* after Septimius Severus, A.D. 193–211.

THE CHIEF NAMES IN THE LITERARY HISTORY OF THE FIRST TWO CENTURIES

LATIN WRITERS

THE AUGUSTAN AGE.

P. VERGILIUS MARO, 70–19 B.C. Born near Mantua.

Q. HORATIUS FLACCUS, 65–8 B.C. Born at Venusia.

ALBIUS TIBULLUS, 54–19 B.C. Elegiac poet.

SEXTUS PROPERTIUS, 49–15 B.C. Imitator of the Alexandrine elegiac poets, but his poetry has much force and originality.

P. OVIDIUS NASO, 43 B.C.–A.D. 17. Exiled to Tomi in A.D. 8.

T. LIVIUS, 59 B.C.–A.D. 17. Born at Patavium (Padua). Wrote a history of Rome to 9 B.C. in 142 books, of which thirty-five survive.

JULIO-CLAUDIAN TIMES.

C. VELLEIUS PATERCULUS. Served under Tiberius in the army. Wrote a brief abridgment of Roman History.

VALERIUS MAXIMUS. Wrote a collection of stories chiefly for rhetorical purposes.

PHAEDRUS. Fabulist.

QUINTUS CURTIUS RUFUS. Compiled a History of Alexander the Great.

LUCIUS ANNAEUS SENECA (the Younger), 4 B.C.–A.D. 65. Born at Corduba. Wrote philosophical essays under various titles. The *Letters to Lucilius* are really brief essays. Several ' consolations ', addressed to various people ; the *consolatio ad Polybium* was written chiefly to procure his own return from exile. Several ' Tragedies ' are also extant.

COLUMELLA. Of Gades, contemporary of Seneca. Wrote *De Re Rustica* in twelve books.

A. PERSIUS FLACCUS, A.D. 34–62. Of Volaterrae. He wrote six satires or rather lectures on Stoic themes. They show much sense of the dramatic and are lively, but expressed in obscure Latin.

382 THE ROMAN EMPIRE

M. ANNAEUS LUCANUS, A.D. 39–65. Of Corduba. Nephew of Seneca. Wrote the *Pharsalia* in ten books, an account of the civil war between Caesar and Pompey.

PETRONIUS ARBITER (reign of Nero). Wrote *Satyricon*, of which the *Cena Trimalchionis* is the most famous episode.

THE FLAVIAN AGE.

C. PLINIUS SECUNDUS (Pliny the Elder) of Comum. A voluminous writer, or rather compiler, on almost every subject, e.g. tactics, history, grammar, rhetoric, science. Only his *Naturalis Historia* in thirty-seven books survives.

C. VALERIUS FLACCUS. Died about A.D. 90 ; wrote under Vespasian eight books of *Argonautica*.

SILIUS ITALICUS, *c.* A.D. 25–101. Wrote seventeen books of *Punica* : he borrowed the matter from Livy and imitated the style of Vergil.

P. PAPINIUS STATIUS, A.D. 40–96. Wrote five books of *Silvae* (occasional poems), and the *Thebaid* and *Achilleis*.

M. VALERIUS MARTIALIS, *c.* A.D. 40–102. Of Bilbilis in Spain. Fifteen books of Epigrams are extant.

M. FABIUS QUINTILIANUS, *c.* A.D. 35–95. Of Calagurris in Spain. Educated at Rome. Twelve books on the education of an orator, *Institutio oratoria*, are extant.

SEXTUS JULIUS FRONTINUS, A.D. 40–103. Engineer and officer. His extant works are *Strategemata* and *De aquis* ; he was *curator aquarum* in A.D. 97. Governor of Britain, A.D. 74–77 or 78.

THE REIGNS OF NERVA AND TRAJAN.

D. JUNIUS JUVENALIS, A.D. 60–140. Of Aquinum. Satirist.

CORNELIUS TACITUS, A.D. 55–120. Wrote *Dialogus de oratoribus*, *Agricola* (98), *Germania*. The *Historiae* originally contained a history of the Empire from A.D. 69–96, but only the account of 69 and 70 (incompletely) has survived. The *Annales*, composed after the *Historiae* and published about A.D. 116, originally embraced the years 14–68. The extant parts cover the years A.D. 14–28, 31–37, 47–68.

C. PLINIUS CAECILIUS SECUNDUS (Pliny the Younger), A.D. 62–*c.* 113. Of Comum. Consul A.D. 100 ; in Bithynia A.D. 111. His *Letters* and a *Panegyric* on Trajan survive.

THE SECOND CENTURY.

C. SUETONIUS TRANQUILLUS, *c.* A.D. 75–160. He wrote, about A.D. 120, *de viris illustribus*, and *Vitae duodecim Caesarum*, from Julius Caesar to Domitian.

M. Cornelius Fronto of Cirta, c. A.D. 100–175. His correspondence with Marcus Aurelius and Lucius Verus is extant.

Aulus Gellius. Wrote *Noctes Atticae*, twenty books of notes
on literature, language, science, etc.

L. Apuleius of Madaura, in Africa. Lived in the reigns of
Antoninus Pius and Marcus Aurelius. His most famous work is
the *Metamorphoses*.

M. Minucius Felix. Wrote *Octavius*, a defence of Christianity.

Q. Septimius Tertullianus, c. A.D. 150–230. Of Carthage.

A collection of *Lives of the Emperors*, known as the *Historia
Augusta* and traditionally written by six authors, was put together
perhaps in the reign of the Emperor Julian. It embraces the
years A.D. 117–284 (with a gap from A.D. 244–260). The ' lives '
are poor in quality, scant in quantity, uncritical and uninteresting,
but in default of better authorities they are valuable.

GREEK WRITERS

Dionysius of Halicarnassus. In Rome during the first half
of the reign of Augustus. He wrote (I) rhetorical and critical
treatises, (II) ‘Ρωμαικὴ ’Αρχαιολογία, a history of Rome to 264
B.C., of which eleven books survive.

Diodorus Siculus. Wrote about the same time a long
uncritical world-history to Caesar's Gallic Wars in forty books,
of which several survive.

(Longinus.) The name and date of the author of a valuable
work of literary criticism, Περὶ "Υψους, are unknown.

Strabo, 63 B.C.–A.D. 23. Wrote the *Geographica*, a description
of the known world, in seventeen books ; he relied partly on
older works, but also on first-hand experience, and therefore his
work is often valuable.

Philo Judaeus. A Jewish philosopher with Greek and
Platonic sympathies. A large number of his works is extant,
among them the *Legatio ad Gaium*, see p. 83.

Flavius Josephus, born about A.D. 37. First visited Rome
in A.D. 63. For his part in the Jewish War, see p. 144. His
main works were (I) an account of the *Jewish War*, (II) a treatise
on *Jewish Antiquities*.

Plutarch, born about A.D. 46 at Chaeronea. He visited
Rome in Vespasian's reign. Besides the *Parallel Lives*, he wrote
four biographies, including those of Galba and Otho, and a large
number of essays on ethical, religious and other themes, known
as the *Moralia*.

DIO CHRYSOSTOM, of Prusa in Bithynia. In Rome under Vespasian, and banished by Domitian. A 'sophist', but his discourses are unusually interesting and throw light on the condition of the Eastern provinces.

FLAVIUS ARRIANUS, of Nicomedia, Governor of Cappadocia A.D. 131–7. An admirer of the philosopher Epictetus, he devoted two works, the *Encheiridion* and the *Diatribae Epicteti* (four books survive), to an exposition of his philosophy. Of the other works which are extant the most important are the *Anabasis of Alexander*, the *Periplus*, an account of a survey of the Black Sea, and the *Indica*.

APPIAN, of Alexandria, lived at Rome under Trajan, Hadrian and Antoninus Pius. He wrote a History of Rome to the time of Vespasian in twenty-four books, of which eleven survive. He abandons a chronological scheme and treats of subjects, e.g. the affairs of each country, the Mithridatic Wars, the Civil Wars, etc.

PTOLEMY, of Alexandria, geographer and astronomer, lived in the reign of Marcus Aurelius.

PAUSANIAS wrote in the time of Marcus Aurelius his Περιήγησις τῆς Ἑλλάδος, a valuable account of a tour in Greece.

AELIUS ARISTIDES, of Mysia, born A.D. 117, died about A.D. 185. A travelling 'sophist'. Some of his essays deal with historical and literary themes ; the Ἱεροὶ λόγοι give an account of his travels in search of cures for his illness. The *Panegyric of Rome*, see p. 258, is dated A.D. 160.

LUCIAN, of Samosata ; born about A.D. 125. One of the few original writers of this age. Trained as a rhetorician and philosopher, he discovered the 'satirical dialogue' ; his works throw much light on social conditions and on the philosophical and literary tendencies of the day.

MARCUS AURELIUS, the Emperor, born A.D. 121, died A.D. 180. Wrote the 'Meditations' (Εἰς Ἑαυτόν), see p. 274.

CASSIUS DIO, consul in A.D. 222, wrote a complete history of Rome up to A.D. 229. Only parts survive, often in abridgments made in the eleventh and twelfth centuries. Whether he used Tacitus is disputed : where Tacitus fails us, Dio often remains the sole authority ; he may have used Suetonius. The period from Augustus to Marcus Aurelius is contained in books liii to lxix, liii to lx (the end of Claudius) being the original Dio unabridged (except part of lv, end of lix, beginning of lx).

VI

SELECT BIBLIOGRAPHY

Gibbon : *Decline and Fall of the Roman Empire* (ed. Bury), vol. i.
T. Mommsen : *The Provinces of the Roman Empire.* 1909.
H. F. Pelham : *Outlines of Roman History.* 5th ed. 1915.
H. Stuart Jones : *Companion to Roman History.* 1912.
J. E. Sandys : *A Companion to Latin Studies.*
J. B. Bury : *Student's Roman Empire.* 1893.
M. P. Nilsson : *Imperial Rome.* 1926.
G. H. Stevenson : *The Roman Empire.* 1930.
A. H. J. Greenidge : *Roman Public Life.* 1901.
Universal History of the World, vols. iii–v (Harmsworth), 1928.
M. Rostovtzeff : *Social and Economic History of the Roman
    Empire.* 1926.
Tenney Frank : *Economic History of Rome.* 2nd ed. 1927.
              History of Rome. 1923.
E. S. Bouchier : *Life and Letters in Roman Africa.* 1913.
                Spain Under the Roman Empire. 1914.
                Syria as a Roman Province. 1917.
W. T. Arnold : *Roman Provincial Administration.* 3rd ed. 1914.
H. Mattingly : *The Imperial Civil Service of Rome.* 1910.
F. F. Abbot and A. C. Johnson : *Municipal Administration in
    the Roman Empire.* 1926.
H. M. D. Parker : *The Roman Legions.* 1928.
E. S. Shuckburgh : *Augustus.* 1903.
F. B. Marsh : *The Reign of Tiberius.* 1931.
J. P. V. D. Balsdon : *The Emperor Gaius (Caligula).* 1934.
A. Momigliano (translated by W. D. Hogarth) : *Claudius.* 1934.
B. W. Henderson : *The Life and Principate of the Emperor Nero.*
                  1903.
                  Civil War and Rebellion, A.D. 69–70. 1908.
                  Life and Principate of the Emperor Hadrian.
                  1923.
                  Five Roman Emperors (Vespasian to Trajan).
                  1927.
T. R. Glover : *The Conflict of Religions in the Early Roman
    Empire.* 1918.

E. G. Hardy : *Christianity and the Roman Government.* 1925.

F. Cumont : *Oriental Religions in Roman Paganism.* 1911.

W. R. Halliday : *The Pagan Background of Early Christianity.* 1925.

F. Haverfield : *The Roman Occupation of Britain.* 1924.

R. G. Collingwood : *Roman Britain.* 1923.

The Archæology of Roman Britain. 1930.

J. G. Tucker : *Life in the Roman World of Nero and St. Paul.* 1910.

S. Dill : *Roman Society from Nero to Marcus Aurelius.* 2nd ed. 1905.

R. H. Barrow : *Slavery in the Roman Empire.* 1928.

A. M. Duff : *Freedmen in the Early Roman Empire.* 1928.

M. P. Charlesworth : *Trade Routes and Commerce of the Roman Empire.* 2nd ed. 1926.

M. Cary and E. H. Warmington : *The Ancient Explorers.* 1929.

E. G. Hardy : *Monumentum Ancyranum.* 1923.

R. H. Barrow : *A Selection of Latin Inscriptions.* 1934.

J. E. Sandys : *Latin Epigraphy.* 2nd ed. 1927.

H. Mattingly : *Roman Coins.* 1928.

J. Wight Duff : *A Literary History of Rome in the Silver Age from Tiberius to Hadrian.* 1927.

C. P. Lucas : *Greater Rome and Greater Britain.* 1912.

Murray's Classical Atlas.

The Ordnance Survey Map of Roman Britain.

INDEX

Abae, 239.
Abascantus, 349.
Aberdeen, 284, 290.
Abgarus, 225–6.
Abila, 216.
Ab epistulis, 88, 180, 244, 377.
a cognitionibus, 180.
a libellis, 88, 180, 244, 377.
a rationibus, 88, 180, 377.
a studiis, 88.
Academy, 249.
Achaia, 41, 61, 91, 221.
acta diurna, 112, 360.
Acte, 113.
Actian games, 42.
Actium, 1, 30, 36.
Acumincum, 206.
Adam-Klissi, 199, 207.
Aden, 315.
Adige, 140.
adlectio, 11, 12, 263, 374.
Adrian, 271.
Adua, 137.
advocati fisci, 245, 377.
Aediles, 342, 375.
Aedui, 68, 93.
Aelia Capitolina (Jerusalem), 242, 243.
Aelius Verus, 250, 251.
Aerarium, 9, 10, 87, 102, 179, 188, 245, 262, 338, 379.
–– *militare*, 22, 379.
Afranius Burrus. *See* Burrus.
Africa, 42, 43, 81 ; troubles in, 66 ; Hadrian in, 240 ; economic condition of, 323.
ager publicus, 324, 325.
Agricola, Calpurnius, 267.
–– Cn. Julius, 133, 186, 192–4 ; in Britain, 282–85, 289, 293.
Agriculture, Italian, 324–9, 333–40.
Agri Decumates, 155, 189, 190–4.
Agrippa, M. Vipsanius, 14, 20, 21, 27, 29, 54, 80, 154, 248 ; marriage of, 27 ; in Spain, 44 ; buildings of, 19 ; in Pannonia, 48 ; in the East, 37.
–– Postumus, 58.
Agrippina, daughter of Agrippa and Pomponia, 27.
–– the Elder (daughter of Agrippa and Julia, wife of Germanicus), 29, 59, 64, 65, 73, 81.
–– the Younger (daughter of Germanicus), 81, 96–102, 107 ; murder of, 104 ; memoirs of, 116.
Aixis, 201, 202.
Ajax, 238.
Alamanni, 270, 361, 362.

Alans, 168, 228, 259.
Albinovanus Pedo, 150.
Albis, F. (Elbe), 50, 52, 145, 146, 150.
Alcibiades, 241.
Aldborough, 291.
Alexander, 227, 228, 315.
Alexandria, 41, 82, 94, 242, 314, 315.
Alimenta, 210, 219, 232 ; description of, 334
Aliso, 51, 53, 151.
allocutiones, 240.
Alphabet, Claudian additions to, 86.
Alpine tribes, 46, 47 ; passes, 320.
Alps, Cottian, 108.
–– Julian, 140.
Altinum, 268.
Aluta, R. (Alt), 201.
Annonae cura. 20. *See* Corn supply.
Amasea, 319.
Ambiani, 46.
Amisia, F., 50, 51, 149.
Amisus, 222.
Ammaedara, 42.
Amminus (Adminius), 82.
Ampsaga, F., 42.
Ampsivarii, 151.
Amyntas, 36, 122.
Ananias, 143.
Anauni, 92.
Ancona, 205, 219.
Ancyra, 54, 235, 238, 318, 319.
Angrivarii, 149, 150.
Angusticlavius, 377
Anio, 249.
Anicetus, 105.
Antinoe, 242.
Antinous, 242.
Antioch in Syria, 38, 225, 226, 228, 265, 297, 316, 318 ; in Pisidia, 318.
Antiochus Epiphanes, 38.
Antipater, 39.
Antonia, 26, 28, 84, 86 ; tower of, 144.
Antonine Wall, 289.
ANTONINUS PIUS, 248, 251–60, 308, 339 ; and 'limes Germanicus', 195 ; and 'limes Raeticus', 196 ; 'Pius', 251 ; and Senate, 257 ; private life, 255 ; character, 253, 256, 257.
Antonius Primus, 140, 141, 156.
Antony, 3, 16, 26, 36, 37, 43.
Apamea, 38, 222, 318.
Apocolocyntosis, 85, 99.
Apollo, 16, 19, 42, 177.
Apollodorus, 203, 218, 248.
Appius Silanus, C., 95.
Apuleius, 43, 383.
Apulia, 325.

387

Printed in Great Britain by
Butler & Tanner Ltd.,
Frome and London